MW00809358

CLYMER® MANUALS

HONDA
XR600R • 1991-2000 &
XR650L • 1993-2019

WHAT'S IN YOUR TOOLBOX?

More information available at Clymer.com
Phone: 805-498-6703

Haynes Publishing Group
Sparkford Nr Yeovil
Somerset BA22 7JJ England

Haynes North America, Inc
859 Lawrence Drive
Newbury Park
California 91320 USA

ISBN-10: 1-62092-364-5
ISBN-13: 978-1-62092-364-1
Library of Congress Control Number: 2019950389

Author: Mike Morlan
Technical Photography: Mike Morlan
Technical Illustrations: Mitzi McCarthy
Cover: Mark Clifford Photography at www.markclifford.com.
Motorcycle courtesy Bert's Mega Mall, Covina, California

© Haynes North America, Inc. 2007, 2014, 2019
With permission from J.H. Haynes & Co. Ltd.

Clymer is a registered trademark of Haynes North America, Inc.

Printed in Malaysia

All rights reserved. No part of this book may be reproduced or transmitted in any form or by any means, electronic or mechanical, including photocopying, recording or by any information storage or retrieval system, without permission in writing from the copyright holder.

While every attempt is made to ensure that the information in this manual is correct, no liability can be accepted by the authors or publishers for loss, damage or injury caused by any errors in, or omissions from, the information given.

M221, 2Y5, 19-336
ABCDEFGHIJKLMNO

Common spark plug conditions

NORMAL

Symptoms: Brown to grayish-tan color and slight electrode wear. Correct heat range for engine and operating conditions.
Recommendation: When new spark plugs are installed, replace with plugs of the same heat range.

WORN

Symptoms: Rounded electrodes with a small amount of deposits on the firing end. Normal color. Causes hard starting in damp or cold weather and poor fuel economy.
Recommendation: Plugs have been left in the engine too long. Replace with new plugs of the same heat range. Follow the recommended maintenance schedule.

TOO HOT

Symptoms: Blistered, white insulator, eroded electrode and absence of deposits. Results in shortened plug life.
Recommendation: Check for the correct plug heat range, over-advanced ignition timing, lean fuel mixture, intake manifold vacuum leaks, sticking valves and insufficient engine cooling.

CARBON DEPOSITS

Symptoms: Dry sooty deposits indicate a rich mixture or weak ignition. Causes misfiring, hard starting and hesitation.
Recommendation: Make sure the plug has the correct heat range. Check for a clogged air filter or problem in the fuel system or engine management system. Also check for ignition system problems.

PREIGNITION

Symptoms: Melted electrodes. Insulators are white, but may be dirty due to misfiring or flying debris in the combustion chamber. Can lead to engine damage.
Recommendation: Check for the correct plug heat range, over-advanced ignition timing, lean fuel mixture, insufficient engine cooling and lack of lubrication.

ASH DEPOSITS

Symptoms: Light brown deposits encrusted on the side or center electrodes or both. Derived from oil and/or fuel additives. Excessive amounts may mask the spark, causing misfiring and hesitation during acceleration.
Recommendation: If excessive deposits accumulate over a short time or low mileage, install new valve guide seals to prevent seepage of oil into the combustion chambers. Also try changing gasoline brands.

HIGH SPEED GLAZING

Symptoms: Insulator has yellowish, glazed appearance. Indicates that combustion chamber temperatures have risen suddenly during hard acceleration. Normal deposits melt to form a conductive coating. Causes misfiring at high speeds.
Recommendation: Install new plugs. Consider using a colder plug if driving habits warrant.

OIL DEPOSITS

Symptoms: Oily coating caused by poor oil control. Oil is leaking past worn valve guides or piston rings into the combustion chamber. Causes hard starting, misfiring and hesitation.
Recommendation: Correct the mechanical condition with necessary repairs and install new plugs.

DETONATION

Symptoms: Insulators may be cracked or chipped. Improper gap setting techniques can also result in a fractured insulator tip. Can lead to piston damage.
Recommendation: Make sure the fuel anti-knock values meet engine requirements. Use care when setting the gaps on new plugs. Avoid lugging the engine.

GAP BRIDGING

Symptoms: Combustion deposits lodge between the electrodes. Heavy deposits accumulate and bridge the electrode gap. The plug ceases to fire, resulting in a dead cylinder.
Recommendation: Locate the faulty plug and remove the deposits from between the electrodes.

MECHANICAL DAMAGE

Symptoms: May be caused by a foreign object in the combustion chamber or the piston striking an incorrect reach (too long) plug. Causes a dead cylinder and could result in piston damage.
Recommendation: Repair the mechanical damage. Remove the foreign object from the engine and/or install the correct reach plug.

CONTENTS

QUICK REFERENCE DATA

MOTORCYCLE INFORMATION

MODEL:_____ YEAR:_____

VIN NUMBER:_____

ENGINE SERIAL NUMBER:_____

CARBURETOR SERIAL NUMBER OR I.D. MARK:_____

TIRE INFLATION PRESSURE

	Front and rear
XR600R	14.5 psi (100 kPa)
XR650L	22 psi (150 kPa)

RECOMMENDED LUBRICANTS, FLUIDS AND FUEL

Engine oil	
Classification	API SG or higher*
Viscosity	
XR600R and 1993-2007 XR650L	SAE 10W-40*
2008-on XR650L	SAE 10W-30
Air filter (XR600R)	Foam air filter oil
Brake fluid	DOT 4
Fork oil	
XR600R & 1993-2007 XR650L	Pro-Honda Suspension Fluid SS-7 or equivalent
2008-on XR650L	Pro-Honda Suspension Fluid SS-7, HP Fork Oil SS-19 or equivalent
Steering and suspension lubricant	Multipurpose grease
Fuel	Octane rating of 86 or higher

*See text for additional information.

ENGINE OIL CAPACITY

	Liters	U.S. qt.
Oil change only	1.9	2
Oil and filter change	1.95	2.06
After engine disassembly	2.3	2.4

ENGINE COMPRESSION, DECOMPRESSION LEVER AND VALVE CLEARANCE SPECIFICATIONS

Decompression lever free play	
XR600R	5-8 mm (3/16-5/16 in.)
Engine compression	
XR600R	
Decompressor engaged	400-600 kPa (58-87 psi)
Decompressor disengaged	1300-1500 kPa (188-217 psi)
XR650L	
Decompressor engaged	637 kPa (92 psi) @ 600 rpm on 2008-on
Decompressor disengaged	1373 kPa (199 psi) @ 600 rpm on 2008-on
Valve clearance	
XR600R	
Intake	0.10 mm (0.004 in.)
Exhaust	0.12 mm (0.005 in.)
XR650L	
Intake	0.08-0.12 mm (0.003-0.005 in.)
Exhaust	0.10-0.14 mm (0.004-0.006 in.)

SPARK PLUG SPECIFICATIONS

Spark plug gap	0.8-0.9 mm (0.032-0.036 in.)
Spark plug type	
Standard	NGK DPR8EA-9 or Denso X24EPR-U9
Extended high-speed riding	NGK DPR9EA-9 or Denso X27EPR-U9
Cold weather operation*	NGK DPR7EA-9 or Denso X22EPR-U9

*Below 41° F (4° C).

IDLE SPEED SPECIFICATION

All models	1200-1400 rpm

DRIVE CHAIN AND SLIDER SPECIFICATIONS

Drive chain	
XR600R	DID 520V8 (110 links)
	RK 520MO4X (110 links)
XR650L	DID 520V8 (110 links)
	RK 520MOZ6 (110 links)
Drive chain slack	35-45 mm (1 3/8-1 3/4 in.)
Chain slider groove depth	
XR600R and 1993-2007 XR650L	2 mm (0.08 in.)
2008-on XR650L	4 mm (0.16 in.)
Chain slipper groove depth (max.)	
XR600R and 1993-2007 XR650L	8 mm (0.31 in.)
2008-on XR650L	2 mm (0.08 in.)

MAINTENANCE TORQUE SPECIFICATIONS

Item	N•m	in.-lb.	ft.-lb.
Engine oil drain bolts			
Frame drain bolt	40	–	29
Crankcase drain bolt	25	–	18
Engine oil filter cover			
XR600R & 1993-2007 XR650L	12	106	-
2008-on XR650L	NA	NA	-
Rear axle nut			
XR600R	95	–	70
XR650L	90	–	66
Rear shock absorber spring locknut	90	–	66
Spark plug	17	150	–
Valve adjuster locknut	25	–	18
Wheel rim locknut	13	115	–
Wheel spoke			
XR600R & 1993-2007 XR650L	4	35.00	–
2008-on XR650L	3.7	32.75	–

CHAPTER ONE

GENERAL INFORMATION

This detailed and comprehensive manual covers 1991-2000 Honda XR600R models and 1993-2019 XR650L models.

The text provides complete information on maintenance, tune-up, repair and overhaul. Hundreds of photos and drawings guide the reader through every job. All procedures are in step-by-step format and designed for the reader who may be working on the motorcycle for the first time.

MANUAL ORGANIZATION

A shop manual is a reference tool and, as in all Clymer manuals, the chapters are thumb-tabbed for easy reference. Important items are indexed at the end of the manual. Frequently used specifications and capacities from individual chapters are summarized in the *Quick Reference Data* at the front of the manual.

During some of the procedures there will be references to headings in other chapters or sections of the manual. When a specific heading is called out in a step it is *italicized* as it appears in the manual. If a sub-heading is indicated as being "in this section" it is located within the same main heading. For example, the sub-heading *Handling Gasoline Safely* is located within the main heading *SAFETY*.

This chapter provides general information on shop safety, tool use, service fundamentals and shop supplies. **Tables 1-9** at the end of the chapter provide general motorcycle, mechanical and shop information.

Chapter Two provides methods for quick and accurate diagnoses of problems. Troubleshooting procedures present typical symptoms and logical methods to pinpoint and repair a problem.

Chapter Three explains all routine maintenance.

Subsequent chapters describe specific systems, such as engine, clutch, transmission, fuel system, electrical system, wheels, tires, drive chain, suspension, brakes and body components.

Specification tables, when applicable, are located at the end of each chapter.

WARNINGS, CAUTIONS AND NOTES

The terms WARNING, CAUTION and NOTE have specific meanings in this manual.

A WARNING emphasizes areas where injury or even death could result from negligence. Mechanical damage may also occur. WARNINGS *are to be taken seriously*.

A CAUTION emphasizes areas where equipment damage could result. Disregarding a CAUTION could cause permanent mechanical damage, though injury is unlikely.

A NOTE provides additional information to make a step or procedure easier or clearer. Disregarding a NOTE could cause inconvenience, but would not cause equipment damage or injury.

SAFETY

Follow these guidelines and practice common sense to safely service the motorcycle:

1. Do not operate the motorcycle in an enclosed area. The exhaust gasses contain carbon monoxide, an odorless, colorless and tasteless poisonous gas. Carbon monoxide levels build quickly in small, enclosed areas and can cause unconsciousness and death in a short time. Make sure the work area is properly ventilated, or operate the motorcycle outside.

2. *Never* use gasoline or any flammable liquid to clean parts. Refer to *Handling Gasoline Safely* and *Cleaning Parts* in this section.

3. *Never* smoke or use a torch in the vicinity of flammable liquids, such as gasoline or cleaning solvent.

4. Do not remove the radiator cap or cooling system hose while the engine is hot. The cooling system is pressurized and the high temperature coolant may cause injury.

5. Dispose of and store coolant in a safe manner. Do not allow children or pets access to open containers of coolant. Animals are attracted to antifreeze.

6. Avoid contact with engine oil and other chemicals. Most are known carcinogens. Wash your hands thoroughly after coming in contact with engine oil. If possible, wear a pair of disposable gloves.

7. If welding or brazing on the motorcycle, remove the fuel tank and shocks to a safe distance at least 50 ft. (15 m) away.

8. Use the correct types and sizes of tools to avoid damaging fasteners.

9. Keep tools clean and in good condition. Replace or repair worn or damaged equipment.

10. When loosening a tight fastener, be guided by what would happen if the tool slips.

11. When replacing fasteners, make sure the new fasteners are the same size and strength as the originals.

12. Keep the work area clean and organized.

13. Wear eye protection *any time* the safety of your eyes is in question. This includes procedures involving drilling, grinding, hammering, compressed air and chemicals.

14. Wear the correct clothing for the job. Tie up or cover long hair so it cannot catch in moving equipment.

15. Do not carry sharp tools in clothing pockets.

16. Always have an approved fire extinguisher available. Make sure it is rated for gasoline (Class B) and electrical (Class C) fires.

17. Do not use compressed air to clean clothes, the motorcycle or the work area. Debris may be blown into the eyes or skin. *Never* direct compressed air at

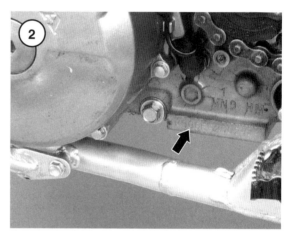

anyone. Do not allow children to use or play with any compressed air equipment.

18. When using compressed air to dry rotating parts, hold the part so it cannot rotate. Do not allow the force of the air to spin the part. The air jet is capable of rotating parts at extreme speeds. The part may be damaged or disintegrate, causing serious injury.

19. Do not inhale the dust created by brake pad and clutch wear. These particles may contain asbestos. In addition, some types of insulating materials and gaskets may contain asbestos. Inhaling asbestos particles is hazardous to health.

20. Never work on the motorcycle while someone is working under it.

21. When placing the motorcycle on a stand or overhead lift, make sure it is secure before walking away.

Handling Gasoline Safely

Gasoline is a volatile flammable liquid and is one of the most dangerous items in the shop. Because gasoline is used so often, many people forget that it is hazardous. Only use gasoline as fuel for gasoline internal combustion engines. Keep in mind when

working on a motorcycle, gasoline is always present in the fuel tank, fuel line and carburetor. To avoid an accident when working around the fuel system, carefully observe the following precautions:

1. *Never* use gasoline to clean parts. Refer to *Cleaning Parts* in this section.
2. When working on the fuel system, work outside or in a well-ventilated area.
3. Do not add fuel to the fuel tank or service the fuel system while the motorcycle is near open flames, sparks or where someone is smoking. Gasoline vapor is heavier than air, collects in low areas and is more easily ignited than liquid gasoline.
4. Allow the engine to cool completely before working on any fuel system component.
5. Do not store gasoline in glass containers. If the glass breaks, an explosion or fire may occur.
6. Immediately wipe up spilled gasoline with rags. Store the rags in a metal container with a lid until they can be properly disposed, or place them outside in a safe place for the fuel to evaporate.
7. Do not pour water onto a gasoline fire. Water spreads the fire and makes it more difficult to put out. Use a class B, BC or ABC fire extinguisher to extinguish the fire.
8. Always turn off the engine before refueling. Do not spill fuel onto the engine or exhaust system. Do not overfill the fuel tank. Leave an air space at the top of the tank to allow room for the fuel to expand due to temperature fluctuations.

Cleaning Parts

Cleaning parts is one of the more tedious and difficult service jobs performed in the home garage. Many types of chemical cleaners and solvents are available for shop use. Most are poisonous and extremely flammable. To prevent chemical exposure, vapor buildup, fire and injury, note the following:

1. Read and observe the entire product label before using any chemical. Always know what type of

chemical is being used and whether it is poisonous and/or flammable.
2. Do not use more than one type of cleaning solvent at a time. If mixing chemicals is required, measure the proper amounts according to the manufacturer.
3. Work in a well-ventilated area.
4. Wear chemical-resistant gloves.
5. Wear safety glasses.
6. Wear a vapor respirator if the instructions call for it.
7. Wash hands and arms thoroughly after cleaning parts.
8. Keep chemicals away from children and pets, especially coolant. Animals are attracted to antifreeze.
9. Thoroughly clean all oil, grease and cleaner residue from any part that must be heated.
10. Use a nylon brush when cleaning parts. Metal brushes may cause a spark.
11. When using a parts washer, only use the solvent recommended by the manufacturer. Make sure the parts washer is equipped with a metal lid that will lower in case of fire.

Warning Labels

Most manufacturers attach information and warning labels to the motorcycle. These labels contain important safety instructions when operating, servicing, transporting and storing the motorcycle. Refer to the owner's manual for the description and location of labels. Order replacement labels from the manufacturer if they are missing or damaged.

SERIAL NUMBERS AND INFORMATION LABELS

Serial numbers are stamped on various locations on the frame, engine and carburetor. Record these numbers in the *Quick Reference Data* section in the front of this manual. Have these numbers available when ordering parts.

The frame serial number (A, **Figure 1**) is stamped on the right side of the steering head.

On XR650L models, the VIN number label (B, **Figure 1**) is located on the left side of the frame adjacent to the steering head.

The engine serial number is stamped on a pad at the left side surface of the lower crankcase (**Figure 2**).

On XR600R models, the carburetor serial number is located on the right side of the carburetor body above the float bowl (**Figure 3**). On XR650L models, the carburetor serial number is located on the left side of the carburetor body above the float bowl (**Figure 4**).

On XR650L models, a tire pressure label is affixed to the chain guard (**Figure 5**). A paint code label is affixed to the left rear frame downtube (**Figure 6**).

FASTENERS

WARNING
Do not install fasteners with a strength classification lower than what was originally installed by the manufacturer. Doing so may cause equipment failure and/or damage.

Proper fastener selection and installation is important to ensure the motorcycle operates as designed and can be serviced efficiently. The choice of original equipment fasteners is not arrived at by chance. Make sure replacement fasteners meet the requirements.

Threaded Fasteners

Threaded fasteners secure most of the components on the motorcycle. Most tighten by turning them clockwise (right-hand threads). If the normal rotation of the component being tightened would loosen the fastener, it may have left-hand threads. If a left-hand threaded fastener is used, it is noted in the text.

Two dimensions are required to match the thread size of the fastener: the number of threads in a given distance and the outside diameter of the threads.

Two systems are currently used to specify threaded fastener dimensions: the U.S. Standard system and the metric system (**Figure 7**). Pay particular attention when working with unidentified fasteners; mismatching thread types can damage threads.

To ensure the fastener threads are not mismatched or cross-threaded, start all fasteners by hand. If a fastener is difficult to start or turn, determine the cause before tightening with a wrench.

Match fasteners by their length (L, **Figure 8**), diameter (D) and distance between thread crests (pitch, T). A typical metric bolt may be identified by the numbers, 8—1.25 × 130. This indicates the bolt has a diameter of 8 mm, the distance between thread crests is 1.25 mm and the length is 130 mm. Always measure bolt length as shown in L, **Figure 8** to avoid installing replacements of the wrong lengths.

If a number is located on the top of a metric fastener (**Figure 8**), this indicates the strength. The higher the number, the stronger the fastener. Typically, unnumbered fasteners are the weakest.

Many screws, bolts and studs are combined with nuts to secure particular components. To indicate the size of a nut, manufacturers specify the internal diameter and thread pitch.

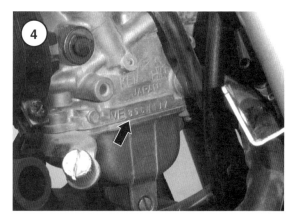

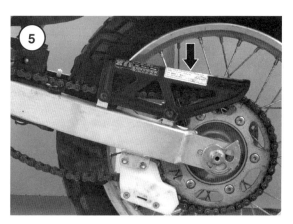

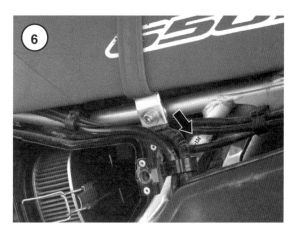

The measurement across two flats on a nut or bolt indicates the wrench size.

Torque Specifications

The materials used in the manufacture of the motorcycle may be subjected to uneven stresses if fasteners are not installed and tightened correctly. Improperly installed fasteners or ones that worked loose can cause extensive damage. It is essential to use an accurate torque wrench, as described in this chapter, with the torque specifications in this manual.

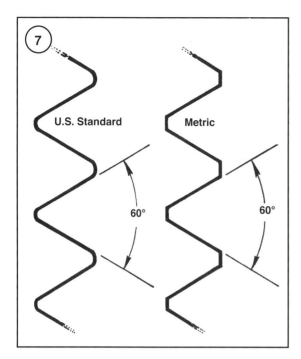

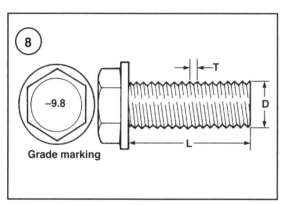

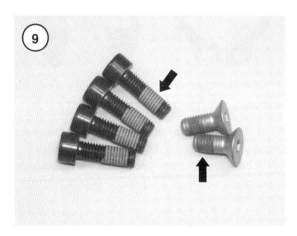

Specifications for torque are provided in Newton-meters (N•m), foot-pounds (ft.-lb.) and inch-pounds (in.-lb.). Refer to **Table 9** for torque recommendations. To use **Table 9**, first determine the size of the fastener as described in *Threaded Fasteners* in this section. Torque specifications for specific components are at the end of the appropriate chapters. Torque wrenches are covered in the *Tools* section.

Self-Locking Fasteners

Several types of bolts, screws and nuts incorporate a system that creates interference between the two fasteners. Interference is achieved in various ways. The most common type used is the nylon insert nut. A dry adhesive coating on the threads of a bolt is another type.

Self-locking fasteners offer greater holding strength than standard fasteners, which improves their resistance to vibration. Self-locking fasteners cannot be reused. The materials used to form the lock become distorted after the initial installation and removal. Do not replace self-locking fasteners with standard fasteners.

Some Honda fasteners are equipped with a threadlock pre-applied to the fastener threads (**Figure 9**). When replacing these fasteners, do not apply additional threadlock. When it is necessary to reuse one of these fasteners, remove the threadlock residue from the threads. Then apply the threadlock specified in the text.

Washers

The two basic types of washers are flat washers and lockwashers. Flat washers are simple discs with a hole to fit a screw or bolt. Lockwashers are used to prevent a fastener from working loose. Washers can be used as spacers and seals or to help distribute fastener load and prevent the fastener from damaging the component.

As with fasteners, when replacing washers make sure the replacements meet the original specifications.

Cotter Pins

A cotter pin is a split metal pin inserted into a hole or slot to prevent a fastener from loosening. In certain applications, such as the rear axle, the fastener must be secured in this way. For these applications, a cotter pin and castellated (slotted) nut is used.

To use a cotter pin, first make sure the diameter is correct for the hole in the fastener. After correctly tightening the fastener and aligning the holes, insert the cotter pin through the hole and bend the ends over the fastener (**Figure 10**). Unless instructed to do so, never loosen a tightened fastener to align the holes. If the holes do not align, tighten the fastener just enough to achieve alignment.

Cotter pins are available in various diameters and lengths. Measure length from the bottom of the head to the tip of the shortest pin.

Snap Rings and E-clips

Snap rings (**Figure 11**) are circular-shaped metal retaining clips. They are required to secure parts and gears in place on parts such as shafts, pins or rods. External type snap rings are used to retain items on shafts. Internal type snap rings secure parts within housing bores. In some applications, in addition to securing the component(s), snap rings of varying thickness also determine endplay. These are usually called selective snap rings.

The two basic types of snap rings are machined and stamped snap rings. Machined snap rings (**Figure 12**) can be installed in either direction because both faces have sharp edges. Stamped snap rings (**Figure 13**) are manufactured with a sharp edge and round edge. When installing a stamped snap ring in a thrust application, install the sharp edge facing away from the part producing the thrust.

E-clips are also used on shafts and rods. Remove E-clips with a flat blade screwdriver by prying between the shaft and E-clip. To install an E-clip, center it over the shaft groove and push or tap it into place.

Observe the following when installing snap rings:
1. Remove and install snap rings with snap ring pliers. Refer to *Tools* in this chapter.
2. In some applications, it may be necessary to replace snap rings after removing them.
3. Compress or expand snap rings only enough to install them. If overly expanded, they lose their retaining ability.
4. After installing a snap ring, make sure it seats completely.
5. Wear eye protection when removing and installing snap rings.

SHOP SUPPLIES

Lubricants and Fluids

Periodic lubrication helps ensure a long service life for any type of equipment. Using the correct type of lubricant is as important as performing the lubrication service, although in an emergency the wrong type is better than not using one. The following section describes the types of lubricants most often required. Make sure to follow the manufacturer's recommendations.

Engine oils

Engine oil for a four-stroke motorcycle engine use is classified by three standards: the American Petroleum Institute (API) service classification, the Society of Automotive Engineers (SAE) viscos-

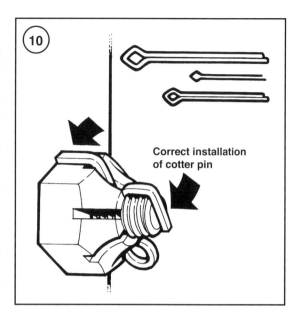

Correct installation of cotter pin

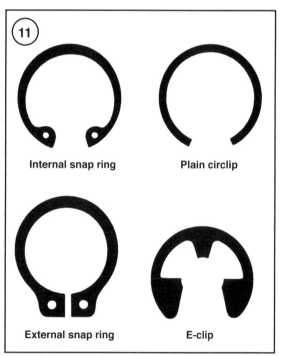

Internal snap ring

Plain circlip

External snap ring

E-clip

ity rating and the Japanese Automobile Standards Organization (JASO) T 903 certification standard.

The JASO certification specifies the oil has passed requirements specified by Japanese motorcycle manufacturers.

The API and SAE information is on all oil container labels. The JASO information is found on oil containers sold by the oil manufacturer specifically for motorcycle use.

The API two-letter service classification indicates the oil meets specific lubrication standards and is not an indication of oil quality. The first letter in the

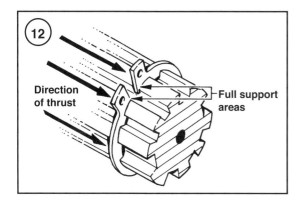

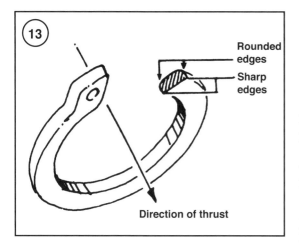

classification *S* indicates that the oil is for gasoline engines. The second letter indicates the standard the oil satisfies.

The JASO certification label identifies two separate oil classifications and a registration number to ensure the oil has passed all JASO certification standards for use in four-stroke motorcycle engines. The classifications are: MA (high friction applications) and MB (low friction applications).

The number or sequence of numbers and a letter (10W-40, for example) is the oil's viscosity.

Viscosity is an indication of the oil's thickness. Thin oils have a lower number while thick oils have a higher number. Engine oils fall into the 5- to 50-weight range for single-grade oils.

Most manufacturers recommend multi-grade oil. These oils perform efficiently across a wide range of operating conditions. Multi-grade oils are identified by a *W* after the first number, which indicates the low-temperature viscosity.

Engine oils are most commonly mineral (petroleum) based; however, synthetic and semi-synthetic types are used more frequently. Always use oil with a classification recommended by the manufacturer (Chapter Three). Using oil with a different classification can cause engine damage.

Greases

Grease is lubricating oil with thickening agents added to it. The National Lubricating Grease Institute (NLGI) grades grease. Grades range from No. 000 to No. 6, with No. 6 being the thickest. Typical multipurpose grease is NLGI No. 2. For specific applications, manufacturers may recommend a water-resistant type grease or one with an additive, such as molybdenum disulfide (MoS_2).

Brake fluid

> *WARNING*
> *Never put a mineral-based (petroleum) oil into the brake system. Mineral oil causes rubber parts in the system to swell and break apart, causing complete brake failure.*

Brake fluid is the hydraulic fluid used to transmit hydraulic pressure (force) to the wheel brakes. Brake fluid is classified by the Department of Transportation (DOT). The classification appears on the fluid container. The models covered in this manual require DOT 4 brake fluid.

Each type of brake fluid has its own definite characteristics. Do not intermix different types of brake fluid; this may cause brake system failure. DOT 5 brake fluid is silicone based. DOT 5 is not compatible with other brake fluids or in systems for which it was not designed. Mixing DOT 5 fluid with other fluids may cause brake system failure. When adding brake fluid, *only* use DOT 4 brake fluid.

Brake fluid damages any plastic, painted or plated surface it contacts. Use extreme care when working with brake fluid, and remove any spills immediately with soap and water.

Hydraulic brake systems require clean and moisture free brake fluid. Never reuse brake fluid. Keep containers and reservoirs properly sealed.

Cleaners, Degreasers and Solvents

Many chemicals are available to remove oil, grease and other residue from the motorcycle. Before using cleaning solvents, consider their uses and disposal methods, particularly if they are not water-soluble. Local ordinances may require special procedures for the disposal of many types of cleaning chemicals. Refer to *Safety* and *Cleaning Parts* in this chapter for more information on their uses.

Use brake parts cleaner to clean brake system components when contact with petroleum-based products will damage seals. Brake parts cleaner leaves no residue. Use electrical contact cleaner to clean electrical connections and components without leaving any residue. Carburetor cleaner is a powerful solvent used to remove fuel deposits and varnish from fuel system components. Use this cleaner carefully; it may damage finishes.

Generally, degreasers are strong cleaners used to remove heavy accumulations of grease from engine and frame components.

Most solvents are designed to be used with a parts washing cabinet for individual component cleaning. For safety, use only nonflammable or high flash point solvents.

Gasket Sealant

Sealants are used in combination with a gasket or seal or occasionally alone. Use extreme care when choosing a sealant different from the type originally recommended. Choose sealants based on their resistance to heat, various fluids and their sealing capabilities.

One of the most common sealants is RTV, or room temperature vulcanizing, sealant. This sealant cures at room temperature over a specific time period. This allows the repositioning of components without damaging gaskets.

Moisture in the air causes the RTV sealant to cure. Always install the tube cap as soon as possible after applying RTV sealant. RTV sealant has a limited shelf life and will not cure properly if the shelf life has expired. Keep partial tubes sealed and discard them if they have surpassed the expiration date. If there is no expiration date on a sealant tube, use a permanent marker and write the date on the tube when it is first opened. Manufacturers usually specify a shelf life of one year after a container is opened, though it is recommended to contact the sealant manufacturer to confirm shelf life.

Removing RTV sealant

Silicone sealant may be used on gasket surfaces. When cleaning parts after disassembly, a razor blade or gasket scraper is required to remove the silicone residue that cannot be pulled off by hand from the gasket surfaces. To avoid damaging gasket surfaces, use Permatex Silicone Stripper (part No. 80647) to help soften the residue before scraping.

Applying RTV sealant

Clean all old sealer residue from the mating surfaces. Then inspect the mating surfaces for damage. Remove all sealer material from blind threaded holes; it can cause inaccurate bolt torque. Spray the mating surfaces with aerosol parts cleaner, and then wipe with a lint-free cloth. Because gasket surfaces

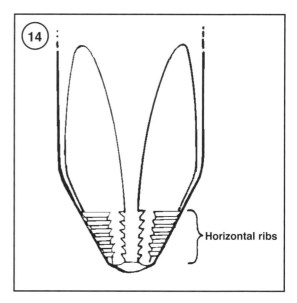

must be dry and oil-free for the sealant to adhere, be thorough when cleaning and drying the parts.

Apply RTV sealant in a continuous bead 2-3 mm (0.08-0.12 in.) thick. Circle all the fastener holes unless otherwise specified. Do not allow any sealant to enter these holes. Drawings in specific chapters show how to apply the sealer to specific gasket surfaces. Assemble and tighten the fasteners to the specified torque within the time frame recommended by the RTV sealant manufacturer.

Gasket Remover

Aerosol gasket remover can help remove stubborn gaskets. This product can speed up the removal process and prevent damage to the mating surface that may be caused by using a scraping tool. Most of these types of products are very caustic. Follow the gasket remover manufacturer's instructions for use.

Threadlocking Compound

CAUTION
Threadlocking compounds are anaerobic and damage most plastic parts and surfaces. Use caution when using these products in areas where plastic components are located.

A threadlocking compound is a fluid applied to the threads of fasteners. After tightening the fastener, the fluid dries and becomes a solid filler between the threads. This makes it difficult for the fastener to work loose from vibration or heat expansion and contraction. Some threadlocking compounds also provide a seal against fluid leaks.

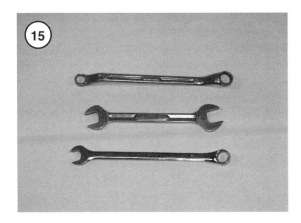

Before applying threadlocking compound, remove any old compound from both thread areas and clean them with aerosol parts cleaner. Use the compound sparingly. Excess fluid can run into adjoining parts.

Threadlocking compounds are available in various strengths, temperatures and repair applications.

TOOLS

Most of the procedures in this manual can be carried out with hand tools and test equipment familiar to the home mechanic. Always use the correct tools for the job. Keep tools organized and clean and store them in a tool chest with related tools organized together.

Quality tools are essential. The best are constructed of high-strength alloy steel. These tools are light, easy-to-use and resistant to wear. Their working surfaces are devoid of sharp edges and the tools are carefully polished. They have an easy-to-clean finish and are comfortable to use. Quality tools are a good investment.

When purchasing tools to perform the procedures covered in this manual, consider the tool's potential frequency of use. If a tool kit is just now being started, consider purchasing a tool set from a quality tool supplier. These sets are available in many tool combinations and offer substantial savings when compared to individually purchased tools. As work experience grows and tasks become more complicated, specialized tools can be added.

Some of the procedures in this manual specify special tools. In most cases, the tool is illustrated in use. In some case it may be possible to substitute similar tools or fabricate a suitable replacement. However, at times, the specialized equipment or expertise may make it impractical for the home mechanic to perform the procedure. When necessary, such operations are identified in the text with the recommendation to have a dealership or specialist perform the task.

If a part number for a tool is provided, it is correct at the time of publication. The publisher cannot guarantee part number accuracy or tool availability in the future.

Screwdrivers

The two basic types of screwdrivers are the slotted tip (flat blade) and the Phillips tip. These are available in sets that often include an assortment of tip sizes and shaft lengths.

As with all tools, use the correct screwdriver. Make sure the size of the tip conforms to the size and shape of the fastener. Use them only for driving screws. Never use a screwdriver for prying or chiseling. Repair or replace worn or damaged screwdrivers. A worn tip may damage the fastener, making it difficult to remove.

Phillips-head screws are often damaged by incorrectly fitting screwdrivers. Quality Phillips screwdrivers are manufactured with their crosshead tip machined to Phillips Screw Company specifications. Poor quality or damaged Phillips screwdrivers can back out and round over the screw head (camout). Compounding the problem of using poor quality screwdrivers are Phillips-head screws made from weak or soft materials and screws initially installed with air tools.

To prevent camout, use an ACR Phillips II screwdriver. The horizontal anti-camout ribs on the driving faces or flutes of the screwdrivers tip (**Figure 14**) grip the screw more securely. ACR Phillips II screwdrivers are designed for use with ACR Phillips II screws, but they work well on all Phillips screws. ACR Phillips II screwdrivers are available in different tip sizes and interchangeable bits to fit screwdriver bit holders.

Another way to prevent camout and increase the grip of a Phillips screwdriver is to apply valve grinding compound or Permatex Screw & Socket Gripper onto the screwdriver tip. After loosening/tightening the screw, clean the screw recess to prevent possible contamination.

Wrenches

Open-end, box-end and combination wrenches (**Figure 15**) are available in a variety of types and sizes.

The number stamped on the wrench refers to the distance between the work areas. This size must match the size of the fastener head.

The box-end wrench is an excellent tool because it grips the fastener on all sides. This reduces the chance of the tool slipping. The box-end wrench is designed with either a 6- or 12-point opening. For stubborn or damaged fasteners, the 6-point provides superior holding ability by contacting the fastener across a wider area at all six edges. For general use, the 12-point works well. It allows the wrench to be removed and reinstalled without moving the handle over such a wide arc.

An open-end wrench is fast and works best in areas with limited overhead access. It contacts the fastener at only two points, and is subject to slipping under heavy force or if the tool or fastener is worn. A box-end wrench is preferred in most instances, especially when breaking loose and applying the final tightness to a fastener.

The combination wrench has a box-end on one end, and an open-end on the other. This combination makes it a convenient tool.

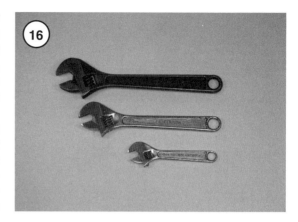

Adjustable Wrenches

An adjustable wrench (**Figure 16**) can fit nearly any nut or bolt head that has clear access around its entire perimeter.

Adjustable wrenches contact the fastener at only two points, which makes them more subject to slipping off the fastener. One jaw is adjustable and may loosen, which increases this possibility. Make certain the solid jaw is the one transmitting the force.

Adjustable wrenches are typically used to prevent a large nut or bolt from turning while the other end is being loosened or tightened with a box-end or socket wrench.

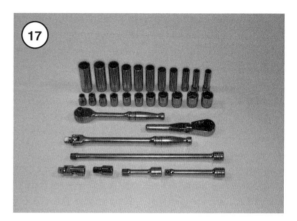

Socket Wrenches, Ratchets and Handles

> *WARNING*
> *Do not use hand sockets with air or impact tools; they may shatter and cause injury. Always wear eye protection when using impact or air tools.*

Sockets that attach to a ratchet handle (**Figure 17**) are available with 6-point (A, **Figure 18**) or 12-point (B) openings and different drive sizes. The drive size indicates the size of the square hole that accepts the ratchet handle. The number stamped on the socket is the size of the work area and must match the fastener head.

As with wrenches, a 6-point socket provides superior-holding ability, while a 12-point socket needs to be moved only half as far to reposition it on the fastener.

Sockets are designated for either hand or impact use. Impact sockets are made of a thicker material

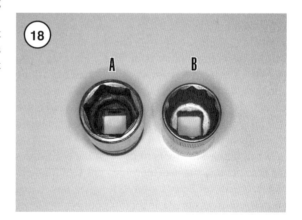

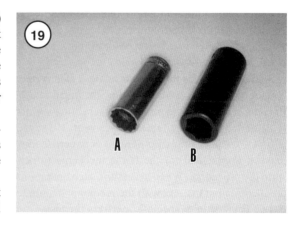

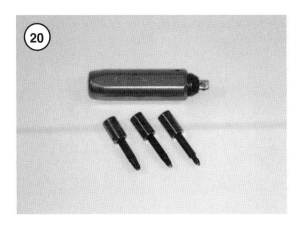

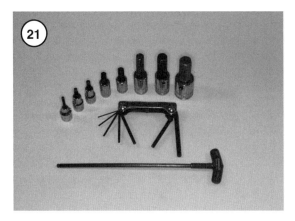

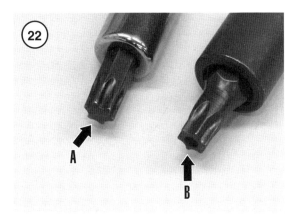

Sockets combined with any number of drivers make them undoubtedly the fastest, safest and most convenient tool for fastener removal and installation.

Impact Driver

> *WARNING*
> *Do not use hand sockets with air or impact tools because they may shatter and cause injury. Always wear eye protection when using impact or air tools.*

An impact driver provides extra force for removing fasteners by converting the impact of a hammer into a turning motion. This makes it possible to remove stubborn fasteners without damaging them. Impact drivers and interchangeable bits (**Figure 20**) are available from most tool suppliers. When using a socket with an impact driver make sure the socket is designed for impact use. Refer to *Socket Wrenches, Ratchets and Handles* in this section.

Allen Wrenches

Allen, or setscrew wrenches (**Figure 21**), are used on fasteners with hexagonal recesses in the fastener head. These wrenches are available in a L-shaped bar, socket and T-handle types. Allen bolts are sometimes called socket bolts.

Torx Fasteners

A Torx fastener head is a 6-point star-shaped pattern (A, **Figure 22**). Torx fasteners are identified with a T and a number indicating their drive size. For example, T25. Torx drivers are available in L-shaped bars, sockets and T-handles. Tamper-resistant Torx fasteners are also used and have a round shaft in the center of the fastener head. Tamper-resistance Torx fasteners require a Torx bit with a hole in the center of the bit (B, **Figure 22**).

for more durability. Compare the size and wall thickness of a 19-mm hand socket (A, **Figure 19**) and the 19-mm impact socket (B). Use impact sockets when using an impact driver or air tool. Use hand sockets with hand-driven attachments.

Various handles are available for sockets. The speed handle is used for fast operation. Flexible ratchet heads in varying lengths allow the socket to be turned with varying force and at odd angles. Extension bars allow the socket setup to reach difficult areas. The ratchet is the most versatile. It allows the user to install or remove the nut without removing the socket.

Torque Wrenches

A torque wrench (**Figure 23**) is used with a socket, torque adapter or similar extension to tighten a fastener to a measured torque. Torque wrenches come in several drive sizes (1/4, 3/8, 1/2 and 3/4) and have various methods of reading the torque value. The drive size indicates the size of the square drive that accepts the socket, adapter or extension. Common methods of reading the torque value are the deflecting beam, the dial indicator and the audible click.

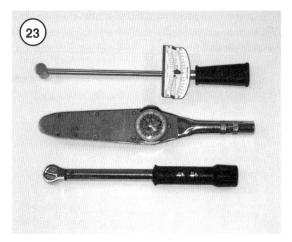

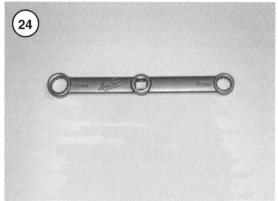

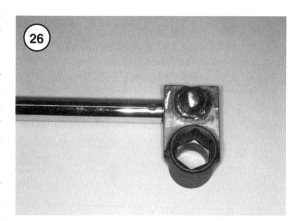

When choosing a torque wrench, consider the torque range, drive size and accuracy. The torque specifications in this manual provide an indication of the range required.

A torque wrench is a precision tool that must be properly cared for to remain accurate. Store torque wrenches in cases or separate padded drawers within a toolbox. Follow the manufacturer's instructions for their care and calibration.

Torque Adapters

Torque adapters (**Figure 24**), or extensions, extend or reduce the reach of a torque wrench. These are available from the motorcycle manufacturer, aftermarket tool suppliers, or can be fabricated by welding a socket (A, **Figure 25**) that matches the fastener onto a metal plate (B). Use another socket or extension (C, **Figure 25**) welded to the plate to attach to the torque wrench drive (**Figure 26**). The adapter shown (**Figure 27**) is used to tighten a fastener while preventing another fastener on the same shaft from turning.

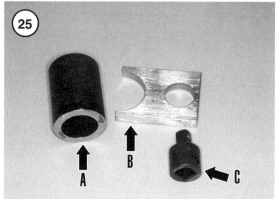

If a torque adapter changes the effective lever length, the torque reading on the wrench will not equal the actual torque applied to the fastener. It is necessary to recalibrate the torque setting on the wrench to compensate for the change of lever length. When a torque adapter is used at a right angle to the drive head, calibration is not required because the lever length has not changed.

To recalculate a torque reading when using a torque adapter, use the following formula, and refer to **Figure 28**.

$$TW = \frac{TA \times L}{L + A}$$

TW is the torque setting or dial reading on the wrench.

TA is the torque specification and the actual amount of torque that will be applied to the fastener.

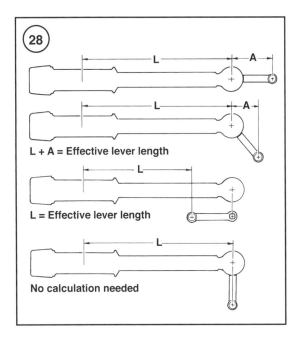

L + A = Effective lever length

L = Effective lever length

No calculation needed

The effective lever length is the sum of *L* and *A*.
Example:

TA = 20 ft.-lb.

A = 3 in.

L = 14 in.

$$TW = \frac{20 \times 14}{14 + 3} = \frac{280}{17} = 16.5 \text{ ft.-lb.}$$

In this example, the torque wrench would be set to the recalculated torque value (TW = 16.5 ft.-lb.). When using a beam-type wrench, tighten the fastener until the pointer aligns with 16.5 ft.-lb. In this example, although the torque wrench is pre set to 16.5 ft.-lb., the actual torque is 20 ft.-lb.

Pliers

Pliers come in a wide range of types and sizes. Pliers are useful for holding, cutting, bending, and crimping. Do not use them to turn fasteners unless they are designed to do so. **Figure 29** and **Figure 30** show several types of pliers. Each design has a specialized function. Slip-joint pliers are general-purpose pliers used for gripping and bending. Diagonal cutting pliers are needed to cut wire and can be used to remove cotter pins. Needlenose pliers are used to hold or bend small objects. Locking pliers (**Figure 30**), sometimes called Vise Grips, hold objects tightly. They have many uses ranging from holding two parts together, to gripping the end of a broken stud. Use caution when using locking pliers; the sharp jaws will damage the objects they hold.

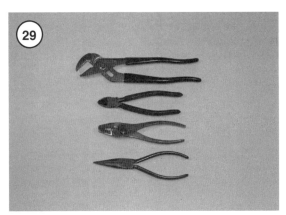

Snap Ring Pliers

> *WARNING*
> *Snap rings can slip and fly off when removing and installing them. In addition, the tips of snap ring pliers may break. Always wear eye protection when using snap ring pliers.*

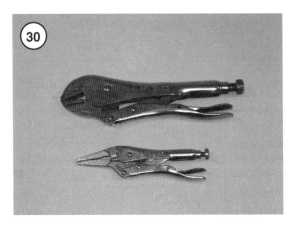

Snap ring pliers are specialized pliers with tips that fit into the ends of snap rings to remove and install them.

Snap ring pliers (**Figure 31**) are available with a fixed action (either internal or external) or are convertible (one tool works on both internal and external snap rings). They may have fixed tips or interchangeable ones of various sizes and angles. For general use, select convertible type pliers with interchangeable tips.

A is the amount the adapter increases (or in some cases reduces) the effective lever length as measured along the centerline of the torque wrench.

L is the lever length of the wrench as measured from the center of the drive to the center of the grip.

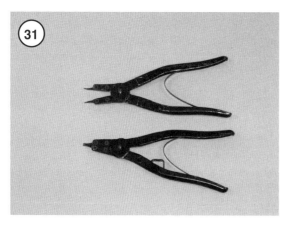

Hammers

WARNING
Always wear eye protection when using
hammers. Make sure the hammer face
is in good condition and the handle is
not cracked. Select the correct hammer
for the job and make sure to strike the
object squarely. Do not use the handle
or the side of the hammer to strike an
object.

Various types of hammers are available to fit a number of applications. A ball-peen hammer is used to strike another tool, such as a punch or chisel. Soft-faced hammers are required when a metal object must be struck without damaging it. *Never* use a metal-faced hammer on engine and suspension components; damage will occur in most cases.

Ignition Grounding Tool

Some test procedures in this manual require turning the engine over without starting it. Do not remove the spark plug cap(s) and crank the engine without grounding the plug cap(s). Doing so will damage the ignition system.

An effective way to ground the system is to fabricate the tool shown in **Figure 32** from a No. 6 screw, two washers and a length of wire with an alligator clip soldered on one end. To use the tool, insert it into the spark plug cap and attach the alligator clip to a known engine ground.

This tool is safer than a spark plug or spark tester because there is no spark firing across the end of the plug/tester to potentially ignite fuel vapor spraying from an open spark plug hole or leaking fuel component.

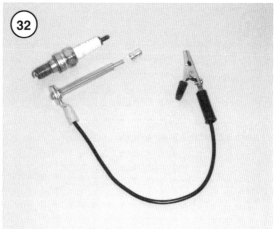

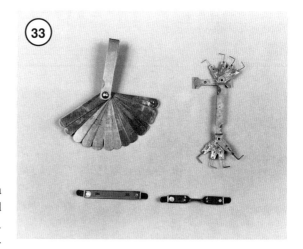

MEASURING TOOLS

The ability to accurately measure components with close tolerances is essential to perform many of the procedures in this manual.

Each type of measuring instrument is designed to measure a dimension with a certain degree of accuracy and within a certain range. When selecting the measuring tool, make sure it is applicable to the task.

As with all tools, measuring tools provide the best results if cared for properly. Improper use can damage the tool and cause inaccurate results. If any measurement is questionable, verify the measurement using another tool. A standard gauge is usually provided with measuring tools to check accuracy and calibrate the tool if necessary.

Accurate measurements are only possible if the mechanic possesses a feel for using the tool. Heavy-handed use of measuring tools produces less accurate results. Hold the tool gently by the fingertips so the point at which the tool contacts the object is easily felt. This feel for the equipment will produce more accurate measurements and reduce the risk of dam-

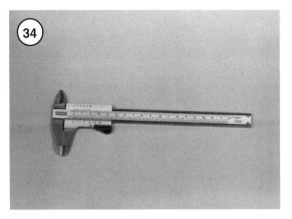

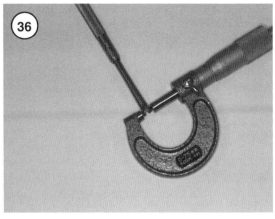

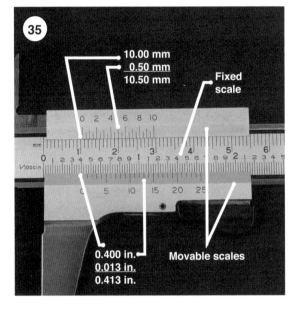

aging the tool or component. Refer to the following sections for specific measuring tools.

Feeler Gauge

The feeler, or thickness gauge (**Figure 33**), is used for measuring the distance between two surfaces.

A feeler gauge set consists of an assortment of steel strips of graduated thickness. Each blade is marked with its thickness. Blades can be of various lengths and angles for different procedures.

A common use for a feeler gauge is to measure valve clearance. Wire (round) type gauges are used to measure spark plug gap.

Calipers

Calipers (**Figure 34**) are excellent tools for obtaining inside, outside and depth measurements. Although not as precise as a micrometer, they allow reasonable precision, typically to within 0.05

mm (0.001 in.). Most calipers have a range up to 150 mm (6 in.).

Calipers are available in dial, vernier or digital versions. Dial calipers have a dial readout that provides convenient reading. Vernier calipers have marked scales that must be compared to determine the measurement. The digital caliper uses a LCD to show the measurement.

Properly maintain the measuring surfaces of the caliper. There must not be any dirt or burrs between the tool and the object being measured. Never force the caliper closed around an object; close the caliper around the highest point so it can be removed with a slight drag. Some calipers require calibration. Always refer to the manufacturer's instructions when using a new or unfamiliar caliper.

To read a vernier caliper refer to **Figure 35**. The fixed scale is marked in 1 mm increments. Ten individual lines on the fixed scale equal 1 cm. The moveable scale is marked in 0.05 mm (hundredth) increments. To obtain a reading, establish the first number by the location of the 0 line on the moveable scale in relation to the first line to the left on the fixed scale. In this example, the number is 10 mm. To determine the next number, note which of the lines on the movable scale align with a mark on the fixed scale. A number of lines will seem close, but only one will align exactly. In this case, 0.50 mm is the reading to add to the first number. The result of adding 10 mm and 0.50 mm is a measurement of 10.50 mm.

Micrometers

A micrometer (**Figure 36**) is an instrument designed for linear measurement using the decimal divisions of the inch or meter. While there are many types and styles of micrometers, most of the procedures in this manual call for an outside micrometer. The outside micrometer is used to measure the outside diameter of cylindrical forms and the thickness of materials.

A micrometer's size indicates the minimum and maximum size of a part that it can measure. The usual sizes are 0-25 mm (0-1 in.), 25-50 mm (1-2 in.), 50-75 mm (2-3 in.) and 75-100 mm (3-4 in.).

Micrometers that cover a wider range of measurements are available. These use a large frame with interchangeable anvils of various lengths. This type of micrometer offers a cost savings; however, its overall size may make it less convenient.

Adjustment

Before using a micrometer, check its adjustment as follows.

1. Clean the anvil and spindle faces.
2A. To check a 0-1 in. or 0-25 mm micrometer:
   a. Turn the thimble until the spindle contacts the anvil. If the micrometer has a ratchet stop, use it to ensure the proper amount of pressure is applied.
   b. If the adjustment is correct, the 0 mark on the thimble will align exactly with the 0 mark on the sleeve line. If the marks do not align, the micrometer is out of adjustment.
   c. Follow the manufacturer's instructions to adjust the micrometer.
2B. To check a micrometer larger than 1 in. or 25 mm, use the standard gauge supplied by the manufacturer. A standard gauge is a steel block, disc or rod that is machined to an exact size.
   a. Place the standard gauge between the spindle and anvil and measure its outside diameter or length. If the micrometer has a ratchet stop, use it to ensure the proper amount of pressure is applied.
   b. If the adjustment is correct, the 0 mark on the thimble will align exactly with the 0 mark on the sleeve line. If the marks do not align, the micrometer is out of adjustment.
   c. Follow the manufacturer's instructions to adjust the micrometer.

Care

Micrometers are precision instruments. They must be used and maintained with great care. Note the following:

1. Store micrometers in protective cases or separate padded drawers in a toolbox.
2. When in storage, make sure the spindle and anvil faces do not contact each other or another object. If they do, temperature changes and corrosion may damage the contact faces.
3. Do not clean a micrometer with compressed air. Dirt forced into the tool causes wear.
4. Lubricate micrometers to prevent corrosion.

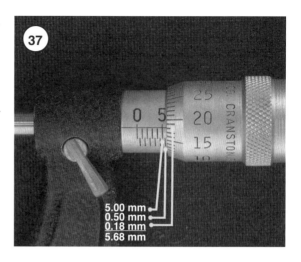

5.00 mm
0.50 mm
0.18 mm
5.68 mm

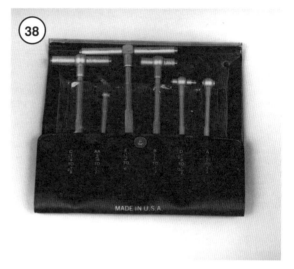

MADE IN U.S.A.

Reading

When reading a micrometer, numbers are taken from different scales and added together.

For accurate results, properly maintain the measuring surfaces of the micrometer. There cannot be any dirt or burrs between the tool and the measured object. Never force the micrometer closed around an object. Close the micrometer around the highest point so it can be removed with a slight drag.

The standard metric micrometer is accurate to one one-hundredth of a millimeter (0.01 mm). The sleeve line is graduated in millimeter and half millimeter increments. The marks on the upper half of the sleeve line equal 1.00 mm. Each fifth mark above the sleeve line is identified with a number. The number sequence depends on the size of the micrometer. A 0-25 mm micrometer, for example, will have sleeve marks numbered 0 through 25 in 5 mm increments. This numbering sequence continues with larger micrometers. On all metric micrometers, each mark on the lower half of the sleeve equals 0.50 mm.

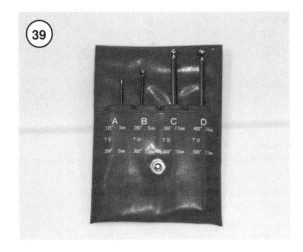

Telescoping and Small Hole Gauges

Use telescoping gauges (**Figure 38**) and small hole gauges (**Figure 39**) to measure bores. Neither gauge has a scale for direct readings. An outside micrometer must be used to determine the reading.

To use a telescoping gauge, select the correct size gauge for the bore. Compress the moveable post and carefully insert the gauge into the bore. Carefully move the gauge in the bore to make sure it is centered. Tighten the knurled end of the gauge to hold the moveable post in position. Remove the gauge and measure the length of the posts. Telescoping gauges are typically used to measure cylinder bores.

To use a small hole gauge, select the correct size gauge for the bore. Carefully insert the gauge into the bore. Tighten the knurled end of the gauge to carefully expand the gauge fingers to the limit within the bore. Do not overtighten the gauge; there is no built-in release. Excessive tightening can damage the bore surface and tool. Remove the gauge and measure the outside dimension with a micrometer (**Figure 36**). Small hole gauges are typically used to measure valve guides.

Dial Indicator

A dial indicator (**Figure 40**) is a gauge with a dial face and needle used to measure variations in dimensions and movements. Measuring brake rotor runout is a typical use for a dial indicator.

Dial indicators are available in various ranges and graduations and with three types of mounting bases: magnetic, clamp or screw-in stud.

Cylinder Bore Gauge

A cylinder bore gauge is similar to a dial indicator. These typically consist of a dial indicator, handle and different length adapters (anvils) to fit the gauge to various bore sizes. The bore gauge is used to measure bore size, taper and out-of-round. When using a bore gauge, follow the manufacturer's instructions.

Compression Gauge

A compression gauge (**Figure 41**) measures combustion chamber (cylinder) pressure, usually in psi or kg/cm². The gauge adapter is either inserted and held in place or screwed into the spark plug hole to obtain the reading. Disable the engine so it will not start and hold the throttle in the wide-open position when performing a compression test. An engine that does not have adequate compression cannot be properly tuned. Refer to Chapter Three.

The tapered end of the thimble has 50 lines marked around it. Each mark equals 0.01 mm. One complete turn of the thimble aligns its 0 mark with the first line on the lower half of the sleeve line, or 0.50 mm.

When reading a metric micrometer, add the number of millimeters and half-millimeters on the sleeve line to the number of one one-hundredth millimeters on the thimble. Perform the following steps while referring to **Figure 37**.

1. Read the upper half of the sleeve line and count the number of lines visible. Each upper line equals 1 mm.

2. See if the half-millimeter line is visible on the lower sleeve line. If so, add 0.50 mm to the reading in Step 1.

3. Read the thimble mark that aligns with the sleeve line. Each thimble mark equals 0.01 mm.

4. If a thimble mark does not align exactly with the sleeve line, estimate the amount between the lines. For accurate readings in two-thousandths of a millimeter (0.002 mm), use a metric vernier micrometer.

5. Add the readings from Steps 1-4.

Multimeter

A multimeter (**Figure 42**) is an essential tool for electrical system diagnosis. The voltage function indicates the voltage applied or available to various electrical components. The ohmmeter function tests circuits for continuity, or lack of continuity, and measures the resistance of a circuit.

Some manufacturers' specifications for electrical components are based on results using a specific test meter. Results may vary if using a meter not recommend by the manufacturer. Such requirements are noted when applicable.

Ohmmeter (analog) calibration

Each time an analog ohmmeter is used or the scale is changed, the ohmmeter must be calibrated.

Digital ohmmeters do not require calibration.
1. Make sure the meter battery is in good condition.
2. Make sure the meter probes are in good condition.
3. Touch the two probes together and observe the needle location on the ohms scale. The needle must align with the 0 mark to obtain accurate measurements.
4. If necessary, rotate the meter ohms adjust knob until the needle and 0 mark align.

ELECTRICAL SYSTEM FUNDAMENTALS

A thorough study of the many types of electrical systems used in today's motorcycles is beyond the scope of this manual. However, a basic understanding of voltage, resistance and amperage is necessary to perform diagnostic tests. Refer to Chapter Two, Chapter Ten (XR600R) and Chapter Eleven (XR650L) for troubleshooting and testing procedures.

Voltage

Voltage is the electrical potential or pressure in an electrical circuit and is expressed in volts. The more pressure (voltage) in a circuit, the more work can be performed.

Direct current (DC) voltage means the electricity flows in one direction. All circuits powered by a battery are DC circuits.

Alternating current (AC) means the electricity flows in one direction momentarily and then switches to the opposite direction. Alternator output is an example of AC voltage. This voltage must be changed or rectified to direct current to operate in a battery powered system.

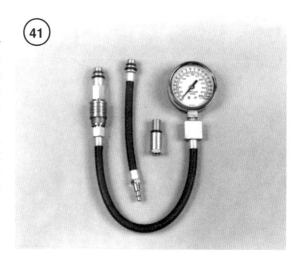

Resistance

Resistance is the opposition to the flow of electricity within a circuit or component and is measured in ohms. Resistance causes a reduction in available current and voltage.

Resistance is measured in an inactive circuit with an ohmmeter. The ohmmeter sends a small amount of current into the circuit and measures how difficult it is to push the current through the circuit.

An ohmmeter, although useful, is not always a good indicator of a circuit's actual ability under operating conditions. This is due to the low voltage (6-9 volts) that the meter uses to test the circuit. The voltage in an ignition coil secondary winding can be several thousand volts. Such high voltage can cause the coil to malfunction, even though it tests acceptable during a resistance test.

Resistance generally increases with temperature. Perform all testing with the component or circuit at room temperature. Resistance tests performed at high temperatures may indicate false resistance readings and cause the unnecessary replacement of a component.

Amperage

Amperage is the unit of measure for the amount of current within a circuit. Current is the actual flow of electricity. The higher the current, the more work can be performed up to a given point. If the current flow exceeds the circuit or component capacity, the system will be damaged.

SERVICE METHODS

Many of the procedures in this manual are straightforward and can be performed by anyone reasonably competent with tools. However, consider previous

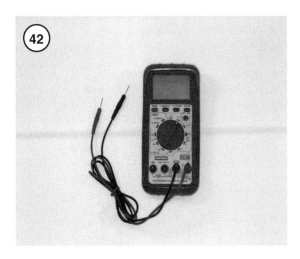

experience carefully before performing any operation involving complicated procedures.

1. Front, in this manual, refers to the front of the motorcycle. The front of any component is the end closest to the front of the motorcycle. The left and right sides refer to the position of the parts as viewed by the rider sitting on the seat facing forward.

2. When servicing the motorcycle, secure it in a safe manner.

3. Label all similar parts for location and mark all mating parts for position. If possible, photograph or draw the number and thickness of any shim as it is removed. Identify parts by placing them in sealed and labeled plastic bags. It is possible for carefully laid out parts to become disturbed, making it difficult to reassemble the components correctly without a diagram.

4. Label disconnected wires and connectors with masking tape and a marking pen. Do not rely on memory alone.

5. Protect finished surfaces from physical damage or corrosion. Keep gasoline and other chemicals off painted surfaces.

6. Use penetrating oil on frozen or tight bolts. Avoid using heat where possible. Heat can warp, melt or affect the temper of parts. Heat also damages the finish of paint and plastics. Refer to *Heating Components* in this section.

7. When a part is a press fit or requires a special tool for removal, the information or type of tool is identified in the text. Otherwise, if a part is difficult to remove or install, determine the cause before proceeding.

8. To prevent objects or debris from falling into the engine, cover all openings.

9. Read each procedure thoroughly and compare the figures to the actual components before starting the procedure. Perform the procedure in sequence.

10. Recommendations are occasionally made to refer service to a dealership or specialist. In these cases, the work can be performed more economically by the specialist than by the home mechanic.

11. The term *replace* means to discard a defective part and replace it with a new part. *Overhaul* means to remove, disassemble, inspect, measure, repair and/or replace parts as required to recondition an assembly.

12. Some operations require the use of a hydraulic press. If a press is not available, have these operations performed by a shop equipped with the necessary equipment. Do not use makeshift equipment that may damage the motorcycle. Do not direct high-pressure water at steering bearings, fuel body hoses, wheel bearings, suspension and electrical components. The water forces the grease out of the bearings and could damage the seals.

13. Repairs are much faster and easier if the motorcycle is clean before starting work. Degrease the motorcycle with a commercial degreaser; follow the directions on the container for the best results. Clean all parts with cleaning solvent.

14. If special tools are required, have them available before starting the procedure. When special tools are required, they will be described at the beginning of the procedure.

15. Make sure all shims and washers are reinstalled in the same location and position.

16. Whenever rotating parts contact a stationary part, look for a shim or washer.

17. Use new gaskets if there is any doubt about the condition of old ones.

18. If self-locking fasteners are used, replace them. Do not install standard fasteners in place of self-locking ones.

19. Use grease to hold small parts in place if they tend to fall out during assembly. Do not apply grease to electrical or brake components.

Heating Components

> *WARNING*
> *Wear protective gloves to prevent burns*
> *and injury when heating parts.*

> *CAUTION*
> *Do not use a welding torch when heating parts. A welding torch applies excessive heat to a small area very quickly, which can damage parts.*

A heat gun or propane torch is required to disassemble, assemble, remove and install many components in this manual. Read the safety and operating information supplied by the manufacturer of the heat gun or propane torch while also noting the following:

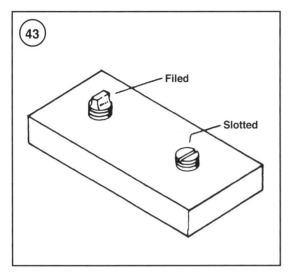

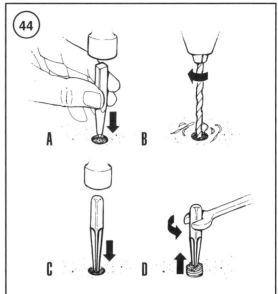

1. The work area should be clean and dry. Remove all combustible components and materials from the work area. Wipe up all grease, oil and other fluids from parts. Check for leaking or damaged fuel system components. Repair or remove these parts before beginning work.

2. Never use a flame near the battery, fuel tank, fuel lines or other flammable materials.

3. When using a heat gun, remember that the temperature can be in excess of 540° C (1000° F).

4. Have a fire extinguisher near the job.

5. Always wear protective goggles and gloves when heating parts.

6. Before heating a part installed on the motorcycle, check areas around the part and those *hidden* that could be damaged or possibly ignite. Do not heat surfaces than can be damaged by heat. Shield materials near the part or area to be heated. For example, cables and wiring harnesses.

7. Before heating a part, read the entire procedure to make sure the required tools are available. This allows quick work while the part is at its optimum temperature.

8. The amount of heat recommended to remove or install a part is typically listed in the procedure. However, before heating parts without a specific recommendation, consider the possible effects. To avoid damaging a part, monitor the temperature with heat sticks or an infrared thermometer, if possible. Another way, though not as accurate, is to place tiny drops of water on the part. When the water starts to sizzle, the part is hot enough. Keep the heat in motion to prevent overheating.

Removing Frozen Fasteners

If a fastener cannot be removed, several methods may be used to loosen it. First, liberally apply pen-

etrating oil, and let it penetrate for 10-15 minutes. Rap the fastener several times with a small hammer. Do not hit it hard enough to cause damage. Reapply the penetrating oil if necessary.

For frozen screws, apply penetrating oil as described, and then insert a screwdriver in the slot and rap the top of the screwdriver with a hammer. This loosens the rust so the screw can be removed in the normal way. If the screw head is too damaged to use this method, grip the head with locking pliers and twist it out.

If heat is required, refer to *Heating Components* in this section.

Removing Broken Fasteners

If the head breaks off a screw or bolt, several methods are available for removing the remaining portion. If a large portion of the remainder projects out, try gripping it with locking pliers. If the projecting portion is too small, file it to fit a wrench or cut a slot in it to fit a screwdriver (**Figure 43**).

If the head breaks off flush, use a screw extractor. To do this, center punch the exact center of the screw or bolt (A, **Figure 44**), and then drill a small hole in the screw (B) and tap the extractor into the hole (C). Back the screw out with a wrench on the extractor (D, **Figure 44**).

Repairing Damaged Threads

Occasionally, threads are stripped through carelessness or impact damage. Often the threads can be repaired by running a tap (for internal threads on nuts) or die (for external threads on bolts) through

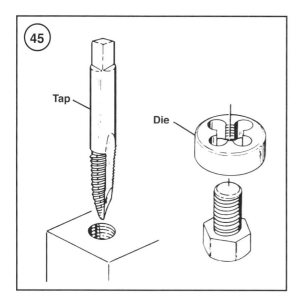

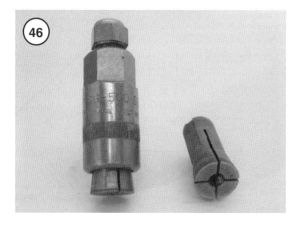

the threads (**Figure 45**). To clean or repair spark plug threads, use a spark plug tap.

If an internal thread is damaged, it may be necessary to install a Helicoil or some other type of thread insert. Follow the manufacturer's instructions when installing its insert.

If it is necessary to drill and tap a hole, refer to **Table 8** for metric tap and drill sizes.

Stud Removal/Installation

A stud removal tool (**Figure 46**) is available from most tool suppliers. This tool makes the removal and installation of studs easier. If one is not available and the threads on the stud are not damaged, thread two nuts onto the stud and tighten them against each other. Remove the stud by turning the lower nut.

1. Measure the height of the stud above the surface.
2. Thread the stud removal tool onto the stud and tighten it, or thread two nuts onto the stud.
3. Remove the stud by turning the stud remover or the lower nut.

4. Remove any threadlocking compound from the threaded hole. Clean the threads with an aerosol parts cleaner.
5. Install the stud removal tool onto the new stud, or thread two nuts onto the stud.
6. Apply threadlocking compound to the threads of the stud.
7. Install the stud and tighten with the stud removal tool or the top nut.
8. Install the stud to the height noted in Step 1 or its torque specification.
9. Remove the stud removal tool or the two nuts.

Removing Hoses

When removing stubborn hoses, do not exert excessive force on the hose or fitting. Remove the hose clamp and carefully insert a small screwdriver or pick tool between the fitting and hose. Apply a spray lubricant under the hose and carefully twist the hose off the fitting. Clean the fitting of any corrosion or rubber hose material with a wire brush. Clean the inside of the hose thoroughly. Do not use any lubricant when installing the hose (new or old). The lubricant may allow the hose to come off the fitting, even with the clamp secure.

Bearings

Bearings are precision parts, they must be maintained with proper lubrication and maintenance. If a bearing is damaged, replace it immediately. When installing a new bearing, make sure to prevent damaging it. Bearing replacement procedures are included in the individual chapters where applicable; however, use the following sections as a guideline.

Unless otherwise specified, install bearings with the manufacturer's mark or number facing outward.

Removal

While bearings are normally removed only when damaged, there may be times when it is necessary to remove a bearing that is in good condition. However, improper bearing removal will damage the bearing and possibly the shaft or housing. Note the following when removing bearings:

1. Before removing the bearings, note the following:
   a. Refer to the bearing replacement procedure in the appropriate chapter for any special instructions.
   b. Remove any seals that interfere with bearing removal. Refer to *Seal Replacement* in this section.

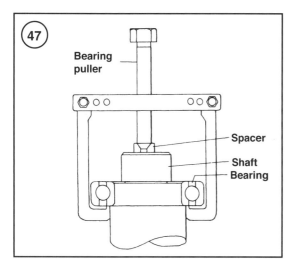

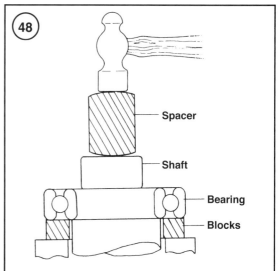

c. When removing more than one bearing, identify the bearings before removing them. Refer to the bearing manufacturer's numbers on the bearing.

d. Note and record the direction in which the bearing numbers face for proper installation.

e. Remove any set plates or bearing retainers before removing the bearings.

2. When using a puller to remove a bearing from a shaft, make sure the shaft is not damaged. Always place a piece of metal between the end of the shaft and the puller screw. In addition, place the puller arms next to the inner bearing race. Refer to **Figure 47**.

3. When using a hammer to remove a bearing from a shaft, do not strike the hammer directly against the shaft. Instead, use a brass or aluminum rod between the hammer and shaft (**Figure 48**) and make sure to support both bearing races with wooden blocks as shown.

4. The ideal method of bearing removal is with a hydraulic press. Note the following when using a press:

a. Always support the inner and outer bearing races with a suitable size wooden or aluminum ring (**Figure 49**). If only the outer race is supported, pressure applied against the balls and/or the inner race will damage them.

b. Always make sure the press arm (**Figure 49**) aligns with the center of the shaft. If the arm is not centered, it may damage the bearing and/or shaft.

c. The moment the shaft is free of the bearing, it will drop to the floor. Secure or hold the shaft to prevent it from falling.

d. When removing bearings from a housing, support the housing with wooden blocks to prevent damage to gasket surfaces.

5. Use a blind bearing puller to remove bearings installed in blind holes (**Figure 50**).

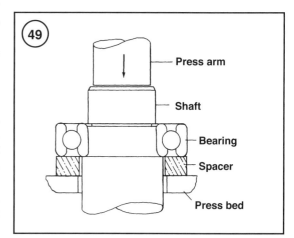

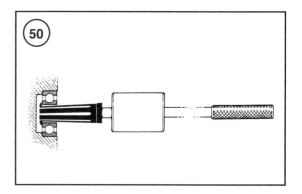

Installation

1. When installing a bearing in a housing, apply pressure to the *outer* bearing race (**Figure 51**). When installing a bearing on a shaft, apply pressure to the *inner* bearing race (**Figure 52**).

2. When installing a bearing as described in Step 1, a driver is required. Never strike the bearing directly with a hammer or the bearing will be damaged.

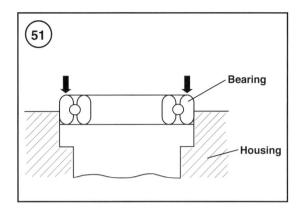

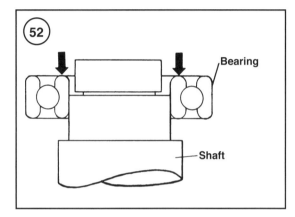

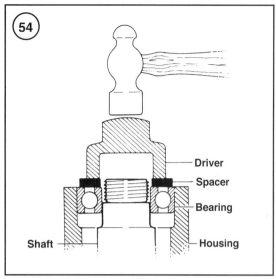

er underneath the driver tool so pressure is applied evenly across both races. Refer to **Figure 54**. If the outer race is not supported, the balls push against the outer bearing race and damage it.

Interference fit

1. Follow this procedure when installing a bearing over a shaft. When a tight fit is required, the bearing inside diameter will be smaller than the shaft. In this case, driving the bearing on the shaft using normal methods may cause bearing damage. Instead, heat the bearing before installation. Note the following:
   a. Secure the shaft so it is ready for bearing installation.
   b. Clean all residue from the bearing surface of the shaft. Remove burrs with a file.
   c. Fill a suitable pot or beaker with clean mineral oil. Place a thermometer rated above 120° C (248° F) in the oil. Support the thermometer so it does not rest on the bottom or side of the pot.
   d. Remove the bearing from its wrapper and secure it with a piece of heavy wire bent to hold it in the pot. Hang the bearing in the pot so it does not touch the bottom or sides of the pot.
   e. Turn the heat on and monitor the thermometer. When the oil temperature rises to approximately 120° C (248° F), remove the bearing from the pot and quickly install it. If necessary, place a socket on the inner bearing race and tap the bearing into place. As the bearing chills, it tightens on the shaft, so installation must be done quickly. Make sure the bearing is installed completely.

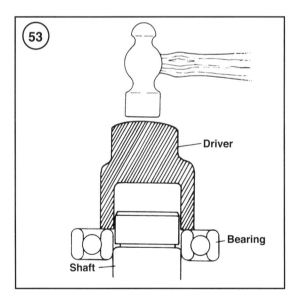

When installing a bearing, use a piece of pipe or a driver with a diameter that matches the bearing race. **Figure 53** shows the correct way to use a driver and hammer to install a bearing on a shaft.

3. Step 1 describes how to install a bearing in a housing or over a shaft. However, when installing a bearing over a shaft and into the housing at the *same time*, a tight fit will be required for both outer and inner bearing races. In this situation, install a spac-

2. Follow this step when installing a bearing in a housing. Bearings are generally installed in a housing with a slight interference fit. Driving the

bearing into the housing using normal methods may damage the housing or cause bearing damage. Instead, heat the housing before the bearing is installed. Note the following:

a. Before heating the housing in this procedure, wash the housing thoroughly with detergent and water. Rinse and rewash the housing as required to remove all oil and chemicals.

b. Heat the housing to approximately 100° C (212° F) with a heat gun or on a hot plate. Monitor temperature with an infrared thermometer, heat sticks or place tiny drops of water on the housing; if they sizzle and evaporate immediately, the temperature is correct. Heat only one housing at a time.

c. If a hot plate is used, remove the housing and place it on wooden blocks.

d. Hold the housing with the bearing side down and tap the bearing out with a suitable size socket and extension. Repeat for all bearings in the housing.

e. Before heating the bearing housing, place the new bearing in a freezer, if possible. Chilling a bearing slightly reduces its outside diameter while the heated bearing housing assembly is slightly larger due to heat expansion. This makes bearing installation easier.

f. While the housing is still hot, install the new bearing(s) into the housing. Install the bearings by hand, if possible. If necessary, lightly tap the bearing(s) into the housing with a socket placed on the outer bearing race (**Figure 51**). Do not install bearings by driving on the inner-bearing race. Install the bearing(s) until it seats completely.

Seal Replacement

Seals are used to contain oil, water, grease or combustion gasses in a housing or shaft. Improper removal of a seal can damage the housing or shaft. Improper installation of the seal can damage the seal.

Before replacing a seal, identify it as a rubber or Teflon seal. On a rubber seal (**Figure 55**), the body and sealing element will be made of the same material. The seal lip (element) will also be equipped with a garter spring. On a Teflon seal, the body and seal lip will be noticeably different. The outer part is normally made of rubber and the sealing lip, placed in the middle of the seal, is Teflon. A garter spring is not used.When replacing seals, consider the following:

1. Prying is generally the easiest and most effective method of removing a seal from the housing. However, always place a rag under the pry tool (**Figure 56**) to prevent damage to the housing.

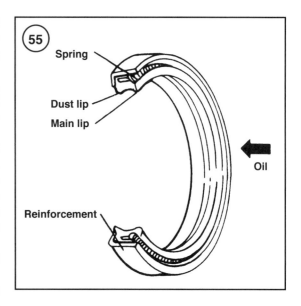

2. Before installing a typical rubber seal, pack waterproof grease in the seal lips.

3. In most cases, install seals with the manufacturer's numbers or marks face out.

4. Install seals either by hand or with tools. Center the seal in its bore and attempt to install it by hand. If necessary, install the seal with a socket or bearing driver placed on the outside of the seal as shown in **Figure 57**. Drive the seal squarely into the housing until it is flush with its mounting bore. Never install a seal by hitting against the top of the seal with a hammer.

STORAGE

Several months of non-use can cause a general deterioration of the motorcycle. This is especially true in areas of extreme temperature variations. This deterioration can be minimized with careful preparation for storage. A properly stored motorcycle is much easier to return to service.

Storage Area Selection

When selecting a storage area, consider the following:

1. The storage area must be dry. A heated area is best, but not necessary. It should be insulated to minimize extreme temperature variations.

2. If the building has large window areas, mask them to keep sunlight off the motorcycle.

3. Avoid storage areas close to saltwater.

4. Consider the area's risk of fire, theft or vandalism. Check with your insurer regarding motorcycle coverage while in storage.

riding time since the last service. Fill the engine with the recommended type and quantity of oil.

3. Fill the fuel tank completely.

4. Remove the spark plug from the cylinder head. Ground the spark plug cap to the engine. Refer to *Ignition Ground Tool* in this chapter. Pour a teaspoon (15-20 ml) of engine oil into the cylinders. Place a rag over the openings and slowly turn the engine over to distribute the oil. Reinstall the spark plug.

5. On XR650L models, remove the battery. Store it in a cool, dry location. Charge the battery once a month. Refer to *Battery* in Chapter Eleven for service.

6. Cover the exhaust and intake openings.

7. Apply a protective substance to the plastic and rubber components, including the tires. Make sure to follow the manufacturer's instructions for each type of product being used.

8. Rotate the front tire periodically to prevent a flat spot from developing and damaging the tire.

9. Cover the motorcycle with old bed sheets or something similar. Do not cover it with any plastic material that will trap moisture.

Preparing the Motorcycle for Storage

The amount of preparation a motorcycle should undergo before storage depends on the expected length of non-use, storage area conditions and personal preference. Consider the following list the minimum requirement:

1. Wash the motorcycle thoroughly. Make sure all dirt, mud and road debris are removed.

2. Start the engine and allow it to reach operating temperature. Drain the engine oil regardless of the

Returning the Motorcycle to Service

The amount of service required when returning a motorcycle to service after storage depends on the length of non-use and storage conditions. In addition to performing the reverse of the above procedure, make sure the brakes, clutch, throttle and engine stop switch work properly before operating the motorcycle. Refer to Chapter Three and evaluate the service intervals to determine which areas require service.

Table 1 MOTORCYCLE DIMENSIONS (XR600R)

Footpeg height	
1991-1992	
Left	426 mm (16.8 in.)
Right	424 mm (16.7 in.)
1993-2000	430 mm (16.9 in.)
Ground clearance	345 mm (13.6 in.)
Overall height	
1991	1230 mm (48.4 in.)
1992-2000	1215 mm (47.8 in.)
Overall length	2160 mm (85.0 in.)
Overall width	900 mm (35.5 in.)
Seat height	955 mm (37.6 in.)
Wheel base	1455 mm (57.3 in.)

Table 2 MOTORCYCLE DIMENSIONS (XR650L)

Footpeg height	
1993	415 mm (16.3 in.)
1994-on	419 mm (16.5 in.)
Ground clearance	330 mm (13.0 in.)
Overall height	1245 mm (49.0 in.)
Overall length	
1993	2185 mm (86.0 in.)
1994-on	2190 mm (86.2 in.)
Overall width	855 mm (33.7 in.)
Seat height	
1993	950 mm (37.4 in.)
1994-on	940 mm (37.0 in.)
Wheel base	1455 mm (57.3 in.)

Table 3 MOTORCYCLE WEIGHT

Dry weight	
XR600R	
1991	122 kg (269 lb.)
1992-2000	123 kg (272 lb.)
1997-2000 (CA)	124 kg (273 lb.)
XR650L (U.S. and CA)	
1993	147 kg (324 lb.)
1994-2007	149 kg (328 lb.)
2008-on	NA*
XR650L (Canada)	
1993	145 kg (320 lb.)
1994-1996	148 kg (326 lb.)
1997-on	149 kg (328 lb.)
Curb weight	
XR650L (U.S. and CA)	
1993	157 kg (346 lb.)
1994-2007	157.4 kg (347 lb.)
2008-on	157 kg (346 lb.)
XR650L (Canada)	
1993	155 kg (342 lb.)
1994-1996	156 kg (345 lb.)
1997-2007	157.5 kg (347.2 lb.)
2008-on	158 kg (348 lb.)

Table 4 FUEL TANK CAPACITY

Total (including reserve)	
XR600R	10.0 liters (2.7 U.S. gal.) (2.24 Imp. gal.)
XR650L	10.5 liters (2.8 U.S. gal.) (2.31 Imp. gal.)
Reserve	
XR600R	2.0 liters (0.50 U.S. gal.) (0.42 Imp. gal.)
XR650L	
1993 - 2007	2.3 liters (0.60 U.S. gal.) (0.50 Imp. gal.)
2008-on	2.8 liters (0.74 U.S. gal.) (0.62 Imp.gal.)

Table 5 CONVERSION FORMULAS

Multiply:	By:	To get the equivalent of:
Length		
Inches	25.4	Millimeter
Inches	2.54	Centimeter
Miles	1.609	Kilometer
Feet	0.3048	Meter
Millimeter	0.03937	Inches
Centimeter	0.3937	Inches

(continued)

Table 5 CONVERSION FORMULAS (continued)

Multiply:	By:	To get the equivalent of:
Kilometer	0.6214	Mile
Meter	3.281	Feet
Fluid volume		
U.S. quarts	0.9463	Liters
U.S. gallons	3.785	Liters
U.S. ounces	29.573529	Milliliters
Liters	0.2641721	U.S. gallons
Liters	1.0566882	U.S. quarts
Liters	33.814023	U.S. ounces
Milliliters	0.033814	U.S. ounces
Milliliters	1.0	Cubic centimeters
Milliliters	0.001	Liters
Torque		
Foot-pounds	1.3558	Newton-meters
Foot-pounds	0.138255	Meters-kilograms
Inch-pounds	0.11299	Newton-meters
Newton-meters	0.7375622	Foot-pounds
Newton-meters	8.8507	Inch-pounds
Meters-kilograms	7.2330139	Foot-pounds
Volume		
Cubic inches	16.387064	Cubic centimeters
Cubic centimeters	0.0610237	Cubic inches
Temperature		
Fahrenheit	(°F − 32) × 0.556	Centigrade
Centigrade	(°C × 1.8) + 32	Fahrenheit
Weight		
Ounces	28.3495	Grams
Pounds	0.4535924	Kilograms
Grams	0.035274	Ounces
Kilograms	2.2046224	Pounds
Pressure		
Pounds per square inch	0.070307	Kilograms per square centimeter
Kilograms per square centimeter	14.223343	Pounds per square inch
Kilopascals	0.1450	Pounds per square inch
Pounds per square inch	6.895	Kilopascals
Speed		
Miles per hour	1.609344	Kilometers per hour
Kilometers per hour	0.6213712	Miles per hour

Table 6 TECHNICAL ABBREVIATIONS

A	Ampere
AC	Alternating current
A.h.	Ampere hour
C	Celsius
cc	Cubic centimeter
CDI	Capacitor discharge ignition
CKP sensor	Crankshaft position sensor
cm	Centimeter
cu. in.	Cubic inch and cubic inches
cyl.	Cylinder
DC	Direct current
DOHC	Dual overhead camshaft
F	Fahrenheit
fl. oz.	Fluid ounces
ft.	Foot
ft.-lb.	Foot-pounds
gal.	Gallon and gallons
hp	Horsepower

(continued)

Table 6 TECHNICAL ABBREVIATIONS (continued)

Hz	Hertz
in.	Inch and inches
in.-lb.	Inch-pounds
in. Hg	Inches of mercury
kg	Kilogram
kg/cm^2	Kilogram per square centimeter
kgm	Kilogram meter
km	Kilometer
km/h	Kilometer per hour
kPa	Kilopascals
kW	Kilowatt
L	Liter and liters
L/m	Liters per minute
lb.	Pound and pounds
m	Meter
mL	Milliliter
mm	Millimeter
MPa	Megapascal
N	Newton
NA	Specification not available from the manufacturer
N·m	Newton meter
oz.	Ounce and ounces
p	Pascal
PAIR	Pulsed secondary air injection
psi	Pounds per square inch
pt.	Pint and pints
qt.	Quart and quarts
RFVC	Radial four valve combustion
rpm	Revolution per minute
SOHC	Single overhead camshaft
TDC	Top dead center
V	Volt
VAC	Alternating current voltage
VDC	Direct current voltage
W	Watt

Table 7 METRIC, DECIMAL AND FRACTIONAL EQUIVALENTS

mm	in.	Nearest fraction	mm	in.	Nearest fraction
1	0.0394	1/32	26	1.0236	1 1/32
2	0.0787	3/32	27	1.0630	1 1/16
3	0.1181	1/8	28	1.1024	1 3/32
4	0.1575	5/32	29	1.1417	1 5/32
5	0.1969	3/16	30	1.1811	1 3/16
6	0.2362	1/4	31	1.2205	1 7/32
7	0.2756	9/32	32	1.2598	1 1/4
8	0.3150	5/16	33	1.2992	1 5/16
9	0.3543	11/32	34	1.3386	1 11/32
10	0.3937	13/32	35	1.3780	1 3/8
11	0.4331	7/16	36	1.4173	1 13/32
12	0.4724	15/32	37	1.4567	1 15/32
13	0.5118	1/2	38	1.4961	1 1/2
14	0.5512	9/16	39	1.5354	1 17/32
15	0.5906	19/32	40	1.5748	1 9/16
16	0.6299	5/8	41	1.6142	1 5/8
17	0.6693	21/32	42	1.6535	1 21/32
18	0.7087	23/32	43	1.6929	1 11/16
19	0.7480	3/4	44	1.7323	1 23/32
20	0.7874	25/32	45	1.7717	1 25/32
21	0.8268	13/16	46	1.8110	1 13/16
22	0.8661	7/8	47	1.8504	1 27/32
23	0.9055	29/32	48	1.8898	1 7/8
24	0.9449	15/16	49	1.9291	1 15/16
25	0.9843	31/32	50	1.9685	1 31/32

Table 8 METRIC TAP AND DRILL SIZES

Metric size	Drill equivalent	Decimal fraction	Nearest fraction
3 × 0.50	No. 39	0.0995	3/32
3 × 0.60	3/32	0.0937	3/32
4 × 0.70	No. 30	0.1285	1/8
4 × 0.75	1/8	0.125	1/8
5 × 0.80	No. 19	0.166	11/64
5 × 0.90	No. 20	0.161	5/32
6 × 1.00	No. 9	0.196	13/64
7 × 1.00	16/64	0.234	15/64
8 × 1.00	J	0.277	9/32
8 × 1.25	17/64	0.265	17/64
9 × 1.00	5/16	0.3125	5/16
9 × 1.25	5/16	0.3125	5/16
10 × 1.25	11/32	0.3437	11/32
10 × 1.50	R	0.339	11/32
11 × 1.50	3/8	0.375	3/8
12 × 1.50	13/32	0.406	13/32
12 × 1.75	13/32	0.406	13/32

Table 9 TORQUE RECOMMENDATIONS*

Thread diameter	N•m	in.-lb.	ft.-lb.
5 mm			
Hex bolt and nut	5	44	–
Screw	4	35	–
6 mm			
Hex bolt and nut	10	88	–
Screw	9	80	–
Flange bolt with 10 mm head	12	106	–
Flange bolt with 8 mm head			
XR600R and 1993-2007 XR650L	9	80	–
2008-on XR650L			
Flange bolt with 8 mm head, small flange	10	88	–
Flange bolt with 8 mm head, large flange	12	106	–
Flange bolt with 10 mm head and nut	12	106	–
8 mm			
Hex bolt and nut	22	–	16
Flange bolt and nut	27	–	20
10 mm			
Hex bolt and nut			
XR600R and 1993-2007 XR650L	35	–	26
2008-on XR650L	34	–	25
Flange bolt and nut			
XR600R and 1993-2007 XR650L	40	–	30
2008-on XR650L	39	–	29
12 mm			
Hex bolt and nut			
XR600R and 1993-2007 XR650L	55	–	41
2008-on XR650L	54	–	40

*Torque recommendations for fasteners without a specification. Refer to the torque specification table at the end of each applicable chapter for specific applications.

CHAPTER TWO

TROUBLESHOOTING

The troubleshooting procedures described in this chapter provide typical symptoms and logical methods for isolating the cause(s). There may be several ways to solve a problem, but only a systematic approach will be successful in avoiding wasted time and possibly unnecessary parts replacement. Gather as much information as possible to aid in diagnosis. Never assume anything and do not overlook the obvious. Make sure the kill switch is in the run position and there is fuel in the tank.

An engine needs three basics to run properly: correct air/ fuel mixture, compression and a spark at the correct time. If one of these is missing, the engine will not run.

Learning to recognize symptoms makes troubleshooting easier. In most cases, expensive and complicated test equipment is not needed to determine whether repairs can be performed at home. On the other hand, be realistic and do not start procedures that are beyond your experience and equipment available. If the motorcycle requires the attention of a professional, describe symptoms and conditions accurately and fully. The more information a technician has available, the easier it is to diagnose the problem.

ELECTRICAL COMPONENT REPLACEMENT

Most parts suppliers will not accept returned electrical components. If the exact cause of any electrical system malfunction has not been determined, do not attempt to remedy the problem through parts replacement. If an accurate diagnosis cannot be performed, have the suspect component or system tested by a professional technician before purchasing electrical components.

Consider any test results carefully before replacing a component that tests only slightly out of specification, especially resistance. A number of variables can affect test results dramatically. These include: the internal tester circuitry, ambient temperature and motorcycle operating conditions. All instructions and specifications have been checked for accuracy; however, successful test results depend to a great degree upon individual accuracy.

STARTING THE ENGINE

When experiencing engine-starting troubles, it is easy to work out of sequence and forget basic start-

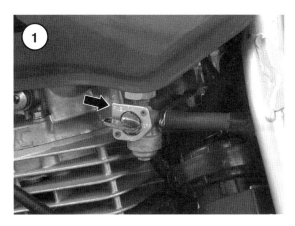

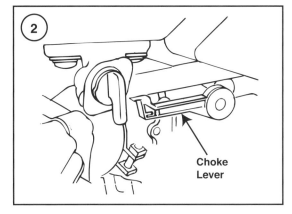

Choke
Lever

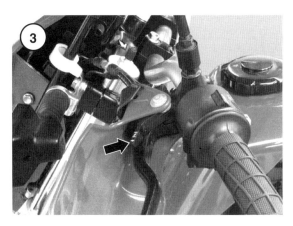

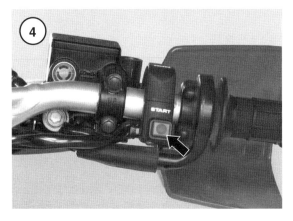

ing procedures. The following sections describe the
recommended starting procedures.

Before starting the engine, perform the pre-ride inspection as described in Chapter Three.

Starting Procedure

Engine is cold

1. Shift the transmission into neutral.
2. Turn the fuel valve (**Figure 1**) on.
3A. On XR600R models, if the air temperature is
below 35° C (95° F), push down the choke lever
(**Figure 2**) all the way to richen the air/fuel mixture.
3B. On XR650L models, if the air temperature is below 35° C (95° F), pull the choke lever (**Figure 3**) all
the way toward the handlebar to richen the air/fuel
mixture.
4. On XR650L models, turn the ignition switch on.
5. On XR600R models, pull in the decompression
lever on the handlebar.
6A. On XR600R models, while keeping the throttle
closed, pull the clutch lever fully in and firmly operate the kickstarter through its entire stroke.
6B. On XR650L models, while keeping the throttle
closed, pull the clutch lever fully in and press the
starter button (**Figure 4**).
7. When the engine starts, use the throttle to keep
the engine running until the engine warms up and
the choke can be fully closed. On XR600R models,
release the decompression lever.
8. If the temperature is 10°-35° C (50°-95° F), move
the choke lever to the midpoint position until the engine will run smoothly without the choke.

Engine is warm

1. Shift the transmission into neutral.
2. Turn the fuel valve (**Figure 1**) on.
3. On XR650L models, turn the ignition switch on.
4. On XR600R models, pull in the decompression
lever on the handlebar.
5A. On XR600R models, while keeping the throttle
closed, pull the clutch lever fully in and firmly operate the kickstarter through its entire stroke.
5B. On XR650L models, while keeping the throttle
closed, pull the clutch lever fully in and press the
starter button (**Figure 4**).

NOTE
*If the engine is not at normal operat-
ing temperature, it may be necessary to
place the choke lever at the midpoint to
prevent engine stumbling.*

6. On XR600R models, when the engine starts, release the decompressor lever.

Flooded engine

If the engine fails to start after several attempts, it is probably flooded. This occurs when too much fuel is drawn into the engine and the spark plug fails to ignite it. The smell of gasoline is often evident when the engine is flooded. Troubleshoot a flooded engine as follows:

1. Look for gasoline overflowing from the carburetor or overflow hose. If gasoline is evident, the engine is flooded and/or the float in the carburetor bowl is stuck. If the carburetor float is stuck, remove and repair the float assembly as described in Chapter Eight or Chapter Nine.

2. Shift the transmission into neutral.

3. Check that the choke lever (**Figure 2** or **Figure 3**) is fully open.

4. Press the engine stop button or switch to off.

5. On XR600R models, pull in the decompression lever on the handlebar.

6A. On XR600R models, hold the throttle in the fully open position. Then kick the kickstarter firmly through its entire stroke ten times to clear the engine. Close the throttle.

6B. On XR650L models, hold the throttle in the fully open position. Press the starter button (**Figure 4**) for 5 seconds, then release and wait 10 seconds.

> *NOTE*
> *On XR650L models, move the engine stop switch to run before performing Step 7.*

7. Attempt to start the engine. Make sure the choke is off. If the engine fails to start, repeat the procedure.

8. If the engine still does not start, refer to *Engine Will Not Start* in this chapter.

ENGINE WILL NOT START

Identifying the Problem

If the engine does not start, perform the following steps in order. If the engine fails to start after performing these checks, refer to the troubleshooting procedures indicated in the steps. If the engine starts, but idles or runs roughly, refer to *Poor Engine Performance* in this chapter.

1. Refer to *Starting the Engine* in this chapter to make sure all starting procedures are correct.

2. On XR650L models, if the starter does not operate, refer to *Starting System* in this chapter.

3. If the engine seems flooded, refer to *Starting The Engine* in this chapter. If the engine is not flooded, continue with Step 4.

4. Remove the cap from the fuel tank and make sure the fuel tank has a sufficient amount of fuel to start the engine.

5. If there is sufficient fuel in the fuel tank, remove the spark plug immediately after attempting to start the engine. The plug insulator should be wet, indicating that fuel is reaching the engine. If the plug tip is dry, fuel is not reaching the engine. Refer to *Fuel System* in this chapter. If there is fuel on the spark plug and the engine will not start, the engine may not have adequate spark. Continue with Step 6.

6. Make sure the spark plug wire is secure. Push the spark plug cap and slightly rotate it to clean the electrical connection between the plug and the connector. If the engine does not start, continue with Step 7.

> *NOTE*
> *A cracked or damaged spark plug cap and cable can cause intermittent problems that are difficult to diagnose. If the engine occasionally misfires or cuts out, use a spray bottle to wet the plug cap and plug cable while the engine is running. Water that enters one of these areas can cause an arc through the insulating material, causing an engine misfire.*

> *NOTE*
> *Engine misfire can also be caused by water that enters through connectors. Check the connectors for loose wire ends. On waterproof connectors, check for damage where the wires enter the connector.*

7. Perform the *Spark Test* in this section. If there is a strong spark, perform Step 8. If there is no spark or

if the spark is very weak, refer to *Ignition System* in this chapter.

8. If the fuel and ignition systems are working correctly, perform a *Leakdown Test* (this chapter) and *Compression Test* (Chapter Three). If the leakdown test indicates a problem, or the compression is low, refer to *Low Compression* under *Engine* in this chapter.

Spark Test

Perform a spark test to determine if the ignition system is producing adequate spark. A spark tester, with an adjustable gap between the center electrode and grounded base, is a convenient way to test the spark. Do not assume that because a spark jumped across a spark plug gap, the ignition system is working correctly.

If possible, perform this test on the engine when it is both cold and hot. If the test results are positive for each test, the ignition system is functioning correctly.

CAUTION
After removing the direct ignition coil or spark plug cap and before removing the spark plug in Step 1, clean the area around the spark plug with compressed air. Dirt that falls into the cylinder causes rapid engine wear.

1. If necessary, remove the air shroud as described in Chapter Sixteen.
2. Disconnect the spark plug cap (**Figure 5**). Check for the presence of water.
3. Visually inspect the spark plug for damage.
4. Set the spark tester gap to 6 mm (0.24 in.).
5. Connect the spark tester to the spark plug cap. Ground the spark tester base (or spark plug) to a good ground (**Figure 6**). Position the spark tester or spark plug firing tip away from the open spark plug hole. Position the spark tester so the electrodes are visible.
6. Shift the transmission into neutral.

WARNING
Do not hold the spark tester, spark plug or connector or a serious electrical shock may result.

7. On XR650L models, make sure the ignition switch is on and engine stop switch is set to run. Turn the engine over with the starter. A fat blue spark must be evident between the spark tester or spark plug terminals.
8. If there is a strong, blue spark, the ignition system is functioning properly. Check for one or more of the following possible malfunctions:
    a. Faulty fuel system component.
    b. Flooded engine.
    c. Engine damage (low compression).
9. If the spark was weak (white or yellow) or if there was no spark, refer to *Ignition System*.

POOR ENGINE PERFORMANCE

If the engine runs, but performance is unsatisfactory, refer to the following section that best describes the symptoms.

Engine Starts but Stalls and is Hard to Restart

Check for the following:
1. Incorrect choke operation. This can be due to improper use or a stuck choke valve in the carburetor.
2. Plugged fuel tank vent hose, if so equipped.
3. Plugged fuel hose, fuel shutoff valve or fuel filter.
4. Incorrect carburetor adjustment.
5. Incorrect float level adjustment.
6. Plugged carburetor jets.

NOTE
If a warm or hot engine will start with the choke on, or if a cold engine starts and runs until the choke is turned off, check for a plugged pilot jet.

7. Contaminated or stale fuel.
8. Clogged air filter.
9. Intake pipe air leak.
10. Plugged exhaust system. Check the silencer or muffler, especially if the motorcycle was just returned from storage.
11. Faulty ignition system component.

Engine Backfires, Cuts Out or Misfires During Acceleration

1. A lean air/fuel mixture can cause these engine performance problems. Check for the following conditions:

a. Incorrect float level adjustment.

b. Plugged pilot jet or pilot system.

2. Faulty accelerator pump.

3. Loose exhaust pipe-to-cylinder head connection.

4. Intake air leak.

5. Incorrect ignition timing or a damaged ignition system can cause these conditions. Refer to *Ignition System* in this chapter to isolate the damaged ignition system component. Check the ignition timing as described in Chapter Three.

6. Check the following engine components:

a. Broken valve springs.

b. Stuck or leaking valves.

c. Worn or damaged camshaft lobes.

d. Incorrect valve timing due to incorrect camshaft installation or a mechanical failure.

Engine Backfires on Deceleration

If the engine backfires when the throttle is released, check the following:

1. Lean carburetor pilot system.

2. Loose exhaust pipe-to-cylinder head connection.

3. On models so equipped, check for a faulty pulse secondary air injection system.

4. Faulty ignition system component.

5. Check the following engine components:

a. Broken valve springs.

b. Stuck or leaking valves.

c. Worn or damaged camshaft lobes.

d. Incorrect valve timing due to incorrect camshaft installation or a mechanical failure.

Poor Fuel Mileage

1. Clogged fuel system.

2. Dirty or clogged air filter.

3. Incorrect ignition timing (defective ICM or ignition pulse generator).

Engine Will Not Idle or Idles Roughly

1. Clogged air filter element.

2. Poor fuel flow resulting from a partially clogged fuel valve, fuel filter or fuel hose.

3. Contaminated or stale fuel.

4. Incorrect carburetor adjustment.

5. Leaking head gasket.

6. Intake air leak.

7. Incorrect ignition timing (defective ICM or ignition pulse generator).

8. Low engine compression.

Low Engine Power

1. Support the motorcycle on a stand with the rear wheel off the ground, then spin the rear wheel by hand. If the wheel spins freely, perform Step 2. If the wheel does not spin freely, check for the following conditions:

a. Dragging brakes. Check for this condition immediately after riding the motorcycle.

NOTE
After riding the motorcycle, come to a stop on a level surface. Turn the engine off and shift the transmission into neutral. Walk or push the motorcycle forward. If the motorcycle is harder to push than normal, check for dragging brakes.

b. Damaged or binding drive chain.

c. Damaged wheel bearings.

2. Test ride the motorcycle and accelerate quickly from first to second gear. If the engine speed increased according to throttle position, perform Step 3. If the engine speed did not increase, check for one or more of the following problems:

a. Slipping clutch.

b. Warped clutch plates.

c. Worn clutch plates.

d. Weak or damaged clutch springs.

3. Test ride the motorcycle and accelerate lightly. If the engine speed increased according to throttle position, perform Step 4. If the engine speed did not increase, check for one or more of the following problems:

a. Clogged air filter.

b. Restricted fuel flow.

c. Pinched fuel tank breather hose, if so equipped.

d. Clogged or damaged silencer or muffler.

4. Check for retarded ignition timing as described in Chapter Three. A decrease in power results when the plug fires later than normal.

5. Check for one or more of the following problems:

a. Low engine compression.

b. Worn spark plug.

c. Fouled spark plug.

d. Incorrect spark plug heat range.

e. Weak ignition coil.

f. Incorrect ignition timing (defective ICM or ignition pulse generator).

g. Plugged carburetor passages.

h. Incorrect oil level (too high or too low).

i. Contaminated oil.

j. Worn or damaged valve train assembly.

k. Engine overheating.

6. If the engine knocks when it is accelerated or when running at high speed, check for one or more of the following possible malfunctions:

    a. Incorrect type of fuel.

    b. Lean fuel mixture.

    c. Advanced ignition timing (defective ICM). May also cause engine overheating and hard starting.

    d. Excessive carbon buildup in combustion chamber.

    e. Worn pistons and/or cylinder bores.

Poor Idle or Low Speed Performance

1. Check for an incorrect pilot screw adjustment.

2. Check for damaged or loose intake pipe and air filter housing hose clamps. These conditions will cause an air leak.

3. Perform the *Spark Test* described in this chapter. Note the following:

    a. If the spark is good, go to Step 4.

    b. If the spark is weak, refer to *Ignition System* in this chapter to isolate the damaged ignition system component.

4. Check the ignition timing as described in Chapter Three. If ignition timing is correct, perform Step 5. If the timing is incorrect, refer to *Ignition System* in this chapter to isolate the damaged ignition system component.

5. Check the fuel system as described in this chapter.

Poor High Speed Performance

1. Check ignition timing as described in Chapter Three. If the ignition timing is correct, perform Step 3.

2. If the timing is incorrect, refer to *Ignition System* in this chapter to isolate the damaged ignition system component.

3. Check the fuel system as described in this chapter.

4. Check the valve clearance as described in Chapter Three. Note the following:

    a. If the valve clearance is correct, refer to Step 5.

    b. If the clearance is incorrect, adjust the valves as described in Chapter Three.

5. Incorrect valve timing and worn or damaged valve springs can cause poor high-speed performance. If the camshaft was timed just before the motorcycle experiencing this type of problem, the cam timing may be incorrect. If the cam timing was not set or changed, and all the other inspection procedures in this section failed to locate the problem, inspect the camshaft and valve assembly.

FUEL SYSTEM

The following section isolates common fuel system problems under specific complaints. If there is a good spark, poor fuel flow may be preventing the correct amount of fuel from being supplied to the spark plug. Troubleshoot the fuel system as follows:

1. Clogged fuel tank breather hose, if so equipped.

2. Check that there is a sufficient amount of fuel in the tank.

3. After attempting to start the engine, remove the spark plug (Chapter Three) and check for fuel on the plug tip. Note the following:

    a. If there is no fuel visible on the plug, check for a clogged fuel shutoff valve, fuel filter or fuel line.

    b. If there is fuel present on the plug tip, and the engine has spark, check for an intake air leak or the possibility of contaminated or stale fuel.

NOTE
If the motorcycle was not used for some time, and was not properly stored, the fuel may be stale. Depending on the condition of the fuel, a no-start condition can result.

    c. If there is an excessive amount of fuel on the plug, check for a clogged air filter or flooded carburetor.

Rich Mixture

1. Clogged air filter.
2. Choke valve stuck open.
3. Float level too high.
4. Contaminated float valve seat.
5. Worn or damaged float valve and seat.
6. Leaking or damaged float.
7. Clogged carburetor jets.
8. Incorrect carburetor jetting.

Lean Mixture

1. Intake air leak.
2. Float level too low.
3. Clogged fuel line, fuel filter or fuel shutoff valve.
4. Partially restricted fuel tank breather hose, if so equipped.
5. Plugged carburetor air vent hose.
6. Damaged float.
7. Damaged float valve.
8. Incorrect carburetor jetting.

ENGINE

Black Smoke

Black smoke is an indication of a rich air/fuel mixture.

Blue Smoke

Blue smoke indicates that the engine is burning oil in the combustion chamber as it leaks past worn valve stem seals or piston rings. Excessive oil consumption is another indicator of an engine that is burning oil. Perform a *Leakdown Test* (this chapter) to isolate the problem.

White Smoke or Steam

It is normal to see white smoke or steam from the exhaust after first starting the engine in cold weather. This is actually condensation formed during combustion. Once the engine heats up to normal operating temperature, the water evaporates and exits the engine through the crankcase vent system. However, if the motorcycle is ridden for short trips or repeatedly started and stopped and allowed to cool off without the engine getting warm enough, water will start to collect in the crankcase. With each short run of the engine, more water collects. As this water mixes with the oil in the crankcase, sludge is produced. Sludge can eventually cause engine damage as it circulates through the lubrication system and blocks off oil passages.

Low Compression

Problems with the engine top end will affect engine performance. When the engine is suspect, perform the *Leakdown Test* in this chapter and the *Compression Test* described in Chapter Three. An engine can lose compression through the following areas:
1. Valves:
   a. Incorrect valve adjustment.
   b. Incorrect valve timing.
   c. Worn or damaged valve seat surfaces.
   d. Bent valves.
   e. Weak or broken valve springs.
2. Cylinder head:
   a. Loose spark plug or damaged spark plug hole.
   b. Damaged cylinder head gasket.
   c. Warped or cracked cylinder head.
3. Damaged decompression lever assembly.

High Compression

1. Faulty decompression lever assembly.

2. Excessive carbon buildup in the combustion chamber.

Engine Overheating

1. Improper spark plug heat range.
2. Low oil level.
3. Oil not circulating properly.
4. Valves leaking.
5. Heavy carbon deposits in the combustion chamber.
6. Dragging brake(s).
7. Slipping clutch.

Preignition

Preignition is the premature burning of fuel and is caused by hot spots in the combustion chamber. Glowing deposits in the combustion chamber, inadequate cooling or an overheated spark plug can all cause preignition. This is first noticed as a power loss but eventually causes damage to the internal parts of the engine because of the high combustion chamber temperature.

Detonation

Detonation is the violent explosion of fuel in the combustion chamber before the proper time of ignition. Using low octane gasoline is a common cause of detonation.

Even when using a high-octane gasoline, detonation can still occur. Other causes are over-advanced ignition timing, lean air/fuel mixture at or near full throttle, inadequate engine cooling, or the excessive accumulation of carbon deposits in the combustion chamber.

Continued detonation can result in engine damage.

Power Loss

Refer to *Poor Engine Performance* in this chapter.

Engine Noises

Unusual noises are often the first indication of a developing problem. Investigate any new noises as soon as possible. Something that may be a minor problem, if corrected, could prevent the possibility of more extensive damage.

Use a mechanic's stethoscope or a small section of hose held near your ear (not directly on your ear) with the other end close to the source of the noise to isolate the location. Determining the exact cause of a noise can be difficult. If this is the case, consult with a professional mechanic to determine the cause. Do not disassemble major components until all other possibilities have been eliminated.

Consider the following when troubleshooting engine noises:

1. A knocking or pinging during acceleration can be caused by using a lower octane fuel than recommended. It may also be caused by poor quality fuel. Pinging can also be caused by an incorrect spark plug heat range or carbon buildup in the combustion chamber.

2. A slapping or rattling noise at low speed or during acceleration may be caused by excessive piston-to-cylinder wall clearance (piston slap). Piston slap is easier to detect when the engine is cold and before the piston has expanded. Once the engine has warmed up, piston expansion reduces piston-to-cylinder clearance.

3. A knocking or rapping while decelerating is usually caused by excessive rod bearing clearance.

4. A persistent knocking and vibration occurring every crankshaft rotation is usually caused by worn rod or main bearing(s). It can also be caused by broken piston rings or a damaged piston pin.

5. A rapid on-off squeal may indicate a compression leak around cylinder head gasket or spark plug(s).

6. For valve train noise(s), check the following:
   a. Excessive valve clearance.
   b. Worn or damaged camshaft.
   c. Worn or damaged valve train components.
   d. Valve sticking in guide.
   e. Broken valve spring.
   f. Low oil pressure.
   g. Clogged cylinder oil hole or oil passage.

Engine Vibration

1. Incorrect balancer shaft timing.
2. Excessive crankshaft runout.
3. Damaged crankshaft and balancer shaft bearings.

ENGINE LUBRICATION

An improperly operating engine lubrication system can quickly lead to engine seizure. Check the engine oil level and oil pressure as described in Chapter Three. Oil pump service is described in Chapter Five.

High Oil Consumption or Excessive Exhaust Smoke

1. Worn valve guides.
2. Worn valve guide seals.
3. Worn or damaged piston rings.

4. Incorrect piston ring installation.

Low Oil Pressure

1. Low oil level.
2. Worn or damaged oil pump.
3. Clogged oil strainer screen.
4. Clogged oil filter.
5. Internal oil leaks.
6. Oil relief valve stuck open.
7. Incorrect type of engine oil.

High Oil Pressure

1. Oil relief valve stuck closed.
2. Clogged oil filter.
3. Clogged oil gallery or metering orifices.

No Oil Pressure

1. Low oil level.
2. Oil relief valve stuck closed.
3. Damaged oil pump.
4. Incorrect oil pump installation.
5. Internal oil leak.

Low Oil Level

1. Oil level not maintained at correct level.
2. Worn piston rings.
3. Worn cylinder.
4. Worn valve guides.
5. Worn valve guide seals.
6. Piston rings incorrectly installed during engine overhaul.
7. External oil leaks.
8. Oil leaking into the cooling system.

Oil Contamination

Change the oil and filter at the specified intervals or when operating conditions demand more frequent changes.

LEAKDOWN TEST

A leakdown test can accurately pinpoint engine problems from the head gasket, valves and valve seats, and piston rings. This test is performed by applying compressed air to the cylinder through a leakdown tester (**Figure 7**) and then measuring the leak rate percentage.

When performing a leakdown test, the engine is first set at TDC on its compression stroke so that the valves are closed. When the combustion chamber is pressurized, very little air should escape.

In this procedure it will be necessary to lock the engine at top dead center (TDC) on its compression stroke and then perform the leakdown test. Follow the manufacturer's directions along with the following information when performing a cylinder leakdown test.

1. Support the motorcycle on a workstand with the rear wheel off the ground.

2. Remove the air filter assembly (Chapter Three). Open and secure the throttle so it is at its wide-open position.

3A. On XR600R models, remove the master link and slide the drive chain off the drive sprocket.

3B. On XR650L models, the drive chain is an endless type. Loosen the rear axle nut and move the rear wheel forward to obtain as much chain slack as possible. Then remove the drive sprocket cover and the drive sprocket as described in Chapter Twelve. Reinstall the drive sprocket without the drive chain.

4. Remove the spark plug (Chapter Three).

5. Install the threaded hose adapter from the leakdown kit. Then install the leakdown gauge onto the hose.

6. Remove the timing hole cap (A, **Figure 8**) from the left crankcase cover.

7. Remove the flywheel bolt cap (B, **Figure 8**) from the left crankcase cover.

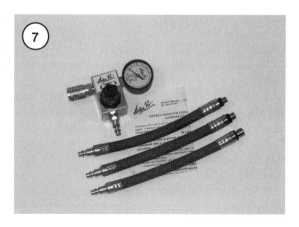

NOTE
The decompression mechanism will click loudly once during each crankshaft revolution. This is normal.

8. Using the flywheel bolt, rotate the engine *counterclockwise* until the engine is at TDC on the compression stroke. Make sure the *T* mark aligns with the index mark on the crankcase (**Figure 9**). Verify the engine is at TDC on the compression stroke as follows:

   a. When aligning the index marks, listen for pressure building inside the combustion chamber, indicating that the piston is on its compression stroke.

   b. View the leakdown tester when turning the engine. As the piston starts its compression stroke, compression building inside the combustion chamber may cause the gauge needle to move slightly.

   c. If the crankshaft is 360° off, these indicators will not be present.

9. Perform the following to lock the transmission so the engine remains at TDC on its compression stroke:

WARNING
Attempting to lock the engine with a tool on the flywheel bolt can cause serious injury. Once the combustion chamber is pressurized, any crankshaft movement can throw the tool away from the engine with considerable force. Lock the engine as described in this procedure.

NOTE
Because of play in the transmission gears, it may be necessary to reposition the countershaft slightly and then relock it in position with the holding tool. Several attempts may be required to determine the amount of transmission play and which direction the countershaft should be turned and locked.

   a. Turn the drive sprocket by hand and shift the transmission into top gear with the shift pedal.

   b. Attach a holding tool such as a clutch holding tool or equivalent to the drive sprocket (**Figure 10**). Use a wooden block and clamp to hold the tool so it cannot move when the combustion chamber is pressurized.

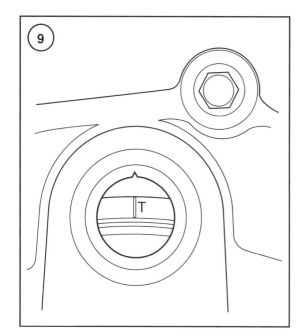

c. Check that the TDC marks are still aligned. If not, turn the crankshaft as required, then relock the holding tool in position.

10. Detach the crankcase breather hose from the fitting on the rear of the crankcase.

11. Apply air pressure to the combustion chamber. Follow the manufacturer's instructions while reading the leak rate on the gauge. Listen for air leaking while noting the following:

NOTE
If a large amount of air escapes from the exhaust pipe and/or through the carburetor, the engine is not at TDC on the compression stroke.

a. Air leaking through the exhaust pipe indicates a leaking exhaust valve.

b. Air leaking through the carburetor indicates a leaking intake valve.

c. Air leaking through the crankcase breather hole indicates the rings are not sealing properly in the bore.

12. If the cylinder leak rate is 10 percent or higher, engine repair is required.

13. Disconnect the test equipment and install all the parts previously removed. On XR650L models, readjust the drive chain (Chapter Three).

CLUTCH

Refer to Chapter Six for clutch service.

No Pressure at Clutch Lever

1. Incorrect clutch adjustment.
2. Broken clutch cable.
3. Damaged clutch lifter mechanism.

Clutch Lever Hard to Pull In

1. Dry or damaged clutch cable.
2. Kinked or stuck clutch cable.
3. Incorrect clutch cable routing.
4. Damaged clutch lifter mechanism.

Rough Clutch Operation

Worn, grooved or damaged clutch hub and clutch housing slots.

Clutch Slip

If the engine speed increases without an increase in motorcycle speed, the clutch is probably slipping. The main causes of clutch slip are:
1. No clutch lever free play.
2. Worn clutch plates.
3. Weak clutch springs.
4. Sticking or damaged clutch lifter.
5. Clutch plates contaminated by oil additive.

Clutch Drag

If the clutch does not disengage or if the motorcycle creeps with the transmission in gear and the clutch disengaged, the clutch is dragging. Some main causes of clutch drag are:
1. Excessive clutch lever free play.
2. Warped clutch plates.
3. Damaged clutch lifter assembly.
4. Loose clutch housing locknut.
5. High oil level.
6. Incorrect oil viscosity.

7. Engine oil additive being used.
8. Damaged clutch hub and clutch housing splines.

GEARSHIFT LINKAGE

The gearshift linkage assembly connects the shift pedal (external shift mechanism) to the shift drum (internal shift mechanism). Refer to Chapter Six and Chapter Seven for component service.

Transmission Jumps Out of Gear

1. Damaged stopper arm.
2. Damaged stopper arm spring.
3. Loose stopper arm mounting bolt.
4. Loose guide plate mounting bolts.
5. Damaged shifter collar.
6. Worn or damaged shift drum cam.
7. Damaged shift shaft spring.

Difficult Shifting

1. Incorrect clutch operation.
2. Incorrect oil viscosity.
3. Loose or damaged stopper arm assembly.
4. Bent shift fork shaft(s).
5. Bent or damaged shift fork(s).
6. Worn gear dogs or slots.
7. Damaged shift drum grooves.
8. Damaged shift shaft spindle.
9. Incorrect gearshift linkage installation.
10. Damaged shift lever assembly.

Shift Pedal Does Not Return

1. Bent shift shaft spindle.
2. Bent shift shaft engagement arm.
3. Damaged shift lever assembly.
4. Weak or damaged shift shaft arm return spring.
5. Shift shaft incorrectly installed (return spring not indexed around pin).

Excessive Transmission Noise

1. Damaged primary drive and driven gears or bearing.
2. Incorrect primary drive and drive gear installation.
3. Damaged transmission bearings or gears.

TRANSMISSION

Transmission symptoms are sometimes hard to distinguish from clutch symptoms. Refer to Chapter Seven for transmission service procedures. Before working on the transmission, make sure the clutch and gearshift linkage assembly are not causing the problem.

Difficult Shifting

1. Incorrect clutch operation.
2. Bent shift fork(s).
3. Damaged shift fork guide pin(s).
4. Bent shift fork shaft(s).
5. Damaged shift drum grooves.
6. Damaged gears.

Jumps Out of Gear

1. Loose or damaged shift drum cam mounting bolt.
2. Bent or damaged shift fork(s).
3. Bent shift fork shaft(s).
4. Damaged shift drum grooves.
5. Worn gear dogs or slots.

Incorrect Shift Lever Operation

1. Bent shift pedal or linkage.
2. Stripped shift pedal splines.
3. Damaged shift linkage.
4. Damaged shift shaft spindle.

Excessive Gear Noise

1. Worn or damaged transmission bearings.
2. Worn or damaged gears.
3. Excessive gear backlash.

ELECTRICAL TESTING

This section describes electrical troubleshooting and test equipment use. Never assume anything and do not overlook the obvious, such as a blown fuse or an electrical connector that has separated. Test the simplest and most obvious items first and try to make tests at easily accessible points on the motorcycle. Make sure to troubleshoot systematically.

Refer to the color wiring diagrams at the end of the manual for component and connector identification. Use the wiring diagrams to determine how the circuit should work by tracing the current paths from the power source through the circuit components to ground. Also check any circuits that share the same fuse, ground or switch. If the other circuits work properly and the shared wiring is good, the cause must be in the wiring used only by the suspect circuit. If all related circuits are faulty at the same time, the probable cause is a poor ground connection or a blown fuse(s).

Preliminary Checks and Precautions

Before starting any electrical troubleshooting, perform the following:
1. On XR650L models, inspect the fuse for the suspected circuit, and replace it if blown. Refer to *Fuses* in Chapter Eleven.
2. On XR650L models, inspect the battery (Chapter Eleven). Make sure it is fully charged and the battery leads are clean and securely attached to the battery terminals.
3. Electrical connectors are often the cause of electrical system problems. Inspect the connectors as follows:
   a. Disconnect each electrical connector in the suspect circuit and make sure there are no bent terminals in the electrical connector. A bent terminal will not connect to its mate, causing an open circuit.
   b. Make sure the terminals are pushed all the way into the connector. If not, carefully push them in with a narrow blade screwdriver.
   c. Check the wires where they attach to the terminals for damage.
   d. Make sure each terminal is clean and free of corrosion. Clean them, if necessary, and pack the connectors with dielectric grease.
   e. Push the connector halves together. Make sure the connectors are fully engaged and locked together.
   f. Never pull the wires when disconnecting a connector. Pull only on the connector housing.
4. Never use a self-powered test light on circuits containing solid-state devices. The solid-state devices may be damaged.

Intermittent Problems

Problems that do not occur all the time can be difficult to isolate during testing. For example, when a problem only occurs when the motorcycle is ridden over rough roads (vibration) or in wet conditions (water penetration). Note the following:
1. Vibration is a common problem with loose or damaged electrical connectors.
   a. Perform a continuity test as described in the appropriate service procedure or under *Continuity Test* in this section. An analog ohmmeter is useful for this type of test, as slight needle movements, indicating a loose connection, are readily visible on the meter display.
   b. Lightly pull or wiggle the connectors while repeating the test. Do the same when checking the wiring harness and individual components, especially where the wires enter a housing or connector.
   c. A change in meter readings indicates a poor connection. Find and repair the problem or replace the part. Check for wires with cracked or broken insulation.
2. Heat is a common problem with connectors or joints having loose or poor connections. As these connections heat up, the connection or joint expands and separates, causing an open circuit. Other heat related problems occur when a component starts to fail as it heats up.
   a. Use a heat gun to quickly raise the temperature of the component being tested. Do not apply heat directly to solid-state devices or use heat in excess of 60° C (140° F) on any electrical component.
   b. To check a connector, perform the *Continuity Test* described in this section. Then repeat the same test while heating the connector with a heat gun. If the meter reading was normal (continuity) when the connector was cold, and then fluctuated or read infinity when heat was applied, the connection is bad.
   c. To check a component, allow the engine to cool, and then start and run the engine. Note operational differences when the engine is cold and hot.
   d. If the engine will not start, isolate and remove the suspect component. Test it at room temperature and again after heating it with a heat gun. A change in meter readings indicates a temperature problem.
3. Water problems occur when riding in wet conditions or in areas with high humidity. Start and run the engine in a dry area. Then, with the engine running, spray water onto the suspected component/circuit. Water-related problems often stop after the component heats up and dries.

Test Light and Voltmeter

Use a test light to check for voltage in a circuit. Attach one lead to ground and the other lead to various points along the circuit. It does not make a difference which test lead is attached to ground. The bulb lights when voltage is present.

Use a voltmeter in the same manner as the test light to find out if voltage is present in any given circuit. The voltmeter, unlike the test light, also indicates how much voltage is present at each test point.

Voltage test

Unless otherwise specified, make all voltage tests with the electrical connectors still connected. Insert the test leads into the backside of the connector and make sure the test lead touches the electrical terminal within the connector housing. If the test lead only touches the wire insulation, it will cause a false reading.

Always check both sides of the connector because one side may be loose or corroded, thus preventing electrical flow through the connector. This type of test can be performed with a test light or a voltmeter.

1. Attach the voltmeter negative test lead to a confirmed ground location. If possible, use the battery ground connection. Make sure the ground is not insulated.

2. Attach the voltmeter positive test lead to the point to be tested (**Figure 11**).

3. Turn the ignition switch on. If using a test light, the test light will come on if voltage is present. If using a voltmeter, note the voltage reading. The reading should be within 1 volt of battery voltage. If the voltage is less there is a problem in the circuit.

Voltage drop test

The wires, cables, connectors and switches in the electrical circuit are designed to carry current with low resistance. This ensures current can flow through the circuit with a minimum loss of voltage. Voltage drop indicates where there is resistance in a circuit. A higher-than-normal amount of resistance in a circuit decreases the flow of current and causes the voltage to drop between the source and destination in the circuit.

Because resistance causes voltage to drop, a voltmeter is used to measure voltage drop when current is running through the circuit. If the circuit has no resistance, there is no voltage drop so the voltmeter indicates 0 volts. The greater the resistance in a circuit, the greater the voltage drop reading.

To perform a voltage drop:

1. Connect the positive meter test lead to the electrical source (where electricity is coming from).

2. Connect the voltmeter negative test lead to the electrical load (where the electricity is going). Refer to **Figure 12**.

3. If necessary, activate the component(s) in the circuit.

4. Read the voltage drop (difference in voltage between the source and destination) on the voltmeter. Note the following:

   a. The voltmeter should indicate 0 volts. If there is a drop of 1 volt or more, there is a problem

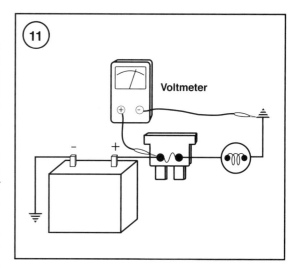

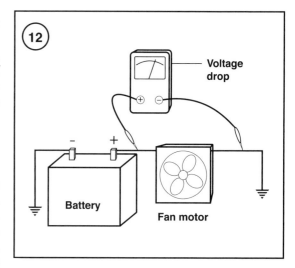

within the circuit. A voltage drop reading of 12 volts indicates an open in the circuit.

   b. A voltage drop of 1 or more volts indicates that a circuit has excessive resistance.

   c. For example, consider a starting problem where the battery is fully charged but the starter turns over slowly. Voltage drop would be the difference in the voltage at the battery (source) and the voltage at the starter (destination) as the engine is being started (current is flowing through the battery cables). A corroded battery cable would cause a high voltage drop (high resistance) and slow engine cranking.

   d. Common sources of voltage drop are loose or contaminated connectors and poor ground connections.

Test for a Short with a Voltmeter

A test light may also be used.

1. Remove the blown fuse from the fuse panel.

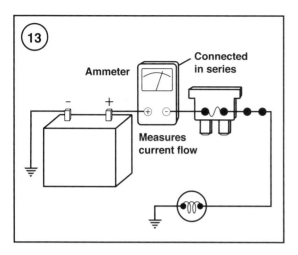

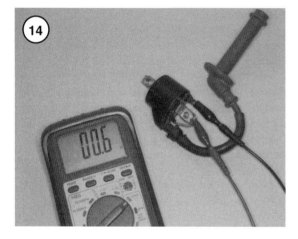

2. Connect the voltmeter across the fuse terminals in the fuse panel. Turn the ignition switch on and check for battery voltage.

3. With the voltmeter attached to the fuse terminals, wiggle the wiring harness relating to the suspect circuit at approximately 15.2 cm (6 in.) intervals. Start next to the fuse panel and work systematically away from the panel. Note the voltmeter reading while progressing along the harness.

4. If the voltmeter reading changes (test light blinks), there is a short-to-ground at that point in the harness.

Ammeter

Use an ammeter to measure the flow of current (amps) in a circuit (**Figure 13**). When connected in series in a circuit, the ammeter determines if current is flowing through the circuit and if that current flow is excessive because of a short in the circuit. Current flow is often referred to as current draw. Comparing actual current draw in the circuit or component to current draw specification (if specified by the manufacturer) provides useful diagnostic information.

Self-powered Test Light

A self-powered test light can be constructed from a 12-volt light bulb, a pair of test leads and a 12-volt battery. When the test leads are touched together the light bulb should go on.

Use a self-powered test light as follows:
1. Touch the test leads together to make sure the light bulb goes on. If not, correct the problem.
2. Disconnect the motorcycle's battery or remove the fuse(s) that protects the circuit to be tested. Do not connect a self-powered test light to a circuit that has power applied to it.
3. Select two points within the circuit where there should be continuity.
4. Attach one lead of the test light to each point.
5. If there is continuity, the test light bulb will come on.
6. If there is no continuity, the test light bulb will not come on, indicating an open circuit.

Ohmmeter

CAUTION
To prevent damage to the ohmmeter, never connect it to a circuit that has power applied to it. Always disconnect the battery negative lead before using an ohmmeter.

Use an ohmmeter to measure the resistance (in ohms) to current flow in a circuit or component.

Ohmmeters may be analog type (needle scale) or digital type (LCD or LED readout). Both types of ohmmeters have a switch that allows the user to select different ranges of resistance for accurate readings. The analog ohmmeter also has a set-adjust control that is used to zero or calibrate the meter (digital ohmmeters do not require calibration). Refer to the ohmmeter's instructions to determine the correct scale setting.

Use an ohmmeter by connecting its test leads to the circuit or component to be tested (**Figure 14**). If an analog meter is used, it must be calibrated by touching the test leads together and turning the set-adjust knob until the meter needle reads zero. When the leads are uncrossed, the needle should move to the other end of the scale, indicating infinite resistance.

During a continuity test, a reading of infinite resistance indicates there is an open in the circuit or component. A reading of zero indicates continuity, that is, there is no measurable resistance in the circuit or component. A measured reading indicates the actual resistance to current flow that is present in that circuit. Even though resistance is present, the circuit has continuity.

Continuity test

Perform a continuity test to determine the integrity of a circuit, wire or component. A circuit has continuity if it forms a complete circuit; that is if there are no opens in either the electrical wires or components within the circuit. A circuit with an open, on the other hand, has no continuity.

This type of test can be performed with a self-powered test light or an ohmmeter. An ohmmeter gives the best results.

1. Disconnect the negative battery cable or disconnect the test circuit/component from its power source.

2. Attach one test lead (test light or ohmmeter) to one end of the part of the circuit to be tested.

3. Attach the other test lead to the other end of the part or the circuit to be tested.

4. The self-powered test light comes on if there is continuity. An ohmmeter reads 0 or low resistance if there is continuity. A reading of infinite resistance indicates no continuity; the circuit is open.

5. If testing a component, note the resistance and compare this to the specification if available.

Test for short with an ohmmeter

An analog ohmmeter or one with an audible continuity indicator works best for short testing. A self-powered test light may also be used.

1. On XR650L models, disconnect the negative battery cable.

2. On XR650L models, if necessary, remove the blown fuse from the fuse panel.

3A. On XR600R models, connect one test lead to the power side of the circuit.

3B. On XR650L models, connect one test lead of the ohmmeter to the load side (component side) of the fuse terminal in the fuse panel.

4. Connect the other test lead to a confirmed ground location. Make sure the ground is not insulated. If possible, use the battery ground connection.

5. Wiggle the wiring harness relating to the suspect circuit at approximately 15.2 cm (6 in.) intervals. Watch the ohmmeter while progressing along the harness.

6. If the ohmmeter needle moves or the ohmmeter beeps, there is a short-to-ground at that point in the harness.

Jumper Wire

Use a jumper wire to bypass a potential problem and isolate it to a particular point in a circuit. If a faulty circuit works properly with a jumper wire

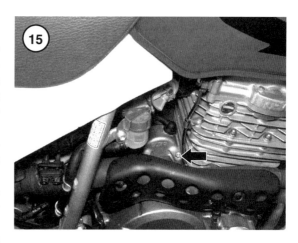

installed, an open exists between the two jumped points in the circuit.

To troubleshoot with a jumper wire, first use the wire to determine if the problem is on the ground side or the load side of a device. Test the ground by connecting the wire between the lamp and a good ground. If the lamp comes on, the problem is the connection between the lamp and ground. If the lamp does not come on with the wire installed, the lamp's connection to ground is good, so the problem is between the lamp and the power source.

To isolate the problem, connect the wire between the battery and the lamp. If it comes on, the problem is between these two points. Next, connect the wire between the battery and the fuse side of the switch. If the lamp comes on, the switch is good. By successively moving the wire from one point to another, the problem can be isolated to a particular place in the circuit.

Note the following when using a jumper wire:

1. Make sure the wire gauge (thickness) is the same as that used in the circuit being tested. Smaller gauge wire rapidly overheats and could melt.

2. Make sure the jumper wire has insulated alligator clips. This prevents accidental grounding (sparks) or possible shock. Install an inline fuse/fuse holder in the jumper wire.

3. A jumper wire is a temporary test measure. Do not leave a jumper wire installed as a permanent solution. This creates a fire hazard.

4. Never use a jumper wire across any load (a component that is connected and turned on). This would cause a direct short and blow the fuse(s).

STARTING SYSTEM (XR650L)

Description

The starting circuit consists of the battery, starter, clutch lever switch, neutral switch, sidestand switch, starter relay, ignition switch and engine stop switch.

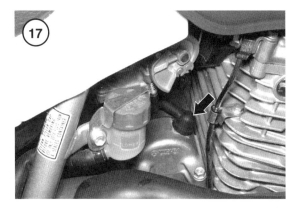

The starter is mounted horizontally at the rear of the engine behind the cylinder (**Figure 15**).

The starter relay (**Figure 16**) carries the current to the starter. Depressing the starter switch allows current to flow through the starter relay coil. The starter relay contacts close and allow current to flow from the battery through the starter relay to the starter.

When the ignition switch is turned on and the engine stop switch is in run, the starter can be operated only if the transmission is in neutral or the clutch lever is pulled in.

If the sidestand is down, the engine will stop if the transmission is shifted into gear.

CAUTION
Do not operate a starter continuously for more than 5 seconds. Allow the motor to cool for at least 10 seconds between attempts to start the engine.

Troubleshooting

Before troubleshooting the starting circuit, make sure that:
1. The battery is fully charged.
2. The battery cables are the proper size and length. Replace cables that are undersize or damaged.
3. All electrical connections are clean and tight.

4. The wiring harness is in good condition, with no worn or frayed insulation or loose harness sockets.
5. The fuel system is filled with an adequate supply of fresh gasoline.

Starter Does Not Operate

When operating the starter switch, turn the engine stop switch to run, and the ignition switch on. Make sure the transmission is in neutral.

NOTE
The following procedure isolates a starter problem when attempting to start in neutral. If the starter operates in neutral but not when the transmission is in gear and the clutch lever is gripped, check the clutch lever switch circuit.

1. Refer to Chapter Eleven and check the 20 amp main fuse. If the fuse is blown, replace it. If the main fuse is good, reinstall it, then continue with Step 2.
2. Test the *Battery* as described in Chapter Eleven. Note the following:
   a. If the battery is fully charged, perform Step 3.
   b. If necessary, clean and recharge the battery. If the battery is damaged, replace it.
3. Check for loose, corroded or damaged battery cables. Check at the battery, starter, starter relay and all cable-to-frame connections.
4. Turn the ignition switch on, then push the starter button and listen for a click sound at the starter relay (**Figure 16**). Note the following:
   a. If the relay clicked, perform Step 5.
   b. If the relay did not click, go to Step 6.
5. Test the battery as follows:
   a. Park the motorcycle on level ground. Make sure the transmission is in neutral.
   b. Disconnect the cable from the starter terminal (**Figure 17**).

WARNING
Because a spark will be produced in the following steps, perform this procedure away from gasoline or other volatile liquids. Make sure that there is no spilled gasoline on the motorcycle or gasoline fumes in the work area.

   c. Momentarily connect a jumper cable (thick gauge wire) from the positive battery terminal to the starter terminal (**Figure 17**). If the starter is working properly, it will turn when making the jumper cable connection.
   d. If the starter did not turn, remove the starter and service it as described in Chapter Eleven.

e. If the starter turned, check for a loose or damaged starter cable. If the cable is good, the starter relay (**Figure 16**) is faulty. Replace the starter relay and retest.

6. Test the following items as described in Chapter Eleven:

a. Neutral switch.

b. Clutch lever switch

c. Sidestand switch

d. Ignition switch.

e. Diode.

7. Perform the starter relay voltage test as described in Chapter Eleven. Note the following:

a. If the voltmeter shows battery voltage, continue with Step 8.

b. If there was no voltage reading, check the ignition switch and starter switch as described in Chapter Eleven. If both switches are good, check the continuity of the yellow/red wire between the starter switch and the starter relay.

8. Perform the starter relay continuity test as described in Chapter Eleven. Note the following:

a. If the meter reading is correct, continue with Step 9.

b. If the meter reading is incorrect, check for an open circuit in the yellow/red and green/red wires. Check the wire ends for loose or damaged connectors.

9. If the starting system problem was not found after performing these steps in order, recheck the wiring system for dirty or loose-fitting terminals or damaged wires; clean and repair as required.

10. Make sure all connectors disconnected during this procedure are free of corrosion and reconnected properly.

Starter Turns Slowly

If the starter turns slowly and all engine components are normal, perform the following:

1. Test the battery as described in Chapter Eleven.

2. Check for the following:

a. Loose or corroded battery terminals.

b. Loose or corroded battery ground cable.

c. Loose starter cable.

3. Remove, disassemble and bench test the starter as described in Chapter Eleven.

4. Check the starter for binding during operation. Disassemble the starter and check the armature shaft for bending or damage. Also, check the starter clutch as described in Chapter Five.

Starter Turns, but Engine Does Not

1. Check for a damaged starter clutch (Chapter Five).

2. Check for a damaged starter gear assembly (Chapter Five).

CHARGING SYSTEM (XR650L)

The charging system consists of the battery, alternator and a voltage regulator/rectifier. A 20 amp main fuse (**Figure 18**) protects the circuit.

A malfunction in the charging system generally causes the battery to remain undercharged.

Battery Discharging

1. Check all of the connections. Make sure they are tight and free of corrosion.

2. Disconnect the negative battery cable (**Figure 19**).

CAUTION
Before connecting the ammeter into the circuit in Step 3, set the meter to its highest amperage scale. This will prevent a large current flow from damaging the meter or blowing the meter's fuse, if so equipped.

3. Connect an ammeter between the battery ground cable and the negative battery terminal.

4. If the ammeter reading exceeds 1.0 mA, perform Step 5. If the current draw is 1.0 mA or less, perform Step 6.

5. Disconnect the 2-wire regulator/rectifier connector (**Figure 20**), then repeat Step 3. Note the following:

   a. If the test results are incorrect, the ignition switch may be faulty or the wiring harness is shorted; test the ignition switch as described in Chapter Eleven.

   b. If the test readings are correct, replace the regulator/rectifier unit (**Figure 21**) and retest.

6. Test the *Charging System* as described in Chapter Eleven. Note the following:

   a. If the test readings are correct, perform Step 7.

   b. If the test readings are incorrect, go to Step 8.

7. Test the battery with a battery tester and note the following:

   a. If the test readings are correct, check for an open circuit in the wiring harness and for dirty or loose-fitting terminals; clean and repair as required.

   b. If the test readings are incorrect, the battery is faulty or electrical components are overloading the charging system.

8. Refer to *Voltage Regulator/Rectifier* in Chapter Eleven and test the harness. Note the following:

   a. If the test readings are correct, perform Step 9.

   b. If the test readings are incorrect, check for an open circuit in the wiring harness and for dirty or loose-fitting terminals; clean and repair as required.

9. Refer to *Alternator* in Chapter Eleven, and test the stator coil. Note the following:

   a. If the test readings are incorrect, replace the alternator and retest.

   b. If the test readings are correct, replace the regulator/rectifier unit and retest.

Battery Overcharging

If the battery is overcharging, the regulator/rectifier unit is faulty. Replace the regulator/rectifier unit as described in Chapter Eleven.

IGNITION SYSTEM

Troubleshooting

> *NOTE*
> *If the problem is intermittent, perform the tests with the engine cold, then hot. Then compare the test results.*

1. Perform the *Spark Test* described in this chapter.

2. Test the ignition coil as described in Chapter Ten or Chapter Eleven. Note the following:

   a. If the ignition coil is good, perform Step 4.

   b. If the ignition coil fails to pass the tests described in Chapter Ten or Chapter Eleven, the ignition coil is probably faulty. However, before replacing the ignition coil, take it to a dealership and have them test the spark with an ignition coil tester. Replace the ignition coil if faulty and retest the ignition system.

3A. On XR600R models, test the engine stop switch as described in *Switches* in Chapter Ten. Note the following:

   a. If the switch is good, perform Step 6.

   b. If the switch fails the test, then the switch is faulty and must be replaced. Replace the switch and retest the ignition system.

3B. On XR650L models, test the engine stop switch as described in *Switches* in Chapter Eleven. Note the following:

   a. If the switch is good, perform Step 5.

   b. If the switch fails the test, then the switch is faulty and must be replaced. Replace the switch and retest the ignition system.

4. On XR650L models, test the ignition switch as described in *Switches* in Chapter Eleven. Note the following:

   a. If the switch is good, perform Step 6.

b. If the switch fails the test, then the switch is faulty and must be replaced. Replace the switch and retest the ignition system.

5. Test the *Pulse Generator* (**Figure 22**) as described in Chapter Ten or Chapter Eleven. Note the following:

a. If the test reading is correct, perform Step 7.

b. If the test reading is incorrect, replace the pulse generator as described in Chapter Ten or Chapter Eleven.

6. If a damaged component was not identified, check the ignition system wiring harness and connectors. Check for damaged wires or loose, dirty or damaged connectors. If the wiring and connectors are good, proceed to Step 8.

7. If all preceding steps do not identify the fault, consider the ICM unit faulty by a process of elimination. The ICM unit cannot be tested. Replace the ICM unit only after determining that all other ignition system components, connectors and wiring are functioning properly.

8. Install all parts previously removed. Make sure all of the connections are free of corrosion and are reconnected properly.

FRONT SUSPENSION AND STEERING

Steering is Sluggish

1. Tight steering adjustment.
2. Damaged steering head bearings.
3. Low tire pressure.
4. Damaged tire.

Motorcycle Steers to One Side

1. Bent axle.
2. Bent frame.
3. Worn or damaged wheel bearings.
4. Worn or damaged swing arm pivot bearings.
5. Damaged steering head bearings.
6. Bent swing arm.
7. Incorrectly installed wheels.
8. Front and rear wheels are not aligned.
9. Front fork legs positioned unevenly in steering stem.
10. Damaged tire.

Front Suspension Noise

1. Loose mounting fasteners.
2. Damaged fork.
3. Low fork oil capacity.

Front Wheel Wobble/Vibration

1. Loose front wheel axle.
2. Loose or damaged wheel bearing(s).
3. Damaged wheel rim(s).
4. Damaged tire(s).
5. Loose or damaged spokes.

Front End Too Stiff

1. Decrease the fork compression damping.
2. Decrease the fork oil capacity.
3. Change to a lighter weight fork oil.
4. Install softer fork springs.

Front End Oversteers

1. Install stiffer fork springs.
2. Increase fork oil capacity.

Front End Washes Out or Understeers

1. Decrease fork oil capacity.
2. Install softer fork springs.

Front End Shakes or Jumps Under Heavy Braking

1. Increase fork oil capacity.
2. Increase shock rebound damping.
3. Reduce the shock spring preload.

Front End is Unstable at High Speed

1. Increase fork oil capacity.
2. Increase rear shock spring preload.

REAR SUSPENSION

Poor Traction During Acceleration

1. Decrease shock compression damping adjustment.
2. Decrease shock spring preload.

Rear End Hops During Acceleration

1. Decrease shock compression damping adjustment.
2. Decrease shock spring preload.

BRAKE SYSTEM

The brake system is critical to performance and safety. Inspect the front and rear brakes frequently and repair any problem immediately. When replacing or refilling the brake fluid, use only DOT 4 brake fluid from a closed container. Refer to Chapter Three for routine brake inspection and service.

Soft or Spongy Brake Lever or Pedal

WARNING
If the fluid level drops too low, air can enter the hydraulic system through the master cylinder. Air can also enter the system from loose or damaged hose fittings. Air in the hydraulic system causes a soft or spongy brake lever action. This condition is noticeable and reduces brake performance. If air has entered the hydraulic system, flush the brake system and bleed the brakes as described in Chapter Fifteen.

WARNING
As the brake pads wear, the brake fluid level in the master cylinder reservoir drops. Whenever adding brake fluid to the reservoir, visually check the brake pads for wear. If it does not appear that there is an increase in pad wear, check the brake hoses, lines and fittings for leaks.

Operate the front brake lever or rear brake pedal and check to see if the lever travel distance increases. If lever travel increases during operation, or feels soft or spongy, there may be air in the brake line. In this condition, the brake system is not capable of producing sufficient brake force. When there is an increase in lever or pedal travel or when the brake feels soft or spongy, check the following possible causes:
1. Air in system.
2. Low brake fluid level.
3. Leak in the brake system.
4. Contaminated brake fluid.
5. Plugged brake fluid passages.
6. Damaged brake lever or pedal assembly.
7. Worn or damaged brake pads.
8. Worn or damaged brake disc.
9. Warped brake disc.
10. Contaminated brake pads and disc. Check for a leaking fork seal.
11. Worn or damaged master cylinder cups and/or cylinder bore.
12. Worn or damaged brake caliper piston seals.
13. Contaminated master cylinder assembly.
14. Contaminated brake caliper assembly.
15. Brake caliper not sliding correctly on slide pins.
16. Sticking master cylinder piston assembly.
17. Sticking brake caliper pistons.

Brake Drag

If the brakes drag when the brake lever or pedal is released, check for the following causes:
1. Warped or damaged brake disc.
2. Brake caliper not sliding correctly on slide pins.
3. Sticking or damaged brake caliper pistons.
4. Contaminated brake pads and disc.
5. Plugged master cylinder port.
6. Contaminated brake fluid and hydraulic passages.
7. Restricted brake hose joint.
8. Loose brake disc mounting bolts.
9. Damaged or misaligned wheel.
10. Incorrect wheel alignment.
11. Incorrectly installed brake caliper.
12. Damaged front or rear wheel.

Hard Brake Lever or Pedal Operation

When applying the brakes and there is sufficient brake performance but the operation of brake lever feels excessively hard, check for the following possible causes:
1. Clogged brake hydraulic system.
2. Sticking caliper piston.
3. Sticking master cylinder piston.
4. Glazed or worn brake pads.
5. Mismatched brake pads.
6. Damaged front brake lever.
7. Damaged rear brake pedal.
8. Brake caliper not sliding correctly on slide pins.
9. Worn or damaged brake caliper seals.

Brake Grabs

1. Damaged brake pad pin bolt. Look for steps or cracks along the pad pin bolt surface.

2. Contaminated brake pads and disc.
3. Incorrect wheel alignment.
4. Warped brake disc.
5. Loose brake disc mounting bolts.
6. Brake caliper not sliding correctly on slide pins.
7. Mismatched brake pads.
8. Damaged wheel bearings.

Brake Squeal or Chatter

1. Contaminated brake pads and disc.
2. Incorrectly installed brake caliper.
3. Warped brake disc.
4. Incorrect wheel alignment.
5. Mismatched brake pads.
6. Incorrectly installed brake pads.
7. Damaged or missing brake pad spring or pad retainer.

Leaking Brake Caliper

1. Damaged dust and piston seals.
2. Damaged cylinder bore.
3. Loose caliper body bolts.
4. Loose union bolt.
5. Damaged union bolt washers.
6. Damaged union bolt threads in caliper body.

Leaking Master Cylinder

1. Damaged piston secondary seal.
2. Damaged piston snap ring/snap ring groove.
3. Worn or damaged master cylinder bore.
4. Loose union bolt.
5. Damaged union bolt washers.
6. Damaged union bolt threads in master cylinder body.
7. Loose or damaged reservoir cap.

CHAPTER THREE

LUBRICATION, MAINTENANCE AND TUNE-UP

This chapter describes lubrication, maintenance, and tune-up procedures. Procedures that require more than minor disassembly or adjustment are covered in the appropriate subsequent chapter. Specifications are in **Tables 1-15** located at the end of this chapter.

Tables 1-4 list the recommended lubrication, maintenance and tune-up intervals. If the motorcycle is operated in extreme conditions, it may be appropriate to reduce the interval between some maintenance items.

Refer to *Safety* in Chapter One before servicing the motorcycle.

PRE-RIDE INSPECTION

Perform the following checks before the first ride of the day. If a component requires service, refer to the appropriate section or chapter. Refer to **Table 3** for pre-race inspection procedures.

1. Inspect all fuel lines and fittings for leaks.
2. Check fuel tank level.
3. Check engine oil level.
4. Check the throttle operation in all steering positions. Open the throttle all the way and release it. The throttle should close quickly with no binding or roughness.
5. Make sure the brake levers operate properly with no binding.
6. Check the brake fluid level in the brake reservoirs. Add DOT 4 brake fluid if necessary.
7. Check clutch operation.
8. Inspect the front and rear suspension. Make sure they have a good solid feel with no looseness. Turn the handlebar from side to side to check steering play. Service the steering assembly if excessive play is noted. Make sure the handlebar cables do not bind.
9. Check tire pressure.
10. Check wheel condition and spoke tightness.
11. Check drive chain condition and adjustment.
12. Check the exhaust system for looseness or damage.
13. Check fastener tightness, especially engine, steering and suspension mounting hardware.
14. Check headlight and taillight operation.
15. On XR650L models, check turn signal operation.
16. On XR650L models, check horn operation.
17. Make sure all switches work properly, including the engine stop switch. If the engine stop switch does not operate properly, test the switch as described in Chapter Ten or Chapter Eleven.

ENGINE OIL

Regular oil and filter changes contribute more to engine longevity than any other maintenance procedure. **Tables 1-4** list the recommended oil and filter change intervals.

Oil Selection

Make sure that the engine oil meets either the JASO (**Figure 1**) or API (**Figure 2**) service classification. Make sure the viscosity is appropriate for the anticipated ambient temperatures (**Figure 3**). Refer to **Table 5**.

Refer to *Shop Supplies* in Chapter One for additional engine oil information.

> *NOTE*
> *There are a number of ways to discard used oil properly. The easiest way is to pour it from the drain pan into a gallon plastic container for disposal. Many service stations and oil retailers accept used oil for recycling. Do not discard oil in household trash or pour it onto the ground.*

Oil Level Check

The majority of the engine oil is stored in a closed-off section of the motorcycle frame while some of the oil is carried in the crankcase. The engine oil level is checked at the dipstick on the frame and the oil level check bolt on the crankcase.

1. Start the engine and allow it to warm up for 3 to 5 minutes. In colder weather, allow the engine to idle for at least 5 minutes.

2. Support the motorcycle so it is vertical and level. Allow the engine to rest in this position for 2 to 3 minutes before checking the oil level.

3. Unscrew the dipstick (**Figure 4**) from the frame between the steering head and the fuel tank.

4. Wipe the dipstick clean and reinsert the dipstick onto the threads in the hole; do not screw it in.

5. Remove the dipstick and check the oil level. The level should be between the two lines and not above the upper one. If the level is below the lower line, add the recommended type engine oil to correct the level.

6. Install the dipstick and tighten securely.

7. Restart the engine and allow it to run for a couple of minutes.

8. Shut off the engine and allow the oil to settle.

9. Unscrew the crankcase oil level check bolt (**Figure 5**).

10. The crankcase oil level is correct if the oil is up to the bottom surface of the threads in the hole.

JASO CERTIFICATION LABEL

Sales company oil code number

M001XXXXX

MA

OIL CLASSIFICATION
MA: Designed for high-friction applications
MB: Designed for low-friction applications

API SERVICE SYMBOL

Oil classification

API SERVICE SJ
SAE 10W-40
ENERGY CONSERVING

When **ENERGY CONSERVING** is listed in this part of the label, the oil has demonstrated energy-conserving properties in standard tests. Do not use **ENERGY CONSERVING** classified oil in motorcycle engines. Instead, look for this API service symbol

API SERVICE SJ
SAE 10W-40

Oil viscosity

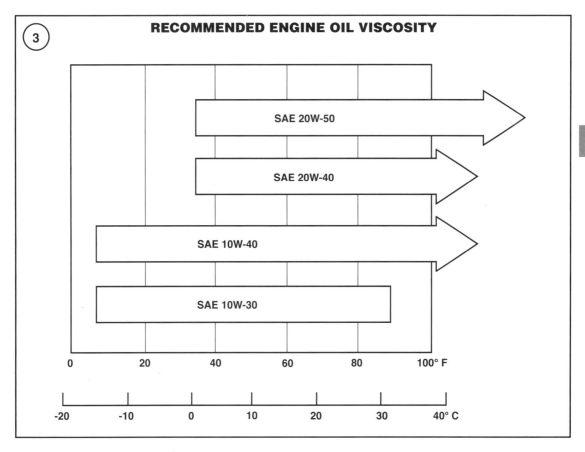

RECOMMENDED ENGINE OIL VISCOSITY

SAE 20W-50

SAE 20W-40

SAE 10W-40

SAE 10W-30

| 0 | 20 | 40 | 60 | 80 | 100° F |

| -20 | -10 | 0 | 10 | 20 | 30 | 40° C |

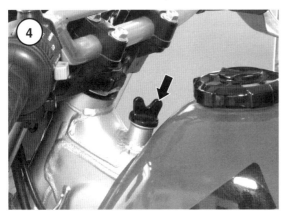

11. If the oil level is correct on the dipstick but the crankcase oil level is incorrect, some part of the oil system is not operating properly. Do not operate the bike until the problem is found and fixed. Perform the following:

    a. Recheck the oil level on the dipstick.

    b. Inspect the oil lines and fittings from the engine to the motorcycle frame.

    c. Inspect the oil pump as described in Chapter Five.

12. Reinstall the oil level check bolt and tighten securely.

Oil and Filter Change

Change the engine oil and filter at the intervals recommended in **Tables 1-4**. Use the classification and viscosity recommended in **Table 5**.

Change the oil when the engine is warm. Contaminants will remain suspended in the oil and it will drain more completely. The following procedure includes oil filter replacement. If the oil filter does not require replacement or removal, skip those steps.

1. Start the engine and allow it to warm up for several minutes. Shut off the engine.

2. Remove the dipstick (**Figure 4**).

3. Place a drain pan below the oil drain bolts (**Figure 6** and **Figure 7**).

4. Remove the oil drain bolt and washer on the lower end of the front frame downtube (**Figure 6**) and allow the oil to drain.

5. Remove the oil drain bolt (**Figure 7**) and washer on the left side of the crankcase and allow the oil to drain.

6. After the oil stops draining from the oil drain holes, reinstall the oil drain bolts and new washers. Tighten the frame drain bolt to 40 N•m (29 ft.-lb.). Tighten the crankcase drain bolt to 25 N•m (18 ft.-lb.).

7. Place a drain pan under the right crankcase cover.

8. Remove the bolts, then remove the oil filter cover (**Figure 8**).

9. Remove the oil filter (**Figure 9**). Discard the oil filter.

10. If necessary, remove the spring (**Figure 10**).

11. If removed, install the spring into the holder in the crankcase.

CAUTION
Installing the oil filter backward will cause engine damage.

12. Install the oil filter with the OUTSIDE mark facing out (**Figure 9**).

13. Replace the oil filter cover O-ring (**Figure 11**) if damaged. Lubricate the O-ring with engine oil and install in the cover groove.

14. Install the oil filter cover. Tighten the bolts to the specification in Table 15.

CAUTION
The engine must be run to transfer oil to the engine before final filling of the frame oil tank. The frame oil tank will not hold the total oil quantity.

15. Fill the frame oil tank with oil until the level reaches the full mark on the dipstick.

16. Install the dipstick, then run the engine at idle speed for 5 minutes. Check for leaks.

17. Recheck the oil level and add oil as described in this section.

OIL LINE STRAINER

Inspect the oil line strainer (**Figure 12**) at the specified intervals. Refer to *Oil Lines* in Chapter Five.

OIL STRAINER SCREEN

The engine is equipped with an oil strainer in the right crankcase half and is accessible after removing the right crankcase cover. Periodic cleaning is not recommended in the maintenance schedule.

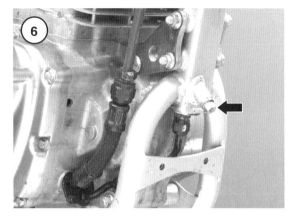

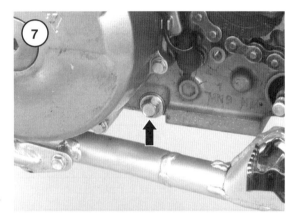

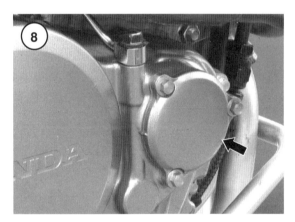

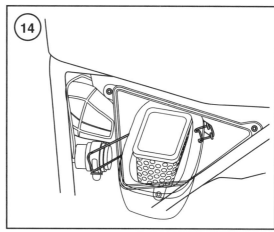

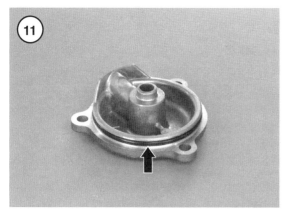

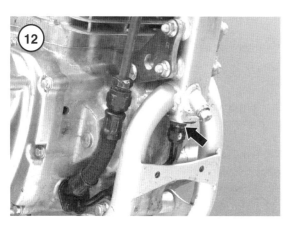

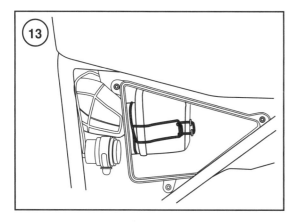

However, remove and clean the strainer whenever the right crankcase cover is removed or debris enters the engine. Refer to Chapter Five.

AIR FILTER

The air filter removes dust and debris from the air before the air enters the carburetor and engine. Without the air filter, very fine particles could enter the engine and cause rapid wear. Never run the engine without the air filter element installed.

Service the air filter at the intervals in **Tables 1-4**.

Removal/Cleaning/Installation (XR600R Models)

1. Remove the left side cover as described in Chapter Sixteen.
2. Unhook the element retaining strap (**Figure 13**).
3. Remove the element assembly from the air box.
4. Separate the air filter element from the holder (**Figure 14**).
5. Clean the interior of the air box with a shop rag dampened with cleaning solvent. Remove any debris that may have passed through a broken element.
6. Before cleaning the air filter element, check it for brittleness, separation or other damage. Replace the element if it is damaged. If there is no visible damage, clean the air filter element as follows.

> *WARNING*
> *Do not clean the air filter element or holder with gasoline.*

> *CAUTION*
> *Do not wring or twist the filter element when cleaning it. This could damage filter pores or tear the filter element loose at a seam and allow unfiltered air to enter the engine.*

7. Soak the air filter element in a container filled with a high flash point solvent, kerosene or an air filter cleaning solution. *Gently* squeeze the filter to dislodge and remove the oil and dirt from the filter pores. Swish the filter around in the cleaner while repeating this step a few times, then remove the air filter and set it aside to dry.

8. Fill a clean pan with warm soapy water.

9. Submerge the filter element into the cleaning solution and gently work the soap solution into the filter pores. Soak and squeeze the filter element gently to clean it.

10. Rinse the filter element under clear water while gently squeezing it.

11. Repeat these steps until the filter element is clean.

12. After cleaning the filter element, inspect it carefully. Replace it if it is torn or damaged. Do not run the engine with a damaged air filter element as it allows dirt to enter the engine.

13. Allow the filter element to dry thoroughly. Make sure the filter element is dry before oiling it.

> *CAUTION*
> *Do not use engine oil to lubricate the foam air filter. Foam air filter oil is specifically formulated for easy and thorough application into the filter pores and provides a tacky viscous medium to trap air borne contaminants. Engine oil is too thin to remain suspended in the filter and will be drawn into the engine, allowing dirt to pass through the filter.*

14. Properly oiling an air filter element is a messy job. Wear a pair of disposable rubber gloves when performing this procedure. Oil the filter element as follows:

   a. Place the air filter element into a one gallon-sized storage bag.

   b. Pour foam air filter oil into the bag and onto the filter element to soak it.

   c. Gently squeeze and release the filter element, from the outside of the bag, to soak the filter oil into the filter element pores. Repeat until all of the pores are saturated.

   d. Remove the filter element from the bag and check the pores for uneven oiling. Light or dark areas on the filter indicate this condition. If necessary, work more oil into the filter and repeat substep c.

   e. When the filter is oiled evenly, squeeze the filter a final time to remove excess oil.

   f. Remove the air filter element from the bag.

15. Install by reversing the removal steps. Make sure the element is correctly seated in the air box so there are no air leaks.

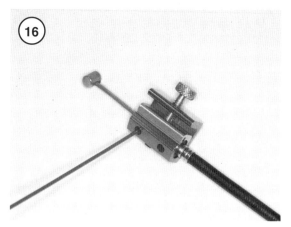

Removal/Inspection/Installation (XR650L)

1. Remove the left side cover as described in Chapter Sixteen.

2. Unhook the element retaining strap (A, **Figure 15**).

3. Remove the element (B, **Figure 15**) from the air box.

4. At the service intervals in **Table 4**, replace the air filter element. If the motorcycle has not yet reached the mileage interval for replacement, check the element for damage or dirt buildup. Replace the element if necessary.

5. Gently tap the air filter element to loosen the dust.

> *CAUTION*
> *Do not direct compressed air toward the outside surface of the element. This forces the dirt and dust into the pores of the element.*

6. Apply compressed air to the inside surface of the element to remove all loosened debris.

7. Inspect the element. If it is torn or broken in any area, replace it.

8. If necessary, clean out the air box and air box drain hose.

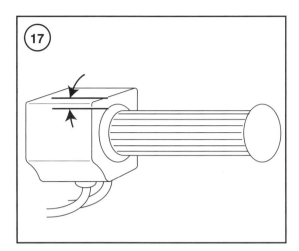

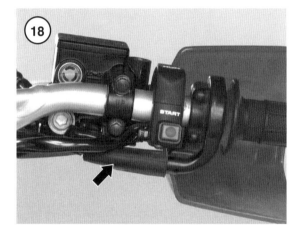

9. Install by reversing the removal steps. Make sure the element is correctly seated in the air box so there are no air leaks.

CONTROL CABLE INSPECTION AND LUBRICATION

Periodically clean and lubricate the throttle, clutch and choke cables. At the same time, check the cables for wear and damage that could cause the cables to bind or break.

CAUTION
Do not use chain lubricant to flush and lubricate the control cables.

1. Disconnect both clutch cable ends as described in Chapter Six.
2. Disconnect both throttle cable ends as described in Chapter Eight or Chapter Nine.
3. On XR650L models, disconnect the upper choke cable end as described in Chapter Nine.
4. Attach a cable lubricator to one end of the cable (**Figure 16**), following the manufacturer's instructions.

5. Tie a plastic bag around the opposite cable end to catch the lubricant.
6. Fit the nozzle of the cable lubricant into the hole in the lubricator.
7. Hold a rag over the lubricator, then press and hold the button on the lubricant can. Continue until lubricant drips from the opposite end.
8. Disconnect the cable lubricator, then pull the inner cable back and forth to help distribute the lubricant.
9. Allow time for excess lubricant to drain from the cable before reconnecting it.
10. Apply a light coat of grease to the upper throttle cable ends before reconnecting them.
11. Lubricate the upper clutch and choke cable ends with grease.
12. Reconnect the cables as described in the appropriate chapter.
13. Adjust the cables as described in this chapter.

THROTTLE CABLE ADJUSTMENT

Free play is the distance the throttle grip can be rotated, measured at the throttle grip flange (**Figure 17**), until resistance from the throttle shaft is felt. Throttle cable free play is necessary to prevent variation in the idle speed when turning the handlebars. In time, the throttle cable free play increases as the cable stretches. This delays throttle response and affects low speed operation. On the other hand, if there is no throttle cable free play, an excessively high idle speed can result.
1. Rotate the throttle grip from low idle position as if accelerating, with the handlebar pointed in different steering positions. In each position, the throttle must open and close smoothly and completely. If the throttle cables bind or move roughly, inspect the cables for kinks, bends or other damage. Replace damaged cables. If the cables move smoothly and are not damaged, continue with Step 2.
2. Determine the throttle grip free play as shown in **Figure 17**. If the free play is more or less than 2-6 mm (1/8-1/4 in.), adjust the cables as described in the following steps.

NOTE
Throttle cable adjustment is made at either end of the pull cable. Make minor adjustments at the upper end of the pull cable. Make major adjustments at the lower end of the pull cable.

3. Slide the rubber cover (**Figure 18**) away from the throttle housing.

4A. On XR600R models, loosen the pull cable lock-nut (**Figure 19**) and turn the cable adjuster in or out to achieve the correct free play. Tighten the locknut.

4B. On XR650L models, loosen the pull cable lock-nut (A, **Figure 20**) and turn the cable adjuster (B) in or out to achieve the correct free play. Tighten the locknut.

5. Recheck the free play and note the following:

    a. If the free play is correct, reposition the rubber cover (**Figure 18**) over the throttle housing.

    b. If further adjustment is required, continue with Step 6.

6. Remove the fuel tank as described in Chapter Eight or Chapter Nine.

7A. On XR600R models, loosen the pull cable lock-nut (A, **Figure 21**) and turn the adjuster (B) in or out to achieve the correct free play. Tighten the locknut.

7B. On XR650L models, loosen the pull cable lock-nut (A, **Figure 22**) and turn the adjuster (B) in or out to achieve the correct free play. Tighten the locknut.

8. If the correct free play cannot be achieved, the throttle cables have stretched to the point where they need to be replaced. Replace both throttle cables as described in Chapter Eight or Chapter Nine.

9. Reinstall the fuel tank.

10. Recheck the throttle cable free play.

11. Slide the rubber cover (**Figure 18**) over the throttle housing.

12. Make sure the throttle grip rotates freely from a fully closed to fully open position.

13. Start the engine and allow it to idle in neutral. Turn the handlebar from side to side. If the idle increases, the throttle cable is routed incorrectly or there is not enough throttle cable free play. Repair this condition before riding the motorcycle.

CHOKE CABLE ADJUSTMENT (XR650L)

The choke cable operates the starter enrichment valve in the carburetor. Adjust the choke cable as described in Chapter Nine.

CLUTCH LEVER ADJUSTMENT

The clutch lever free play changes due to clutch cable stretching and clutch plate wear. Maintain the clutch lever free play within specification. Insufficient free play causes clutch slip and premature clutch plate wear. Excessive free play causes clutch drag and difficult shifting.

1. Determine the clutch lever free play at the end of the clutch lever as shown in **Figure 23**. If the free play is more or less than 10-20 mm (3/8-3/4 in.), adjust the cable as described in the following steps.

2. Slide the cover away from the adjuster. Loosen the locknut (A, **Figure 24**) and turn the cable end

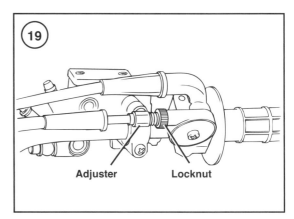

Adjuster   Locknut

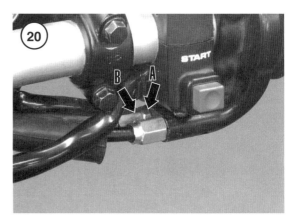

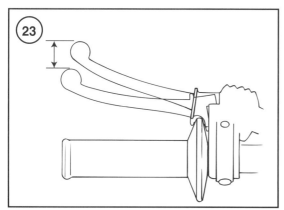

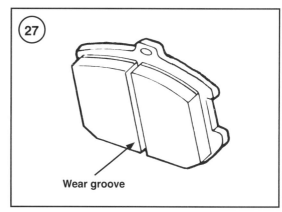

Wear groove

3

adjuster (B) either in or out as required to achieve the specified amount of free play. Tighten the lock-nut.

3. If the proper amount of free play cannot be achieved by adjusting the clutch lever adjuster, the cable inline adjuster must be changed. Perform the following:

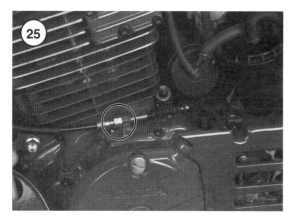

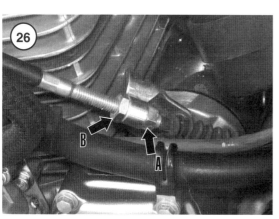

    a. Turn the clutch lever adjuster (B, **Figure 24**) in all the way and then back out one turn.

    b. On XR600R models, loosen the clutch cable locknut (**Figure 25**), then turn the adjuster nut as required to obtain the free play specified in Step 1. Tighten the locknut against the adjuster nut. If necessary, fine-tune the adjustment at the clutch lever adjuster.

    c. On XR650L models, loosen the clutch cable inline adjuster locknut (A, **Figure 26**). Turn the adjuster nut (B, **Figure 26**) as required to obtain the free play specified in Step 1. Tighten the locknut. If necessary, fine-tune the adjustment at the clutch lever adjuster.

4. If the correct free play cannot be obtained, either the cable has stretched or the clutch discs are worn. Refer to Chapter Six for clutch cable and clutch service.

5. Make sure the locknut(s) are tight.

6. Reinstall the clutch lever cover.

BRAKES

This section describes routine service procedures for the front and rear brakes. Refer to **Tables 1-4** for service intervals.

Brake Pad Wear

Inspect the brake pads for wear, contamination or damage. Inspect the thickness of the friction material on each pad. Each brake pad is equipped with a wear groove (**Figure 27**). If any one pad on the front or rear is worn to its wear limit grooves, or measures 1.0 mm (0.04 in.) or less, replace both pads. Refer to Chapter Fifteen for brake pad service.

Front Brake Lever Adjustment (XR600R)

The position of the brake lever, in relation to the handlebar, can be adjusted.
1. Remove the dust cover from the adjuster.
2. To move the brake lever closer to or farther away from the handlebar, loosen the locknut (A, **Figure 28**) and turn the adjuster (B) in or out. Tighten the locknut.
3. Check the front brake lever free play (C, **Figure 28**). The free play should be 0.6-8.0 mm (0.02-0.31 in.). If the brake lever free play exceeds 8 mm (0.31 in.) and the clearance between the front master cylinder piston and the adjuster (D, **Figure 28**) is less than 1.4 mm (0.06 in.) there is probably air in the brake system and it must be bled. Refer to Chapter Fifteen.
4. Support the motorcycle with the front wheel off the ground. Rotate the front wheel and check for brake drag. Operate the front brake lever several times to make sure it returns to the at-rest position after releasing it.
5. Tighten the locknut, making sure the adjuster does not move, and recheck the free play.
6. Move the brake lever away from the handlebar and lubricate the end of the adjuster and piston contact surfaces with silicone brake grease.
7. Install the dust cover.

Rear Brake Pedal Height Adjustment

1. Apply the rear brake a few times and allow the pedal to come to rest. Make sure the return spring is installed and in good condition.
2. Measure the pushrod height dimension as shown in **Figure 29**.
   a. If necessary, loosen the locknut (**Figure 29**) and turn the pushrod to adjust the height to 71 mm (2.8 in.).
   b. Tighten the locknut securely and recheck the height dimension.

Rear Brake Light Switch Adjustment

1. Turn the ignition switch on.
2. Depress the brake pedal and watch the brake light. The brake light should come on just before feeling pressure at the brake pedal. If necessary, adjust the switch by performing the following:
   a. Hold the switch body (A, **Figure 30**) and turn the adjusting nut (B). To make the light come on earlier, turn the adjusting nut and move the

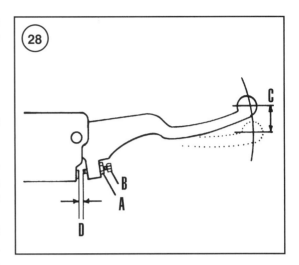

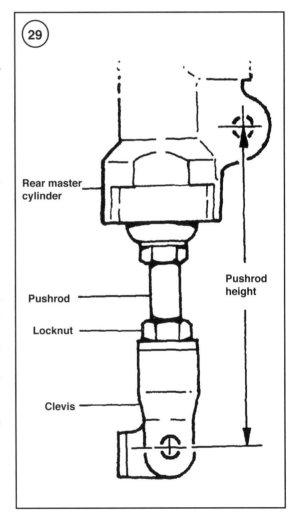

switch body up. Move the switch body down to delay the light coming on.
   b. Make sure the brake light comes on when the pedal is depressed and goes off when the pedal is released. Readjust if necessary.
3. Turn the ignition switch off.

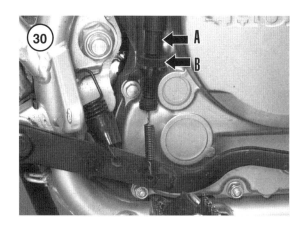

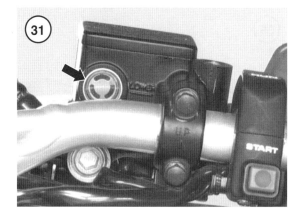

Brake Fluid Level Inspection

> *WARNING*
> *If any reservoir is empty, or if the brake fluid level is so low that air is entering the brake system, bleed the brake system as described in Chapter Fifteen. Simply adding brake fluid to the reservoir does not restore the brake system to its full effectiveness.*

> *WARNING*
> *Use DOT 4 brake fluid specified for disc brakes. Others may vaporize and cause brake failure. Do not intermix different brands or types of brake fluid, as they may not be compatible. Do not intermix a silicone-based (DOT 5) brake fluid, as it can cause brake component damage leading to brake system failure.*

Maintain the brake fluid level in the front and rear master cylinder reservoirs above the minimum level line. If the fluid level is low in either reservoir, check for loose or damaged hoses or loose fittings. If there are no visible fluid leaks, check the brake pads for wear. As the brake pads wear, the caliper pistons move farther out of their bores, causing the brake fluid level to drop in the reservoir. Also, check the master cylinder bore and the brake caliper for brake fluid leaks. If there is a noticeable fluid leak, inspect the components carefully. Check the brake pads for wear as described in this section. Refer to Chapter Fifteen for brake service.

1. Park the motorcycle on level ground.

2. Clean the master cylinder area before removing the cover to avoid contaminating the fluid.

3A. On the front master cylinder, perform the following:

    a. Turn the handlebar so the master cylinder reservoir is level.

    b. Observe the brake fluid level through the inspection window (**Figure 31**).

    c. The brake fluid level must be above the lower level line.

    d. Remove the two screws and remove the cover (**Figure 32**) and diaphragm.

    e. Add DOT 4 brake fluid up to the upper level mark inside the reservoir (**Figure 33**).

    f. Replace the cover and diaphragm if damaged.

    g. Install the diaphragm and cover and tighten the screws securely.

3B. On the rear master cylinder, perform the following:

a. Make sure the brake fluid level is above the lower level mark on the reservoir (A, **Figure 34**).

b. On XR600R models, unscrew the top cap. Pull up and loosen the top cap and the diaphragm.

c. On XR650L models, remove the mounting bolt and bracket (B, **Figure 34**). Reposition the reservoir on the frame and reinstall the mounting bolt without the bracket. Unscrew the top cap. Pull up and loosen the top cap and the diaphragm.

d. Add DOT 4 brake fluid up to the upper level mark on the reservoir.

e. Replace the cover and diaphragm. Install the bracket on XR650L models and tighten the bolt securely.

Brake Hose Replacement

Periodically inspect the brake hoses. If necessary, refer to Chapter Fifteen for replacement.

Brake Fluid Change

Every time a fluid reservoir cap is removed, a small amount of dirt and moisture enters the brake system. The same thing happens if a leak occurs or if any of the hydraulic system is loosened or disconnected. Dirt can clog the system and cause unnecessary wear. Water in the brake fluid can vaporize at high brake system temperatures, impairing the hydraulic action and reducing stopping ability.

To maintain peak performance, change the brake fluid every year. To change brake fluid, follow the brake bleeding procedure in Chapter Fifteen.

DRIVE CHAIN

Drive Chain Lubrication

Lubricate the drive chain frequently. A properly maintained chain provides maximum service life and reliability.

1. Ride the motorcycle approximately 5 minutes to heat the chain.

2. Support the motorcycle so the rear wheel is off the ground.

3. Shift the transmission into neutral.

4A. For a non-O-ring chain, perform the following:

a. Turn the rear wheel and lubricate the chain with an SAE 80 or 90-weight gear oil or a chain spray lubricant. Do not over-lubricate, as this causes dirt to collect on the chain and sprockets.

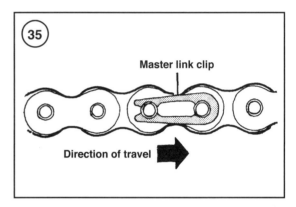

b. Wipe off all excess oil from the rear hub, wheel and tire.

4B. For an O-ring chain, perform the following:

> *CAUTION*
> *Do not use a tacky chain lubricant on O-ring chains. Dirt and other abrasive material that sticks to the lubricant also sticks against the O-rings and damages them. Clean the chain as described in this chapter.*

a. Lubricate the chain with a chain lubricant (non-tacky) specifically formulated for O-ring chains. If unavailable, lubricate the chain with an SAE 80 or 90-weight gear oil.

b. Wipe off all excess oil from the rear hub, wheel and tire.

5. After lubricating the chain with gear oil, support the motorcycle with the rear wheel off the ground. Then hold a cloth against the chain and rear sprocket and slowly turn the wheel to remove excess oil.

6. Make sure the master link, if so equipped, is properly installed and secured (**Figure 35**).

Drive Chain Adjustment

The drive chain must have adequate free play to accommodate swing arm movement. A tight chain

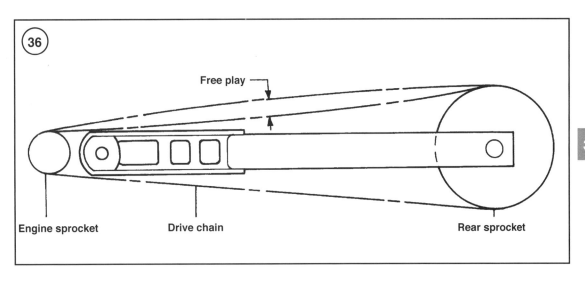

Free play

Engine sprocket   Drive chain   Rear sprocket

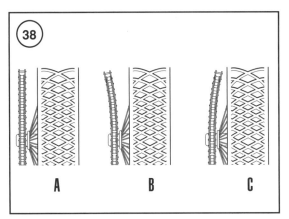

A   B   C

causes unnecessary wear to the driveline components while a loose chain may jump off the sprockets, possibly causing damage.

1. Support the motorcycle with the rear wheel off the ground.

2. Slowly turn the rear wheel and check the chain for binding and tight spots by moving the links up and down by hand. If a link or group of links does not move freely, remove and clean the chain. Check for swollen or damaged O-rings.

3. Check the amount of free play by measuring midway between the two sprockets at the upper chain run (**Figure 36**) on XR600R and 1993-2007 XR650L models. On 2008-on XR650L, check free play on the lower chain run. Chains do not wear evenly. Check several sections of the chain to find the tightest length (least amount of play) and measure free play at this point. The correct amount of free play is 35-45 mm (1.38-1.75 in.). Continue with the next steps to adjust the chain if the free play is out of specification.

4. Mark the tight spot on the chain with chalk. After adjusting and spinning the chain, recheck free play at the same spot. Because drive chains do not wear evenly, always measure and adjust the chain at its tightest spot.

NOTE
On XR600R models, the rear axle nut is on the left side. On XR650L models it is on the right side. This procedure is shown on a XR650L model. The adjustment procedure is the same for both models except for the axle nut location.

5. Loosen the rear axle nut (A, **Figure 37**).

6. Rotate the chain adjuster (B, **Figure 37**) on each side of the swing arm to adjust the chain. Turn the adjusters equally so the same chain adjuster plate index marks align with the index pin on each side of the swing arm. Remeasure chain free play at the original spot.

7. When the chain free play is correct, verify proper wheel alignment by sighting along the chain from the rear sprocket. The chain must leave the sprocket in a straight line (A, **Figure 38**). If it is turned to one side or the other (B and C, **Figure 38**), perform the following:

   a. Adjust wheel alignment by turning one adjuster or the other. Recheck chain free play.

b. Confirm swing arm index mark accuracy, if necessary, by measuring from the center of the swing arm pivot shaft to the center of the rear axle.

8A. On XR600R models, tighten the rear axle nut to 95 N•m (70 ft.-lb.).

8B. On XR650L models, tighten the rear axle nut (A, **Figure 37**) to the specification in Table 15.

9. Spin the wheel several times and note the following:

a. Recheck the free play at its tightest point. Make sure the free play is within specification.

b. Check the chain alignment as it runs through the chain guide.

c. Check rear brake operation.

d. Make sure the drive sprocket cover is installed and tightened securely.

Drive Chain Cleaning

NOTE
XR650L models are equipped with an endless chain, which requires swing arm dislocation to remove the chain.

1. If desired, remove the drive chain as described in Chapter Twelve.

2A. With the chain installed, proceed as follows:

a. Support the motorcycle so the rear wheel is off the ground.

b. Increase chain free play as described in this section so the chain is as loose as possible.

c. Liberally apply kerosene to the drive chain while turning the rear wheel for complete coverage.

2B. With the chain removed, proceed as follows:

a. Immerse the chain in a pan of kerosene.

b. Flex the chain to loosen dirt and increase kerosene penetration.

3. Allow the kerosene to soak into the drive chain.

CAUTION
Brushes with coarse or wire bristles may damage the O-rings.

4. Using a soft brush, clean dirt and debris from all exterior chain surfaces.

5. Check for binding or kinked links and damaged pins.

6. Clean the sprockets.

7. Rinse the chain with clean kerosene and allow it to dry.

8. If removed, install the drive chain as described in Chapter Twelve.

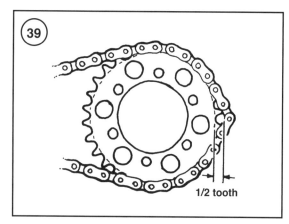

1/2 tooth

Drive Chain and Sprocket Wear Inspection

A worn drive chain and sprockets are both unreliable and potentially dangerous. Inspect the chain and both sprockets for wear and replace if necessary. If there is wear, replace both sprockets and the chain. Mixing old and new parts will prematurely wear the new parts.

1. Perform a quick inspection of the chain by pulling one link away from the rear sprocket. If more than half the height of the tooth is visible (**Figure 39**), the chain is probably worn out. Also refer to *Drive Chain Wear Inspection* in this section.

2. Inspect the inner plate chain faces (**Figure 40**). They should be polished on both sides. If they show considerable uneven wear on one side, the sprockets are not aligned properly. Severe wear requires replacement of not only the drive chain but also the drive and driven sprockets. Also check for a damaged chain guide, and worn bushings and bearings in the swing arm and drive system.

3. Inspect the teeth on each sprocket. The teeth should be symmetrical and uniform. Look for hooked and broken teeth (**Figure 41**). Check the rear sprocket for cracks and damaged Allen bolt recesses.

NOTE
If both sprockets and chain were replaced as a set, and the driven sprocket wore out quickly, inspect the condition of the sprocket teeth. If the worn area is halfway up on the sprocket teeth, the chain was adjusted too tightly. Sprocket wear only on one side of the sprocket is normally caused by incorrect chain alignment. A bent or damaged chain guide will also cause the sprocket to wear on one side. Also, consider the condition of the swing arm bearings. Worn or damaged bearings will affect swing arm and chain alignment, even when the chain adjuster marks are correctly aligned.

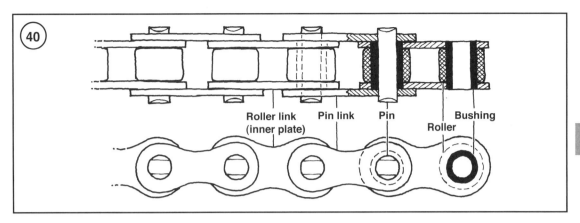

Roller link Pin link Pin Bushing
(inner plate) Roller

3

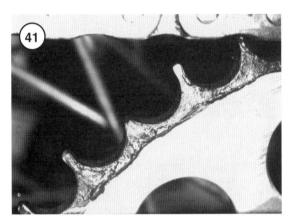

Drive Chain Wear Inspection

Drive chain wear is indicated by a green and red line on the chain adjuster (B, **Figure 37**). Determine chain wear as follows:

1. Check the chain adjustment and adjust if necessary as described in this section.

2. If any part of the red zone on the indicator line aligns with the index pin (C, **Figure 37**) on the swing arm, and chain free play is correct, the drive chain is excessively worn. Replace the drive chain.

Drive Chain Slider Inspection

The chain slider protects the swing arm from chain damage. The chain slipper protects the frame tube.

1. Remove the drive sprocket cover.

2. Inspect the chain slider (A, **Figure 42**) for excessive wear or damage.

3. Measure the depth of the chain slider wear grooves. Replace the chain slider if the groove depth exceeds the specification in Table 8. If there is extensive damage or wear, inspect the swing arm. To replace the slider and inspect the swing arm, remove the swing arm as described in Chapter Fourteen.

4. Inspect the chain slipper (B, **Figure 42**) for excessive wear or damage.

5. Measure the depth of the chain slipper wear grooves. Replace the chain slipper if the groove depth exceeds the specification in Table 8. If there is extensive damage or wear, inspect the frame tube.

6. Install the drive sprocket cover.

Chain Guide Inspection

1. Inspect the chain guide (A, **Figure 43**) for loose mounting bolts or damage.

2. Inspect the chain guide for wear and damage. Replace the chain guide when the chain is visible in the wear limit slot (B, **Figure 43**).

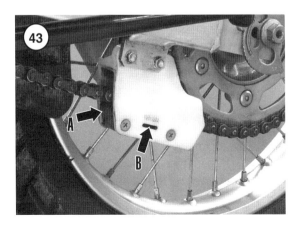

TIRES AND WHEELS

Tire Pressure

Periodically check the tire pressure to maintain good handling and to prevent unnecessary wear or damage. Refer to **Table 9** for the standard tire pressures. Check the tire pressure when the tires are cold.

Tire Inspection

Inspect the tires weekly for damage. Check the sidewalls for damage. Inspect the tire tread for tears or objects embedded in the tire.

Tube Alignment

Check the valve stem. If a valve stem is turned sideways (**Figure 44**), the tire and tube have slipped on the wheel. The valve will eventually pull out of the tube, causing a flat. To realign the tube and tire:

1. Wash the tire and rim.
2. Remove the valve stem core to deflate the tire.
3. Loosen the rim locknuts, if so equipped.
4. With an assistant steadying the motorcycle, break the tire-to-rim seal all the way around the wheel on both sides.
5. Put the motorcycle on a stand with the wheel off the ground.
6. Spray soapy water along both tire beads.
7. Have an assistant apply the brake.
8. Grab the tire at two opposite places and turn it and the tube to straighten the valve stem.
9. Install the valve stem core and inflate the tire. If necessary, reapply the soap and water to help the tire seat on the rim. Check the tire to make sure it seats evenly around the rim.

WARNING
Do not over-inflate the tire and tube. If the tire does not seat properly, remove the valve stem core and re-lubricate the tire with soap and water again.

10. If so equipped, tighten the rim locknut(s) to 13 N•m (115 in.-lb.).
11. Adjust the tire pressure (**Table 9**) and install the valve stem nut and cap.

Wheel Inspection

Inspect wheel runout and check spoke tension as follows:

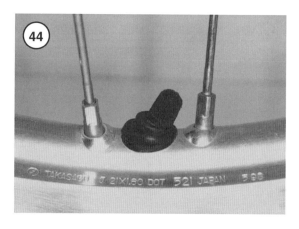

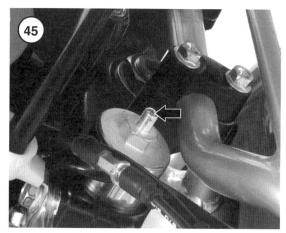

CAUTION
Most spokes loosen as a group rather than individually. Tighten loose spokes carefully. Over-tightened spokes put excessive pressure across the wheel. Never tighten spokes so tight that the spoke wrench rounds off the spoke nipples. If the spokes are stuck, apply penetrating oil into the top of each nipple and allow time for it to soak in and dissolve rust and corrosion on the mating threads.

NOTE
During break-in for a new or a re-spoked wheel, check the spoke tension at the end of each 15-minute interval for the first hour of riding. Most spoke seating takes place during initial use.

1. Inspect the wheels for cracks, warp or dents. Replace damaged wheels.
2. Support the motorcycle with the wheel off the ground, then spin it while watching the rim. If there is appreciable wobble or runout, note the following:
   a. Refer to *Wheel Bearing Inspection* in this chapter to check the bearings.

b. If the wheel bearings are good, check the wheel runout and true the wheel as described in Chapter Twelve.

3. Tap each spoke in the same spot with a spoke wrench. Tight spokes will ring and loose spokes will make a dull, flat sound.

4. If only a few spokes are loose, tighten them with a spoke wrench. If a group of spokes are loose, tighten them while truing the wheel as described in Chapter Twelve.

5. When using a spoke torque wrench, tighten the spokes to the specification in Table 15.

WHEEL BEARING INSPECTION

Inspect the wheels at the intervals in **Tables 1-4**. Check the condition of the seals and bearings as well. If the seals are in good condition, wipe off their outer surface, then pack the lip of each seal with grease. To replace the seals and wheel bearings, refer to the service procedures in Chapter Twelve.

Check the front and rear wheel bearings as follows:

1. Support the motorcycle with the wheel off the ground.

2. Push the caliper in to push the piston(s) into its bore. This will move the pads away from the disc.

3. Spin the wheel while checking for excessive wheel bearing noise or other damage. Stop the wheel.

4. Grab the wheel at two points and rock it. There should be no perceptible play at the wheel bearings. If any movement can be seen or felt, check the wheel bearings for excessive wear or damage (Chapter Twelve).

5. Spin the wheel while applying the brake several times to reposition the pads against the disc.

FRONT FORK

Oil Change

There is no fork oil change interval specified. However, a one-year interval is a typical recommendation. Refer to Chapter Thirteen.

Air Pressure Adjustment

Adjust the fork air pressure (**Table 10**) to match rider and load weight as follows:

1. Place the motorcycle on a workstand with the front wheel off the ground.

2. Remove the cap on the air valve (**Figure 45**).

NOTE
Using an air pressure gauge may allow the release of air while connecting and disconnecting it from the air valve. Compensate accordingly.

3. Using a low-pressure gauge, measure the air pressure in the fork leg.

4. Depress the air valve core stem to release air pressure.

5. Use a low-volume pump, such as a bicycle air pump, to increase air pressure.

6. Adjust the air pressure in the other fork. The air pressure in both fork legs must be the same.

7. Install the air valve caps.

Compression Damping Adjustment

The compression damping adjuster is located in the center of the compression valve in the bottom of the fork. Compression damping adjustment affects the rate of fork compression. Turning the adjuster clockwise increases damping (stiffens). Turning the adjuster counterclockwise decreases damping (softens). Refer to **Table 10** for the standard compression setting. Set compression damping as follows:

1. Remove the plug from the bottom of the fork leg (**Figure 46**).

2. Turn the adjuster (**Figure 47**) to the maximum hard position (clockwise). Do not force the adjuster beyond its range of travel.

3. Turn the adjuster counterclockwise while counting the number of clicks, as recommended in **Table 10**. Make sure the compression damping adjusters in both fork legs are set in the same positions.

4. Reinstall the plug into the bottom of the fork leg.

STEERING

Steering Head Bearing Inspection

Inspect the steering head bearings at the intervals specified in **Tables 1-4**. Lubricate the bearings when necessary. Remove the steering stem to clean and lubricate the bearings. Refer to Chapter Thirteen for service procedures.

Steering Head Adjustment

The steering head assembly consists of upper and lower tapered roller bearings, the steering stem and the steering head. Because the motorcycle may be subjected to rough terrain and conditions, check the bearing play at the specified intervals (**Tables 1-4**) or whenever it feels loose. A loose bearing adjustment hampers steering and causes premature bearing and race wear. In extreme conditions, a loose bearing adjustment can cause loss of control. Refer to *Steering Play Check and Adjustment* in Chapter Thirteen.

To check steering play:

1. Apply the front brake while compressing the fork. If the steering head pulls away from the frame, or looseness is felt, the steering is too loose.

2. Support the motorcycle with the front wheel off the ground. Turn the handlebar from side to side. Roughness or binding indicates a tight steering adjustment or damaged bearings.

Front Suspension Inspection

1. With the front wheel touching the ground, apply the front brake and pump the fork up and down vigorously. Check fork movement, paying attention to any abnormal noises or oil leaks.

2. Make sure the upper and lower fork tube pinch bolts are secure (Chapter Thirteen).

REAR SUSPENSION ADJUSTMENT

Shock Spring Preload Adjustment

The spring preload adjustment can be performed with the shock mounted on the motorcycle. Adjust spring preload by changing the position of the adjuster on the shock body (**Figure 48**). One complete turn of the adjuster moves the spring 1.5 mm (0.06

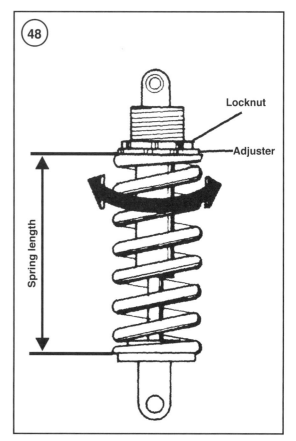

in.). Tightening the adjuster increases spring preload and loosening it decreases preload.

1. Support the motorcycle with the rear wheel off the ground.

2. Remove the left side cover as described in Chapter Sixteen.

3. Clean the threads on the shock body.

4. Measure the existing spring preload length. Measure the spring from end to end. Do not include the thickness of the adjuster or the spring seat. Record the measurement for reference.

5. Loosen the spring locknut (**Figure 48**) with a spanner wrench. If the adjuster turns with the lock-

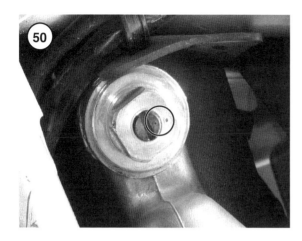

nut, strike the locknut with a punch and hammer to break it from the locknut.

6. Turn the adjuster to change the spring preload dimension within the limits specified in **Table 11**. Usually, turning the spring by hand also turns the adjuster. Measure and record the dimension for reference.

> *CAUTION*
> *Maintain the spring preload within the specifications in **Table 11**. If the minimum specification is exceeded, the spring may coil bind when the shock comes near full compression. This will overload and weaken the spring.*

7. Lightly lubricate the threads on the shock body with engine oil. Then hold the adjuster and tighten the spring locknut (**Figure 48**) to the specification in Table 15.

8. Install the left side cover (Chapter Sixteen).

Compression Damping

Compression damping controls the shock absorber rate after hitting a bump. This setting has no effect on the rebound rate of the shock. The compression damping adjuster is located above the shock reservoir (**Figure 49**). Turning the adjuster clockwise increases damping (stiffens). Turning the adjuster counterclockwise decreases damping (softens). Refer to **Table 11** for the standard compression setting. Set compression damping as follows:

1. Remove the left side cover as described in Chapter Sixteen.

2. Turn the adjuster to the maximum hard position (clockwise). Do not force the adjuster beyond its normal range of travel.

3. Turn the adjuster counterclockwise 7-11 positions so the reference punch marks align (**Figure 50**). This is the standard position.

4. Turn the adjuster as needed to obtain the desired compression damping.

Rebound Damping

The rebound damping adjustment affects the rate of shock absorber extension after it has been compressed. This adjustment has no effect on shock compression. If rebound damping is set too low, the rear wheel may bottom on subsequent bumps.

The rebound damping adjuster is mounted at the bottom of the shock (**Figure 51**). A clicker type adjuster is used; each click of the adjuster screw represents one adjustment or position change. Turning the adjuster one full turn changes the adjuster by eight positions. Refer to **Table 11** for standard and total adjustment positions.

For the standard setting, turn the adjuster screw clockwise until it stops (this is the full hard position). Then turn it counterclockwise the number of clicks (standard) in **Table 11**. When the standard setting is set, the slit on the adjuster will align with the reference mark on the shock body.

To increase the rebound damping, turn the adjuster clockwise. To decrease the rebound damping, turn the adjuster counterclockwise.

Make sure the adjuster is located in one of the detent positions and not in between any two settings.

Nitrogen Pressure

Refer all nitrogen pressure adjustment to a dealership or suspension specialist.

REAR SUSPENSION LUBRICATION

Swing Arm Bearing Lubrication

Lubricate the swing arm bushings at the interval in **Tables 1-4**. Apply molybdenum disulfide grease (NLGI No. 2) with a grease gun.

1. Clean all dirt and grease residue off the grease fitting (**Figure 52**). With the grease gun, force the grease into the fitting until the grease runs out of both ends of the swing arm.

2. Clean the excess grease off all parts.

3. If the grease will not run out of the ends of the swing arm, unscrew the grease fitting from the swing arm. Clean it out with solvent; make sure the ball check valve is free. Reinstall the fitting or replace with a new one.

4. Apply the grease gun again. If the grease still does not run out of both ends of the swing arm, remove the swing arm as described in Chapter Fourteen. Disassemble the swing arm, thoroughly clean it and regrease.

Pro-Link Suspension Lubrication

Lubricate the rear suspension at the interval in **Tables 1-4**. Apply molybdenum disulfide grease (NLGI No. 2) with a grease gun.

1. Clean all dirt and grease residue off the grease fitting.

2. With the grease gun, force the grease into the fitting until the grease runs out past the dust seals on each of the links. There is a fitting on the shock arm (**Figure 53**) and two fittings on the shock link (**Figure 54**).

NOTE
The shock linkage on 2009-on XR650L models does not have grease fittings. Lubricate the dust seals and spacers as described in Shock Linkage Removal/ Installation in Chapter Fourteen.

3. Clean the excess grease off all parts.

4. If the grease will not run out of the ends of the joints, unscrew the grease fitting from the arm or link. Clean it out with solvent and make sure the ball check valve is free. Reinstall the fitting or replace with a new one.

5. Apply the grease gun again. If the grease still does not run out of both ends, remove the suspension components as described in Chapter Fourteen.

BATTERY (XR650L)

The original equipment battery is a sealed, maintenance-free type. The electrolyte level on a sealed battery cannot be adjusted because there are no filler caps and the top is permanently attached.

Removal/Installation

1. Remove the left side cover as described in Chapter Sixteen.

2. Turn the ignition switch off.

3. Release the rubber hooks at the top of the battery box cover (**Figure 55**) and lower the cover.

4. First disconnect the negative battery cable (A, **Figure 56**) and then the positive cable (B) from the battery.

5. Remove the screws securing the battery holder and remove the holder (C, **Figure 56**).

6. Slide the battery out of the battery box.

Inspection

For a preliminary test, connect a digital voltmeter to the battery negative and positive terminals and measure battery voltage. A fully charged battery should read 13.0 volts or greater. If the voltmeter reads less, the battery is under charged. If necessary, charge the battery as described in this section.

Charging

CAUTION
Always follow the manufacturer's instructions when using a battery charger. Never connect a battery charger to the battery with the cables still connected. Always disconnect the leads from the battery. During the charging procedure the charger may damage the voltage regulator/rectifier if the battery cables are connected.

1. Remove the battery as described in this section.
2. Connect the positive charger lead to the positive battery terminal and the negative charger lead to the negative battery terminal.

CAUTION
Do not exceed the recommended charging amperage rate or charging time on the battery label.

3. Set the charger to 12 volts. If the output of the charger is variable, it is best to select a low setting. Use the following suggested charging amperage and length of charge time:
   a. Standard charge: 0.9 amps for 5 to 10 hours.
   b. Quick charge: 4.0 amps for 1 hour.
4. Turn on the charger.
5. After the battery has been charged for the specified amount of time, turn the charger off and disconnect the charger leads.
6. Connect a voltmeter between the battery negative and positive terminals and measure the battery voltage. A fully charged battery should read 13.0-13.2 volts. If necessary, continue charging.
7. After charging, the battery should remain stable for 1 hour at the specified voltage.
8. Clean the battery terminals and case. Coat the terminals and cables with dielectric grease or silicone spray to prevent corrosion.
9. Reinstall the battery as described in this section.

New Battery Installation

Always replace the battery with another maintenance-free type. The charging system and battery box are designed for this type of battery.

When replacing the old battery with a new one, be sure to charge it completely before installing it in the motorcycle. Failure to do so will permanently damage the battery.

NOTE
Recycle the old battery. Most motorcycle dealers accept battery's for recycling. Never place an old battery in household trash.

CARBURETOR

Idle Speed Adjustment

1. Check the air filter for cleanliness. Clean if necessary as described in this chapter.
2. Connect a tachometer to the engine following the manufacturer's instructions.
3. Make sure the throttle cable free play is correct. Check and adjust as described in this chapter.
4. Start and allow the engine to reach operating temperature.
5A. On XR600R models, adjust the idle speed using the idle speed screw (**Figure 57**).
5B. On XR650L models, adjust the idle speed using the throttle stop screw (**Figure 58**).

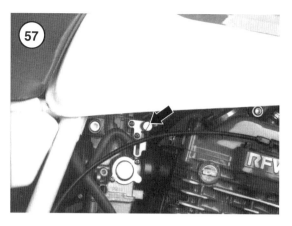

6. Adjust the idle speed to 1200-1400 rpm. Open and close the throttle a few times to make sure the idle speed returns to the rpm.

7. Turn off the engine and disconnect the tachometer.

Pilot Screw Adjustment

Pilot screw adjustment is not necessary unless the carburetor has been overhauled or it has been misadjusted. Refer to Chapter Eight or Chapter Nine.

FUEL SYSTEM

Fuel Shutoff Valve and Filter
Removal/Installation

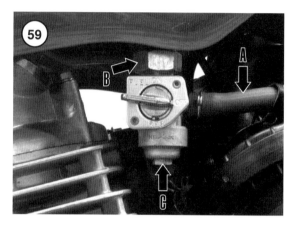

The fuel filter is built into the shutoff valve.

1. Turn the shutoff valve off and detach the fuel line (A, **Figure 59**) from the carburetor.

2. Place the loose end in a clean, sealable metal container. This fuel can be reused if it is kept clean.

3. Turn the shutoff valve to reserve and remove the fuel filler cap. This will allow air to enter the fuel tank and speed up the flow of fuel. Drain the fuel tank completely.

4A. On XR600R models, remove the screws securing the fuel shutoff valve to the fuel tank. Remove the metal collars that surround the screws and remove the valve.

4B. On XR650L models, unscrew the locknut (B, **Figure 59**) securing the fuel shutoff valve to the fuel tank. Remove the valve.

5. After removing the valve from the fuel tank, insert a corner of a shop cloth into the opening in the tank to prevent fuel from leaking onto the engine and frame.

NOTE
The filter is replaceable on XR650L models; on XR600R models, it is not.

6. Clean the filter screen (**Figure 60**) with a soft toothbrush and carefully blow out with compressed air. Replace the filter (XR650L models) or valve as-

sembly (XR600R models) if the filter is broken in any area.

7. Install by reversing the removal steps, noting the following.

   a. On XR600R models, be sure to install the O-ring seal onto the valve. Do not forget to install the collars that surround the screws. Tighten the screws securely.

   b. On XR650L models, be sure to install the O-ring seal onto the valve. Tighten the locknut securely.

   c. Turn the fuel shutoff valve on and check for leaks.

Fuel Strainer Cleaning (XR650L)

In addition to the internal fuel filter, the fuel shutoff valve is equipped with a fuel strainer on the bottom of the valve (C, **Figure 59**).

1. Turn the shutoff valve off.

2. Unscrew the fuel cap (C, **Figure 59**), then remove the O-ring and screen from the shutoff valve. Dispose of fuel remaining in the fuel cup properly.

3. Clean the screen with a soft toothbrush and blow out with compressed air. Replace the screen if it is broken in any area.

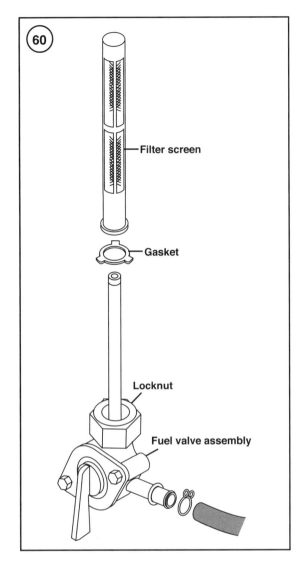

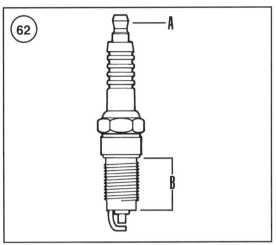

4. Install the O-ring seal and screw on the fuel cup.

Do not overtighten the fuel cup as it may be damaged.

5. Turn the fuel shutoff valve on and check for leaks.

Fuel Line Inspection

Inspect the fuel line (A, **Figure 59**) from the fuel shutoff valve to the carburetor. If it is cracked or starting to deteriorate, replace it. Make sure the hose clamps are in place and holding securely.

EMISSION CONTROL SYSTEM (XR650L)

Periodically inspect the emission control system hoses and fittings. Make sure the hoses are correctly routed and attached. Refer to Chapter Nine.

SPARK PLUG

Removal

1. Grasp the spark plug lead (**Figure 61**) as near the plug as possible and pull it off the plug. If it is stuck to the plug, twist it slightly to break it loose.

> *CAUTION*
> *Whenever the spark plug is removed, dirt around it can fall into the plug hole causing engine wear and/or damage.*

2. Blow away any dirt that has collected around the spark plug.

> *CAUTION*
> *If the plug is difficult to remove, apply penetrating oil around the base of the plug and let it soak about 10-20 minutes. If necessary, work the plug in and out while continuing to apply oil.*

3. Remove the spark plug using a spark plug socket.
4. Inspect the plug carefully. Look for a broken center porcelain, excessively eroded electrodes and excessive carbon or oil fouling.

Gapping and Installation

Carefully adjust the electrode gap on a new spark plug to ensure a reliable, consistent spark. Use a spark plug gapping tool and a wire feeler gauge.

1. Remove the terminal nut from the end of the plug (A, **Figure 62**).

2. Insert a wire feeler gauge between the center and side electrode of the plug (**Figure 63**). Refer to **Table 12** for the gap specifications. If the gap is correct, a slight drag will be felt while pulling the wire through. If there is no drag, or the gauge will not pass through, bend the side electrode with a gaping tool (**Figure 64**) to set the proper gap.

3. Apply an antiseize compound to the plug threads before installing the spark plug. Do not use engine oil on the plug threads.

4. Screw the spark plug in by hand until it seats. Very little effort should be required. If force is necessary, the plug may be cross-threaded. Unscrew it and try again.

5A. When installing a new spark plug without a torque wrench, tighten the spark plug 1/2-3/4 turn after it seats.

5B. When installing a used spark plug without a torque wrench, tighten the spark plug an additional 1/8 turn after it seats.

5C. When installing a spark plug with a torque wrench, tighten it to 17 N•m (150 in.-lb.).

Inspection

Reading a spark plug that has been in use can provide information about spark plug operation, air/fuel mixture composition and engine operating conditions (oil consumption due to wear for example). Before checking the spark plug, operate the motorcycle under a medium load for approximately 6 miles (10 km). Avoid prolonged idling before shutting off the engine. Remove the spark plug as described in this section. Examine the plug and compare it to the typical plugs and conditions shown in **Figure 65**.

When reading a plug to evaluate carburetor jetting, start with a new plug and operate the motorcycle at the load that corresponds to the jetting information desired. For example, if the main jet is in question, operate the motorcycle at full throttle, shut off the engine and coast to a stop.

Heat range

Spark plugs are available in various heat ranges that are either hotter or colder than the original plugs (**Figure 66**). Select plugs of the heat range designed for the anticipated loads and operating conditions.

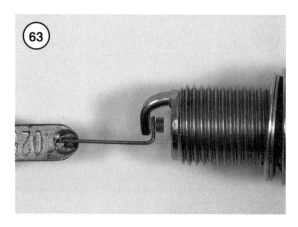

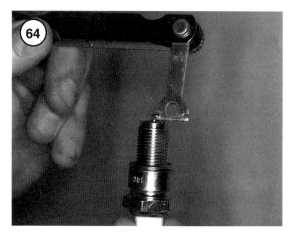

Use of the incorrect heat range can cause the plug to foul or overheat and cause piston damage.

In general, use a hot plug for low speeds and low temperatures. Use a cold plug for high speeds, high engine loads and high temperatures. The plug should operate hot enough to burn off unwanted deposits, but not so hot that it causes preignition. A spark plug of the correct heat range shows a light tan color on the insulator after the plug has been in service.

The reach, or length, of a plug is also important (B, **Figure 62**). A plug that is too short causes excessive carbon buildup, hard starting and plug fouling. A plug that is too long causes overheating or may contact the top of the piston. Both conditions cause engine damage.

Table 12 lists the standard heat range spark plug.

Normal condition

If the plug has a light tan- or gray-colored deposit and no abnormal gap wear or erosion, good engine, carburetion and ignition conditions are indicated. The plug in use is of the proper heat range and may be serviced and returned to use.

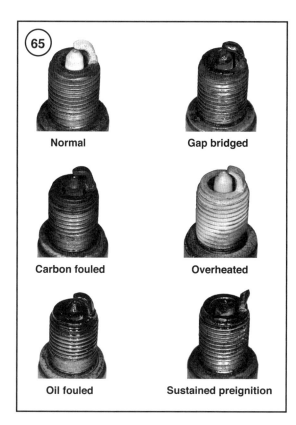

Normal — Gap bridged

Carbon fouled — Overheated

Oil fouled — Sustained preignition

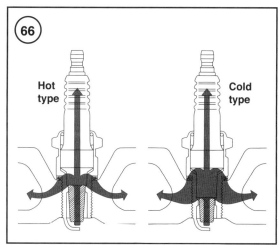

Hot type — Cold type

Carbon fouled

Soft, dry, sooty deposits covering the entire firing end of the plug are evidence of incomplete combustion. Even though the firing end of the plug is dry, the plug's insulation decreases. An electrical path is formed that lowers the voltage from the ignition system. Engine misfiring is a sign of carbon fouling. One or more of the following can cause carbon fouling:
1. Rich fuel mixture.
2. Spark plug heat range too cold.
3. Clogged air filter.
4. Retarded ignition timing. Timing is not adjustable.

5. Ignition component failure.
6. Low engine compression.
7. Prolonged idling.

Oil fouled

The tip of an oil fouled plug has a black insulator tip, a damp oily film over the firing end and a carbon layer over the entire nose. The electrodes are not worn. An oil fouled spark plug may be cleaned in an emergency, but it is better to replace it. It is important to correct the cause of fouling before the engine is returned to service. Common causes for this condition are:
1. Incorrect carburetor jetting.
2. Low idle speed or prolonged idling.
3. Ignition component failure.
4. Spark plug heat range too cold.
5. Engine still being broken in.

Gap bridging

Plugs with this condition exhibit gaps shorted out by combustion deposits between the electrodes. If this condition is encountered, check for an improper oil type or excessive carbon in the combustion chamber. Make sure to locate and correct the cause of this condition.

Overheating

Badly worn electrodes and premature gap wear, along with a gray or white blistered porcelain insulator surface are signs of overheating. The most common cause for this condition is using a spark plug of the wrong heat range (too hot). If a hotter spark plug has not been installed, but the plug is overheated, consider the following causes:
1. Lean fuel mixture.
2. Advanced ignition timing. Timing is not adjustable.
3. Engine lubrication system malfunction.
4. Intake vacuum leak.
5. Improper spark plug installation (too tight).
6. No spark plug gasket.

Worn out

Corrosive gasses formed by combustion and high voltage sparks have eroded the electrodes. Spark plugs in this condition require more voltage to fire under hard acceleration. Replace with a new spark plug.

Preignition

If the electrodes are melted, preignition is almost certainly the cause. Check for carburetor mounting or intake manifold leaks and over-advanced ignition timing. It is also possible that a plug of the wrong heat range (too hot) is being used. Find the cause of the preignition before returning the engine into service.

IGNITION TIMING

All models are equipped with a capacitor discharge ignition system (CDI). Ignition timing is not adjustable. Check the ignition timing to make sure all components within the ignition system are working correctly.

1. Start the engine and let it warm approximately 2-3 minutes. Shut off the engine.

2. Park the motorcycle on level ground.

3. Remove the timing hole cap (A, **Figure 67**) and O-ring.

4. Connect a tachometer following the manufacturer's instructions.

5. Connect a timing light following the manufacturer's instructions.

6. Restart the engine and let it run at 1200-1400 rpm. Adjust the idle speed if necessary as described in this chapter.

7. Aim the timing light at the timing hole and pull the trigger. The *F* mark on the flywheel should align with the index mark on the crankcase cover as shown in **Figure 68**.

8. Increase engine speed to 4000 rpm and check the ignition timing. The index mark on the crankcase cover should be between the twin vertical flywheel marks as shown in **Figure 69**.

9. If the ignition timing is incorrect, troubleshoot the ignition system as described in Chapter Two.

10. Turn off the ignition switch, and disconnect the timing light and tachometer.

11. Install the timing hole cap and O-ring, and tighten securely.

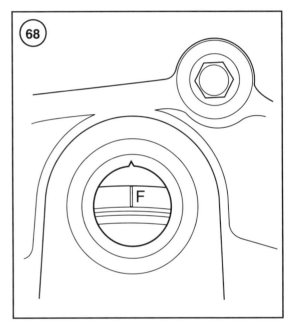

VALVE CLEARANCE ADJUSTMENT

CAUTION
On XR600R models, the decompression system affects the valve adjustment procedure. Adjustment of the right exhaust valve is critical and must be followed exactly. Make sure there is free play in the starter decompression lever. If not, it will hold down the right exhaust valve and make the exhaust valve clearance incorrect. If necessary, adjust the starter decompression lever, as described in this chapter.

The XR600R model is equipped with a manual decompression system that requires additional steps

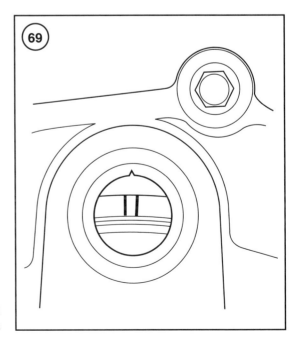

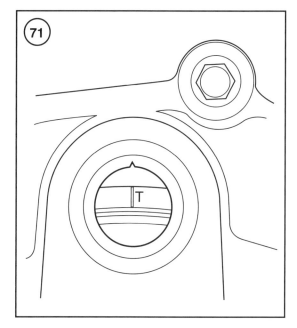

of the engine and the intake valves are located at the rear of the engine.

NOTE
A cylinder at TDC on its compression stroke will have free play in all of its rocker arms, indicating that the intake valves and exhaust valves are closed.

1. Remove the fuel tank as described in Chapter Eight or Chapter Nine.
2. Remove the timing hole cap (A, **Figure 67**) and the flywheel bolt cap (B) on the left crankcase cover.
3. Unscrew each valve adjustment cover (**Figure 70**).
4. Remove the spark plug. This will make it easier to rotate the engine.
5. Insert a wrench through the crankcase cover hole and rotate the engine using the flywheel bolt. Rotate the engine counterclockwise until the *T* mark aligns with the index mark on the crankcase (**Figure 71**).
6. With the marks aligned, all rocker arms should be loose, indicating the engine is at top dead center (TDC) of the compression stroke.
7. If the rockers are not loose, rotate the engine an additional 360° (one revolution) until the rockers have free play.
8A. On XR600R models, check the clearance of the left exhaust valve and both intake valves. The right exhaust valve will be checked later.
8B. On XR650L models, check the clearance of all valves.
9. Insert a flat feeler gauge between the adjusting screw and the valve stem (**Figure 72**). When the clearance is correct, there will be a slight drag on the feeler gauge when it is inserted and withdrawn.
10. To correct the clearance, perform the following:
   a. Loosen the adjuster locknut (A, **Figure 72**).
   b. Screw the adjuster (B, **Figure 72**) in or out so there is a slight resistance felt on the feeler gauge.
   c. Hold the adjuster to prevent it from turning any farther and tighten the locknut to 25 N•m (18 ft.-lb.).
   d. Recheck the clearance to make sure the adjuster did not turn after the clearance was set; readjust if necessary.
11. On XR600R models, adjust the starter decompression lever as described in this chapter.

CAUTION
Prior to checking the clearance of the right exhaust valve, make sure the engine is set to TDC. The decompressor cam on the right end of the camshaft slightly opens the right exhaust valve when the engine is slightly before TDC on the compression stroke. Therefore the engine must be at the TDC position.

to adjust the valve clearance. The XR650L model is equipped with an automatic decompression system.

Perform the valve clearance measurements and adjustments with the engine cool, at room temperature (below 35° C/95° F). The valve clearance is listed in **Table 14**. The exhaust valves are located at the front

CAUTION
Do not rotate the engine clockwise. Due
to the design of the decompression sys-
tem, the engine must always be rotated
counterclockwise for this procedure. If
the engine is rotated clockwise the de-
compression cam may be slightly raised,
thus lifting the rocker arm and decreas-
ing any valve clearance. This would lead
to a false valve clearance indication.

12. On XR600R models, make sure the *T* mark is
still aligned with the index mark on the crankcase
(**Figure 71**). If the *T* mark has passed by the index
mark, even the slightest amount, it must be realigned
as follows:
  a. Rotate the engine *counterclockwise* using the
     flywheel bolt until the engine is at TDC on the
     compression stroke.
  b. Make sure the *T* mark aligns with the index
     mark on the crankcase (**Figure 71**). Do not go
     past the *T* mark.
  c. Check the clearance of the right exhaust valve
     as described in Step 10. If necessary, adjust the
     clearance.
  d. If necessary, adjust the starter decompression
     lever as described in this chapter.
13. Inspect the rubber gaskets on each valve adjustment cover. Replace if damaged or hardened. Install
the covers and tighten securely.
14. Install the two caps (A and B, **Figure 67**) on the
left crankcase cover and tighten securely.
15. Install the fuel tank as described in Chapter
Eight or Chapter Nine.

STARTER DECOMPRESSION LEVER ADJUSTMENT (XR600R)

NOTE
Valve clearance must be correctly ad-
justed before adjusting the decompres-
*sion lever. Refer to **Valve Clearance***
***Adjustment** in this chapter.*

1. Measure free play at the tip of the decompression
lever on the left handlebar. Correct free play is 5-8
mm (3/16-5/16 in.).
2. To adjust the free play, loosen the locknut (A,
Figure 73) and turn the adjuster (B) as needed to obtain the correct free play.
3. Tighten the locknut securely.

EXHAUST SYSTEM

Refer to Chapter Eight or Chapter Nine for service
and repair procedures.

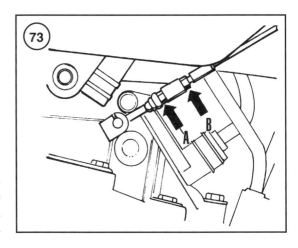

Inspection

1. Inspect the exhaust pipe for cracks or dents that
could alter performance. Refer all repairs to a qualified dealership or welding shop.
2. Check all the exhaust pipe fasteners and mounting points for loose or damaged parts.

Spark Arrestor Cleaning

Remove and clean the spark arrestor at the intervals specified in **Tables 1-4**.

WARNING
Perform this procedure when the ex-
haust system is cold. Work in a well-
ventilated area. Wear safety eyewear
and clothing.

1. Remove the bolts securing the rear port cover
(**Figure 74**). Remove the cover and gasket.
2. On XR650L models, also remove the front port
cover at the forward end of the muffler.
3. Insert heavy shop cloths or rags into the end of the
muffler to create back pressure. This will force the
exhaust and carbon deposits out of the port(s).
4. Start the engine. Increase engine speed several
times.
5. Run the engine until carbon no longer blows out
of the port(s).
6. Reinstall the port cover(s). If necessary, install a
new gasket on the port cover.

COMPRESSION TEST

A compression test is one of the quickest ways to
check the internal condition of the engine (piston
rings, piston, head gasket, valves and cylinder). It is
a good idea to check compression at each major service interval, record it and compare it with the reading obtained at the next service.

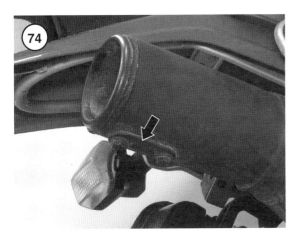

Use a screw-in type compression gauge with a flexible adapter. Before using the gauge, check that the rubber gasket on the end of the adapter is not cracked or damaged; this gasket seals the cylinder to ensure accurate compression readings.

1. On XR650L models, make sure the battery is fully charged to ensure proper engine cranking speed.

2. Run the engine until it reaches normal operating temperature, then turn it off.

3. Remove the spark plug as described in this chapter.

4. Carefully thread the gauge into the spark plug hole. Tighten the hose by hand to form a good seal.

CAUTION
*When the spark plug lead is disconnected, the electronic ignition will produce the highest voltage possible. This can damage the ignition control module. To protect the ignition system, install a grounding tool in the spark plug cap. Refer to **Ignition Grounding Tool** in Chapter One. Do not crank the engine more than necessary.*

5A. On XR600R models, open the throttle completely, press the engine stop switch and kick the engine over while reading the compression gauge until there is no further rise in pressure. The compression reading should increase on each stroke. Record the reading.

5B. On XR650L models, open the throttle completely and operate the starter to turn the engine over while reading the compression gauge until there is no further rise in pressure. The compression reading should increase on each stroke. Record the reading. If the starter does not turn the engine over fast enough, press the engine stop switch and use the kickstarter.

6. Refer to **Table 14** for the compression specification. If the compression reading is low, go to Step 7. If the compression reading is high, go to Step 8.

7. A low compression reading can be caused by the following:
   a. Incorrect valve adjustment.
   b. Worn piston rings, piston or cylinder bore.
   c. Leaking valve seat.
   d. Damaged cylinder head gasket.

8. A high compression reading can be caused by the following:
   a. Damaged decompression assembly.
   b. Excessive carbon deposits on the piston crown or combustion chamber.

9. To isolate the problem, perform a wet compression test. Pour about a teaspoon of engine oil into the spark plug hole. Repeat the compression test and record the reading. If the compression increases significantly, the valves are good but the piston rings are defective. If compression does not increase, the valves require servicing.

10. Reverse the steps to complete installation. Reinstall the spark plug as described in this chapter.

TUNE UP

When performing a tune up refer to the appropriate sections in this chapter and service/check the following items in order:

1. Air filter element.
2. Valve clearance.
3. Compression test.
4. Spark plug.
5. Carburetor idle speed.

Table 1 MAINTENANCE SCHEDULE (1991-1997 XR600R)

Initial maintenance after 200 miles (350 km) or one week
Inspect valve clearance
Replace engine oil and filter
Check engine idle speed
Inspect decompression system
Inspect brake system
Inspect clutch system
(continued)

Table 1 MAINTENANCE SCHEDULE (1991-1997 XR600R) (continued)

Check for loose or missing fasteners
Inspect wheels and tires*
Check steering free play
Every 300 miles (500 km) or ten operating days
  Lubricate and adjust drive chain*
Every 1000 miles (1600 km) or 30 operating days
  Replace engine oil and filter
  Clean oil line strainer
  Clean air filter
  Inspect spark plug, regap if necessary
  Check and adjust valve clearance
  Inspect decompression system
  Check and adjust carburetor idle speed
  Inspect throttle operation
  Clean and inspect fuel filter screen
  Inspect fuel lines for chafed, cracked or swollen ends
  Check and adjust clutch free play
  Inspect and repack wheel bearings
  Check brake fluid level
  Adjust front and rear brake levers
  Inspect brake pads for wear
  Inspect brake system
  Inspect drive chain sliders
  Check steering free play
  Check all suspension components
  Lubricate rear suspension linkage
  Lubricate swing arm bearings
  Check and adjust headlight aim
  Clean muffler
  Check all fasteners for tightness*
Every 1000 miles (1600 km) or two years, whichever occurs first
  Replace brake fluid

*Service more frequently when operated in severe conditions.

Table 2 MAINTENANCE SCHEDULE (1998-2000 XR600R)

Initial maintenance after 100 miles (150 km) or one month
  Inspect valve clearance
  Replace engine oil and filter
  Check engine idle speed
  Inspect decompression system
  Inspect brake system
  Inspect clutch system
  Check for loose or missing fasteners
  Inspect wheels and tires*
  Check steering for free play
Every 300 miles (500 km) or three months
  Lubricate and adjust drive chain*
Every 600 miles (1000 km) or six months
  Replace engine oil and filter
  Clean air filter
  Inspect spark plug, regap if necessary
  Check and adjust valve clearance
  Inspect decompression system
  Check and adjust carburetor idle speed
  Check and adjust clutch free play
  Inspect and repack wheel bearings
  Check brake fluid level
  Adjust front and rear brake levers
  Inspect brake pads for wear
  Inspect brake system
  Inspect drive chain sliders
  Clean muffler

(continued)

Table 2 MAINTENANCE SCHEDULE (1998-2000 XR600R) (continued)

Every 600 miles (1000 km) or two years, whichever occurs first
  Replace brake fluid
Every 1200 miles (2000 km) or one year
  Clean and inspect fuel filter screen
  Inspect fuel lines for chafed, cracked or swollen ends
  Clean oil line strainer
  Inspect throttle operation
  Check all fasteners for tightness*
  Check steering free play
  Check all suspension components
  Check and adjust headlight aim
  Lubricate rear suspension linkage
  Lubricate swing arm bearings

*Service more frequently when operated in severe conditions.

Table 3 PRE-RACE INSPECTION (XR600R)

Engine oil	Check for contamination, change if dirty
Fuel line	Check for leaks and deterioration, replace
Air filter	Check for tears and contamination, replace or clean
Valve clearance	Adjust if necessary to correct clearance
Camshaft chain tensioner	Check for abnormal noise
Carburetor idle speed	Check and adjust if necessary
Spark plug	Check for proper heat range, gap, tightness and plug cap tightness
Starter decompression lever	Check for correct free play, adjust if necessary
Clutch disc wear	Check for abnormal wear and/or discoloration
Steering head	Check for free rotation of handlebar, check tightness of steering stem nut, adjust and/or tighten if necessary
Front suspension	Check for oil leaks, tight boot clamps and smooth action of fork
Rear suspension	Check for oil leaks and smooth operation
Swing arm bearings	Check for abnormal side play, replace if necessary
Drive chain	Inspect for damage and chain stretch, replace if necessary
Sprockets	Inspect for wear and tightness
Seat	Check mounting hardware
Control cables	Check for smooth operation and frayed outer sheath, lubricate or replace
Engine mounting bolts	Check tightness
Headlight	Check headlight adjustment
Instrument lights	Check operation
Tires	Check inflation and inspect for damage, replace if necessary

Table 4 MAINTENANCE SCHEDULE (XR650L)

Initial maintenance after 600 miles (1000 km)
  Inspect valve clearance
  Replace engine oil and filter
  Check engine idle speed
  Inspect brake fluid level
  Inspect brake system
  Inspect clutch system
  Check for loose or missing fasteners
  Inspect wheels and tires*
  Check steering free play
Every 500 miles (800 km)
  Lubricate and adjust drive chain*
Every 2000 miles (3000 km) or 6 months
  Change engine oil
Every 4000 miles (6400 km)
  Inspect spark plug, regap if necessary
  Check and adjust valve clearance
  Check and adjust carburetor idle speed
  Check clutch operation
  Check and adjust clutch free play
  Clean and inspect fuel filter screen
  Inspect and repack wheel bearings

(continued)

Table 4 MAINTENANCE SCHEDULE (XR650L) (continued)

Every 4000 miles (6400 km) (continued)
  Adjust front and rear brake levers
  Inspect brake pads for wear
  Check and adjust the front and rear brake fluid levels
  Inspect drive chain sliders
  Clean and inspect the spark arrester/muffler
  Inspect the wheels and tires
Every 8000 miles (12,800 km)
  Replace engine oil filter*
  Clean oil line strainer*
  Replace spark plug
  Inspect fuel lines for chafed, cracked or swollen ends
  Inspect throttle operation
  Inspect the carburetor choke
  Inspect the secondary air supply system
  Check all fasteners for tightness*
  Check steering for free play
  Check all suspension components
  Inspect entire brake system
  Check the front and rear brake light switches
  Inspect the sidestand
  Inspect the wheels and tires
  Check and adjust headlight aim
  Lubricate rear suspension linkage
  Lubricate swing arm bearings
  Inspect crankcase and emission hoses for cracks or loose hose clamps
Every 12,000 miles (19,200 km)
  Replace air filter and clean air box drain hose*
  On California models, inspect the evaporative emission control system
Every 12,000 miles (19,200 km) or two years, whichever occurs first
  Replace brake fluid

*Service more frequently when operated in severe conditions.

Table 5 RECOMMENDED LUBRICANTS, FLUIDS AND FUEL

Engine oil
  Classification   API SG or higher/JASO MA*
  Viscosity
    XR600R and 1993-2007 XR650L   SAE 10W-40*
    2008-on XR650L   SAE 10W-30
Air filter (XR600R)   Foam air filter oil
Brake fluid   DOT 4
Fork oil
  XR600R & 1993-2007 XR650L   Pro-Honda Suspension Fluid SS-7 or equivalent
  2008-on XR650L   Pro-Honda Suspension Fluid SS-7, HP Fork Oil SS-19
                                               or equivalent
Steering and suspension lubricant   Multipurpose grease
Fuel   Octane rating of 86 or higher

*See text for additional information.

Table 6 ENGINE OIL CAPACITY

	Liters	U.S. qt.
Oil change only	1.9	2.0
Oil and filter change	1.95	2.06
After engine disassembly	2.3	2.4

Table 7 CLUTCH, BRAKE AND THROTTLE ADJUSTMENTS

Clutch lever free play	10-20 mm (3/8-3/4 in.)
Front brake lever free play (XR600R)	0.6-8.0 mm (0.02-0.31 in.)
Rear brake pedal pushrod height	71 mm (2.8 in.)
Throttle grip free play	2-6 mm (1/8-1/4 in.)

Table 8 DRIVE CHAIN AND SLIDER SPECIFICATIONS

Drive chain	
XR600R	DID 520V8 (110 links)
	RK 520MO4X (110 links)
XR650L	DID 520V8 (110 links)
	RK 520MOZ6 (110 links)

(continued)

Table 8 DRIVE CHAIN AND SLIDER SPECIFICATIONS (continued)

Drive chain slack	35-45 mm (1 3/8-1 3/4 in.)
Chain slider groove depth (max.)	2 mm (0.08 in.)
XR600R and 1993-2007 XR650L	2 mm (0.08 in.)
2008-on XR650L	4 mm (0.16 in.)
Chain slipper groove depth (max.)	8 mm (0.31 in.)
XR600R and 1993-2007 XR650L	8 mm (0.31 in.)
2008-on XR650L	2 mm (0.08 in.)

Table 9 TIRE INFLATION PRESSURE

	Front and rear
XR600R	14.5 psi (100 kPa)
XR650L	22 psi (150 kPa)

3

Table 10 FRONT FORK ADJUSTMENT SPECIFICATIONS

XR600R	
Air pressure	
Standard	0 psi (0 kPa)
Maximum	15 psi (98 kPa)
Compression damping adjusting positions*	
Minimum	16
Standard	3
Maximum	1
XR650L	
Air pressure	
Standard	0 psi (0 kPa)
Maximum	
1993-2007	6 psi (40 kPa)
2008-on	5.7 psi (39 kPa)
Compression damping adjusting positions*	
Minimum	
1993-2007	14
2008-on	NA
Standard	3
Maximum	
1993-2007	1
2008-on	NA

*Number of turns from the fully turned-in position.

Table 11 REAR SHOCK ABSORBER ADJUSTMENT SPECIFICATIONS

XR600R	
Shock absorber spring adjustable range	195-205 mm (7.7-8.1 in.)
Compression damping adjusting positions*	
Minimum	16
Standard	10
Maximum	1
Rebound damping adjusting positions*	
Minimum	19
Standard	14
Maximum	1
XR650L	
Shock absorber spring adjustable range	
1993	195-205 mm (7.7-8.1 in.)
1994-2006	203-210 mm (8.0-8.3 in.)
2007-on	NA
Shock absorber spring installed length	
2008-on	206.5 mm (8.13 in.)
Compression damping adjusting positions*	
Minimum	
1993-2007	20
2008-on	NA
Standard	
1993-2007	11
2008-on	7-11
Maximum	
1993-2007	1
2008-on	NA
Rebound damping adjusting positions*	
Minimum	
1993-2007	19
2008-on	NA

(continued)

Table 11 REAR SHOCK ABSORBER ADJUSTMENT SPECIFICATIONS (continued)

Rebound damping adjusting positions* (continued)	
Standard	
1993-2007	15
2008-on	13-17
Maximum	
1993-2007	1
2008-on	NA

*Number of turns from the fully turned-in position.

Table 12 SPARK PLUG SPECIFICATIONS

Spark plug gap	0.8-0.9 mm (0.032-0.036 in.)
Spark plug type	
Standard	NGK DPR8EA-9 or Denso X24EPR-U9
Extended high-speed riding	NGK DPR9EA-9 or Denso X27EPR-U9
Cold weather operation*	NGK DPR7EA-9 or Denso X22EPR-U9

*Below 41° F (4° C).

Table 13 IDLE SPEED SPECIFICATION

All models	1200-1400 rpm

Table 14 ENGINE COMPRESSION, DECOMPRESSION LEVER AND VALVE CLEARANCE SPECIFICATIONS

Decompression lever free play	
XR600R	5-8 mm (3/16-5/16 in.)
Engine compression	
XR600R	
Decompressor engaged	400-600 kPa (58-87 psi)
Decompressor disengaged	1300-1500 kPa (188-217 psi)
XR650L	
1993-2007 models	
Decompressor engaged	637 kPa (92 psi)
Decompressor disengaged	1373 kPa (199 psi)
2008-on	
Decompressor engaged	637 kPa (92 psi) @ 600 rpm
Decompressor disengaged	1373 kPa (199 psi) @ 600 rpm
Valve clearance	
XR600R	
Intake	0.10 mm (0.004 in.)
Exhaust	0.12 mm (0.005 in.)
XR650L	
Intake	0.08-0.12 mm (0.003-0.005 in.)
Exhaust	0.10-0.14 mm (0.004-0.006 in.)

Table 15 MAINTENANCE TORQUE SPECIFICATIONS

Item	N•m	in.-lb.	ft.-lb.
Engine oil drain bolts			
Frame drain bolt	40	–	29
Crankcase drain bolt	25	–	18
Engine oil filter cover bolts			
XR600R & 1993-2007 XR650L	12	106	–
2008-on XR650L	NA	NA	–
Rear axle nut			
XR600R	95	–	70
XR650L			
1993-2007	90	–	66
2008-on	88	–	65
Rear shock absorber spring locknut			
1993-2007	90	–	66
2008-on	88	–	65
Spark plug	17	150	–
Valve adjuster locknut	25	–	18
Wheel rim locknut	13	115	–
Wheel spoke			
XR600R & 1993-2007 XR650L	4	35.00	–
2008-on XR650L	3.7	32.75	–

CHAPTER FOUR

ENGINE TOP END

This chapter provides service and overhaul procedures for the engine top end components. **Tables 1-3**, at the end of the chapter, provide engine specifications.

Throughout the text there is frequent mention of the right and left side of the engine. This refers to the engine as it sits in the motorcycle frame, not as it sits on the workbench.

The motorcycle is equipped with a Radial Four Valve Combustion (RFVC), air-cooled, four-stroke, single-cylinder engine. The cylinder head incorporates two intake and two exhaust valves arranged radially. Each pair of valves has its own set of rocker arms and each valve has its own adjuster. The valves are actuated by a single overhead camshaft (SOHC).

To ease starting, the engine has a cylinder decompression mechanism. When the starter is operated, a decompression cam on the camshaft opens an exhaust valve momentarily to reduce compression pressure. Reduced compression pressure improves starter performance.

CYLINDER HEAD COVER AND CAMSHAFT

The cylinder head cover contains the rocker arm assemblies. The camshaft is held in place between the cylinder head cover and the cylinder head. The camshaft is driven by a chain attached to the crankshaft sprocket.

Cylinder Head Cover Removal

CAUTION
Remove the cylinder head cover when the engine is at room temperature to prevent damage.

1. Remove the carburetor as described in Chapter Eight or Chapter Nine.
2. Detach the spark plug wire (A, **Figure 1**) from the spark plug.
3. Loosen the clamp and detach the breather tube (B, **Figure 1**) from the cylinder head cover.
4. On XR600R models, detach the decompression cable from the cylinder head cover.
5. Remove the intake tube retaining bolts and remove the intake tube (A, **Figure 2**). Remove the O-ring if it does not remain on the intake tube flange.
6. Remove the valve adjuster covers (B, **Figure 2**).
7. Remove the inspection plugs (**Figure 3**) on the left crankcase cover.
8. Using the bolt on the alternator rotor, rotate the crankshaft counterclockwise until the piston is at top dead center (TDC) on the compression stroke. Check

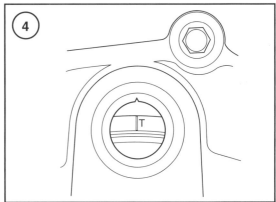

that the alternator rotor *T* mark aligns with the stationary pointer on the crankcase cover (**Figure 4**).

NOTE
When the piston is at TDC on the compression stroke there will be free play in all rocker arms, indicating that both the intake and exhaust valves are closed. If the rocker arms are tight, the piston is on the exhaust stroke. Rotate the crankshaft one full turn and check again to make sure the rocker arms are loose.

9. Remove the upper oil union bolt (A, **Figure 5**) and washers.

10. Remove the upper oil tube retaining bolt (B, **Figure 5**).

11. Remove the lower oil union bolt (A, **Figure 6**) and washers.

12. Remove the lower oil tube retaining bolt (B, **Figure 6**), then remove the oil tube.

13. Remove the engine hanger plate retaining bolts, and then remove the hanger plate (**Figure 7**).

14. Loosen the center cylinder head cover retaining bolts (**Figure 8**). Due to limited space, remove the retaining bolts after removing the cover from the engine.

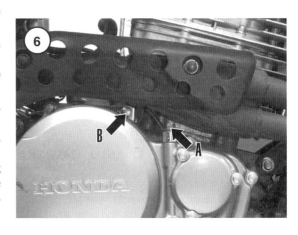

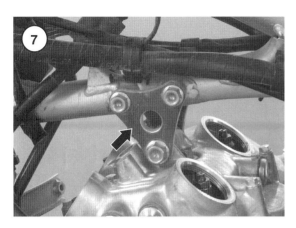

4

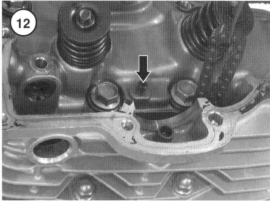

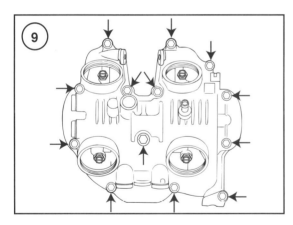

15. Using a crossing pattern, remove the remaining bolts securing the cylinder head cover. Refer to **Figure 9**.

16. Remove the cylinder head cover and gasket. Do not lose the locating dowels.

17. Remove the camshaft chain tensioner as described in this chapter.

18. Using the alternator rotor, rotate the engine counterclockwise until one of the camshaft sprocket bolts is visible (**Figure 10**). Remove that bolt.

19. Again rotate the engine until the other camshaft sprocket bolt is visible. Remove that bolt.

20. Remove the camshaft chain from the camshaft sprocket (**Figure 11**).

21. Tie a piece of wire to the camshaft chain and secure the loose end to the exterior of the engine. This will prevent the camshaft chain from falling into the crankcase.

22. Remove the camshaft and sprocket from the cylinder head.

23. Do not damage or lose the decompression pin (**Figure 12**) and spring in the cylinder head.

CAUTION
If the crankshaft must be rotated when the camshaft is removed, pull up on the camshaft chain and keep it taut while rotating the crankshaft. Make certain

that the chain is positioned correctly on the crankshaft sprocket. If this is not done, the chain may become kinked and may damage both the chain and the sprocket on the crankshaft.

Camshaft Inspection

1. Rotate the camshaft bearings (A, **Figure 13**) and check for roughness, pitting, galling and play. If any roughness or play can be felt in a bearing, replace it.
2. Check the camshaft lobes for wear. The lobes must be smooth with no scoring, galling or roughness.

> *NOTE*
> *The cam is dark in color due to the manufacturing heat treating process. It is not due to lack of oil pressure or excessive engine heat.*

3. Measure both the intake (B, **Figure 13**) and exhaust (C) lobes of the camshaft. Compare to the specifications in **Table 2**.
4. Inspect the camshaft sprocket for wear and replace if necessary.
5. Inspect the starter decompression mechanism for wear or damage. Disassemble it if necessary as described in this section.

Starter Decompression Mechanism Disassembly/Inspection/Assembly

The spring-loaded decompression cam on the camshaft projects above the exhaust camshaft lobe to hold the exhaust valve open during starting, thereby reducing cylinder compression. When the engine runs, centrifugal force positions the decompression cam below the camshaft lobe.

The reverse decompression cam rides on a one-way roller bearing. Should engine kickback occur during starting, the bearing locks, which projects the cam above the camshaft exhaust cam lobe. The exhaust valve opens slightly to reduce engine compression and lessen the kickback force.

Refer to **Figure 14**.
1. Remove the bearing from each end of the camshaft.
2. Install the insert under the camshaft sprocket holder on the camshaft.
3. Install the camshaft and an insert into the press.
4. Place a suitable size rod or socket extension onto the end of the camshaft. The extension must be small enough to pass through the inner diameter of the camshaft sprocket holder being pressed off the camshaft.
5. While holding the camshaft, slowly press the camshaft sprocket holder off the end of the camshaft.

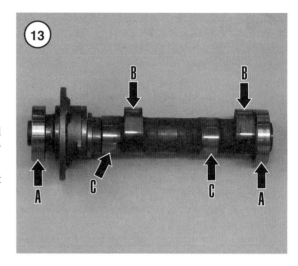

6. Remove the camshaft from the press while holding the camshaft so the decompression parts will not fall off.
7. Take the camshaft assembly to the workbench.
8. Remove the sprocket holder (**Figure 15**).
9. Slide off the thrust washer (**Figure 16**).

> *CAUTION*
> *When the one-way clutch is removed from the end of the camshaft, the small rollers and springs will pop out of the one-way clutch. Do not lose them.*

10. Slide off the one-way clutch (**Figure 17**) along with the rollers and springs. Do not lose the small pin in the backside of the one-way clutch.
11. Slide off the reverse decompressor cam (**Figure 18**).
12. Slide off the decompression cam (A, **Figure 19**). Remove the small spring (B, **Figure 19**). Do not remove the pin (C, **Figure 19**) from the camshaft.
13. Clean all parts in solvent and thoroughly dry with compressed air.
14. Inspect all parts for wear or damage and replace if necessary. There are no service specifications for any of these parts.
15. Apply clean engine oil to all parts prior to installation.
16. Install the small spring into the hole in the camshaft (B, **Figure 19**).
17. Position the decompression cam with the side marked *M* toward the shaft end and install the decompression cam onto the camshaft (**Figure 20**). Carefully index the slot in the decompression cam with the spring in the camshaft and the locating pin. Make sure they are properly meshed.
18. Position the reverse decompression cam with the cam lobe side going on first and install the reverse decompression cam onto the camshaft (**Figure 18**).

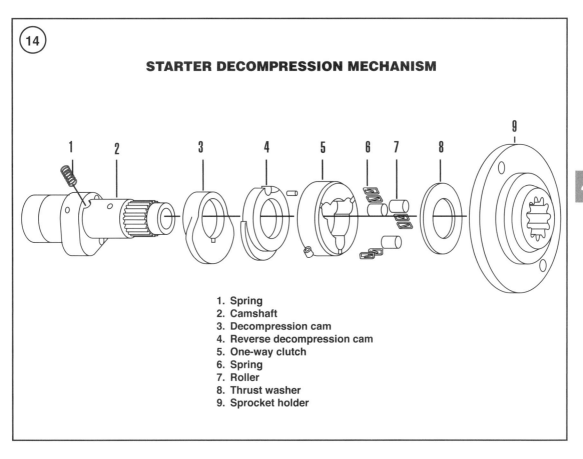

STARTER DECOMPRESSION MECHANISM

1. Spring
2. Camshaft
3. Decompression cam
4. Reverse decompression cam
5. One-way clutch
6. Spring
7. Roller
8. Thrust washer
9. Sprocket holder

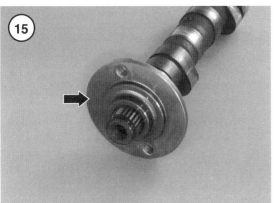

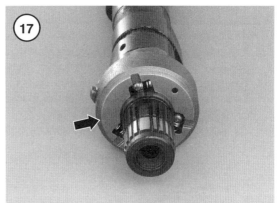

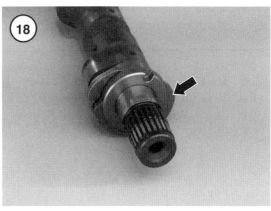

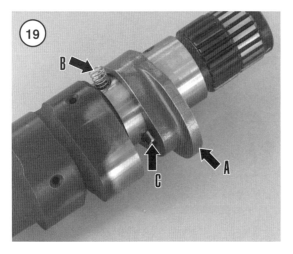

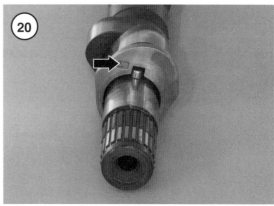

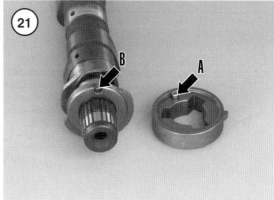

19. Align the pin on the backside of the one-way clutch with the receptacle in the reverse decompression cam (**Figure 21**) and push the one-way clutch all the way on until it bottoms. Install the springs and rollers (**Figure 22**) into the one-way clutch (**Figure 17**).

20. Install the thrust washer (**Figure 16**).

21. Refer to **Figure 14** to check the assembly. Reassemble if necessary.

22. Hold the thrust washer up against the one-way clutch and rotate the one-way clutch counterclockwise as viewed from the decompression end of the camshaft. The one-way clutch should only be able to rotate *counterclockwise* and not in the other direction. If it can rotate in both directions the springs or rollers within the one-way clutch are either installed incorrectly or are faulty and must be replaced.

23. The sprocket holder can be installed onto the camshaft in only one position. Align the master splines on the sprocket holder and camshaft.

24. Press the cam sprocket holder onto the camshaft until it bottoms on the camshaft shoulder.

25. Install the bearing onto each end of the camshaft.

Cylinder Head Cover
Disassembly/Inspection/Assembly

The intake valve sub-rocker arms are identical. To avoid intermixing parts, inspect and install one rocker arm assembly (**Figure 23**) at a time. Individual parts develop specific wear patterns.

Refer to **Table 2** during inspection.

1. On XR600R models, to remove the starter decompression valve lifter lever, perform the following:
   a. Remove the dowel pin (**Figure 24**) securing the lever.
   b. Remove the lifter lever and return spring from the cylinder head cover.

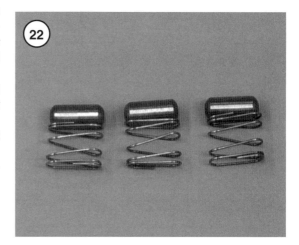

2. Unscrew the valve adjuster covers.

CAUTION
Identify the intake and exhaust sub-rocker arms and shafts for inspection and reassembly.

3. To remove the sub-rocker arm assembly, perform the following:
   a. Unscrew the exhaust valve sub-rocker arm shaft (A, **Figure 25**).

CYLINDER HEAD COVER

1. Wave washer
2. Left exhaust sub-rocker arm
3. Left exhaust rocker arm
4. Left intake rocker arm
5. Copper washer
6. Main rocker arm shaft
7. Wave washer
8. Intake sub-rocker arm
9. Copper washer
10. Intake sub-rocker arm shaft
11. Cylinder head cover
12. Right intake rocker arm
13. Right exhaust rocker arm
14. Exhaust sub-rocker arm shaft
15. Copper washer
16. Right exhaust sub-rocker arm

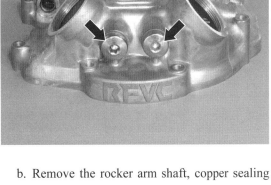

b. Remove the rocker arm shaft, copper sealing washer and wave washer (B, **Figure 25**).

c. Remove the sub-rocker arm (C, **Figure 25**).

d. Repeat Steps a-c for the intake valve sub-rocker arm shaft and sub-rocker arm.

4. To remove the main rocker arm assemblies, perform the following:

a. Unscrew the main rocker arm shaft (**Figure 26**).

b. Remove the main rocker arm shaft and copper sealing washer.

c. Remove the main rocker arms.

5. Wash all parts in cleaning solvent and dry thoroughly.

6. Inspect the sub-rocker arm components as follows:

   a. Inspect the sub-rocker arm valve stem contact pad (**Figure 27**). If the pad is scratched or unevenly worn, inspect the main rocker arm where the sub-rocker arm rides for scoring, chipping or flat spots. Replace the rocker arm if defective.

   b. Measure the inside diameter of the sub-rocker arm bore. Replace if worn to the service limit or greater.

   c. Inspect the rocker arm shafts (**Figure 28**) for signs of wear or scoring. Measure the outside diameter of the shafts. Replace any worn to the service limit or less.

7. Inspect the main rocker arm components as follows:

   a. Inspect the main rocker arm camshaft lobe contact pad (**Figure 29**) and where the adjuster rides on the sub-rocker arm. If the pad is scratched or unevenly worn, inspect the cam lobe for scoring, chipping or flat spots. Replace the rocker arm if defective.

   b. Measure the inside diameter of the main rocker arm bore. Replace if worn to the service limit or greater.

   c. Inspect the rocker arm shafts (**Figure 28**) for signs of wear or scoring. Measure the outside diameter of the shafts. Replace any worn to the service limit or less.

8. Lubricate the rocker arm shaft and rocker arm bores with engine oil.

9. All the main rocker arms are dissimilar. Each main rocker arm has an identifying mark (A, **Figure 30**) or tab (B). Identify the main rocker arms as follows:

   a. Left exhaust rocker arm–identification letter *M* and no identification tab.

   b. Right exhaust rocker arm–no identification letter and an identification tab.

   c. Left intake rocker arm–identification letter *M* and an identification tab.

   d. Right intake rocker arm–identification number *26* and no identification tab.

10. To install the main rocker arm assemblies perform the following:

   a. Install the left exhaust rocker arm (A, **Figure 31**), right exhaust rocker arm (B), left intake rocker arm (C) and right intake rocker arm (D).

   b. Place a copper sealing washer on each rocker arm shaft.

   c. Push the main rocker arm shaft through the cylinder head cover, rocker arm, wave washer, cover boss, wave washer and rocker arm.

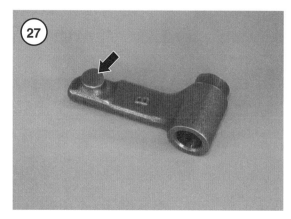

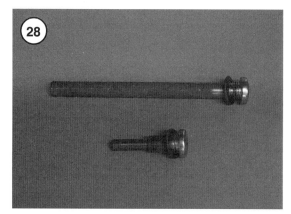

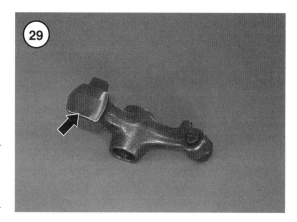

   d. Screw in the main rocker arm shaft and tighten to 27 N•m (20 ft.-lb.).

11. To install the sub-rocker arm assemblies, perform the following:

   a. Position the main rocker arms as shown in **Figure 32**. Each sub-rocker arm has its own identifying mark (A, **Figure 32**). The exhaust valves are identified A (left side) or B (right side). The intake valves are marked with an *IN*.

   b. Place a wave washer on the intake valve sub-rocker arm (B, **Figure 32**) and on the

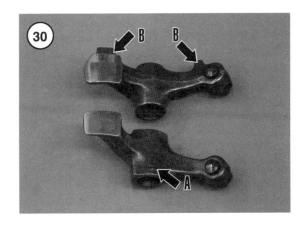

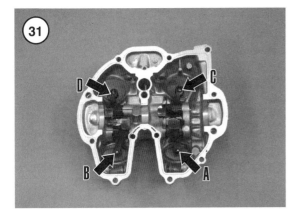

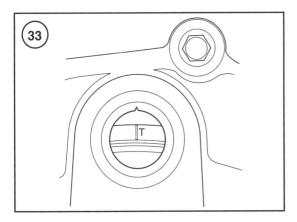

exhaust valve sub-rocker arm as shown in B, **Figure 25**.

 c. Place a copper sealing washer on each rocker arm shaft.

 d. On the intake valve sub-rocker arm, push the sub-rocker arm shafts through the cylinder head cover, rocker arm, wave washer and cover boss.

 e. On the exhaust valve sub-rocker arm, push the sub-rocker arm shafts through the cylinder head cover, wave washer, rocker arm and cover boss.

 f. Screw in each sub-rocker arm shaft. Tighten the intake sub-rocker arm shafts to 27 N•m (20 ft.-lb.). Tighten the exhaust sub-rocker arm shafts to the specification in Table 3.

12. On XR600R models, install the starter decompression lever, as follows:

 a. Install the spring into the lifter lever.

 b. Install the lifter lever into the cylinder head cover and position the spring onto the boss.

 c. Align the cutout in the lifter lever shaft with the dowel pin hole in the cylinder head cover.

 d. Apply a light coat of grease to the dowel pin. This will hold the dowel in place when the cylinder head cover is turned upside down during installation.

 e. Install the dowel pin (**Figure 24**) into the cylinder head cover and past the lifter lever shaft.

Cylinder Head Cover Installation

1. Lubricate all camshaft lobes with molybdenum disulfide grease. Apply clean engine oil to the camshaft bearings.

2. If removed, install the bearings onto the camshaft so the sealed side faces out.

CAUTION
When rotating the crankshaft, keep the camshaft chain taut and engaged with the timing sprocket on the crankshaft.

3. The engine must be at top dead center (TDC) for the following steps for correct valve timing. Hold the camshaft chain out and taut while rotating the crankshaft to avoid damage to the chain and/or the crankcase.

4. Pull up on the chain, making sure it is properly engaged on the crankshaft sprocket. Rotate the engine until the *T* mark on the alternator rotor aligns with the crankcase cover notch (**Figure 33**).

5. If removed, install the camshaft bearing locating pins (**Figure 34**) into the cylinder head.

6. If removed, install the decompression stop pin and spring in the hole in the cylinder head (**Figure 35**).

7. Place the camshaft sprocket onto the camshaft so the OUT mark on the sprocket is toward the end of the camshaft. Do not fasten the sprocket to the camshaft at this time.

8. Install the camshaft through the camshaft chain and into position in the cylinder head.

9. Position the camshaft sprocket so the alignment marks are aligned with the top surface of the cylinder head (**Figure 36**).

10. Make sure the camshaft chain is meshed properly with the drive sprocket on the crankshaft.

11. Hold the camshaft sprocket in this position and install the chain onto the camshaft sprocket.

NOTE
*The camshaft can be positioned with the lobes up or down as long as the bolt holes align with the camshaft sprocket and the timing marks on the sprocket align with the cylinder head (***Figure 36***). It is easier if the lobes are facing down, as this will place less of a load on the rocker arms during cylinder head cover installation.*

12. Pull the camshaft chain and sprocket assembly up onto the shoulder on the camshaft. Make sure the alignment marks still align with the top surface of the cylinder head (**Figure 36**) and the alternator rotor *T* mark aligns with the crankcase cover notch (**Figure 33**).

13. If alignment is incorrect, reposition the camshaft chain on the sprocket and recheck the alignment.

CAUTION
Make sure camshaft and camshaft chain alignment is correct. Engine damage can occur if the cam timing is incorrect.

14. Rotate the camshaft until the sprocket boss bolt hole aligns with the bolt hole in the camshaft sprocket.

15. When alignment is correct, perform the following:
  a. Install the bolt into the exposed bolt hole. Tighten only finger-tight at this time.
  b. Rotate the engine to expose the other bolt hole and install the remaining bolt.
  c. Make sure the camshaft sprocket is correctly seated on the camshaft boss.
  d. Tighten both bolts to 20 N•m (15 ft.-lb.).

CAUTION
If there is any binding while rotating the crankshaft, stop. Determine the cause before proceeding.

16. After installation is complete, rotate the crankshaft several times using the alternator rotor bolt.

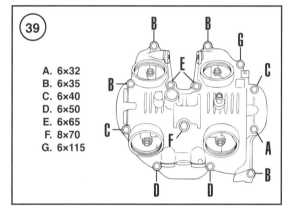

A. 6×32
B. 6×35
C. 6×40
D. 6×50
E. 6×65
F. 8×70
G. 6×115

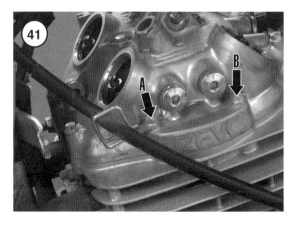

17. Make one final check to make sure alignment is correct. The *T* mark must align with the crankcase cover notch and the camshaft sprocket marks must align with the top surface of the cylinder head.

18. Install the camshaft chain tensioner as described in this section.

19. Fill the oil pocket in the cylinder head with engine oil so the cam lobes are submerged in the oil for the initial start up.

20. Make sure all locating dowels are in place in the cylinder head (**Figure 37**).

21. Loosen the valve adjusters fully. This will relieve strain on the rocker arms and cylinder head cover during installation.

22. Wrap a small rubber band (**Figure 38**) around each sub-rocker arm and then attach it to the exterior of the cylinder head cover. This will hold the main and sub-rocker arms up during cylinder head cover installation.

23. Make sure all sealing surfaces of the cylinder head and the cylinder head cover are completely clean. Spray both sealing surfaces with contact cleaner and wipe dry with a clean lint-free cloth.

CAUTION
*Do not damage the silicone surface on
the cylinder head cover gasket.*

24. Install a new cylinder head cover gasket.

25. Due to the limited space available with the cylinder head cover installed, place the center cover retaining bolts (**Figure 8**) in the cover before installing it.

26. Install the cylinder head cover.

27. Remove the rubber bands.

28. Install the 6-mm and 8-mm bolts in the locations shown in **Figure 39** while noting the following:

    a. The oil pipe fitting retainer is secured by the corner bolt (**Figure 40**).

    b. The clutch cable retainer is secured by the front, side bolt (A, **Figure 41**).

    c. On California models, the EVAP canister hoses are held by a retainer that is secured by the rear, side bolt (B, **Figure 41**).

29. Tighten the bolts in a crossing pattern in 2-3 steps to the torque specification in **Table 3**.

30. Install the engine hanger plate (**Figure 7**). Note that the plates are not flat. Position each plate so the lower end contacts the cylinder head cover. Tighten the 8 mm bolts to the specification in **Table 3**. Tighten the 10 mm bolt to specification (**Table 3**).

31. Install a *new* O-ring onto the intake tube flange. Install the intake tube and tighten the retaining bolts securely.

32. Install the oil tube, including new washers on both sides of the end fittings. Tighten the oil tube

union bolts to 18 N•m (159 in.-lb.). Tighten the upper retaining bolt to 18 N•m (159 in.-lb.). Tighten the lower retaining bolt (also retains right crankcase cover) to 12 N•m (106 in.-lb.).

33. Attach the breather tube to the cylinder head cover.

34. Install the carburetor as described in Chapter Eight or Chapter Nine.

35. Adjust the valves.

36. On XR600R models, adjust the starter decompression lever as described in Chapter Three.

CAMSHAFT CHAIN TENSIONER

Removal

1. Unscrew the bolt securing the camshaft chain tensioner shaft (A, **Figure 42**).

> *NOTE*
> *The camshaft chain tensioner contains a one-way bearing that allows rotation in one direction only.*

2. Withdraw the camshaft chain tensioner shaft (B, **Figure 42**) by turning it *clockwise* while pulling it out.

> *WARNING*
> *In the next step, the camshaft chain tensioner is under spring tension. As the tensioner is removed from the cylinder head the spring will snap but will not fly out. It is captured in the tensioner. Do not place your fingers in the cylinder cavity.*

3. Carefully withdraw the camshaft chain tensioner from the cylinder head.

4. Inspect the spring, bearing and arm on the tensioner (**Figure 43**).

5. Inspect the tensioner shaft (**Figure 44**) for wear. Replace the O-ring.

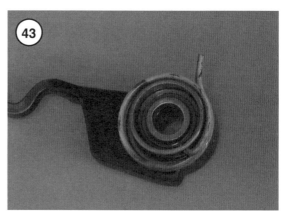

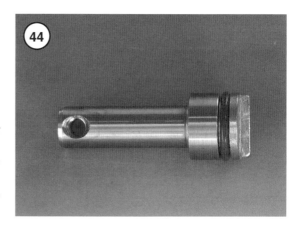

Installation

If removed, install the camshaft chain tensioner spring onto the tensioner lifter as shown in **Figure 43**.

1. Install the tensioner with a special tool, as follows:

  a. Partially install the tensioner lifter assembly into the cylinder head with the curved surface on the arm facing toward the camshaft chain.

  b. Place the tensioner setting holder (Honda part No. 07973-MG30003) onto the tensioner so the tool pin fits into the hole in the tensioner as shown in **Figure 45**.

  c. Using a screwdriver to push against the tensioner arm, push the tensioner down until the shaft hole aligns with the hole in the cylinder head.

  d. Apply clean engine oil to the O-ring seal on the tensioner shaft and install the tensioner shaft by turning it clockwise. Rotate the shaft until the retaining bolt hole aligns with the hole in the cylinder head cover.

  e. Install the bolt securing the tensioner shaft (A, **Figure 42**) and tighten securely.

  f. Remove the tensioner setting holder.

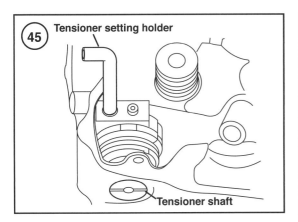

Tensioner setting holder

Tensioner shaft

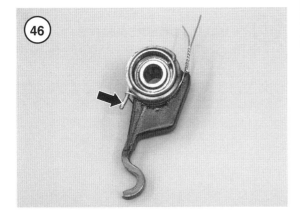

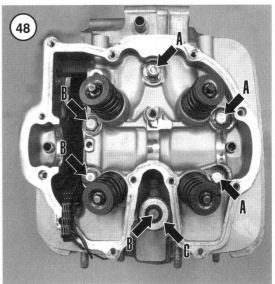

4

help push the spring down into position onto the flat surface within the cylinder head.

d. Apply clean engine oil to the O-ring seal on the tensioner shaft and install the tensioner shaft by turning it clockwise. Rotate the shaft until the retaining bolt hole aligns with the hole in the cylinder head cover.

e. Install the bolt securing the tensioner shaft (A, **Figure 42**) and tighten securely.

f. Cut the wire and pull it out. Make sure that all pieces of wire are removed from the engine.

CYLINDER HEAD

Removal/Installation

> *CAUTION*
> *To prevent damage, remove the cylinder head only when the engine is at room temperature.*

1. Remove the cylinder head cover and camshaft as described in this chapter.

2. Remove the nuts (**Figure 47**) on the right side.

3. Loosen the cylinder head bolts (A and B, **Figure 48**) in a crossing pattern in 2-3 stages. Remove the bolts and nuts. The washers may stay in the bolt receptacles in the cylinder head. After the cylinder head is removed, remove the washers.

4. If the camshaft bearing locating pins (**Figure 34**) are loose, remove them. If they are secure in the cylinder head, do not remove them.

> *CAUTION*
> *The cooling fins are fragile and are easily damaged.*

2. Install the tensioner without a special tool, as follows:

a. Wrap a piece of wire around the tensioner lifter and the spring and compress the spring (**Figure 46**). Locking pliers work well to compress and hold the spring while installing the wire.

b. Partially install the tensioner lifter assembly into the cylinder head with the curved surface on the arm facing toward the camshaft chain.

c. Push the tensioner lifter assembly down until the hole aligns with the hole in the cylinder head. A long narrow-blade screwdriver will

5. Loosen the cylinder head by tapping around the perimeter with a rubber mallet.

6. Untie the wire securing the camshaft chain and retie it to the cylinder head.

7. Lift the cylinder head straight up and off the cylinder. Guide the camshaft chain through the opening in the cylinder head and retie the wire to the exterior of the engine. This will prevent the drive chain from falling into the crankcase.

8. Remove the cylinder head gasket. Do not lose the locating dowels.

9. Place a clean shop cloth into the camshaft chain opening in the cylinder to prevent the entry of debris.

10. Install by reversing the preceding removal steps while noting the following:

    a. Clean the mating surface of the cylinder and cylinder head of any gasket material.

    b. If removed, install the locating dowels in the dowel holes in the cylinder.

    c. Lubricate the cylinder head bolt threads and underside of the bolt head with engine oil prior to installation.

    d. Install the long cylinder head bolts (A, **Figure 48**) and short bolts (B) in the locations shown. Install the large washer (C, **Figure 48**) on the short, center bolt.

    e. Tighten the cylinder head bolts to 36 N•m (26 ft.-lb.) in a crossing pattern in 2-3 stages.

    f. Tighten the cylinder head base nuts securely.

VALVES AND VALVE COMPONENTS

A complete valve job, consisting of reconditioning the valve seats and replacing the valve guides, requires specialized tools and experience. This section describes service procedures used to check the valve components for wear and how to determine what type of service is required. Refer all valve machining and guide replacement work to a qualified machine shop.

A valve spring compressor, designed for motorcycle applications, is required to remove and install the valves.

Solvent Test

For proper engine operation, the valves must seat tightly against their seats. Any condition that prevents the valves from seating properly can cause valve burning and reduced engine performance. Before removing the valves from the cylinder head, perform the following to check valve seating.

1. Remove the cylinder head as described in this chapter.

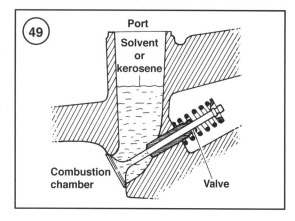

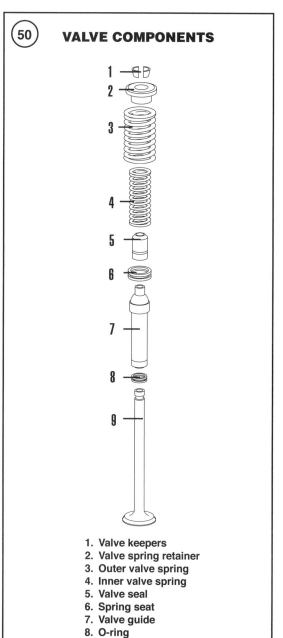

1. Valve keepers
2. Valve spring retainer
3. Outer valve spring
4. Inner valve spring
5. Valve seal
6. Spring seat
7. Valve guide
8. O-ring
9. Valve

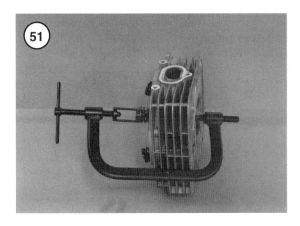

2. Support the cylinder so that the exhaust port faces up (**Figure 49**) and pour solvent or kerosene into the port. Then check the combustion chamber for fluid leaking past each exhaust valve seat.

3. Repeat Step 2 for the intake valves and seats.

4. If there is fluid leaking around a valve seat, the valve is not seating properly on its seat. The following conditions can cause poor valve seating:

    a. A bent valve stem.

    b. A worn or damaged valve seat (in cylinder head).

    c. A worn or damaged valve face.

    d. A crack in the combustion chamber.

Valve Removal

Refer to **Figure 50**.

1. Remove the cylinder head as described in this chapter.

> *WARNING*
> *Wear safety glasses when performing Step 2.*

> *CAUTION*
> *Do not compress the springs any more than necessary to remove the keepers in Step 2.*

2. Compress the valve springs using a valve spring compressor (**Figure 51**). Remove the valve keepers and release the spring. Remove the tool.

3. Remove the valve spring retainer and valve springs (**Figure 52**).

4. Before removing the valve, remove any burrs from the valve stem (**Figure 53**) to prevent valve guide damage.

5. Remove the valve from the cylinder head.

6. Remove the lower spring seat (A, **Figure 54**).

7. Pull the valve stem seal (B, **Figure 54**) off the valve guide and discard it.

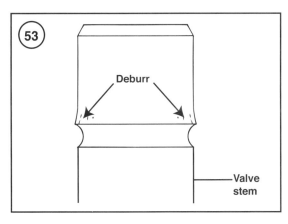

Deburr

Valve stem

> *CAUTION*
> *Keep all parts of each valve assembly together. Do not mix components from the different valves or wear may result.*

8. Repeat Steps 2-7 to remove the remaining valves.

Component Inspection

When measuring the valve components (**Figure 50**) in this section, compare the actual measurements to the specifications in **Table 2**. Replace parts that

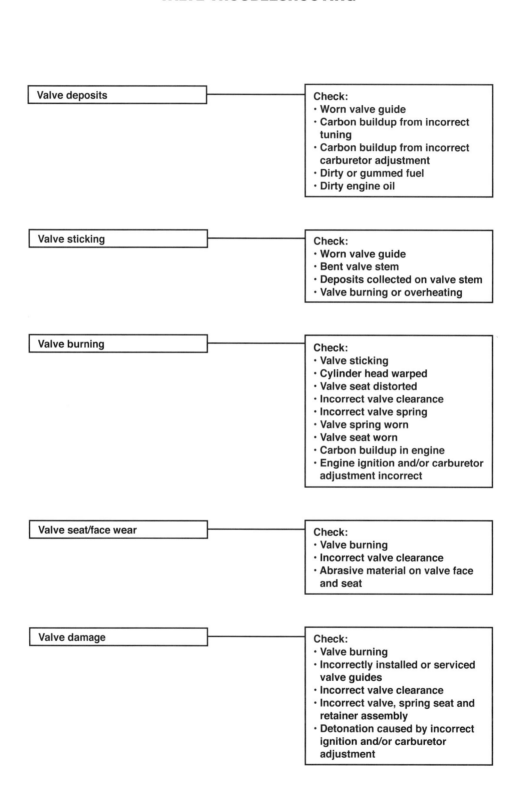

55

VALVE TROUBLESHOOTING

Valve deposits

Check:
- Worn valve guide
- Carbon buildup from incorrect tuning
- Carbon buildup from incorrect carburetor adjustment
- Dirty or gummed fuel
- Dirty engine oil

Valve sticking

Check:
- Worn valve guide
- Bent valve stem
- Deposits collected on valve stem
- Valve burning or overheating

Valve burning

Check:
- Valve sticking
- Cylinder head warped
- Valve seat distorted
- Incorrect valve clearance
- Incorrect valve spring
- Valve spring worn
- Valve seat worn
- Carbon buildup in engine
- Engine ignition and/or carburetor adjustment incorrect

Valve seat/face wear

Check:
- Valve burning
- Incorrect valve clearance
- Abrasive material on valve face and seat

Valve damage

Check:
- Valve burning
- Incorrectly installed or serviced valve guides
- Incorrect valve clearance
- Incorrect valve, spring seat and retainer assembly
- Detonation caused by incorrect ignition and/or carburetor adjustment

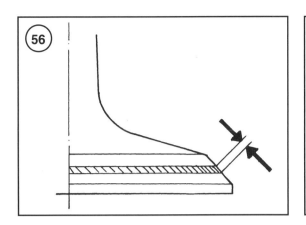

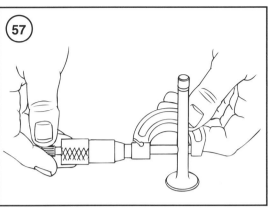

4

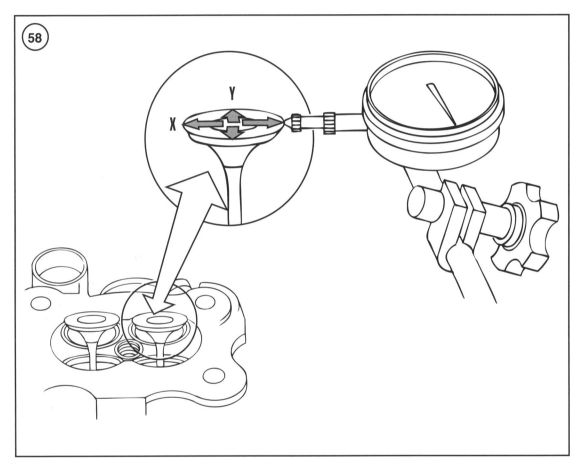

are out of specification or show damage as described in this section.

Refer to **Figure 55**.

1. Clean the valves in solvent. Do not gouge or damage the valve seating surface.

2. Inspect the contact surface (**Figure 56**) of each valve for burning. Minor roughness and pitting can be removed by lapping the valve as described in this chapter. Excessive unevenness in the contact surface is an indication that the valve is not serviceable.

3. Inspect the valve stems for wear and roughness. Measure the valve stem diameter (**Figure 57**) for wear.

4. Remove all carbon and varnish from the valve guides with a stiff spiral wire brush before measuring wear.

5. Measure each valve guide at its top, center and bottom inside diameter with a small bore gauge. Then measure the small bore gauge with a micrometer to determine the valve guide inside diameter.

6. Subtract the measurement made in Step 3 from the measurement made in Step 5. The difference is the valve stem-to-guide clearance. Replace any guide or valve that is not within tolerance.

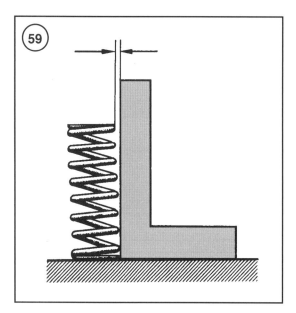

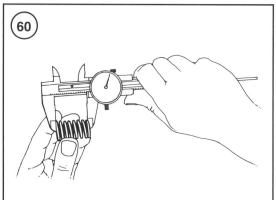

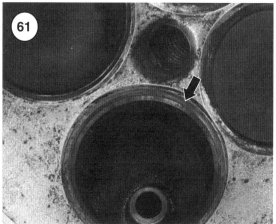

7. If a small bore gauge is not available, insert each valve in its guide. Hold the valve just slightly off its seat and rock it sideways (**Figure 58**). If the valve rocks more than slightly, the guide is probably worn. However, as a final check, take the cylinder head to a dealership and have the valve guides measured.

8. Check the inner and outer valve springs as follows:

   a. Check each valve spring for visual damage.

   b. Use a square and check each spring for distortion or tilt (**Figure 59**).

   c. Measure the valve spring free length with a vernier caliper (**Figure 60**).

   d. Replace worn or damaged springs as a set.

9. Check the valve spring seats and valve keepers for cracks or other damage.

10. Inspect the valve seats (**Figure 61**) for burning, pitting, cracks, excessive wear or other damage. If worn or burned, they may be reconditioned as described in this chapter. Seats and valves in near-perfect condition can be reconditioned by lapping with fine carborundum paste. Check as follows:

   a. Clean the valve seat and valve mating areas with contact cleaner.

   b. Coat the valve seat with machinist's blue.

   c. Install the valve into its guide and rotate it against its seat with a valve lapping tool. Refer to *Valve Lapping* in this section.

   d. Lift the valve out of the guide and measure the seat width (**Figure 62**) with a vernier caliper.

   e. The seat width for intake and exhaust valves should measure within the specification in **Table 2** all the way around the seat. If the seat width exceeds the service limit, have the seats machined.

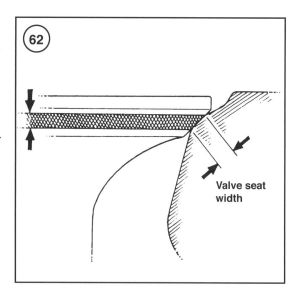

Valve seat width

   f. Remove all residue of machinist's blue from the seats and valves.

Valve Guide Replacement

Refer valve guide replacement to a machine shop. A 6.6 mm valve guide reamer is required.

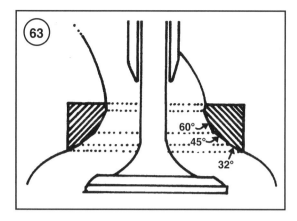

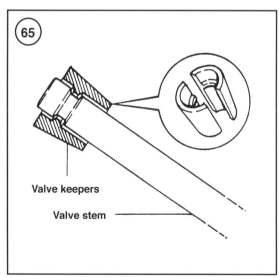

Valve keepers

Valve stem

Valve Seat Reconditioning

The valve seats are an integral part of the cylinder head and cannot be replaced separately. Minor valve seat wear can be repaired by machining them. Due to the number of specialized tools required, refer this service to a machine shop. Refer to **Figure 63** for the required valve seat angles. Refer to **Table 2** for valve specifications.

Valve Lapping

Valve lapping can restore the valve seal without machining if the amount of wear or distortion is not excessive.

Perform this procedure after determining that the valve seat width and outside diameter are within specification. Refer to *Component Inspection*.

1. Smear a light coating of fine grade valve lapping compound on the valve face seating surface.
2. Insert the valve into the head.
3. Wet the suction cup of the lapping stick and stick it onto the head of the valve. Lap the valve to the seat by spinning the lapping stick in both directions. Every 5 to 10 seconds, rotate the valve 180° in the valve seat. Continue this action until the mating surfaces on the valve and seat are smooth and equal in size.
4. Closely examine the valve seat in the cylinder head. It should be smooth and even with a smooth, polished seating ring.
5. Thoroughly clean the valves and cylinder head in solvent, and then with hot soapy water to remove all lapping compound. Any compound left on the valves or the cylinder head will contaminate the engine oil, and cause excessive wear and damage. After drying the cylinder head, lubricate the valve guides with engine oil to prevent rust.
6. After installing the valves into the cylinder, test the valve seat seal as described in *Solvent Test*. If fluid leaks past the seat, remove the valve assembly and repeat the lapping procedure until there are no leaks. When there are no leaks, remove all valve sets and reclean the cylinder head assembly as described in Step 5.

Valve Installation

1. Clean and dry all parts. If the valve seats were reground or lapped, or the valve guides were replaced, thoroughly clean the valves and cylinder head in solvent and then with hot soapy water to remove all lapping and grinding compound. Any abrasive residue left on the valves or in the cylinder head will contaminate the engine oil and cause excessive wear and damage. After drying the cylinder head, lubricate the valve guides with engine oil to prevent rust.
2. Install the new valve seal onto the valve guide and seat it into place (B, **Figure 54**).
3. Install the spring seat (A, **Figure 54**).
4. Coat the valve stem with molybdenum disulfide paste, then install the valve into the correct guide.
5. Install the inner and outer valve springs. Install each outer valve spring so that the end with the coils closest together (**Figure 64**) is toward the cylinder head.

6. Install the valve spring retainer.

> *WARNING*
> *Wear safety glasses or goggles when*
> *performing Step 7.*

7. Install the valve spring compressor (**Figure 51**). Push down on the valve spring retainer and compress the springs, then install the valve keepers (**Figure 65**). Release tension from the compressor and check that the keepers seat evenly around the end of the valve. Tap the end of the valve stem with a rubber mallet to ensure that the keepers are properly seated.

8. Repeat Steps 2-7 for the remaining valves.

9. After installing the cylinder head cover onto the engine, adjust the valve clearance. See Chapter Three.

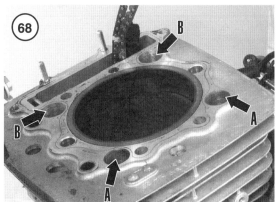

CYLINDER

Removal

1. Remove the cylinder head cover and cylinder head as described in this chapter.

2. Remove the cam chain guide (**Figure 66**).

3. On XR650L models, remove the PAIR control valve, its mounting bracket and the air injection pipes from the cylinder as described in PULSED SECONDARY AIR INJECTION SYSTEM in Chapter Nine.

4. Remove the bolts securing the cylinder base to the crankcase (**Figure 67**).

5. Loosen the cylinder bolts (A and B, **Figure 68**) in a crossing pattern in 2-3 stages. Remove the cylinder bolts and washers.

> *CAUTION*
> *The cooling fins are fragile and easily*
> *damaged.*

6. Loosen the cylinder by tapping around the perimeter with a rubber mallet.

7. Pull the cylinder straight up and off the piston. Pass the camshaft chain wire through the opening in

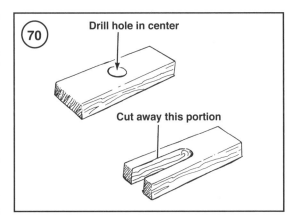

Drill hole in center

Cut away this portion

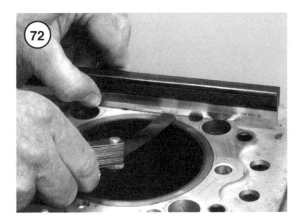

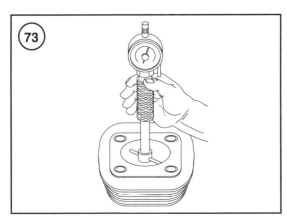

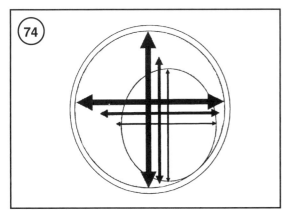

the cylinder. Reattach the wire to the exterior of the crankcase.

8. If the cylinder is difficult to remove, use a heat gun and apply heat to the dowel pin areas on the cylinder.

9. Install a piston holding fixture under the piston (A, **Figure 69**). This can be a purchased unit or a homemade unit (**Figure 70**).

10. Remove the base gasket (B, **Figure 69**).

11. If necessary, remove the piston as described in this chapter.

12. If necessary, remove the two dowel pins (C, **Figure 69**).

13. Cover the crankcase opening to prevent objects from falling into the crankcase.

Inspection

Refer to **Table 2** when measuring the cylinder in this section.

1. Remove all gasket residue from the top and bottom cylinder gasket surfaces.

2. Wash the cylinder (**Figure 71**) in solvent. Dry with compressed air.

3. Check the dowel pin holes for cracks or other damage.

4. Check the cylinder for warp with a feeler gauge and straightedge as shown in **Figure 72**. Check at several places on the cylinder and compare to **Table 2**. If out of specification, refer service to a dealership.

5. Measure the cylinder bore using a bore gauge (**Figure 73**) or inside micrometer aligned with the piston pin and at 90° to the pin. Measure at the top, bottom and middle positions (**Figure 74**). Use the maximum bore dimension to determine cylinder wear. Average the other measurements to determine the taper and out-of-round. If any dimension is out of specification, bore the cylinder and install a new piston and ring assembly. Refer this service to a machine shop.

6. If the cylinder is not worn past the service limit, check the bore for scratches or gouges. The bore still may require boring and reconditioning.

> *CAUTION*
> *The soap and water described in Step 7 is the only solution that can wash the fine grit residue out of the cylinder crevices. Solvent and kerosene cannot do this. Grit residue left in the cylinder will act like a grinding compound and cause rapid and premature wear to the contact surfaces of the piston rings, cylinder bore and piston.*

7. After servicing the cylinder, wash the bore in hot soapy water. This is the only way to clean the cylinder wall of the fine grit material left from the bore or honing job. After washing the cylinder wall, run a clean white cloth through it. The cylinder must be

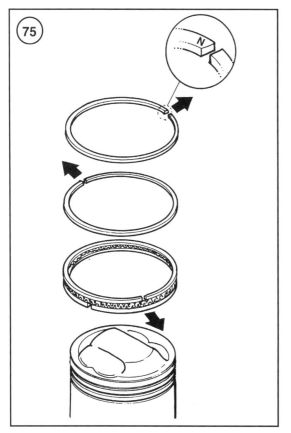

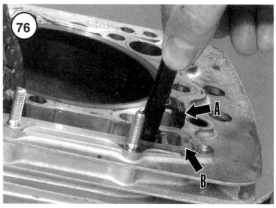

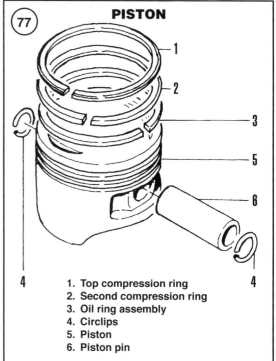

PISTON

1. Top compression ring
2. Second compression ring
3. Oil ring assembly
4. Circlips
5. Piston
6. Piston pin

free of all grit and other residue. If the rag is dirty, rewash the cylinder wall again and recheck with the white cloth. Repeat until the cloth comes out clean. When the cylinder is clean, lubricate it with engine oil to prevent the cylinder liner from rusting.

Installation

1. Make sure that the top surface of the crankcase and the bottom surface of the cylinder are clean before installing a *new* base gasket.

2. Apply a small amount of liquid sealant to the mating surfaces of the crankcase halves in the area where the cylinder base gasket fits. This will help prevent an oil leak.

3. Install the dowel pins (C, **Figure 69**) into the holes in the crankcase.

4. Install a new cylinder base gasket (B, **Figure 69**). Make sure all holes align.

5. Install a piston holding fixture under the piston.

6. Stagger the piston ring end gaps as shown in **Figure 75**. Lightly oil the piston rings and the inside of the cylinder bore with engine oil.

7. Carefully feed the camshaft chain and wire up through the opening in the cylinder and tie it to the engine.

NOTE
It is easier to install the cylinder over the piston in Step 8 by first compressing the rings with a ring compressor. As the cylinder is installed over the piston, the rings pass into the cylinder compressed and then expand out once they are free of the ring compressor. A hose clamp works well for this. Before using a ring compressor or hose clamp, lubricate its ring contact side with engine oil. When using a ring compressor or hose clamp, do not overtighten. The tool should be able to slide freely as the cylinder pushes against it.

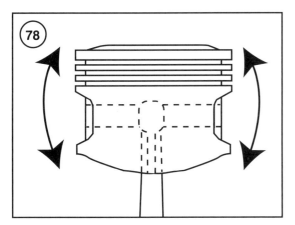

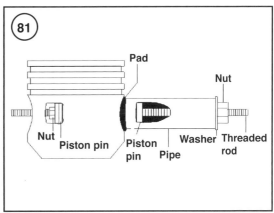

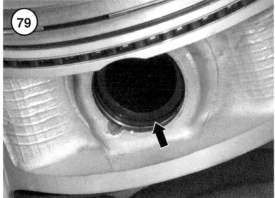

13. Install the cam chain guide (**Figure 66**). Make sure the lower end of the guide enters the recess in the crankcase, and the hook at the upper end (A, **Figure 76**) engages the recess (B) in the cylinder.

14. Install the cylinder head, camshaft and cylinder head cover as described in this chapter.

15. Follow the *Break-in Procedure* in Chapter Five if the cylinder was bored or honed or a new piston or piston rings were installed.

PISTON, PISTON PIN AND PISTON RINGS

Refer to **Figure 77**.

Piston Removal

1. Remove the cylinder as described in this chapter.

2. Block off the crankcase below the piston to prevent the piston pin circlips from falling into the crankcase.

3. Before removing the piston, hold the rod and rock the piston (**Figure 78**). Any rocking motion (do not confuse with the normal sliding motion) indicates wear on the piston pin, rod bore, pin bore, or a combination of all three.

> *WARNING*
> *Wear safety glasses when removing the circlips in Step 4.*

4. Remove the circlips from the piston pin bore grooves (**Figure 79**).

> *CAUTION*
> *Discard the piston circlips. Install new circlips during reassembly.*

5. Push the piston pin (**Figure 80**) out of the piston by hand. If the pin is tight, use a homemade tool (**Figure 81**) to remove it. Do not drive the piston pin out as the force may damage the piston pin, connecting rod or piston.

8. While compressing the piston rings, slide the cylinder down over the piston until it bottoms on the piston holding fixture.

9. Remove the piston holding fixture and slide the cylinder down into place on the crankcase.

10. Lubricate the cylinder bolt threads and underside of the bolt head with engine oil prior to installation.

11. Install the cylinder bolts and washers. Note the location of the long bolts (A, **Figure 68**) and short bolts (B). Tighten the bolts in a crossing pattern in 2-3 steps to the specification in Table 3.

12. Install the cylinder base bolts (**Figure 67**). Tighten the bolts securely.

6. Lift the piston off the connecting rod.
7. Inspect the piston as described in this chapter.

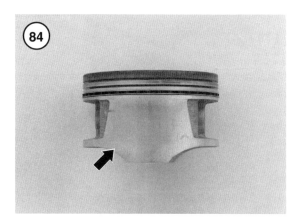

Piston Inspection

1. Remove the piston rings as described in this chapter.
2. Clean the carbon from the piston crown (**Figure 82**) with a soft scraper. Large carbon accumulations reduce piston cooling and result in detonation and piston damage.

> *CAUTION*
> *Do not clean the piston skirt using a wire brush.*

3. After cleaning the piston, examine the crown. The crown must show no signs of wear or damage. If the crown appears pecked or spongy-looking, also check the spark plug, valves and combustion chamber for aluminum deposits. If these deposits are found, the engine is overheating.
4. Examine each ring groove (**Figure 83**) for burrs, dented edges or other damage. Pay particular attention to the top compression ring groove as it usually wears more than the others. Because the oil rings are bathed in oil, their rings and grooves wear less than compression rings and their grooves. If there is evidence of oil ring groove wear or if the oil ring is tight and difficult to remove, the piston skirt may have collapsed due to excessive heat. Replace the piston.
5. Check the piston oil control holes for carbon or oil sludge buildup. Clean the holes with wire.
6. Inspect the piston skirt (**Figure 84**) for cracks or other damage. If the piston shows signs of partial seizure (bits of aluminum on the piston skirt), replace the piston.

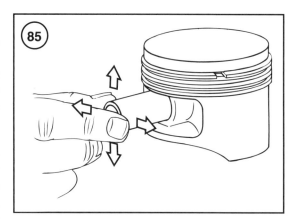

> *CAUTION*
> *If the piston skirt is worn or scuffed unevenly from side-to-side, the connecting rod may be bent or twisted.*

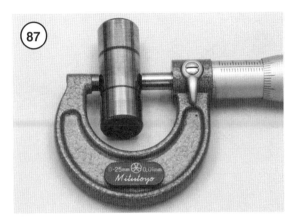

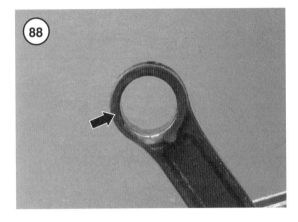

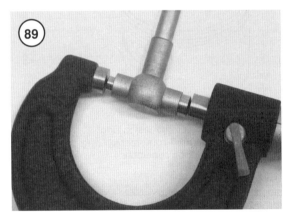

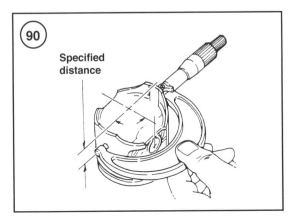

Specified distance

7. Check the piston circlip grooves for wear, cracks or other damage. If a circlip groove is worn, replace the piston.

8. Measure piston-to-cylinder clearance as described in *Piston Clearance*.

Piston Pin Inspection

Refer to **Table 2** when measuring the piston pin components in this section. Replace parts that are out of specification or show damage.

1. Clean and dry the piston pin.

2. Inspect the piston pin for chrome flaking, cracks or signs of heat damage.

3. Lubricate the piston pin and install it in the piston. Slowly rotate the piston pin and check for excessive play as shown in **Figure 85**. Determine piston pin clearance by performing the following steps.

4. Measure the piston pin bore diameter (**Figure 86**) in the piston. If within specification, record the dimension and continue with Step 5.

5. Measure the piston pin outside diameter (**Figure 87**). If within specification, record the dimension and continue with Step 6.

6. Subtract the measurement made in Step 5 from the measurement made in Step 4 to determine the piston-to-piston pin clearance. Replace the piston and/or piston pin if the clearance is excessive.

Connecting Rod Small End Inspection

1. Inspect the connecting rod small end (**Figure 88**) for cracks or signs of heat damage.

2. Measure the connecting rod small end diameter with a snap gauge. Then measure the snap gauge with a micrometer (**Figure 89**, typical) and compare with the dimension in **Table 2**. If the bore wear is excessive, replace the crankshaft assembly. The connecting rod cannot be replaced separately.

Piston Clearance

1. Make sure the piston and cylinder walls are clean and dry.

2. Refer to *Cylinder* in this chapter and measure the cylinder bore. Record the bore diameter measurement.

3. Measure the piston diameter with a micrometer at a right angle to the piston pin bore (**Figure 90**). Measure 25 mm (1.0 in.) from the bottom edge of the piston skirt. Write down the piston diameter measurement.

4. Subtract the piston diameter from the largest bore diameter; the difference is piston-to-cylinder clearance. If clearance exceeds the service limit in **Table 2**, the cylinder must be bored and a new piston/ring assembly installed.

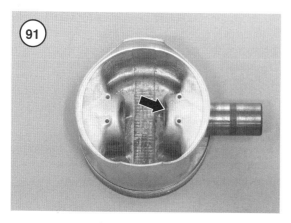

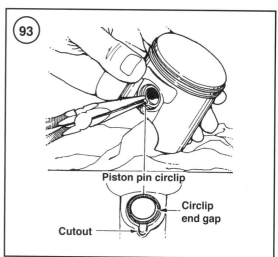

Piston pin circlip

Circlip end gap

Cutout

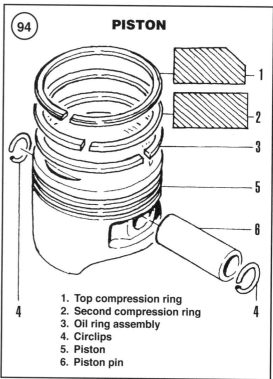

PISTON

1
2
3
5
6
4

4

1. Top compression ring
2. Second compression ring
3. Oil ring assembly
4. Circlips
5. Piston
6. Piston pin

Piston Installation

1. Install the piston rings onto the piston as described in this section.

2. Coat the connecting rod bore, piston pin and piston with engine oil.

3. Slide the piston pin into the piston until its end is flush with the piston pin boss as shown in **Figure 91**.

4. Place the piston onto the connecting rod so the IN mark (**Figure 92**) on the piston crown faces toward the intake side of the engine.

5. Align the piston pin with the hole in the connecting rod. Push the piston pin (**Figure 80**) through the connecting rod and into the other side of the piston and center it in the piston.

6. Cover the crankcase opening with clean rags.

> *WARNING*
> *Wear safety glasses when installing the*
> *piston pin circlips in Step 7.*

7. Install *new* piston pin circlips in both ends of the piston pin bore (**Figure 93**). Make sure the circlips seat in the piston clip grooves completely. Turn the circlips so that their end gaps do not align with the cutout in the piston (**Figure 93**).

8. Install the cylinder as described in this chapter.

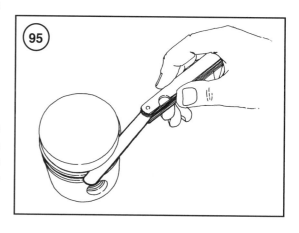

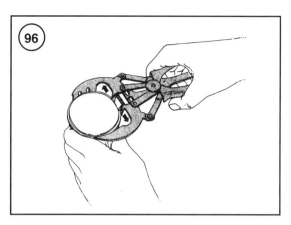

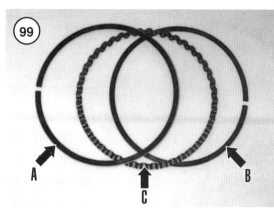

Piston Ring Inspection and Removal

The piston assembly uses three rings (**Figure 94**). The top and second rings are compression rings. The lower ring is an oil control ring assembly (consisting of two ring rails and an expander spacer).

> *WARNING*
> *The edges of all piston rings are very sharp. Be careful when handling them to avoid cut fingers.*

1. Measure the side clearance of each compression ring in its groove with a flat feeler gauge (**Figure 95**) and compare with the specifications in **Table 2**. If the clearance is greater than specified, replace the rings. If the clearance is still excessive with the new rings, replace the piston.

> *NOTE*
> *Store the rings in order of removal.*

2. Remove the compression rings with a ring expander tool (**Figure 96**) or spread the ring ends by hand and lift the rings out of their grooves and up over the piston (**Figure 97**).

3. Remove the oil ring assembly (**Figure 98**) by first removing the upper (A, **Figure 99**) and then the lower (B) ring rails. Then remove the expander spacer (C, **Figure 99**).

> *CAUTION*
> *When cleaning the piston ring grooves in Step 4, use the same type of ring that operates in the groove. Using a ring that is dissimilar to the groove will damage the groove. Do not remove aluminum material from the ring grooves, as this will increase ring side clearance.*

4. Using a broken piston ring, remove carbon and oil residue from the piston ring grooves (**Figure 100**).

5. Inspect the ring grooves for burrs, nicks or broken or cracked lands. Replace the piston if necessary.

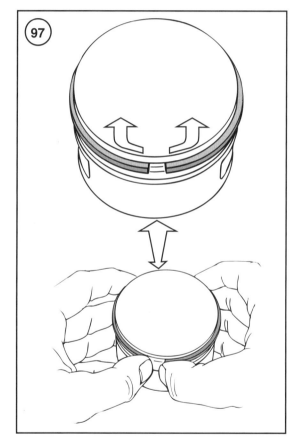

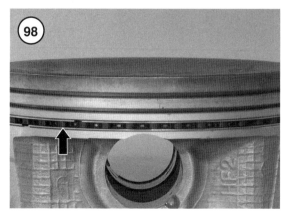

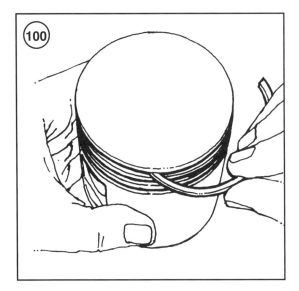

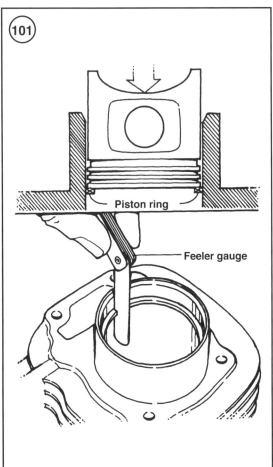

6. Check the end gap of each ring. To check, insert the ring into the bottom of the cylinder bore and square it with the cylinder wall by tapping it with the piston (**Figure 101**). Measure the end gap with a feeler gauge (**Figure 101**). Compare the end gap dimension with **Table 2**. Replace the rings if the gap is too large. If the gap on the new ring is smaller than specified, hold a fine-cut file in a vise. File the ends of the ring to enlarge the gap.

NOTE
*When measuring the oil control ring end gap, measure the upper and lower ring rail end gaps only. Do not measure the expander spacer (C, **Figure 99**).*

7. Roll each ring around its piston groove (**Figure 102**) to check for binding. Repair minor binding with a fine-cut file.

Piston Ring Installation

1. Hone or deglaze the cylinder before installing new piston rings. Honing helps the new rings seat in the cylinder. If necessary, refer this job to a dealership. After honing, measure the end gap of each ring and compare to the dimensions in **Table 2**.
2. Clean the piston and rings with hot soapy water then dry with compressed air.
3. If the cylinder was honed, clean the cylinder as described in *Cylinder, Inspection* in this chapter.
4. Clean the piston and rings in solvent. Dry with compressed air.
5. Refer to **Figure 94** to identify and install the rings as follows:
   a. Install the rings by spreading the ring ends either by hand or with a ring expander tool, and then slipping the rings over the top of the piston.

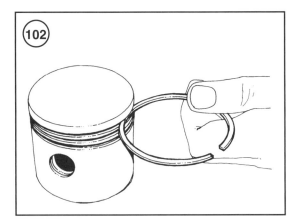

   b. Install the oil ring assembly into the bottom ring groove. First install the expander spacer, then the bottom and top ring rails (**Figure 98**).
   c. Install the second compression ring with the manufacturer's marks facing up.
   d. Install the top compression ring with the manufacturer's marks facing up.
   e. Position the end gaps around the piston as shown in **Figure 75**. Check that the piston rings rotate freely.

Table 1 ENGINE SPECIFICATIONS

Engine	4-stroke, overhead camshaft engine
Displacement	
XR600R	591 cc (36.1 cu. in.)
XR650L	644 cc (39.3 cu. in.)
Bore	
XR600R	97 mm (3.82 in.)
XR650L	100 mm (3.9 in.)
Stroke	
XR600R	80 mm (3.15 in.)
XR650L	82 mm (3.2 in.)
Compression ratio	
XR600R	9.0:1
XR650L	8.3:1
Cooling system	Air cooled
Valve timing*	
Intake valve opens	5° BTDC
Intake valve closes	40° ABDC
Exhaust valve opens	45° BBDC
Exhaust valve closes	5° ATDC

*Specified at 1 mm (0.039 in.) lift.

Table 2 ENGINE TOP END SERVICE SPECIFICATIONS

	New mm (in.)	Service limit mm (in.)
Cam lobe height		
XR600R		
Intake	31.155-31.315 (1.2266-1.2329)	31.05 (31.05)
Exhaust	31.091-31.251 (1.2241-1.2304)	31.00 (1.220)
XR650L		
Intake	31.101-31.341 (1.2244-1.2339)	30.48 (1.200)
Exhaust	31.072-31.312 (1.2233-1.2328)	30.45 (1.199)
Connecting rod small end inside diameter	24.020-24.041 (0.9457-0.9465)	24.07 (0.948)
Connecting rod-to-piston pin clearance	0.024-0.049 (0.0009-0.0019)	0.10 (0.004)
Cylinder bore diameter (standard bore)		
XR600R	97.010-97.020 (3.8193-3.8197)	97.13 (3.824)
XR650L	100.00-100.01 (3.9370-3.9374)	100.12 (3.942)
Cylinder head warpage limit	–	0.10 (0.004)
Cylinder out-of-round limit	–	0.05 (0.002)
Cylinder taper limit	–	0.05 (0.002)
Cylinder warpage limit	–	0.10 (0.004)
Piston diameter (standard piston)		
XR600R	96.96-96.99 (3.8173-3.8197)	96.86 (3.813)
XR650L	99.960-99.980 (3.9354-3.9362)	99.85 (3.931)
Piston diameter measuring point	see text	–
Piston-to-cylinder clearance		
XR600R	0.010-0.050 (0.0004-0.0020)	0.10 (0.004)
XR650L	0.020-0.050 (0.0008-0.0020)	0.12 (0.005)
Piston pin bore diameter	24.002-24.008 (0.9450-0.9452)	24.03 (0.946)
Piston pin outside diameter	23.992-23.996 (0.9446-0.9447)	23.96 (0.943)
Piston-to-piston pin clearance		
XR600R	0.007-0.019 (0.0003-0.0007)	0.07 (0.003)
XR650L	0.006-0.016 (0.0002-0.0006)	0.07 (0.003)
Piston ring end gap		
Top compression ring		
1993-1996	0.20-0.40 (0.008-0.016)	–
1997-2007	0.20-0.35 (0.008-0.014)	–
2008-on	0.20-0.35 (0.008-0.014)	0.5 (0.02)
Second compression ring		
1993-1996	0.35-0.55 (0.014-0.022)	–
1997-2007	0.35-0.50 (0.014-0.020)	–
2008-on	0.35-0.50 (0.014-0.020)	0.65 (0.026)

(continued)

Table 2 ENGINE TOP END SERVICE SPECIFICATIONS (continued)

	New mm (in.)	Service limit mm (in.)
Oil ring (side rails)		
XR600R	0.20-0.90 (0.008-0.028)	–
XR650L		
1993-2007	0.20-0.70 (0.008-0.028)	–
2008-on	0.20-0.70 (0.008-0.028)	0.9 (0.04)
Piston ring side clearance		
Top & second compression ring	0.015-0.045 (0.0006-0.0018)	0.12 (0.005)
Rocker arm bore inside diameter		
Main rocker arms	11.500-11.518 (0.4528-0.4535)11.55 (0.455)	
Sub-rocker arms		
Intake	8.000-8.015 (0.3150-0.3156)	8.05 (0.317)
Exhaust	7.000-7.015 (0.2756-0.2762)	7.05 (0.278)
Rocker arm shaft outside diameter		
Main rocker arm shafts	11.466-11.484 (0.4514-0.4521)11.41 (0.449)	
Sub-rocker arm shafts		
1993 - 2007		
Intake	7.969-7.972 (0.3137-0.3138)	7.92 (0.312)
Exhaust	6.969-6.972 (0.2744-0.2745)	6.92 (0.272)
2008-on		
Intake	7.972-7.987 (0.3139-0.3144)	7.92 (0.312)
Exhaust	6.972-6.987 (0.2745-0.2751)	6.92 (0.272)
Rocker arm-to-shaft clearance		
Main rocker arms	0.016-0.052 (0.0006-0.0020)	0.14 (0.006)
Sub-rocker arms		
1993 - 2007	0.028-0.046 (0.0011-0.0018)	0.10 (0.004)
2008-on	0.013-0.043 (0.0005-0.0017)	0.10 (0.004)
Valve clearance		
Intake	0.08-0.12 (0.003-0.005)	–
Exhaust	0.10-0.14 (0.004-0.006)	–
Valve guide Inside diameter	6.600-6.615 (0.2589-0.2604)	6.63 (0.261)
Valve seat width		
1993-2007	1.2-1.4 (0.05-0.06)	2.0 (0.08)
2008-on	1.0-1.2 (0.04-0.05)	2.0 (0.08)
Valve spring free length		
1993 - 2007		
Inner	35.1 (1.38)	34.1 (1.34)
Outer	36.0 (1.42)	35.0 (1.34)
2008-on		
Inner	34.08 (1.342)	33.0 (1.30)
Outer	38.14 (1.502)	37.1 (1.46)
Valve stem diameter		
Intake	6.575-6.590 (0.2589-0.2594)	6.56 (0.258)
Exhaust		
1993 - 2007	6.565-6.575 (0.2585-0.2589)	6.55 (0.258)
2008-on	6.560-6.575 (0.2583-0.2589)	6.55 (0.258)
Valve stem-to-guide clearance		
Intake	0.010-0.040 (0.0004-0.0016)	0.06 (0.002)
Exhaust		
1993 - 2007	0.030-0.055 (0.0012-0.0022)	0.08 (0.003)
2008-on	0.025-0.055 (0.0010-0.0022)	0.08 (0.003)

Table 3 ENGINE TORQUE SPECIFICATIONS

	N•m	in.-lb.	ft.-lb.
Camshaft sprocket bolts	20	177	---
Cylinder bolts			
XR600R	50		37
XR650L			
1993 - 2007	50		37
2008-on	49		36
Cylinder head bolts	36	---	26
Cylinder head cover			
6 mm	12	106	---
6 mm (small head)	10	88	---
8 mm	23		17
Engine hanger bolts			
XR600R and XR650L (1993 - 2007)			
8 mm	27	---	20
10 mm	50	---	36
XR650L (2008-on)			
8 mm	26	---	19
10 mm	49	---	36
Main rocker arm shaft	27	---	20
Oil tube			
Union bolts	18	159	---
Upper retaining bolt	18	159	---
Lower retaining bolt	12	106	---
Sub rocker arm shafts			
Intake	27		20
Exhaust			
1993 - 2007	23		17
2008-on	22	195	---

4

CHAPTER FIVE

ENGINE LOWER END

This chapter describes service procedures for the engine lower end. Engine removal and installation procedures are also included.

Specifications are located in **Tables 1-3** at the end of this chapter.

SERVICING ENGINE IN FRAME

The following components can be serviced with the engine installed:
1. Camshaft (Chapter Four).
2. Cylinder head (Chapter Four).
3. Piston and cylinder (Chapter Four).
4. Camshaft chain (this chapter).
5. Clutch (Chapter Six).
6. External shift mechanism (Chapter Six).
7. Alternator and flywheel (this chapter).
8. Starter (XR650L models [Chapter Nine]).
9. Carburetor assembly (Chapter Eight or Chapter Nine).
10. Kickstarter (XR600R models [this chapter]).
11. Oil pump (this chapter).

ENGINE REMOVAL/INSTALLATION

WARNING
The engine is heavy. Remove the engine safely with proper tools and techniques to prevent injury.

1. Support the motorcycle securely.
2. Drain the engine oil as described in Chapter Three.
3. Remove the frame guard as described in Chapter Sixteen.
4. Remove both side covers and the seat as described in Chapter Sixteen.
5. Remove the bolt securing the right footpeg and remove the footpeg.
6. Remove the rear brake pedal as described in Chapter Fifteen.
7. Remove the fuel tank as described in Chapter Eight or Chapter Nine.
8. On California XR650L models, remove the EVAP system as described in Chapter Nine.
9. On XR650L models, remove the PAIR system as described in Chapter Nine.
10. Remove the exhaust system as described in Chapter Eight or Chapter Nine.
11. Remove the carburetor as described in Chapter Eight or Chapter Nine.
12. Disconnect the spark plug lead and tie it up out of the way.
13. On XR600R models, disconnect the starter de-compression lever cable(s) (A, **Figure 1**) from the cylinder head cover.
14. Disconnect the oil tank breather tube (B, **Figure 1**) from the cylinder head cover.
15. Remove the bolt securing the gear shift lever and remove the gearshift lever.

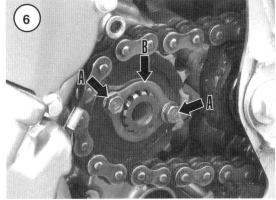

16. On XR600R models, slacken the clutch cable at the hand lever. Turn the lower adjustment nuts (**Figure 2**) as needed, then disconnect the clutch cable from the clutch release lever.

17. On XR650L models, slacken the clutch cable at the hand lever. Remove the clutch cable retainer on the cylinder head cover (**Figure 3**). Remove the clutch cable holder bolt (**Figure 4**). Disconnect the clutch cable from the clutch release lever.

18. On XR600R models, disconnect the alternator wire on the left side of the engine at the electrical connector.

19. On XR650L models, disconnect the alternator and neutral switch wires on the left side of the engine at the electrical connectors above the air box.

20. Disconnect the ignition pulse generator connector or the crankshaft position sensor connector (2008-on XR650L) on the right side of the engine.

21. Remove the bolts securing the drive sprocket cover and remove the cover (**Figure 5**).

22. Remove the bolts (A, **Figure 6**) securing the drive sprocket.

23. Rotate the drive sprocket holder (B, **Figure 6**) in either direction and slide it off the shaft.

24. Loosen the rear axle nut (A, **Figure 7**) and move the chain tension adjuster (B) on both sides to loosen the drive chain.

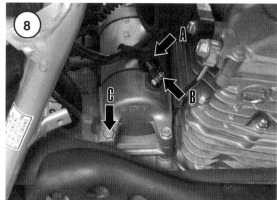

25. Push the rear wheel forward and remove the drive sprocket and drive chain from the shaft.

26. On XR650L models, push back the boot (A, **Figure 8**) on the starter wire. Remove the retaining nut (B, **Figure 8**), and then disconnect the starter wire from the starter terminal.

27. On XR650L models, remove the starter mounting bolt (C, **Figure 8**) and disconnect the ground cable strap.

28. Disconnect the crankcase breather tube from the rear of the crankcase.

29. On XR650L models, remove the rear brake light switch from the right crankcase cover (**Figure 9**).

30. To disconnect the oil lines, perform the following:

   a. Hold onto the fittings either on the metal oil line (A, **Figure 10**) or the frame (B) and unscrew the flexible oil lines (C).

   b. Remove the bolts securing the oil line retainer plate (D, **Figure 10**) to the engine and remove the oil lines. Do not lose the O-rings on the oil line lower ends.

NOTE
If the engine is not being removed for disassembly, skip Step 31. However, the components identified in Step 31 may be more easily serviced with the engine in the frame.

31. If the engine is going to be disassembled, remove the following parts.

   a. Alternator as described in Chapter Ten or Chapter Eleven.

   b. On XR650L models, remove the starter as described in Chapter Eleven.

   c. Camshaft and cylinder head as described in Chapter Four.

   d. Cylinder and piston as described in Chapter Four.

   e. Clutch as described in Chapter Six.

   f. External shift mechanism as described in Chapter Six.

   g. Oil pump as described in this chapter.

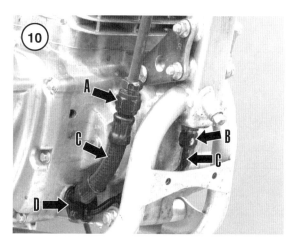

32. Verify that all engine wiring or hoses have been disconnected from the frame.

33. Place tape or other material on the frame to protect it and the engine.

34. Place a suitable size jack, with a piece of wood to protect the crankcase, under the engine. Apply a small amount of jack pressure up on the engine.

CAUTION
Continually adjust jack pressure during engine removal and installation to

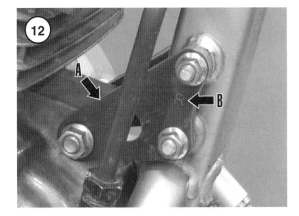

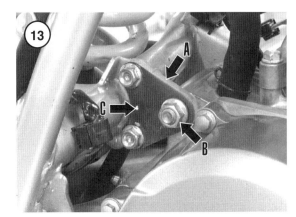

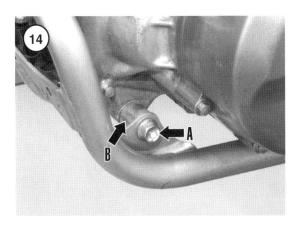

prevent damage to the mounting bolts threads and hardware.

35. Remove the engine upper hanger bolts and nuts and remove the hanger plates (**Figure 11**).

36. Remove the bolts securing the front hanger plates (A, **Figure 12**) and remove the hanger plates.

37. Remove the bolts securing the rear hanger plate (A, **Figure 13**). Remove the throughbolt (B, **Figure 13**).

38. Remove the lower front throughbolt (A, **Figure 14**). Note the spacers (B, **Figure 14**) on each side of the engine.

39. Remove the lower rear throughbolt (**Figure 15**).

40. Remove the engine from the right side of the frame. Take it to a workbench for further disassembly.

41. Install by reversing the preceding removal steps while noting the following.

  a. Make sure to install the spacers (B, **Figure 14**) on both sides of the engine when installing the lower front mounting throughbolt.

  b. The front hanger plates are marked R and L (B, **Figure 12**) to indicate installation on right or left side of frame.

  c. The rear hanger plate has a punch mark (C, **Figure 13**) to indicate which side must face out.

  d. Note that the upper hanger plates (**Figure 11**) are not flat. Position each plate so the lower end contacts the cylinder head cover.

  e. Tighten the 8-mm and 10-mm mounting bolts and nuts to the specifications in Table 3.

  f. Refer to *Oil Lines* and reinstall the oil lines.

  g. Fill the engine with the recommended type and quantity of oil as described in Chapter Three.

  h. Adjust the clutch as described in Chapter Three.

  i. On XR600R models, adjust the starter decompression lever as described in Chapter Three.

  j. Install the drive sprocket so the OUT mark is visible.

  k. Adjust the drive chain as described in Chapter Three.

  l. Start the engine and check for leaks.

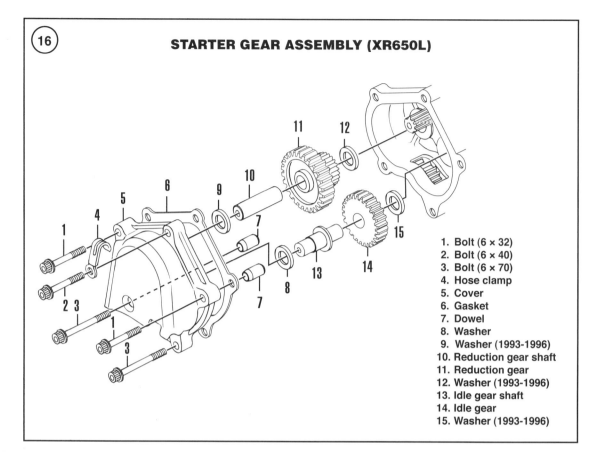

16 **STARTER GEAR ASSEMBLY (XR650L)**

1. Bolt (6 × 32)
2. Bolt (6 × 40)
3. Bolt (6 × 70)
4. Hose clamp
5. Cover
6. Gasket
7. Dowel
8. Washer
9. Washer (1993-1996)
10. Reduction gear shaft
11. Reduction gear
12. Washer (1993-1996)
13. Idle gear shaft
14. Idle gear
15. Washer (1993-1996)

STARTER GEAR ASSEMBLY (XR650L)

Removal/Inspection/Installation

Refer to **Figure 16**.

1. Unhook the air suction valve hose from the clamp (A, **Figure 17**) on the starter gear cover.

2. Remove the bolts securing the starter gear cover (B, **Figure 17**) and remove the cover and gasket. Do not lose the locating dowels on the cover.

3. Remove the washer (**Figure 18**) from the end of the idle gear shaft.

CAUTION
On 1993-1996 models, there is a washer at the inner end of each shaft. Be careful when removing the gear, shaft and washer assembly to prevent these washers from falling into the opening in the left crankcase cover.

4. On 1993-1996 models, remove the washer (**Figure 19**) from the end of the reduction gear shaft.

5. Remove the reduction gear (**Figure 20**), shaft and washer.

6. Remove the idle gear (**Figure 21**), shaft and washer.

7. Inspect the idle gear and shaft (**Figure 22**) for abnormal wear or tooth damage. Replace if necessary.

8. Inspect the reduction gear and shaft (**Figure 23**) for abnormal wear or tooth damage. Replace if necessary.

9. Inspect the bearing (A, **Figure 24**) in the starter gear cover for wear or damage. Replace if necessary.

10. Installation is the reverse of the preceding removal steps. Note the following:

    a. On 1993-1996 models, apply grease to the inner washer prior to installation. This will hold it against the backside of the gear (**Figure 25**) and prevent it from falling off and into the opening in the left crankcase cover.

    b. On gears so marked, install the reduction gear with the OUT mark facing toward the outside.

    c. Make sure the locating dowels (B, **Figure 24**) are in place in the cover.

    d. Install a new gasket.

    e. Install the cover and tighten the bolts securely.

FLYWHEEL AND STARTER CLUTCH (XR650L)

The flywheel/alternator rotor is available only as an assembly. The flywheel (**Figure 26**) can be removed with the engine in the frame.

Tool

A flywheel puller is required to remove the flywheel from the crankshaft. Use one of the following pullers:

1. Flywheel puller (Honda part No. 07733-0020001 or 07933-3290001).

2. Universal flywheel puller (K&L partNo. 35-5944).

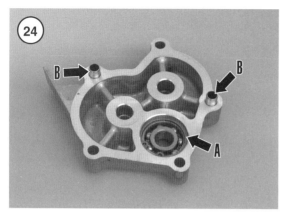

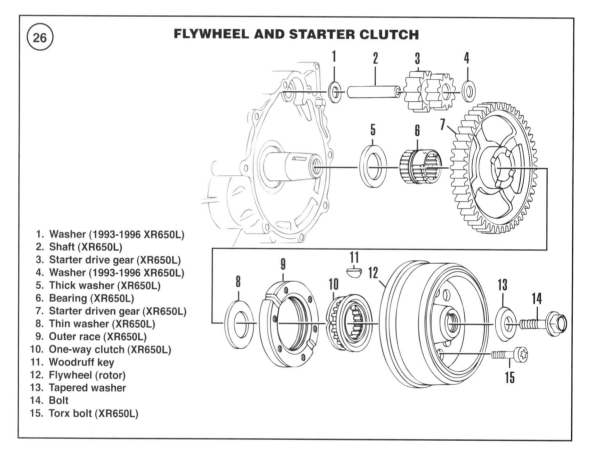

FLYWHEEL AND STARTER CLUTCH

1. Washer (1993-1996 XR650L)
2. Shaft (XR650L)
3. Starter drive gear (XR650L)
4. Washer (1993-1996 XR650L)
5. Thick washer (XR650L)
6. Bearing (XR650L)
7. Starter driven gear (XR650L)
8. Thin washer (XR650L)
9. Outer race (XR650L)
10. One-way clutch (XR650L)
11. Woodruff key
12. Flywheel (rotor)
13. Tapered washer
14. Bolt
15. Torx bolt (XR650L)

Flywheel Removal

1. Support the motorcycle securely.

2. Remove the left side cover and the seat as described in Chapter Sixteen.

3. Disconnect the negative battery cable (**Figure 27**).

4. Drain the engine oil as described in Chapter Three.

5. Remove the clutch cable holder bolt (**Figure 28**). Disconnect the clutch cable from the clutch release lever.

6. Remove the *Starter Gear Assembly* as described in this chapter.

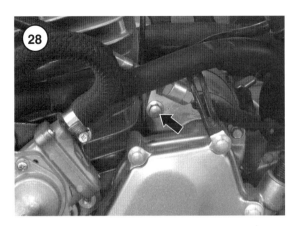

7. Remove the bolt securing the gearshift pedal (A, **Figure 29**) and remove the pedal from the shift shaft.

8. Remove the bolts securing the drive sprocket cover and remove the cover (B, **Figure 29**).

9. Disconnect the electrical connector (**Figure 30**) from the neutral switch.

10. Disconnect the alternator and neutral switch wires on the left side of the engine at the electrical connectors above the air box.

NOTE
*When removing the left crankcase cover do not lose the clutch lifter piece (**Figure 31**). It may fall out or may stay within the recess in the cover.*

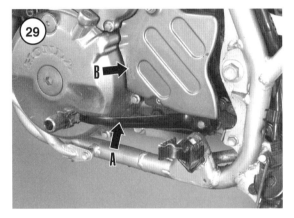

11. Remove the bolts securing the left crankcase cover and remove the cover (**Figure 32**). Do not lose the locating dowels.

12. Hold the flywheel using a strap wrench or a wrench that engages the flats on the flywheel hub.

13. Remove the bolt and washer (A, **Figure 33**) securing the flywheel.

14. Screw in the flywheel puller until it stops (**Figure 34**).

CAUTION
Do not try to remove the flywheel without a puller; doing so will damage the engine and/or flywheel. If a puller is not available, have a dealership remove the flywheel.

15. Turn the flywheel puller with a wrench until the flywheel separates from the crankshaft.

CAUTION
If the flywheel is difficult to remove, strike the puller with a hammer a few times. The shock may break it loose. Do not force the puller as the threads may strip out of the flywheel. Take the motorcycle to a dealership and have the flywheel removed.

16. Remove the flywheel (B, **Figure 33**) and remove the puller from the flywheel.

> *NOTE*
> *When removing the flywheel, the starter driven gear (A, **Figure 35**) may remain on the crankshaft.*

> *NOTE*
> *On 1993-1996 models, washers (1 and 4, **Figure 26**) are located on the inner and outer ends of the starter drive gear.*

17. If necessary, remove the starter drive gear (B, **Figure 35**) and shaft (C).
18. Remove the starter driven gear (A, **Figure 36**) and thin washer (B).
19. Remove the needle bearing (A, **Figure 37**) and thick washer (B).
20. If necessary, remove the Woodruff key (C, **Figure 37**) from the crankshaft keyway.

Starter Clutch Removal/Inspection/Installation

Refer to **Figure 26**.
1. Check the one-way clutch operation as follows:
   a. Place the flywheel and starter clutch on the workbench so that the driven gear faces up as shown in **Figure 38**.
   b. Hold the flywheel and try to turn the driven gear clockwise and then counterclockwise. The driven gear should only turn *counterclockwise* as viewed in **Figure 38**.
   c. If the driven gear turns clockwise, the one-way clutch is damaged and must be replaced as described in this procedure.
2. Rotate the driven gear (**Figure 38**) counterclockwise, and remove the gear from the one-way clutch assembly.
3. Inspect the driven gear (A, **Figure 39**) for the following conditions:
   a. Worn or damaged gear teeth.

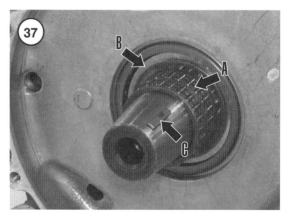

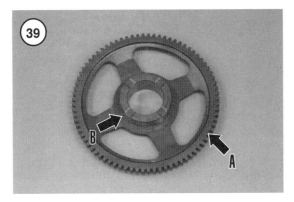

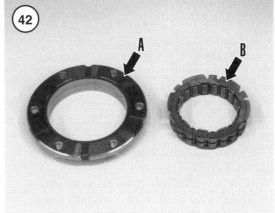

b. Worn or damaged bearing shoulder.

c. Measure the starter driven gear outside diameter-to-needle bearing surface (B, **Figure 39**) and refer to **Table 2**.

4. Inspect the one-way clutch (**Figure 40**) for the following conditions:

  a. Severely worn or damaged one-way clutch rollers.

  b. Loose one-way clutch Torx bolts.

5. To replace the one-way clutch (**Figure 40**), perform the following:

  a. Secure the flywheel with a strap or band wrench.

b. Using an impact driver, remove the one-way clutch bolts (**Figure 41**).

c. Separate the clutch outer race (A, **Figure 42**, typical) and the one-way clutch (B).

d. Install the one-way clutch into the outer race so the flange on the one-way clutch fits into the recess in the outer race as shown in **Figure 43**, typical.

e. Apply a medium strength threadlock to the threads of each bolt.

f. Install the one-way clutch bolts finger-tight and then tighten them to the specification in **Table 3**.

6. Inspect the needle bearing (A, **Figure 37**). The needles should be smooth and polished with no flat spots, cracks or other damage. Inspect the bearing cage for cracks or other damage. Replace the bearing if necessary.

7. Inspect the washer (B, **Figure 37**) for cracks, scoring or other damage.

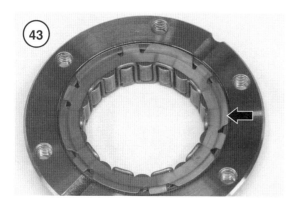

Flywheel Inspection

WARNING
Replace a cracked or chipped flywheel. A damaged flywheel can fly apart at high rpm, throwing metal fragments into the engine. Do not attempt to repair a damaged flywheel.

CAUTION
Carefully inspect the inside of the flywheel for metal objects that may have been picked up by the magnets. Any metal attached to the magnets can damage the alternator stator assembly.

1. Clean and dry the flywheel.
2. Check the flywheel for cracks or breaks.
3. Check the flywheel tapered bore and the crankshaft taper for damage.
4. Replace damaged parts as required.

Flywheel Installation

NOTE
There are two similar washers (Figure 26). The thick washer fits between the crankshaft main bearing and the needle bearing (A, Figure 37). The thin washer fits between the driven gear (A, Figure 36) and the flywheel hub.

1. Apply engine oil to the one-way clutch rollers and the driven gear shoulder.
2. To install the driven gear:
   a. Place the flywheel on the workbench so that the one-way clutch faces up.
   b. Place the thin washer (B, Figure 36) onto the flywheel hub.
   c. Rotate the driven gear counterclockwise and slide it into the one-way clutch (Figure 38).

3. Apply engine oil onto the thick washer and needle bearing before installing them onto the crankshaft.
4. Install the washer (B, Figure 37) and the needle bearing (A) onto the crankshaft.
5. If removed, install the Woodruff key (C, Figure 37) into the crankshaft keyway.
6. Align the keyway in the flywheel with the Woodruff key in the crankshaft and install the flywheel (B, Figure 33).
7. Lubricate the flywheel bolt and flange surface with engine oil. Install the flywheel bolt and washer. The washer is tapered. Position the washer so the larger diameter contacts the flywheel hub. Tighten the flywheel bolt to the specification in Table 3.

NOTE
On 1993-1996 models, install washers (1 and 4, Figure 26) on both ends of the starter drive gear in Step 8.

8. Install the starter drive gear (B, Figure 35) and shaft with the OUT mark on the gear end visible.
9. Lubricate the lifter piece (Figure 31) with molybdenum disulfide oil. If it fell out during the cover removal sequence, install the lifter piece with the concave end facing out so it can mate correctly with the clutch pushrod.

10. Make sure the locating dowels (**Figure 44**) are in place and install a new cover gasket.

11. Install the left crankcase cover. Install the neutral switch wire guide on the bolt indicated in **Figure 45**. Tighten the cover bolts to the specification in **Table 3**.

12. Connect the alternator and neutral switch wires.

CAUTION
Do not overtighten the neutral switch
wire retaining nut. Doing so may break
the switch stud.

13. Connect the electrical connector (**Figure 30**) to the neutral switch. Install the boot around the neutral switch. Fit the switch wire into the guide on the crankcase cover bolt (**Figure 45**).

14. Install the drive sprocket cover (B, **Figure 29**). Apply a medium strength threadlock to the bolts. The longer bolt fits in the upper cover hole. Tighten the bolts securely.

15. Install the gearshift pedal (A, **Figure 29**) onto the shift shaft. Align the punch marks on the pedal and shaft (**Figure 46**). Tighten the pinch bolt to 12 N•m (106 in.-lb.).

16. Install the *Starter Gear Assembly* as described in this chapter.

17. Connect the clutch cable to the clutch release lever. Install the clutch cable holder bolt (**Figure 28**) and tighten securely.

18. Connect the negative battery cable (**Figure 27**).

19. Install the left side cover and the seat as described in Chapter Sixteen.

20. Refill the engine oil as described in Chapter Three.

FLYWHEEL (XR600R)

The flywheel/alternator rotor is available only as a unit assembly. The flywheel (**Figure 26**) can be removed with the engine in the frame.

Tool

A flywheel puller is required to remove the flywheel from the crankshaft. Use one of the following pullers:

1. Flywheel puller (Honda part No. 07733-0020001 or 07933-329001).

2. Universal flywheel puller (K&L part No. 35-5944).

Removal

1. Support the motorcycle securely.

2. Remove the left side cover and the seat as described in Chapter Sixteen.

3. Drain the engine oil as described in Chapter Three.

4. Remove the bolt securing the gearshift pedal and remove the pedal (A, **Figure 47**) from the shift shaft.

5. Remove the clutch cable from the crankcase cover holder and disconnect the clutch cable from the clutch release lever (B, **Figure 47**).

6. Remove the bolts securing the drive sprocket cover and remove the cover (**Figure 48**).

7. Disconnect the alternator wires on the left side of the engine at the electrical connectors above the air box.

NOTE
*When removing the left crankcase cover do not lose the clutch lifter piece (**Figure 31**). It may fall out or may stay within the recess in the cover.*

8. Remove the bolts securing the left crankcase cover and remove the cover (**Figure 49**). Do not lose the locating dowels.
9. Hold the flywheel using a strap wrench.
10. Remove the bolt and washer (**Figure 50**) securing the flywheel.
11. Screw in the flywheel puller until it stops (**Figure 51**).

CAUTION
Do not try to remove the flywheel without a puller; doing so will damage the engine and/or flywheel. If a puller is not available, have a dealership remove the flywheel.

12. Turn the flywheel puller with a wrench until the flywheel separates from the crankshaft.

CAUTION
If the flywheel is difficult to remove, strike the puller with a hammer a few times. The shock may break it loose. Do not force the puller as the threads may strip out of the flywheel. Take the motorcycle to a dealership and have the flywheel removed.

13. Remove the flywheel and remove the puller from the flywheel.
14. If necessary, remove the Woodruff key (**Figure 52**) from the crankshaft keyway.

Flywheel Inspection

WARNING
Replace a cracked or chipped flywheel. A damaged flywheel can fly apart at high rpm, throwing metal fragments into the engine. Do not attempt to repair a damaged flywheel.

CAUTION
Carefully inspect the inside of the flywheel for metal objects that may have been picked up by the magnets. Any metal attached to the magnets can damage the alternator stator assembly.

1. Clean and dry the flywheel.
2. Check the flywheel for cracks or breaks.
3. Check the flywheel tapered bore and the crankshaft taper for damage.
4. Replace damaged parts as required.

Installation

1. If removed, install the Woodruff key (**Figure 52**) into the crankshaft keyway.
2. Align the keyway in the flywheel with the Woodruff key in the crankshaft and install the flywheel.

3. Lubricate the flywheel bolt and flange surface with engine oil. Install the flywheel bolt and washer. The washer is tapered. Position the washer so the larger diameter contacts the flywheel hub. Tighten the flywheel bolt to 125 N•m (92 ft.-lb.).

4. Make sure the clutch lifter piece is still in place in the left crankcase cover (**Figure 31**). If it fell out during the cover removal sequence, install the lifter piece with the concave end facing out so it can mate correctly with the clutch lifter rod.

5. Make sure the locating dowcls (**Figure 44**, typical) are in place and install a new cover gasket.

6. Install the left crankcase cover. Tighten the cover bolts to 12 N•m (106 in.-lb.).

7. Connect the alternator wires.

8. Install the drive sprocket cover. Tighten the bolts securely.

9. Install the gearshift pedal onto the shift shaft. Align the punch marks on the pedal and shaft (**Figure 46**). Tighten the pinch bolt to 12 N•m (106 in.-lb.).

10. Connect the clutch cable to the clutch release lever.

11. Install the left side cover and the seat as described in Chapter Sixteen.

12. Refill the engine oil as described in Chapter Three.

KICKSTARTER (XR600R)

Removal

1. Remove the clutch as described in Chapter Six.

2. Remove the kickstarter idle gear and bushing (**Figure 53**).

3. Using locking pliers, carefully unhook the return spring from the boss on the crankcase.

4. Withdraw the kickstarter assembly from the crankcase.

Disassembly

Refer to **Figure 54**.

1. Clean the assembled shaft in solvent and dry thoroughly with compressed air.

2. Slide off the thrust washer.

3. Remove the spring collar, return spring and spring seat.

4. Remove the ratchet spring and the kickstarter ratchet.

5. Remove the snap ring and slide off the thrust washer.

6. Slide off the kickstarter gear and bushing.

Inspection

1. Measure the inside diameter of the kickstarter idle gear (A, **Figure 55**). Replace if worn to the service limit in **Table 1** or greater.

2. Measure the inside diameter (B, **Figure 55**) and outside diameter (C) of the kickstarter idle gear bushing. Replace if worn to the service limit in **Table 1**.

3. Measure the inside diameter of the kickstarter gear (A, **Figure 56**). Replace if worn to the service limit in **Table 1** or greater.

4. Measure the outside diameter of the kickstarter shaft where the kickstarter gear rides (B, **Figure 56**). Replace if worn to the service limit in **Table 1** or less.

5. Inspect the gears for chipped or missing teeth. Replace any gears as necessary.

6. Inspect the splines on the kickstarter shaft for wear or damage. Replace as necessary.

7. Make sure the ratchet gear operates properly and smoothly on its shaft.

8. Check all parts for uneven wear; replace any that are questionable.

Assembly

1. Apply new engine oil to all sliding surfaces of all parts.

5

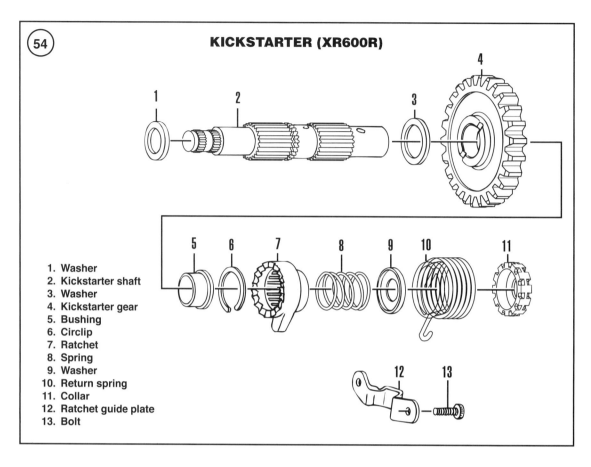

KICKSTARTER (XR600R)

1. Washer
2. Kickstarter shaft
3. Washer
4. Kickstarter gear
5. Bushing
6. Circlip
7. Ratchet
8. Spring
9. Washer
10. Return spring
11. Collar
12. Ratchet guide plate
13. Bolt

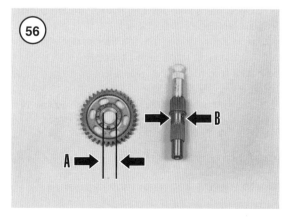

2. Slide on the thrust washer.

3. Slide the kickstarter gear bushing and the kickstarter gear onto the shaft (**Figure 57**).

4. Install the thrust washer and snap ring (**Figure 58**). Make sure the snap ring is correctly seated in the groove in the shaft.

5. Align the punch marks on the kickstarter shaft and the drive ratchet (**Figure 59**). Slide on the ratchet.

6. Install the ratchet spring and spring seat (**Figure 60**).

7. Install the return spring. Place the hook into the hole in the shaft (**Figure 61**).

8. Slide on the collar and push the collar into place within the return spring (**Figure 62**).

9. Slide on the thrust washer.

Installation

1. Install the assembled shaft into the crankcase.

2. Insert the drive ratchet pawl against the ratchet guide plate on the crankcase.

3. Temporarily install the kickstarter pedal onto the shaft.

4. Hook the return spring onto the crankcase.

5. Rotate the assembly clockwise until the ratchet pawl clears the stopper plate. Then push the kickstarter shaft all the way in.

6. Remove the kickstarter pedal.

7. Install the kickstarter idle gear bushing with the shoulder side on first (**Figure 63**).

8. Install the kickstarter idle gear onto the bushing (**Figure 53**).

9. Install the clutch assembly as described in Chapter Six.

OIL PUMP

The oil pump is located on the right side of the engine next to the clutch. The oil pump can be removed with the engine in the frame.

Removal/Installation

1. Remove the clutch as described in Chapter Six.
2. Remove the oil pump driven gear (**Figure 64**).
3. Remove the nut (A, **Figure 65**) and bolt (B) securing the oil tube, and remove the oil tube.
4. Remove the bolts (**Figure 66**) securing the oil pump to the crankcase, and remove the oil pump assembly.
5. Before installing the oil pump, make sure the oil control orifice and O-ring (**Figure 67**) are installed in the inlet on the crankcase.
6. Install the locating dowels in either the oil pump (A, **Figure 68**) or in the crankcase.
7. Pour engine oil into the pump inlet hole (B, **Figure 68**). At the same time rotate the pump shaft counterclockwise until oil flows out the pump outlet hole.
8. Install the oil pump and tighten the bolts securely.
9. Make sure the O-ring seals are in place on each end of the oil tube.
10. Install the oil tube. Tighten the retaining nut and bolt securely.
11. After reassembling the engine, start the engine and let it idle for about one minute. Loosen the oil return tube fitting (**Figure 69**) and make sure oil flows from the connection. Retighten the oil tube fitting.

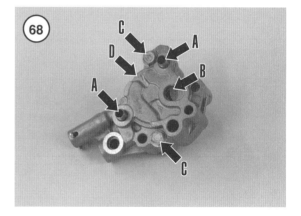

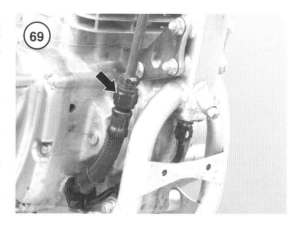

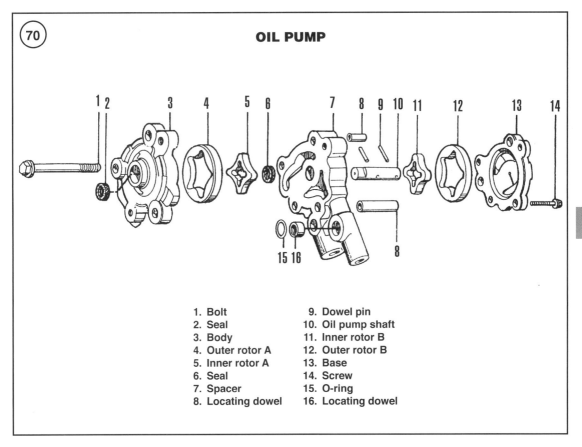

OIL PUMP

1. Bolt
2. Seal
3. Body
4. Outer rotor A
5. Inner rotor A
6. Seal
7. Spacer
8. Locating dowel
9. Dowel pin
10. Oil pump shaft
11. Inner rotor B
12. Outer rotor B
13. Base
14. Screw
15. O-ring
16. Locating dowel

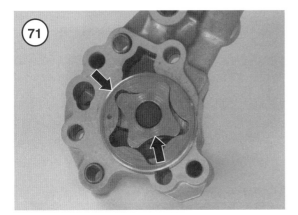

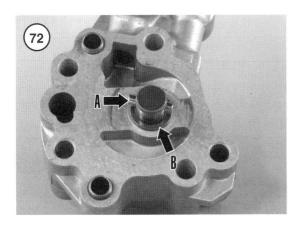

Disassembly/Assembly

The oil pump (**Figure 70**) has dual cavities with main and sub-rotor assemblies. In the inspection steps, the clearance measurements are the same for both the main and sub-rotor assemblies. The main set of rotors is the thicker of the two sets and is assembled into the oil pump body.

1. Remove the bolts (C, **Figure 68**) securing the oil pump body to the base and spacer.

2. Remove the pump inner cover (D, **Figure 68**).

3. Remove outer rotor B and inner rotor B (**Figure 71**).

4. Remove the dowel pin (A, **Figure 72**) and thrust washer (B).

5. Turn the assembly over and remove the outer cover (**Figure 73**).

6. Remove outer rotor A (A, **Figure 74**) and inner rotor A (B).

7. Remove the pump shaft (A, **Figure 75**) and dowel pin (B) from the pump body.

8. Inspect the oil pump components as described in this chapter.

9. To assemble the oil pump, install the pump drive shaft (A, **Figure 75**) and dowel pin (B) into the pump body.

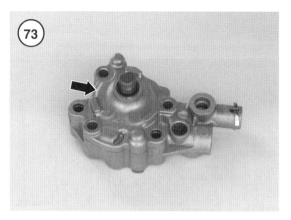

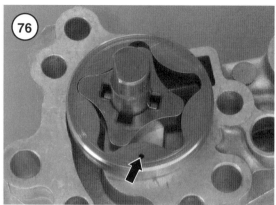

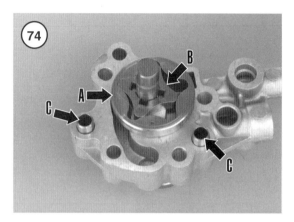

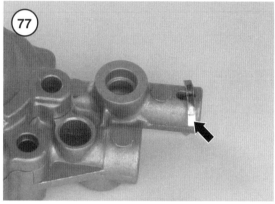

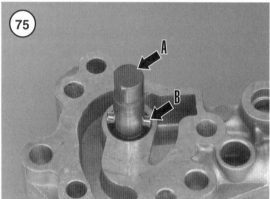

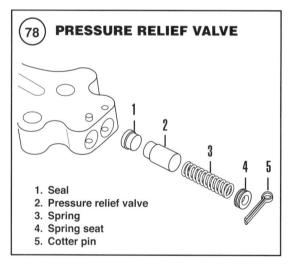

78 PRESSURE RELIEF VALVE

1. Seal
2. Pressure relief valve
3. Spring
4. Spring seat
5. Cotter pin

10. If removed, install the hollow dowels into the pump body (C, **Figure 74**).

11. Install the inner rotor A (B, **Figure 74**) and the outer rotor A. Make sure the punch mark (**Figure 76**) is visible.

12. Install the outer cover onto the body.

13. Turn the assembly over.

14. Install the thrust washer (B, **Figure 72**) and the dowel pin (A).

15. Install the outer rotor B and inner rotor B (**Figure 71**). Make sure the punch mark on the outer rotor is visible.

16. Install the pump inner cover (D, **Figure 68**).

17. Install the bolts (C, **Figure 68**) securing the oil pump body and covers. Tighten the bolt securely.

18. To disassemble the pressure relief valve, perform the following:

   a. Remove the cotter pin at the end of the pressure relief valve housing (**Figure 77**). Discard the cotter pin.

   b. Remove the spring seat (4, **Figure 78**), spring (3), pressure relief valve (2), and seal (1).

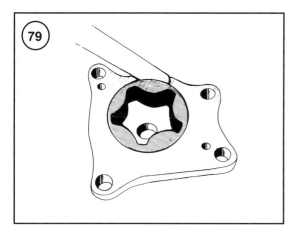

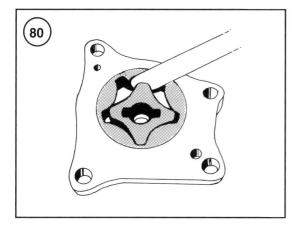

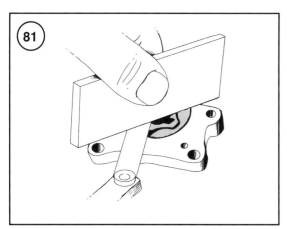

19. Clean all pressure relief valve parts in solvent and thoroughly dry. Coat all parts with fresh engine oil before installation.

20. To assemble the pressure relief valve, perform the following:

a. Install the seal, pressure relief valve (small end in first), spring and spring seat.

b. Install a new cotter pin and bend the ends over completely.

Inspection

1. Inspect both sets of inner and outer rotors for scratches and abrasions. Replace parts of each set if evidence of these are found.

2. Clean all parts in solvent and dry thoroughly. Coat all parts with fresh engine oil before installation.

3. Inspect the teeth on the driven gear. Replace the driven gear if the teeth are damaged or any are missing.

4. Install the correct outer rotor into the corresponding pump cover.

5. Measure the clearance between the outer rotor and the oil pump cover using a flat feeler gauge (**Figure 79**). Compare the clearance to the service limit in **Table 2**.

6. Install the correct inner rotor into the outer rotor that was installed in Step 5.

7. Measure the clearance between the tip of the inner rotor and the outer rotor using a flat feeler gauge (**Figure 80**). Compare the clearance to the service limit in **Table 2**.

8. Measure the side clearance between both rotors and the oil pump cover with a straightedge and a flat feeler gauge (**Figure 81**). Compare the clearance to the service limit in **Table 2**.

9. Inspect the seals in the oil pump body and the outer oil pump cover. If worn or damaged, replace the seals as follows:

a. Note the position of the seal in the body and cover and note which side of the seal faces out. The new seal must face in the same direction.

b. Measure the distance down from the top surface of the body or spacer to the top of the seal. This dimension should be 0.5-1.1 mm (0.020- 0.043 in.).

c. Carefully pry the seal out of the body or spacer.

d. Position the new seal with the same side facing out as the one that was removed.

e. Carefully install the new seal into the body or spacer until it is recessed 0.5-1.1 mm (0.020-0.043 in.) from the top surface of the body or spacer.

OIL LINES

The dry-sump engine lubrication system requires an external oil tank. The motorcycle frame serves this purpose. Engine oil flows between the frame and engine through oil lines at the front of the engine and frame (A, **Figure 82**).

Oil flows from the frame through a fitting threaded into the front downtube (**Figure 83**). The oil must pass through a strainer attached to the fitting. Pressurized return oil travels from the engine through a tube attached to the frame adjacent to the steering head (**Figure 84**).

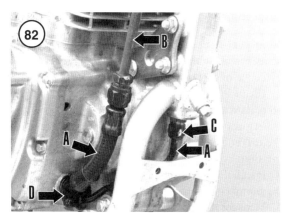

Removal/Inspection/Installation

1. Drain the engine oil as described in Chapter Three.

2. Hold onto the fittings either on the metal oil line (B, **Figure 82**) or the frame (C) and unscrew the flexible oil lines (A).

3. Remove the bolts securing the oil line retainer plate (D, **Figure 82**) to the engine and remove the oil lines. Do not lose the O-rings on the oil line lower ends.

4. Inspect the oil lines (**Figure 85**) for damage or leaks. If damaged, replace both lines.

5. Inspect the O-ring seals on the engine end of the oil lines. If damaged or starting to deteriorate, replace the O-ring on each oil line.

6. Remove the frame fitting (**Figure 83**). Inspect the strainer on the fitting (**Figure 86**). Clean all debris off the strainer. Install the fitting and tighten to the specification in **Table 3**.

7. To remove the metal oil line, perform the following:

    a. Remove the clamping band on the frame.

    b. Disconnect the fitting on the metal oil line from the motorcycle frame.

8. Install by reversing the preceding removal steps while noting the following:

    a. The lower ends of the oil lines are configured differently for proper installation. The oil feed line fitting (A, **Figure 85**) has flat edges, while the return line fitting (B) has rounded edges.

    b. Install the retainer plate so the square slot (A, **Figure 87**) for the oil feed line fitting is down and toward the inside. The rounded slot (B, **Figure 87**) secures the oil return line fitting. Tighten the retainer plate bolts securely.

    c. Do not kink the oil lines during installation. The oil lines must retain a natural curve.

    d. Tighten the oil line fittings to the specification in **Table 3**.

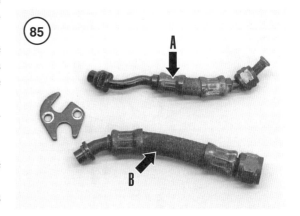

OIL STRAINER SCREEN

An oil strainer screen is located in the bottom of the right crankcase half. The oil strainer prevents debris from entering the intake passage for the oil pump.

Removal/Installation

1. Remove the right crankcase cover as described in Chapter Six.
2. Unscrew the strainer retaining bolt (**Figure 88**), then remove the strainer.
3. Clean the strainer screen (**Figure 89**). Replace the strainer if damaged.
4. Reverse the removal steps to install the strainer. Tighten the strainer retaining bolt securely.

PRIMARY DRIVE GEAR ASSEMBLY

The primary drive gear assembly includes the primary drive gear, pulse-generator/CKP-sensor rotor, and oil pump drive gear.

Removal/Installation

1. Remove the clutch as described in Chapter Six.
2. Remove the pulse generator (XR600R and 1993-2007 XR650L) or the crankshaft position sensor (2008-on XR650L) as described in Chapter Ten or Chapter Eleven.
3. Remove the oil pump driven gear (**Figure 90**).
4. Reinstall the clutch outer housing.
5. Place the gear holder (Honda part No. 07724-0010100 [**Figure 91**]) between the primary drive gear and the primary driven gear on the clutch outer housing (**Figure 92**).

NOTE
If a gear holder tool is not available, a copper penny may be placed between the gear teeth to prevent gear rotation.

6. Remove the nut (**Figure 93**).

7. Remove the Belleville washer (A, **Figure 94**) and oil pump drive gear (B).

8. Remove the pulse-generator/CKP-sensor rotor (A, **Figure 95**) and primary drive gear (B).

9. Reinstall the gear assembly by reversing the removal steps and noting the following:

    a. The gears and rotor have a master spline that must align with the master spline on the crankshaft.

    b. Install the rotor so the boss (C, **Figure 95**) is nearer the end of the crankshaft.

    c. Install the Belleville washer so the side marked OUTSIDE is toward the end of the crankshaft.

    d. Lubricate the nut threads with engine oil and tighten the primary gear nut to the specification in **Table 3**.

CAMSHAFT CHAIN AND GUIDES

Removal/Installation

1. Remove the cylinder head cover and camshaft as described in this chapter.

2. Remove the clutch assembly as described in Chapter Six.

3. Remove the primary drive gear as described in this chapter.

> *NOTE*
> *Do not lose the inner washer when removing the chain guide bolt in Step 4.*

4. Remove the bolt securing the rear camshaft chain guide (A, **Figure 96**), then remove the guide (B).

5. Let the camshaft chain drop down through the passageway in the cylinder head and cylinder, and into the outer portion of the right crankcase half.

6. Remove the camshaft chain (A, **Figure 97**) from the camshaft chain sprocket (B) on the crankshaft.

7. Remove the camshaft chain sprocket from the crankshaft.

8. Inspect the camshaft chain for wear and damage. If chain replacement is necessary, also inspect the drive sprocket and the camshaft sprocket.

9. If the front chain guide must be serviced, remove the cylinder head as described in Chapter Four.

10. Install by reversing the preceding removal steps while noting the following:

    a. Align the master splines on the sprocket and crankshaft during sprocket installation. The flanged end of the sprocket must be toward the crankshaft end.

    b. Attach a piece of wire to the camshaft chain and pull the chain up through the passageway in the cylinder and cylinder head.

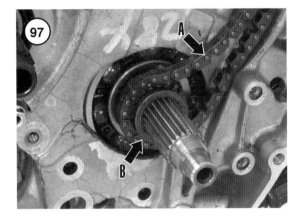

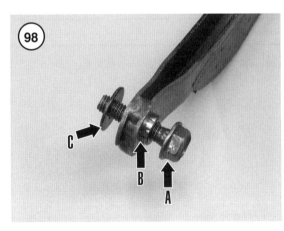

c. When installing the rear chain guide, assemble the bolt (A, **Figure 98**), sleeve (B) and washer (C) as shown. Apply a medium strength threadlock to the bolt threads and tighten the bolt securely.

CRANKCASE AND CRANKSHAFT

Disassembly of the crankcase and removal of the crankshaft assembly requires engine removal from the frame.

The crankshaft, connecting rod and rod bearing are available only as a unit assembly. Service is limited to replacement. Two ball bearings in the crankcase support the crankshaft assembly.

The crankcase is made in two halves of thin-wall, precision diecast aluminum alloy. To avoid damage, do not hammer or pry on any of the interior or exterior projected walls. A gasket seals the crankcase halves while dowel pins align the crankcase halves when mated. The crankcase halves can be replaced separately.

The following procedure describes a complete, step-by-step major lower end overhaul. If only transmission service is necessary, the crankcase may be disassembled and assembled without removing the crankshaft.

Reference in the text to the right and left side of the engine, refer to the engine as it sits in the frame, not as it sits on a workbench.

Tools

A press is required to remove the crankshaft from the crankcase.

To install the crankshaft into the crankcase, the following Honda tools or their equivalents are required:

1. Threaded adapter (part No. 07931-KF00200).
2. Shaft puller (part No. 07931-ME4000A).
3. Attachment (part No. 07746-0030400).
4. Assembly collar (part No. 07931-KF00100).

Crankcase Disassembly

1. Remove all exterior engine assemblies as described in this chapter and other related chapters.
   a. Starter (XR650L models).
   b. Cylinder head cover, camshaft and cylinder head.
   c. Cylinder and piston.
   d. Camshaft chain and tensioner.
   e. Clutch assembly.
   f. Kickstarter (XR600R models).
   g. Flywheel.
   h. External shift mechanism.
   i. Oil pump.
2. Remove the engine as described in this chapter.
3. Before removing the crankcase bolts, cut a cardboard template approximately the size of the crankcase and punch holes in the template for each bolt location. Place each bolt in the template hole as it is removed.
4. Remove the bolts from the left crankcase side that secure the crankcase halves together (**Figure 99**). To prevent warp, loosen them in a crossing pattern.

NOTE
*Set the engine on wood blocks or fabricate a wood fixture (**Figure 100**).*

5. Remove the bolts from the right crankcase side (**Figure 101**).

CAUTION
Perform the next step directly over and close to the workbench as the crankcase halves may separate easily. Do not hammer on the crankcase halves or they will be damaged.

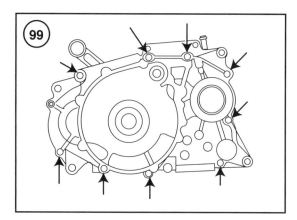

6. Set the crankcase down on the left side. Hold onto the right crankcase half and tap on the right end of the crankshaft and transmission shafts with a plastic or soft-faced mallet until the crankshaft and crankcase separate.

7. If the crankcase and crankshaft will not separate using the procedure in Step 6, check to make sure that all bolts are removed. If the crankcase remains intact, it may be necessary to use a puller to remove the right crankcase half. If the proper tools are not available, take the crankcase assembly to a dealer and have it separated. Do not risk crankcase damage with improper tools or techniques.

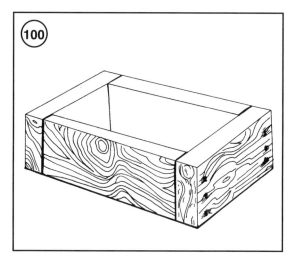

CAUTION
Do not pry between the crankcase mating surfaces when separating the crankcase halves. Doing so may cause an oil leak.

CAUTION
*The crankshaft is pressed into the left crankcase half. Attempting to drive out the crankshaft will damage the crankshaft and crankcase. Refer to **Crankshaft Removal** in this section.*

8. Remove the crankcase gasket. Do not lose the locating dowels if they came out of the case. Dowel removal is not necessary if they are secure.

9. For further disassembly, refer to the appropriate section or chapter. Note that the transmission or balancer may be serviced without removing the crankshaft. The balancer and transmission must be removed for crankshaft removal.

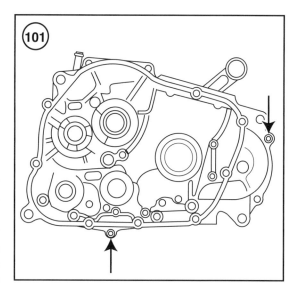

Balancer

The balancer has two gears that engage the crankshaft gear. The gears are spring loaded to remove backlash between the balancer and crankshaft gears.

Removal/Installation

1. Rotate the crankshaft so the balancer can be removed straight out without interference between the crankshaft and balancer weights. Place paint marks on the balancer and crankshaft gear teeth so they can be assembled in their original positions.

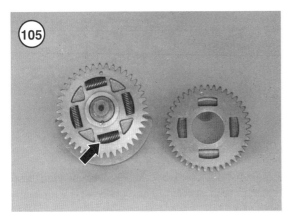

2. On XR600R and 1993-2007 XR650L, insert a punch through the holes in the balancer gears (**Figure 102**). The punch must force the two gears to rotate so the gear teeth on the inner and outer balancer gears align. On 2008-on XR650L, insert a flat-blade screwdriver into the teeth of the inner and outer balancer gears, rotate the screwdriver so the gear teeth align, and insert a suitable size pin into the gear holes to lock the gears in place.

3. Remove the balancer.

4. Reverse the removal steps to install the balancer while noting the following:

   a. Align the paint marks made during disassembly.

   b. After installation remove the punch or pin.

   c. Rotate the crankshaft and verify that the crankshaft gear and balancer gear timing marks align (**Figure 103**). If not, reinstall the balancer.

Disassembly/Inspection/Assembly

1. Remove the snap ring (A, **Figure 104**) and washer (B).

2. Remove the outer driven gear (C, **Figure 104**).

3. If necessary, remove the damper springs (**Figure 105**) from the balancer shaft assembly.

4. Check for broken, chipped or missing teeth on the outer driven gear and the gear on the balancer shaft assembly.

5. Inspect the damper springs. Make sure they are not broken or collapsed. Replace the springs as a set even if only one requires replacement.

6. Inspect the outside diameter of the balancer shaft at each end. Replace if damaged or excessively worn.

7. Install the damper springs into the balancer shaft assembly (**Figure 105**).

8. On XR600R and 1993-2007 XR650L, align the index marks on both gears (**Figure 106**) and install the outer driven gear (C, **Figure 104**). On 2008-on XR650L, align the holes of both gears and then install the outer driven gear.

9. Install the washer (B, **Figure 104**) onto the shaft.

10. Install the snap ring (A, **Figure 104**) with the sharp side facing out. Make sure it is completely seated in the groove in the shaft.

Crankshaft Removal

The balancer and transmission must be removed prior to crankshaft removal.

1. Support the left crankcase half in a press.

CAUTION
When supporting the crankcase half in the press, confirm that there is adequate room to press the crankshaft out without the connecting rod hitting against the press bed. If this happens, a bent connecting rod may result. Check the setup carefully before applying pressure to the crankshaft.

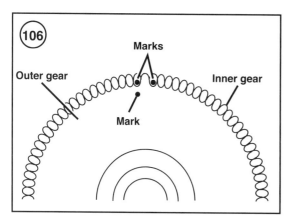

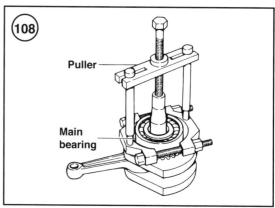

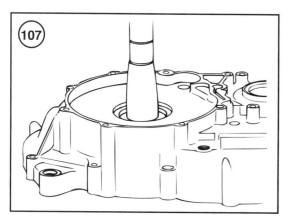

CAUTION
Catch the crankshaft once the crank-
shaft is free of the crankcase half.
Otherwise, these parts can fall to the
floor, causing damage.

2. Center the crankshaft under the press ram
(**Figure 107**) and press the crankshaft out of the
crankcase.
3. Remove the crankshaft from the crankcase half.
4. Remove the rear crankcase from the press.

NOTE
If the crankshaft left main bearing
comes out of the crankcase half with
the crankshaft it must be replaced.
Remove the bearing using a suitable
*puller (***Figure 108***).*

Crankcase Inspection

1. Remove all gasket residue from the crankcase
mating surfaces.
2. Pry out the output shaft seal (A, **Figure 109**) and
shift shaft seal (B) from the right crankcase half using a wide-blade screwdriver or seal puller. Protect
the crankcase surface to prevent damage.

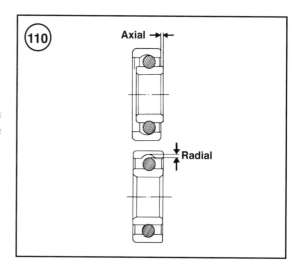

CAUTION
When drying the crankcase bearings in
Step 3, do not allow the inner bearing
races to spin. The bearings are not lubri-
cated and damage may result. When dry-
ing the bearings with compressed air, do
not allow the air jet to spin the bearing.

3. Clean both crankcase halves and all crankcase
bearings with solvent. Thoroughly dry with compressed air.

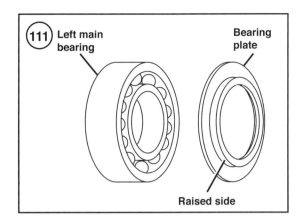

(111) Left main bearing — Bearing plate — Raised side

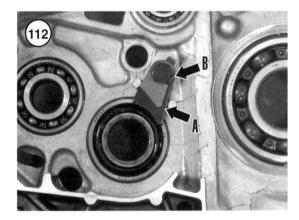

(112)

(113)

4. Flush all crankcase oil passages with compressed air.

5. Lightly oil all of the crankcase bearings with engine oil before checking the bearings in Step 6.

6. Check the bearings for roughness, pitting, galling and play by rotating them slowly by hand. Replace any bearing that turns roughly or has excessive play (**Figure 110**).

7. Replace any worn or damaged bearings as described in this section.

8. Carefully inspect the crankcase for cracks and fractures, especially in the lower areas where it is vulnerable to rock damage.

9. Check the areas around the stiffening ribs, around bearing bosses and threaded holes for damage. Refer crankcase repair to a shop specializing in the repair of precision aluminum castings.

10. Check the threaded holes in both crankcase halves for thread damage, dirt or oil buildup. If necessary, clean or repair the threads with the correct size metric tap. Coat the tap threads with kerosene or an aluminum tap fluid before use.

11. Install the output shaft and shift shaft seals with the flat side (**Figure 109**) facing out. Pack the seal lips with grease.

Crankcase Bearing Replacement

The crankcase contains the crankshaft, transmission and balancer shaft bearings. When replacing bearings, note the following:

1. Before removing the bearings, note and record the direction in which the bearings size codes face for proper reinstallation.

2. Refer to the general bearing replacement procedures in Chapter One and note the following:

   a. When installing the left main bearing, place the bearing plate between the bearing and crankcase half. The raised side of the bearing plate must be toward the outside of the crankcase half (**Figure 111**).

   b. A retainer plate (A, **Figure 112**) holds the transmission bearing in the right crankcase half. During assembly, install a new lock plate under the retainer plate bolt, and tighten the bolt securely on XR600R and 1993-2007 XR650L. On 2008-on XR650L, torque the retainer plate bolt to the specification in **Table 3**. On all models, bend a locking tab (B, **Figure 112**) against a bolt-head flat.

   c. The transmission mainshaft bearing in the left crankcase half includes a separate inner roller bearing (A, **Figure 113**) and outer race (B). The race and bearing are available only as a unit. A retainer plate (C, **Figure 113**) holds the bearing race in the crankcase. Apply a medium-strength threadlock to the threads of the retainer plate bolt. On XR600R and 1993-2007 XR650L, tighten the retainer plate bolt securely. On 2008-on XR650L, tighten the bolt to the specification in **Table 3**

Crankshaft Inspection

Handle the crankshaft carefully when performing the following cleaning and inspection procedures. Individual crankshaft components are not available separately. If the crankshaft is excessively worn or damaged, or if any measurement is out of specification, replace the crankshaft as an assembly.

5

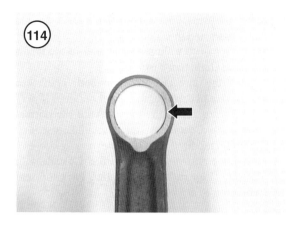

1. Clean the crankshaft thoroughly with solvent. Clean the crankshaft oil passageway with compressed air. Dry the crankshaft with compressed air, then lubricate all bearing surfaces with a light coat of engine oil.

2. Check the crankshaft journals for scratches, heat discoloration or other defects.

3. Check the flywheel taper, threads and keyway for damage.

4. Check the connecting rod big end for signs of damage, as well as bearing or thrust washer damage.

5. Check the connecting rod small end for signs of excessive heat (blue coloration) or other damage.

6. Measure the connecting rod small end inside diameter (**Figure 114**) using a snap gauge or an inside micrometer and compare with the dimension in **Table 2**.

7. Slide the connecting rod to one side and check the connecting rod side clearance with a flat feeler gauge (**Figure 115**) and compare with the dimension in **Table 2**.

8. Place the crankshaft on a set of V-blocks and measure runout with a dial indicator at the points listed in **Table 2**. If the runout exceeds the service limit, take the crankshaft to a dealership for service or replacement.

9. Place the crankshaft on a set of V-blocks and measure the connecting rod big end radial clearance with a dial indicator. Measure in the two directions shown in **Figure 116** and compare with the dimension in **Table 2**.

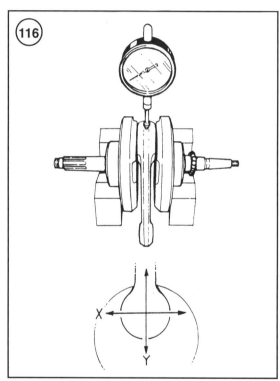

Transmission Inspection

Refer to Chapter Seven.

Crankshaft Installation

> *CAUTION*
> *Refer to **Tools** at the start of this section. Do not attempt to drive the crankshaft into the left main bearing. Doing so will affect crankshaft alignment.*

1. Lubricate the crankshaft main bearing with oil.

2. Insert the crankshaft into the main bearing.

3. Install the threaded adapter into the end of the crankshaft.

4. Install the crankshaft puller assembly (**Figure 117**) onto the end of the crankshaft and thread it into the threaded adapter. Center the tool assembly on the main bearing inner race.

> *CAUTION*
> *When installing the crankshaft in Step 5, position the connecting rod at top dead center. Otherwise, the connecting rod may contact the side of the crankcase, causing damage.*

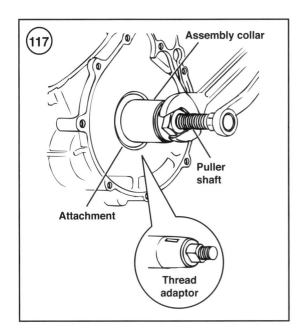

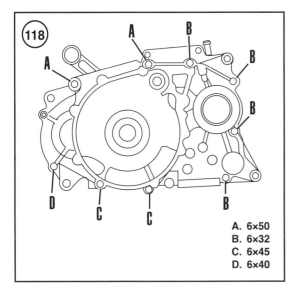

A. 6×50
B. 6×32
C. 6×45
D. 6×40

5. Hold the threaded adapter and turn the puller shaft (**Figure 117**) to pull the crankshaft into the main bearing. When installing the crankshaft, frequently check that it is going straight into the bearing and not binding to one side.

6. Continue to turn the puller shaft until the crankshaft bottoms against the main bearing. Remove the crankshaft tools and turn the crankshaft. The crankshaft must turn with no binding or roughness.

Crankcase Assembly

1. Apply assembly oil to the inner race of all bearings in both crankcase halves and to the crankshaft main bearings.

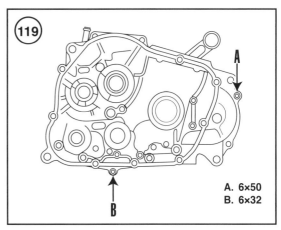

A. 6×50
B. 6×32

NOTE
Set the crankcase half assembly on wood blocks or the wood holding fixture shown in the disassembly procedure.

2. Install the balancer as described in this chapter. Rotate the crankshaft and balancer several times and check for proper timing and smooth operation.

3. Install the transmission assemblies, shift shafts and shift drum in the left crankcase half as described in Chapter Seven. Lubricate all transmission components with engine oil.

NOTE
Make sure the crankcase mating surfaces are clean and free of all old sealant material.

4. Install the locating dowels if they were removed and install a new crankcase gasket.

5. Set the right crankcase half onto the left crankcase half. Push it down squarely into place until it reaches the crankshaft bearing. There is usually about 1/2 inch gap between the halves.

6. Lightly tap the case halves together with a rubber mallet until they mate.

CAUTION
The crankcase halves should fit together without force. Do not attempt to pull the case halves together with the crankcase fasteners. Separate the crankcase and investigate the cause of the interference. If the transmission shafts were disassembled, recheck to make sure that a gear is not installed backwards.

7. After the crankcase halves are completely mated, rotate the crankshaft and transmission shafts to make sure there is no binding. If any is present, disassemble the crankcase and correct the problem.

8. Install the left crankcase half bolts (**Figure 118**). Tighten only fingertight.

9. Securely tighten the bolts in two stages in a crossing pattern to the specification in **Table 3**.

10. Install the bolts into the right crankcase half (**Figure 119**) and tighten to the specification in **Table 3**.

11. After the crankcase halves are completely assembled, again rotate the crankshaft and transmission shafts to make sure there is no binding. If any is present, disassemble the crankcase and correct the problem.

12. After a new crankcase gasket has been installed it must be trimmed. Carefully trim off all excess gasket material where the cylinder base gasket comes in contact with the crankcase. If it is not trimmed the cylinder base gasket will not seal properly.

13. Feed the camshaft chain down through the top of the chain opening in the crankcase and install the chain (A, **Figure 97**) onto the crankshaft sprocket (B). Make sure it is correctly engaged with the sprocket.

14. Install the following components as described in this chapter or the indicated chapter:
   a. Camshaft chain.
   b. Primary gear.
   c. External shift mechanism (Chapter Six).
   d. Oil pump.
   e. Clutch assembly (Chapter Six).
   f. Kickstarter (XR600R models).
   g. Alternator.
   h. Cylinder and piston.
   i. Cylinder head.
   j. Camshaft and tensioner.
   k. Cylinder head cover.
   l. Starter (XR650L models [Chapter Nine]).

ENGINE BREAK-IN

If the piston rings or a new piston were installed, the cylinder was honed or bored, or major lower end work was performed, break in the engine as if new. The performance and service life of the engine depends greatly on a careful and sensible break-in.

For the first 5-10 hours of operation, use no more than one-third throttle and vary the speed as much as possible within the one-third throttle limit. Avoid prolonged or steady running at one speed as well as hard acceleration.

Table 1 ENGINE SPECIFICATIONS

Crankshaft type	Two main journals, unit type
Engine weight (approximate)	51 kg (112 lb.)
Lubrication system	Dry sump, forced pressure

Table 2 ENGINE LOWER END SERVICE SPECIFICATIONS

	New mm (in.)	Service limit mm (in.)
Connecting rod big end radial clearance	0.006-0.018 (0.0002-0.0007)	0.05 (0.002)
Connecting rod side clearance		
XR600R	0.050-0.650 (0.0020-0.0256)	0.80 (0.031)
XR650L	0.05-0.450 (0.002-0.018)	0.60 (0.024)
Connecting rod small end inside diameter	24.020-24.041 (0.9457-0.9465)	24.07 (0.948)
Crankshaft runout*	–	0.10 (0.004)
Oil pump		
Outer rotor-to-cover clearance	0.15-0.21 (0.006-0.008)	0.25 (0.010)
Tip clearance	0.15 (0.006)	0.20 (0.008)
Side clearance	0.02-0.08 (0.001-0.003)	0.12 (0.005)
Starter driven gear OD	57.755-57.768 (2.2738-2.2743)	57.66 (2.270)
Kickstarter		
Idle gear ID	20.000-20.021 (0.7874-0.7882)	20.11 (0.792)
Idle gear bushing		
ID	16.000-16.018 (0.6299-0.6306)	16.03 (0.631)
OD	19.959-19.980 (0.7859-0.7866)	19.90 (0.783)
Gear ID	25.500-25.521 (1.0039-1.0048)	25.58 (1.007)
Shaft OD (at gear location)	21.959-21.980 (0.8645-0.8653)	21.91 (0.863)

*Measure crankshaft runout at each end at a point 6 mm (0.24 in.) in from either crankshaft end

Table 3 ENGINE TORQUE SPECIFICATIONS

	N•m	in.-lb.	ft.-lb.
Crankcase bolts			
XR600R and 1993-2007 XR650L	12	106	–
2008-on XR650L	NA	NA	–
Engine mounts			
XR600R and XR650L (1993 - 2007)			
8 mm	27	–	20
10 mm	50	–	37
XR650L (2008-on)			
8 mm	26	–	19
10 mm	49	–	36
Flywheel bolt			
1993 - 2007	125	–	92
2008-on	123	–	91
Gearshift pedal bolt	12	106	–
Left crankcase cover bolts			
XR600R and 1993-2007 XR650L	12	106	–
2008-on XR650L	NA	NA	–
Left mainshaft bearing			
retainer bolt (2008-on)	12	106	–
Right mainshaft bearing			
retainer bolt (2008-on)	25	–	18
Oil fitting in frame			
1993 - 2007	55	–	41
2008-on	54	–	40
Oil line fittings			
1993- 2007	40	–	30
2008-on	39	–	29
Primary gear nut			
1993- 2007	110	–	81
2008-on	108	–	80
Starter one way clutch mounting bolts (XR650L)			
1993- 2007	30	–	22
2008-on	29	–	21

5

CHAPTER SIX

CLUTCH AND EXTERNAL SHIFT MECHANISM

This chapter provides service procedures for the clutch, clutch release mechanism and external shift mechanism. Specifications are in **Table 1** and **Table 2** located at the end of this chapter.

The clutch is a wet (operates in the engine oil) multi-plate design. The clutch assembly is located on the right side of the engine. The clutch hub is mounted on the splines on the transmission mainshaft. The primary drive gear, which is mounted on the splines of the crankshaft, drives the clutch outer housing.

Clutch release is via a pushrod assembly operating on the pressure plate. The pushrod passes through the transmission mainshaft and is activated by the clutch cable pulling on the clutch release mechanism mounted in the left crankcase cover. This system requires routine adjustment (Chapter Three) to compensate for cable stretch.

CLUTCH CABLE

Replacement

1. Move the rubber boot away from the clutch lever assembly.
2. Increase cable free play by loosening the adjuster nut (A, **Figure 1**), then screwing in the cable adjuster (B).

3. On XR600R models, loosen both cable nuts on the lower end of the clutch cable (**Figure 2**).
4. On XR650L models, loosen the right nut on the lower end of the clutch cable (**Figure 3**).
5. Detach the lower end of the clutch cable from the clutch actuating lever.
6. On models equipped with a hand guard, remove the hand guard retaining bolt (**Figure 4**). Remove the clutch lever pivot bolt nut, then remove the hand guard.
7. Detach the clutch cable from the clutch lever.
8. While noting the routing, remove the clutch cable.
9. Reverse the removal steps to install the clutch cable while noting the following:
   a. Make sure the cable passes through the retainer loops on the steering head and cylinder head cover.
   b. Lubricate the cable.
   c. Adjust the cable free play as described in Chapter Three.

RIGHT CRANKCASE COVER

Removal/Installation

1. Support the motorcycle securely.
2. Drain the engine oil as described in Chapter Three.
3. Remove the frame guard as described in Chapter Sixteen.

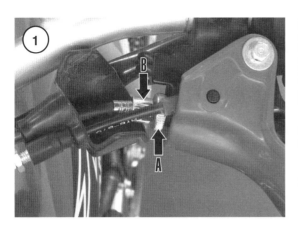

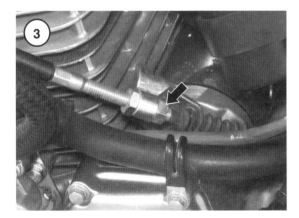

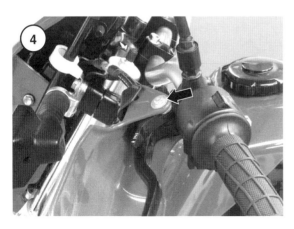

4. Remove the rear brake pedal as described in Chapter Fifteen.

5. On XR600R models, remove the bolt securing the kickstarter pedal and remove the kickstarter pedal.

6. Remove the oil tube bolt and washers (**Figure 5**).

7. Remove the bolts and nuts securing the right crankcase cover (A, **Figure 6**). Remove the right crankcase cover and gasket. Do not lose the locating dowels.

NOTE
*The oil tube and O-ring (A, **Figure 7**)*
may remain in the cover during removal.

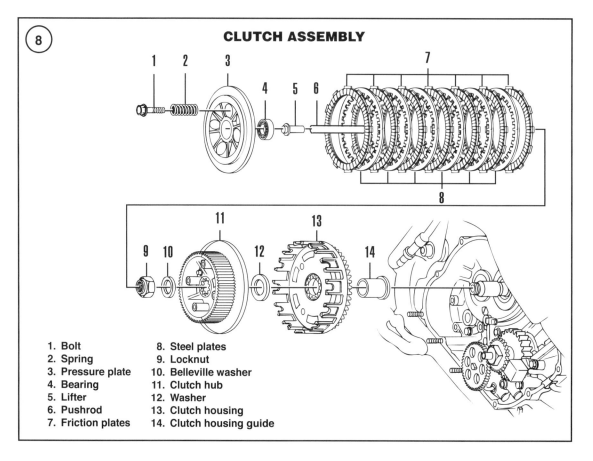

CLUTCH ASSEMBLY

1. Bolt
2. Spring
3. Pressure plate
4. Bearing
5. Lifter
6. Pushrod
7. Friction plates
8. Steel plates
9. Locknut
10. Belleville washer
11. Clutch hub
12. Washer
13. Clutch housing
14. Clutch housing guide

8. Reverse the preceding steps to install the right crankcase cover. Note the following:

   a. Make sure the oil tube and O-ring (A, **Figure 7**) are installed in the cover or in the oil pump (Chapter Five).

   b. Long bolts are located at the front and rear ends (B, **Figure 6**) of the cover.

   c. The rear brake switch holder is retained by the crankcase cover bolt (C, **Figure 6**).

   d. Tighten the cover bolts and nuts to 12 N•m (106 in.-lb.).

   e. Install new washers on the oil tube bolt (**Figure 5**). Tighten the bolt securely.

Inspection

The right crankcase cover contains the oil filter and an oil passage to the oil pump.

1. Inspect the oil passage seal (B, **Figure 7**).
2. To replace the oil seal, remove the snap ring (C, **Figure 7**). Pry the seal out of the crankcase cover. Be careful not to damage the cover.

CLUTCH

Removal/Disassembly

The clutch assembly (**Figure 8**) can be removed with the engine in the frame.

1. Remove the right crankcase cover as described in this chapter.
2. Using a crossing pattern, loosen the clutch pressure plate bolts (**Figure 9**).
3. Remove the bolts (A, **Figure 10**) and clutch springs (B).
4. Remove the pressure plate (**Figure 11**).
5. Remove the friction plates and steel plates (**Figure 12**).
6. Remove the clutch lifter (**Figure 13**) and the pushrod (**Figure 14**) from the transmission

> *CAUTION*
> *Do not clamp the clutch holder too tight as it may damage the grooves in the clutch hub.*

7. To prevent the clutch hub from turning in the next step, attach a clutch holder tool (A, **Figure 15**) to the clutch hub.
8. Using a suitable punch, lift the staked portion of the locknut away from the mainshaft. Remove the locknut (B, **Figure 15**). If necessary, use a die grinder to unstake the locknut. Cover the parts so that metal particles do not enter the clutch or engine.
9. Remove the clutch holder from the clutch hub.
10. Remove the Belleville washer (A, **Figure 16**).

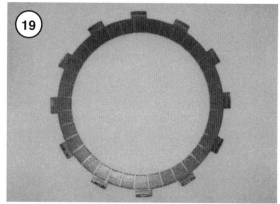

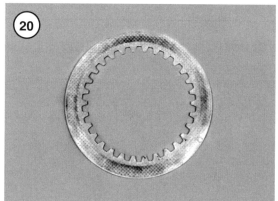

11. Remove the clutch hub (B, **Figure 16**).

12. Remove the washer (A, **Figure 17**) and the clutch housing (B).

13. Slide off the clutch housing guide (**Figure 18**).

14. Inspect all components as described in this section.

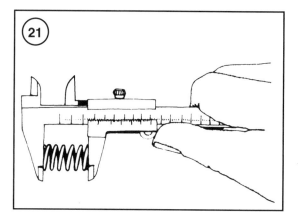

Inspection

The clutch contains two types of clutch plates: friction plates (**Figure 19**) and steel plates (**Figure 20**).

1. Clean clutch parts in solvent and dry thoroughly with compressed air.

2. Measure the free length of each clutch spring as shown in **Figure 21**. Replace any springs that have sagged to the service limit or less.

3. Measure the thickness of each friction plate at several places around the disc as shown in **Figure 22**. Replace any disc that is worn to the service limit or less.

4. Check the steel plates for warp on a flat surface such as a piece of glass (**Figure 23**). Replace any plate that is warped to the service limit or more.

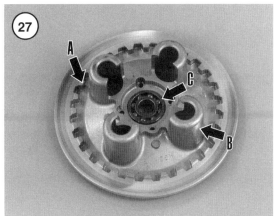

6

NOTE
If any of the friction plates, steel plates or clutch springs require replacement, consider replacing all of them as a set to retain maximum clutch performance.

5. Inspect the slots in the clutch housing (**Figure 24**) for cracks, nicks or galling where they come in contact with the friction plate tabs. If severe damage is evident, replace the housing.

6. Inspect the gear teeth on the housing for damage (A, **Figure 25**). Remove any small nicks with an oilstone. If damage is severe, replace the housing. Also check the teeth on the crankshaft primary drive gear.

7. Inspect the damper springs (B, **Figure 25**). If they are sagged or broken, replace the housing.

8. Measure the inside diameter of the clutch housing. Compare to the service limit in **Table 1**; replace if worn.

9. Measure the inside diameter and the outside diameter of the housing guide (**Figure 26**). Compare to the service limit in **Table 1**; replace if worn.

10. Inspect the slots (A, **Figure 27**) and spring holders (B) in the pressure plate. If either show signs of wear or galling, replace the pressure plate.

11. Inspect the clutch release bearing in the pressure plate (C, **Figure 27**). Replace the bearing if it is rough or otherwise damaged.

12. Inspect the inner splines and outer grooves in the clutch hub (**Figure 28**). If damaged, replace the clutch hub.

13. Inspect the clutch pushrod for bending. Roll it on a flat surface such as a piece of glass. If the rod is bent or deformed in any way, replace it. Otherwise, it may bind in the transmission shaft, causing erratic clutch operation.

14. Inspect the clutch lifter. The concave end must be smooth. Replace the clutch lifter if damaged.

Assembly/Installation

Refer to **Figure 8**.

NOTE
If new friction plates and clutch plates
are being installed, apply new engine
oil to all surfaces.

1. Lubricate the clutch housing guide with engine oil. Install the guide so the flanged end is to the inside (**Figure 18**).
2. Install the clutch housing (B, **Figure 17**) onto the guide.
3. Install the washer (A, **Figure 17**).
4. Install the clutch hub (B, **Figure 16**).
5. Install the Belleville washer (A, **Figure 16**) with the OUTSIDE mark facing toward the outside.
6. Lubricate the threads, then install the clutch locknut (B, **Figure 15**).
7. Hold the clutch hub and tighten the clutch locknut to the specification in **Table 2**.
8. Install the clutch pushrod (**Figure 14**).
9. Install the clutch lifter (**Figure 13**).
10. Install a friction plate and then a steel plate onto the clutch hub.
11. Continue to install the friction plates and steel plates, alternating them until all are installed. The last plate installed is a friction plate.
12. Install the pressure plate (**Figure 11**).
13. Install the clutch bolts (A, **Figure 10**) and the clutch springs (B).
14. Tighten the bolts in a crossing pattern in two to three steps to 12 N•m (106 in.-lb.).
15. Install the right crankcase cover as described in this chapter.

CLUTCH RELEASE LEVER

The clutch cable connects the clutch hand lever to the clutch release lever. The clutch release lever forces the clutch pushrod against the clutch lifter on the clutch pressure plate, thereby disengaging the clutch when the clutch hand lever is pulled. The clutch release lever is mounted in the left crankcase cover.

Removal/Installation

1. Refer to *Flywheel* in Chapter Five and remove the left crankcase cover.
2. Check the movement of the clutch release lever assembly in the crankcase cover. If the lever binds or the return spring is weak or broken, replace it.
3. Remove the clutch lifter (**Figure 29**) from the crankcase cover.
4. Remove the release lever (A, **Figure 30**), spring (B) and washer (C) from the cover.

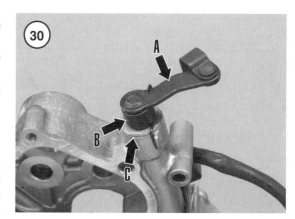

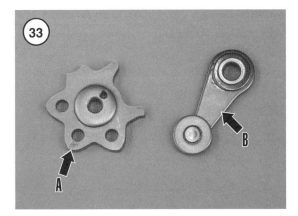

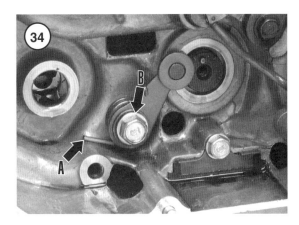

5. Inspect the oil seal (A, **Figure 31**) and bearing (B). Replace if damaged.

6. Install the clutch release lever by reversing the removal steps. Lubricate the lifter piece (**Figure 29**) with molybdenum disulfide oil and install it with the concave end facing out so it mates correctly with the clutch pushrod.

EXTERNAL SHIFT MECHANISM

The external shift mechanism is located on the same side of the crankcase as the clutch assembly. To remove the internal shift mechanism (shift levers, shift drum and shift forks), it is necessary to remove the engine and split the crankcase as described in Chapter Five.

Removal

1. Remove the clutch assembly as described in this chapter.

2. On XR600R models, remove the kickstarter assembly as described in Chapter Five.

3. Remove the bolt (A, **Figure 32**) securing the gearshift cam and remove the cam (B).

4. Remove the bolt (C, **Figure 32**) securing the stopper arm (D) and remove the arm.

Inspection

1. Inspect the ramps of the gearshift cam (A, **Figure 33**). They must be smooth and free from burrs or wear; replace as necessary.

2. Inspect the roller on the stopper arm (B, **Figure 33**). It must rotate smoothly with no signs of wear or binding; replace as necessary.

Installation

1. Install the stopper arm and spring onto the crankcase. Note the position of the spring (A, **Figure 34**). Make sure to install the washer (B, **Figure 34**) on the bolt. Tighten the bolt to 25 N•m (18 ft.-lb.).

2. Hold the stopper arm back and out of the way with a screwdriver.

3. Align the indexing hole in the backside of the gearshift cam with the dowel pin on the shift drum (**Figure 35**). Apply a medium strength threadlock to the bolt threads, then install the gearshift cam and bolt (A, **Figure 32**). Tighten the bolt to 12 N•m (106 in.-lb.).

4. Remove the screwdriver and allow the stopper arm to rest against the gearshift cam.

5. On XR600R models, install the kickstarter as described in Chapter Five.

6. Install the clutch assembly as described in this chapter.

Table 1 CLUTCH SERVICE SPECIFICATIONS

	New mm (in.)	Service limit mm (in.)
Clutch spring free length	44.7 (1.76)	43.1 (1.70)
Friction plate thickness	2.92-3.08 (0.115-0.121)	2.6 (0.10)
Clutch steel plate warp	–	0.15 (0.006)
Clutch housing guide		
Outside diameter	26.959-26.980 (1.0614-1.0622)	26.91 (1.059)
Inside diameter		
1993 - 2007	21.990-22.035 (0.8657-0.8675)	22.05 (0.868)
2008-on	21.990-22.040 (0.8657-0.8677)	22.05 (0.868)
Mainshaft outside diameter at housing guide	21.967-21.980 (0.8648-0.8654)	21.93 (0.863)

Table 2 CLUTCH TORQUE SPECIFICATIONS

	N•m	in.-lb.	ft.-lb.
Clutch locknut			
1993 - 2007	120	–	89
2008-on	118	–	87
Clutch pressure plate bolts	12	106	–
Crankcase cover bolts and nuts	12	106	–
Gearshift cam bolt	12	106	–
Gearshift stopper arm bolt	25	–	18

CHAPTER SEVEN

TRANSMISSION AND INTERNAL SHIFT MECHANISM

This chapter covers the transmission and internal gearshift assemblies. Specifications are in **Tables 1-3** at the end of this chapter.

TRANSMISSION

To gain access to the transmission and internal shift mechanism, it is necessary to remove the engine and disassemble the crankcase as described in Chapter Five.

When the clutch is engaged, the mainshaft is driven by the clutch hub, which is driven by the primary crankshaft drive gear/clutch outer housing. Power flows from the mainshaft through the selected gear combination to the countershaft, which drives the engine drive sprocket.

Removal/Installation

1. Remove the engine and separate the crankcase as described in Chapter Five.
2. Pull back on the gearshift plate (A, **Figure 1**) of the gearshift mechanism to disengage it from the shift drum. Pull up the shift shaft (B, **Figure 1**) and remove the gearshift assembly.
3. Bend down the locking tab (A, **Figure 2**) on the lockplate and remove the bolt (B) and lockplate securing the center shift fork to the shift fork shaft. Discard the lockplate.

4. Pull the shift fork shaft (A, **Figure 3**) out of the crankcase.
5. Pivot the shift forks away from the shift drum (B, **Figure 3**) to allow for shift drum removal.
6. Remove the shift drum and the shift forks.
7. Remove both transmission assemblies.
8. Inspect the shift fork assembly as described in this section.

NOTE
During assembly lubricate all moving contact surfaces with clean engine oil.

9. Install the transmission assemblies as follows:
   a. Mesh both transmission assemblies together in their proper relationship to each other (**Figure 4**).
   b. Hold the thrust washers in place on both shaft assemblies and install the assembled shafts into the left crankcase half (**Figure 5**).
   c. Make sure the thrust washer on both shaft assemblies is still positioned correctly after the assemblies are completely installed. If the thrust washers are not seated correctly, they will prevent the crankcase halves from seating completely.
   d. After both assemblies are installed, tap on the end of both shafts with a plastic or soft-faced mallet to make sure they are completely seated.

10. Identify the shift forks according to position. Each shift fork has a letter L, C or R cast onto it (**Figure 6**) to indicate left, center or right respectively.

11. Install the left shift fork (A, **Figure 7**), center shift fork (B) and right shift fork (C) into the gear slots. The identifying letter on each fork must be up (toward right end of transmission shafts).

NOTE
It may be necessary to move the sliding gears up the transmission shafts so the shift fork pins will fit into the shift drum slots in Step 12.

12. Install the shift drum (**Figure 8**). Insert the end pins of the shift forks into the corresponding slots in the shift drum.

13. Align the bolt hole in the shift fork shaft and the hole in the center shift fork and install the shift fork shaft (**Figure 9**).

14. Install the shift fork shaft bolt and new lockplate (B, **Figure 2**) and tighten to 15 N•m (133 in.-lb.).

15. Bend one of the tabs on the new lockplate so it is against the side of the bolt.

16. Install the gearshift mechanism as follows:

   a. Partially install the gearshift assembly with the splined end (for the gearshift pedal) into the left crankcase half.

   b. Pull back on the shift plate and push the shift mechanism all the way down into position.

   c. Release the shift plate and engage it correctly into the shift drum (**Figure 1**).

17. Turn both transmission shafts. Make sure there is no binding.

18. Tilt the left crankcase half and transmission assemblies up to about a 45° angle from horizontal. This will relieve some of the weight of the gears against each other so the gears will shift properly.

19. Turn the transmission shafts and shift through all five gears using the shift drum. Make sure all gears properly engage. Ensure everything is installed correctly, before the crankcase is completely assembled.

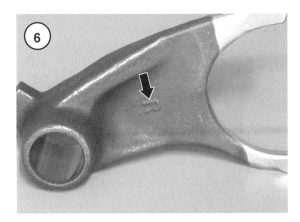

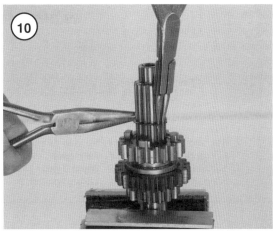

20. Make sure the thrust washer is installed on the end of the countershaft.

21. Reassemble the crankcase and install the engine as described in Chapter Five.

Preliminary Inspection

1. Clean and dry the shaft assembly before inspection.

2. Before disassembling the transmission shafts, perform the following:

   a. Rotate each fixed gear and slide each grooved gear on its shaft. Any roughness or binding may indicate a problem with a gear bore, bushing or shaft.

   b. Hold each transmission shaft, one at a time, and lock each sliding gear against its fixed gear.

   c. Visually check the engagement between the gear dogs on both gears. The dogs should be pointed.

3. Parts with two different sides, such as gears, snap rings and shift forks, can be installed backward. To maintain the correct alignment and position of the parts during disassembly, store each part in order and in a divided container.

4. Before removing the snap rings, try to turn them without spreading them. If they can turn, the thrust washer installed beside the snap ring is probably worn.

5. Because snap rings fatigue and distort during removal, do not reuse them, although they may appear to be in good condition. Install new snap rings during reassembly.

6. To install new snap rings without distorting them, open the new snap ring with a pair of snap ring pliers while holding the back of the snap ring with a pair of pliers (**Figure 10**). Slide the snap ring down the shaft and seat it into the correct groove. This technique can also be used to remove snap rings from a shaft once they are free from their grooves.

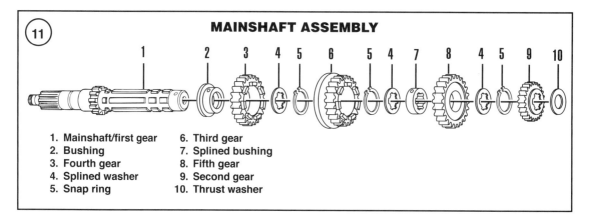

MAINSHAFT ASSEMBLY

1. Mainshaft/first gear
2. Bushing
3. Fourth gear
4. Splined washer
5. Snap ring
6. Third gear
7. Splined bushing
8. Fifth gear
9. Second gear
10. Thrust washer

Mainshaft Disassembly/Inspection/Assembly

Refer to **Figure 11** and **Figure 12** when performing this procedure. Mark the parts with a grease pencil or metal marking pen so they can be installed facing in their original operating position.

1. Hold the mainshaft to keep the parts from sliding off, then clean in solvent and dry with compressed air.

2. Remove the thrust washer (A, **Figure 13**) and second gear (B).

3. Remove the snap ring (A, **Figure 14**) and the splined washer (B).

4. Remove the fifth gear (C, **Figure 14**).

5. Remove the bushing (A, **Figure 15**), splined washer (B) and snap ring (C).

6. Remove the third gear (**Figure 16**).

7. Remove the snap ring (A, **Figure 17**) and splined washer (B).

8. Remove the fourth gear and bushing (C, **Figure 17**).

9. Inspect each gear for excessive wear, burrs, pitting, or chipped or missing teeth.

> *NOTE*
> *Replace defective gears. It is a good idea to replace the mating gear on the countershaft even though it may not show as much wear or damage.*

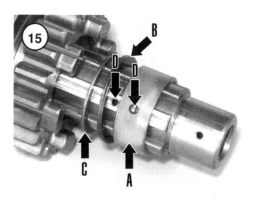

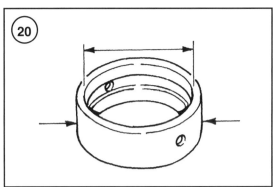

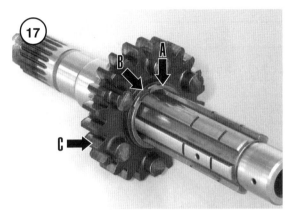

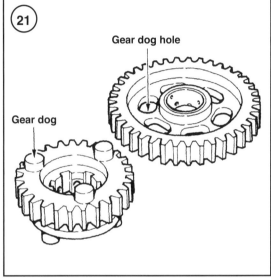

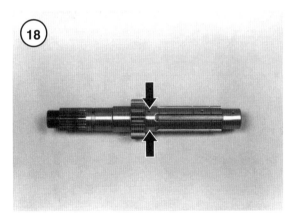

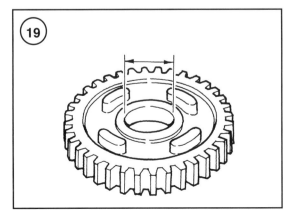

NOTE
The first gear is part of the mainshaft.
Replace the shaft if the gear is defective.

10. Make sure all gears slide smoothly on the mainshaft splines.

11. Measure the outside diameter of the mainshaft at the position shown in **Figure 18**. If the shaft is worn to the service limit in **Table 1** or less, replace the shaft.

12. Measure the inside diameter of the mainshaft fourth and fifth gears (**Figure 19**). If either gear is worn to the service limit in **Table 1** or greater, replace the gear.

13. Measure the outside diameter of the mainshaft fifth gear bushing (**Figure 20**). If the bushing is worn to the service limit in **Table 1** or less, replace the bushing.

14. Measure the inside and outside diameter of the fourth gear bushing. Replace the bushing if it is worn to or beyond the service limit in **Table 1**.

15. Inspect the gear dogs and holes on the gears (**Figure 21**) for rounded or damaged edges. Pay particular attention to the sides that carry the engine

load. Any wear on the dogs or slots should be uniform. If the dogs are not worn evenly, the dogs may fail. Check the engagement of the dogs by placing the gears at their appropriate positions on the shaft, then twist the gears together. Check for positive engagement in both directions. Rounded dogs will cause the transmission to jump out of gear. If damage is evident, also check the condition of the shift forks.

NOTE
*When installing the snap rings, align the end gap with a shaft groove (***Figure 22***).*

NOTE
The snap rings and washers have a flat side and a beveled or rounded side. Refer to **Figure 23** *during assembly.*

16. To assemble the mainshaft, install the fourth gear bushing on the mainshaft with the shoulder side going on first.
17. Install the fourth gear (C, **Figure 17**) with the shift dogs toward the unthreaded shaft end.
18. Install the splined washer (B, **Figure 17**) and snap ring (A).
19. Install the third gear (**Figure 16**) with the shift dogs toward the unthreaded shaft end. Then install the snap ring (C, **Figure 15**) and splined washer (B).
20. Align the oil holes (D, **Figure 15**) in the bushing and the mainshaft, and install the bushing (A) onto mainshaft.
21. Install the fifth gear (C, **Figure 14**) so the side containing the dog slots faces the third gear.
22. Install the splined washer (B, **Figure 14**) and snap ring (A).
23. Install the second gear (B, **Figure 13**) and the thrust washer (A).
24. Before installation, check the placement of all gears (**Figure 12**). Make sure all snap rings are seated correctly in the mainshaft grooves.
25. Make sure each gear engages properly with the adjoining gear where applicable.

Countershaft Disassembly/Inspection/Assembly

Refer to **Figure 24** and **Figure 25** when performing this procedure. Mark the parts with a grease pencil or metal marking pen so they can be installed facing their original operating position.
1. Hold the countershaft to keep the parts from sliding off, then clean in solvent and dry with compressed air.
2. Remove the thrust washer (A, **Figure 26**), second gear (B) and bushing (**Figure 27**).
3. Remove the fifth gear (**Figure 28**).

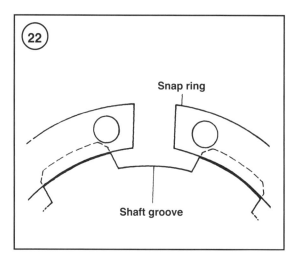

Snap ring

Shaft groove

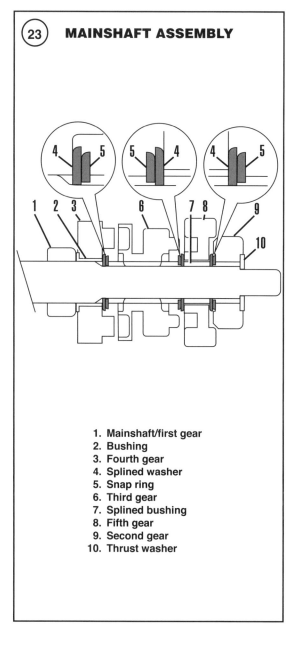

MAINSHAFT ASSEMBLY

1. Mainshaft/first gear
2. Bushing
3. Fourth gear
4. Splined washer
5. Snap ring
6. Third gear
7. Splined bushing
8. Fifth gear
9. Second gear
10. Thrust washer

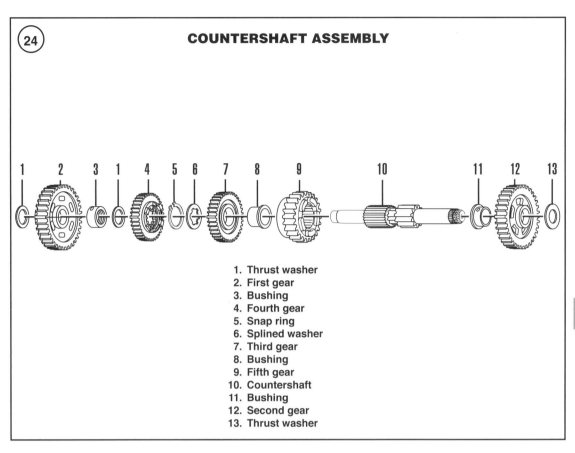

COUNTERSHAFT ASSEMBLY

24

1. Thrust washer
2. First gear
3. Bushing
4. Fourth gear
5. Snap ring
6. Splined washer
7. Third gear
8. Bushing
9. Fifth gear
10. Countershaft
11. Bushing
12. Second gear
13. Thrust washer

7

25

27

26

28

4. From the other end of the shaft, remove the thrust washer (A, **Figure 29**) and first gear (B).

5. Remove the first gear bushing (A, **Figure 30**), thrust washer (B) and fourth gear (C).

6. Remove the snap ring (A, **Figure 31**) and splined washer (B).

7. Remove the third gear (**Figure 32**) and bushing (**Figure 33**).

8. Inspect each gear for excessive wear, burrs, pitting, or chipped or missing teeth.

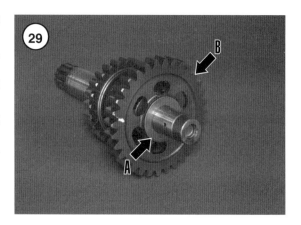

> *NOTE*
> *Replace defective gears. It is a good idea to replace the mating gear on the mainshaft even though it may not show as much wear or damage.*

9. Make sure that all gears slide smoothly on the countershaft splines.

10. Measure the outside diameter of the countershaft at the points shown in **Figure 34**. If the shaft is worn to the service limit in **Table 1** or less at any location, replace the shaft.

11. Measure the inside diameter of the first, second and third gears (**Figure 19**). Replace any gear that is worn to or greater than the service limit in **Table 1**.

12. Measure the inside and outside diameter of the first and second gear bushings (**Figure 20**). Replace any bushing that is worn to or beyond the service limit in **Table 4**.

13. Inspect the engagement dogs and slots on the gears (**Figure 21**) for rounded or damaged edges. Pay particular attention to the side of the gear dogs that carries the engine load. Any wear on the dogs or slots should be uniform. If the dogs are not worn evenly, the dogs may fail. Check the engagement of the dogs by placing the gears at their appropriate positions on the shaft, then twist the gears together. Check for positive engagement in both directions. Rounded dogs will cause the transmission to jump out of gear. If damage is evident, also check the condition of the shift forks.

14. To assemble the countershaft, install the third gear bushing so the flanged end contacts the shoulder on the countershaft (**Figure 33**).

15. Install the third gear (**Figure 32**) so the dog slots are toward the unsplined end of the shaft.

> *NOTE*
> *The snap ring and thrust washer in Step 16 have a flat side and a beveled or rounded side. Install the snap ring and thrust washer so the rounded side is toward the third gear.*

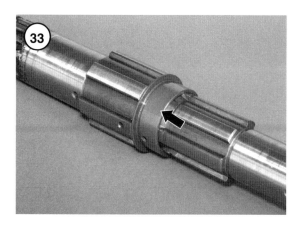

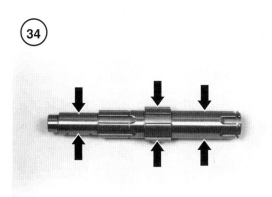

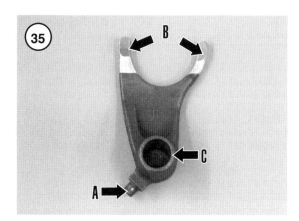

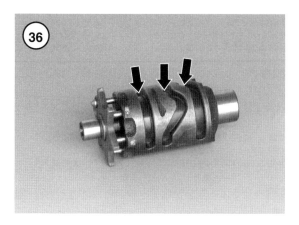

16. Install the splined washer (B, **Figure 31**) and snap ring (A). When installing the snap ring, align the end gap with a shaft groove (**Figure 22**).

17. Install the fourth gear (C, **Figure 30**) so the shift groove end is toward the third gear.

18. Install the thrust washer (B, **Figure 30**) and the first gear bushing (A).

19. Install the first gear (B, **Figure 29**) so the side with the deeper recess is toward the fourth gear.

20. Install the thrust washer (A, **Figure 29**).

21. Onto the opposite end of the shaft, install the fifth gear (**Figure 28**).

22. Install the second gear bushing (**Figure 27**) so the flanged end contacts the shoulder on the countershaft.

23. Install the second gear (B, **Figure 26**) with the raised side toward the shaft end, and then the thrust washer (A).

24. Before installation, check the placement of all gears (**Figure 25**). Make sure the snap ring is seated correctly in the mainshaft groove.

25. Make sure each gear engages properly with the adjoining gear where applicable.

7

INTERNAL SHIFT MECHANISM

Remove and install the internal shift mechanism as described under *Transmission* in this chapter.

Inspection

> *CAUTION*
> *Worn forks can cause the transmission to slip out of gear, leading to extensive damage. Replace questionable shift forks.*

1. Inspect each shift fork (**Figure 35**) for signs of wear or cracking. Check for bending and make sure each fork slides smoothly on the shaft; replace any worn or damaged forks.

2. Check for any arc-shaped wear or burned marks on the shift forks. This indicates that the shift fork has come in contact with the gear. If the fork fingers are excessively worn, replace the fork.

3. Check the grooves in the shift drum (**Figure 36**) for wear or roughness. If any of the groove profiles have excessive wear or damage, replace the shift drum.

4. Check the drum followers (A, **Figure 35**) on each shift fork for wear or damage; replace as necessary.

5. Measure the outside diameter of the gearshift fork shafts. Replace a shaft if worn to the service limit listed in **Table 2** or less.

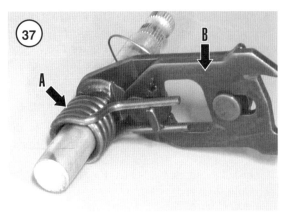

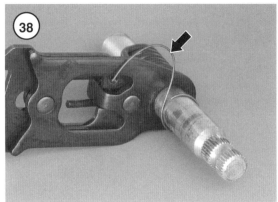

6. Roll each shift fork shaft on a flat surface such as a piece of glass and check for any damage. Replace a bent shaft.

7. Measure the width of the shift fork fingers (B, **Figure 35**). Replace forks that are worn to the service limit in **Table 2** or less.

8. Measure the inside diameter of the shift forks (C, **Figure 35**). Replace shafts that are worn to the service limit in **Table 2** or greater.

9. Apply a light coat of oil to the shift fork shafts and the inside bores of the shift forks before installation.

10. Inspect the shift mechanism for wear or damage. Make sure the return spring (A, **Figure 37**) and reset spring (**Figure 38**) have not sagged or broken; replace as necessary.

11. Move the shift plate back and forth (B, **Figure 37**). It must move freely with no binding. Replace the shift mechanism if necessary.

Table 1 TRANSMISSION SPECIFICATIONS

	New mm (in.)	Service limit mm (in.)
Transmission gears inside diameter		
Mainshaft		
Fourth gear	28.020-28.041 (1.1031-1.1040)	28.10 (1.106)
Fifth gear	28.000-28.021 (1.1024-1.1032)	28.08 (1.106)
Countershaft		
First gear	25.020-25.041 (0.9850-0.9859)	25.10 (0.988)
Second gear	28.020-28.041 (1.1031-1.1040)	28.10 (1.106)
Third gear	28.020-28.041 (1.1031-1.1040)	28.10 (1.106)
Bushings		
Mainshaft		
Fourth gear outside diameter	27.979-28.000 (1.1015-1.1024)	27.93 (1.100)
Fourth gear inside diameter	25.020-25.041 (0.9850-0.9859)	25.10 (0.988)
Fifth gear outside diameter	27.949-27.980 (1.1004-1.1016)	27.90 (1.098)
Countershaft		
First gear inside diameter	20.020-20.041 (0.7882-0.7890)	20.01 (0.788)
First gear outside diameter	24.984-25.005 (0.9836-0.9844)	24.93 (0.981)
Second gear inside diameter	25.020-25.041 (0.9850-0.9859)	25.10 (0.988)
Second gear outside diameter	27.979-28.000 (1.1015-1.1024)	27.93 (1.100)
Third gear inside diameter	25.020-25.041 (0.9850-0.9859)	25.10 (0.988)
Third gear outside diameter	27.979-28.000 (1.1015-1.1024)	27.93 (1.100)
Bushing-to-shaft clearance		
Mainshaft		
Fourth gear	0.040-0.082 (0.0016-0.0032)	0.10 (0.004)
Countershaft		
First gear	0.027-0.061 (0.0011-0.0024)	0.10 (0.004)
Second gear	0.027-0.069 (0.0011-0.0027)	0.10 (0.004)
Third gear	0.040-0.082 (0.0016-0.0032)	0.10 (0.004)

(continued)

Table 1 TRANSMISSION SPECIFICATIONS (continued)

	New mm (in.)	Service limit mm (in.)
Gear-to-bushing clearance		
Mainshaft		
Fourth gear	0.020-0.062 (0.0008-0.0024)	0.10 (0.004)
Fifth gear	0.020-0.072 (0.0008-0.0028)	0.10 (0.004)
Countershaft		
First gear	0.015.0.057 (0.0006-0.0022)	0.10 (0.004)
Second gear	0.020-0.062 (0.0008-0.0024)	0.10 (0.004)
Third gear (2008-on)	0.020-0.062 (0.0008-0.0024)	0.10 (0.004)
Mainshaft outside diameter at:		
Fourth gear bushing		
1993 - 2007	24.972-24.993 (0.9831-0.9840)	24.92 (0.981)
2008-on	24.959-24.980 (0.9826-0.9835)	24.92 (0.981)
Countershaft outside diameter location:		
First gear bushing	19.980-19.993 (0.7866-0.7871)	19.94 (0.785)
Second gear bushing	24.972-24.993 (0.9831-0.9840)	24.92 (0.981)
Third gear bushing	24.959-24.980 (0.9826-0.9835)	24.92 (0.981)

7

Table 2 SHIFT FORK AND SHAFT SPECIFICATIONS

	New mm (in.)	Service limit mm (in.)
Shift fork inside diameter		
C	14.000-14.015 (0.5512-0.5518)	14.05 (0.553)
L and R	14.000-14.018 (0.5512-0.5519)	14.05 (0.553)
Shift fork finger thickness	4.93-5.00 (0.194-0.197)	4.50 (0.18)
Shift fork shaft outside diameter	13.966-13.984 (0.5498-0.5506)	13.90 (0.547)

Table 3 TRANSMISSION TORQUE SPECIFICATIONS

	N•m	in.-lb.	ft.-lb.
Shift fork shaft bolt	15	133	–

CHAPTER EIGHT

FUEL AND EXHAUST SYSTEMS (XR600R)

This chapter covers the fuel system. Air filter service is covered in Chapter Three. Refer to *Safety* in Chapter One when working on the fuel system and related components.

Specification **Tables 1-3** are located at the end of this chapter.

CARBURETOR

Removal/Installation

1. Remove both side covers.
2. Remove the fuel tank as described in this chapter.
3. Loosen the clamp screws on both the front intake tube and rear rubber boot.
4. Note the routing of the drain tube through the frame. Carefully pull the tube free from the frame and leave it attached to the carburetor.
5. Carefully pull the carburetor free of the intake tube and the rear rubber boot. Remove the carburetor out through the right side.
6. Mark the throttle cables for easy identification during assembly. Disconnect the throttle cables from the carburetor pulley.
7. Install by reversing the preceding removal steps while noting the following during installation:

a. Install the carburetor so the boss on the carburetor aligns with the notch in the rubber intake tube.
b. When installing the throttle cables, be sure to install the pull cable to the bottom receptacle on the carburetor pulley and the return cable to the top receptacle.
c. Make sure the screws on the clamping bands are tight to avoid a vacuum leak and possible valve damage.
d. Adjust the throttle cables as described in Chapter Three.

Disassembly/Assembly

Refer to **Figure 1**.
1. Remove the vent and overflow tubes (**Figure 2**).
2. Remove the screws (**Figure 3**) securing the top cover and remove the cover and gasket.
3. Remove the screws (**Figure 4**) securing the valve lever assembly to the throttle valve and pivot the valve lever assembly out of the way.
4. Remove the throttle valve and needle valve from the carburetor. Note the position of the needle valve clip for reassembly.
5. Remove the choke lever and bracket.

6. Remove the screws (**Figure 5**) securing the air cutoff valve cover and remove the cover.

7. Remove the spring and diaphragm (**Figure 6**).

8. Remove the small O-ring (**Figure 7**).

9. Remove the screws securing the float bowl and remove the float bowl (A, **Figure 8**).

10. Unscrew the main jet cover (B, **Figure 8**) from the float bowl.

11. Remove the plastic baffle (**Figure 9**) from the main jet.

12. Carefully turn the pilot screw in until it *lightly* seats. Count and record the number of turns so it can be reinstalled in the same position.

13. Unscrew the pilot screw and spring (**Figure 10**).

14. Remove the O-ring (**Figure 11**) located within the pilot screw hole.

15. Remove the float pivot pin (**Figure 12**).

16. Remove the float and fuel valve (**Figure 13**).

17. Remove the main jet (A, **Figure 14**), needle jet holder (**Figure 15**) and needle jet.

18. Turn the carburetor over and gently tap the side of the body. Catch the needle jet as it falls out. If the needle jet does not fall out, use a plastic tool and gently push the needle jet out. Do not use any metal tools for this purpose.

19. Remove the slow jet (B, **Figure 14**).

20. Remove the idle speed screw assembly.

21. Remove the O-ring gasket from the float bowl.

NOTE
Further disassembly is not necessary. The throttle and choke plates and shafts are available only as part of the carburetor body.

22. Clean and inspect all parts as described in this section.

23. Assembly is the reverse of the disassembly steps. Note the following:

   a. Install the needle jet (**Figure 16**) so the chamfered end faces up toward the needle jet holder.

   b. If removed, install the jet needle clip in its original position. Refer to **Table 1**.

   c. Install the plastic main jet baffle (**Figure 9**) so the cutout notch faces toward the float pin. The notch encloses the overflow tube in the float bowl.

   d. Check the float height. If necessary, adjust it as described in this chapter.

Cleaning/Inspection

1. Clean and dry the carburetor parts.

CAUTION
Do not clean the carburetor body or the O-rings in a carburetor cleaner that damages rubber parts.

2. Clean the overflow tube in the float bowl from both ends (**Figure 17**).

3. Inspect the end of the fuel valve (**Figure 18**) for wear or damage. Also check the inside of the valve seat in the carburetor body. If either part is damaged, replace as a set. A damaged valve or a particle of debris in the valve seat assembly may cause the carburetor to flood and overflow fuel.

4. Inspect all O-ring seals. O-ring seals tend to harden over time from heat.

5. Inspect the pilot screw (**Figure 19**) and spring for damage. Replace the screw if damaged.

6. Inspect the float for deterioration or damage. Check the float by submersing it in a container of water. If water enters the float, replace it.

7. Move the throttle pulley from stop-to-stop and check for free movement. If it does not move freely, replace the carburetor body.

8. Make sure all openings in the carburetor body are clear. Clean with compressed air.

9. Inspect the air cutoff diaphragm (**Figure 6**) for cracks, deterioration or other damage.

CAUTION
Do not use wire or drill bits to clean the jets. Minor gouges in the jets can alter the air/fuel mixture.

10. Make sure all jet openings are clear. Replace any jet that cannot be cleaned.

CARBURETOR ADJUSTMENTS

Idle Speed Adjustment

Refer to Chapter Three.

Float Adjustment

The fuel valve and float maintain a constant fuel level in the carburetor float bowl. Because the float level affects the fuel mixture throughout the engine's operating range, this level must be maintained within the specifications in **Table 1**.

1. Remove the carburetor as described in this chapter.

2. Remove the screws securing the float bowl and remove the float bowl (**Figure 20**).

3. Hold the carburetor assembly with the carburetor inclined 15-45° from vertical so that the float arm is just touching the float needle-not pushing it down. Use a float level gauge (**Figure 21**), vernier caliper or small ruler and measure the distance from the car-

8

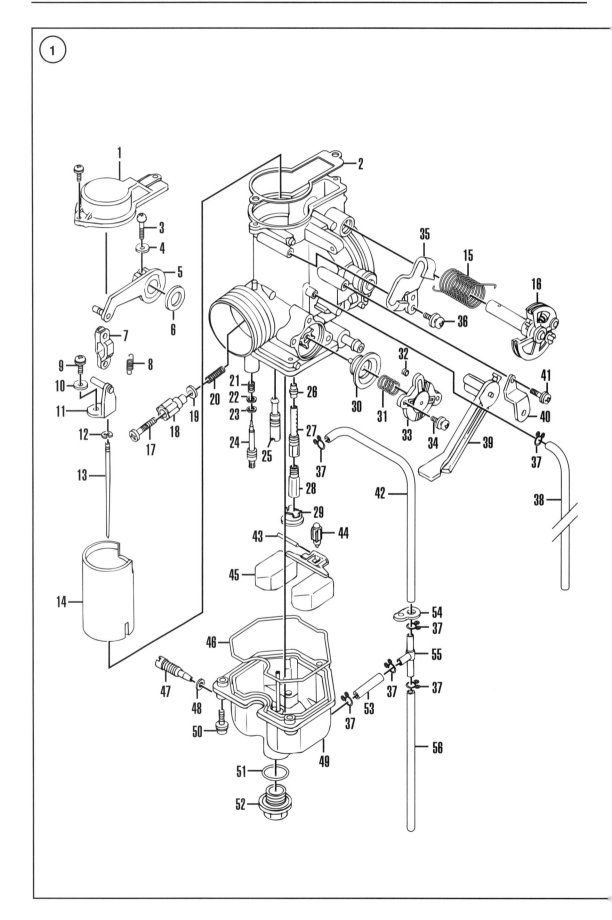

CARBURETOR

1. Cover
2. Gasket
3. Screw
4. Washer
5. Lever
6. Washer
7. Link
8. Spring
9. Screw
10. Washer
11. Plate
12. Jet needle clip
13. Jet needle
14. Throttle valve
15. Spring
16. Throttle pulley and shaft
17. Screw
18. Idle speed knob
19. Washer
20. Spring
21. Spring
22. O-ring
23. Washer
24. Pilot screw
25. Slow jet
26. Needle jet
27. Needle jet holder
28. Main jet
29. Baffle
30. Diaphragm
31. Spring
32. O-ring
33. Air cutoff valve cover
34. Screw
35. Throttle cable bracket
36. Screw
37. Clip
38. Air vent hose
39. Choke lever
40. Bracket
41. Screw
42. Breather hose
43. Fuel valve
44. Float pin
45. Float
46. O-ring
47. Drain screw
48. O-ring
49. Float bowl
50. Screw
51. O-ring
52. Main jet cover
53. Hose
54. Holder
55. T-fitting
56. Hose

8

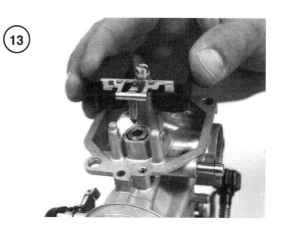

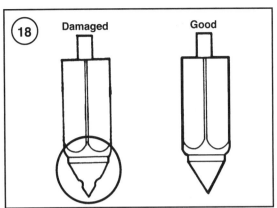

Damaged   Good

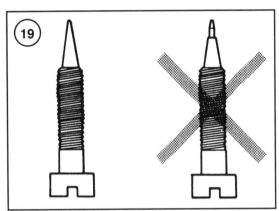

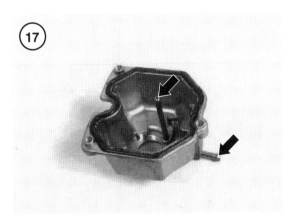

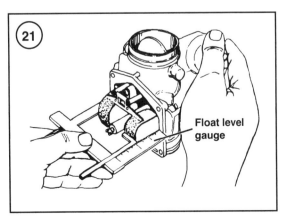

Float level gauge

8

buretor body to the bottom surface of the float body (**Figure 22**).

4. Adjust by carefully bending the tang on the float arm. If the float level is too high, the result will be a rich air/fuel mixture. If it is too low, the mixture will be too lean.

5. Reassemble and install the carburetor.

Pilot Screw Adjustment

> *NOTE*
> *Pilot screw adjustment is not necessary unless the carburetor has been overhauled or it has been misadjusted.*

The air filter element must be clean before starting this procedure or the results will be inaccurate. Refer to Chapter Three.

1. For the preliminary adjustment, carefully turn the pilot screw (**Figure 23**) in until it seats *lightly* and then back it out the number of turns in **Table 1**.

2. Start the engine and let it reach normal operating temperature. Approximately 10 minutes of stop and go riding is sufficient. Shut off the engine.

3. Connect a portable tachometer following the manufacturer's instructions.

4. Turn the idle adjust screw (**Figure 24**) to obtain the idle speed in **Table 1**.

5. Turn the pilot screw as needed to obtain the highest idle speed.

6. Reset the idle speed. Open and close the throttle a couple of times while checking for variation in idle speed. Readjust if necessary.

7A. On 1991-1997 models, repeat Step 5 and Step 6 until the engine runs smoothly at the correct idle speed.

7B. On 1998-2000 models, while running the engine, turn the pilot screw in slowly until the engine speed drops 100 rpm. On California models, turn the pilot screw out 1/2 turn. On all other models, turn the pilot screw out 3/4 turn. Turn the idle adjust screw (**Figure 24**) to obtain the idle speed in **Table 1**.

8. Stop the engine and disconnect the portable tachometer.

Needle Jet Adjustment

1. Remove the carburetor assembly as described in this chapter.

2. Remove the screws (**Figure 25**) securing the cover and remove the cover and gasket.

3. Remove the screws (**Figure 26**) securing the lever assembly to the throttle valve. Then pivot the lever assembly back out of the way.

4. Remove the throttle valve and needle jet.

5. Remove the needle valve and note the original position of the needle clip. The standard setting is in **Table 1**.

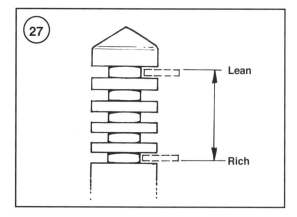

6. Raising the needle (lowering the clip) will enrich the mixture during mid-throttle openings, while lowering the needle (raising the clip) will lean out the mixture (**Figure 27**).

7. Reassemble and install the carburetor by reversing these steps.

High-altitude and Temperature Adjustment

CAUTION
If the carburetor is adjusted for higher elevations, change it back to the standard settings when the bike is returned to lower elevations (near sea level). Engine overheating and piston seizure will occur if the engine runs lean.

High-altitude and temperature adjustments consist of three different changes to the carburetor: main jet size change, a different location of the clip on the jet needle and a different pilot screw setting. Refer to **Figure 28**.

If the motorcycle will be operated for sustained periods at high elevations (above 2000 m [6500 ft.]), change the main jet to a 1-step smaller jet. Never change a jet by more than one size at a time without

test riding the motorcycle and inspecting the spark plug as described in Chapter Three.

Carburetor Rejetting

1. Do not try to solve a poor running engine problem by rejetting the carburetor if all of the following conditions hold true:
   a. The engine maintained a good tune in the past with the standard jetting.
   b. The engine has not been modified.
   c. The motorcycle is being operated in the same geographical region under the same general climatic conditions as in the past.
   d. The motorcycle was and is being ridden at average speeds.

2. If the above conditions all hold true, chances are the problem is due to a malfunction in the carburetor or in another component that needs adjustment or repair. Changing carburetor jet size probably will not solve the problem. Rejetting the carburetor may be necessary if any of the following conditions occurred:
   a. Installation of a non-standard type of air filter element.
   b. Installation of a non-standard exhaust system.
   c. Modification of engine top end components (piston, cams, valves, compression ratio, etc.).
   d. Operation at considerably higher or lower altitudes or in a considerably hotter or colder climate than in the past.
   e. Operation at considerably higher speeds than before and changing to colder spark plugs does not solve the problem.
   f. Previously changed carburetor jetting.
   g. Inconsistent engine tune.

3. If it is necessary to rejet the carburetor due to installation of aftermarket parts, check with the part manufacturer for jetting recommendations.

4. When rejetting a carburetor, change the jets one size at a time, unless specific recommendations are available. After rejetting, test ride the bike and inspect the spark plug as described in Chapter Three.

THROTTLE CABLE REPLACEMENT

WARNING
Do not ride the motorcycle until the throttle cables are installed and properly adjusted.

1. Remove both side covers and the seat.
2. Remove the fuel tank as described in this chapter.
3. Remove the screws securing the throttle body together and separate the parts.

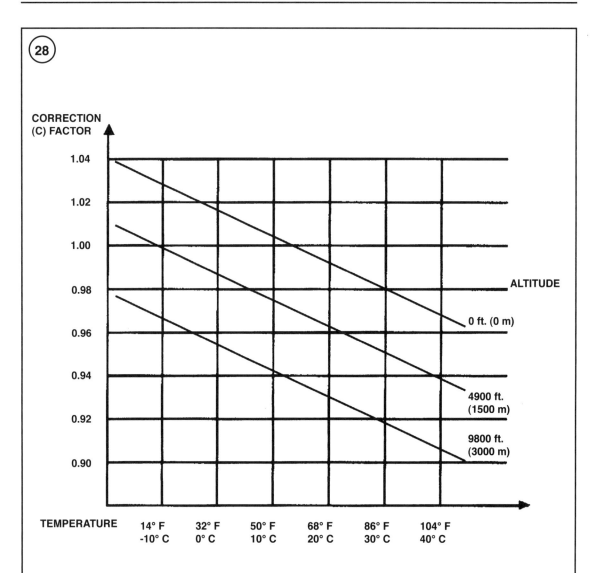

The chart is divided in three directions:
    Ambient temperature—vertical lines at bottom.
    Altitude—Angled lines on right.
    Correction (C) factor—horizontal lines on left.
Determine the approximate altitude and air temperature and note where these two factors intersect (vertical and angled lines). Determine the C factor by moving horizontally to the left from the altitude and temperature intersection.
    For example, at 4900 ft. and 68° F the correction factor is approximately 0.96.

To Determine Main Jet Size
    Multiply the standard main jet number by the C factor. Use the main jet number closest to the result.

    For example, (152 × 0.96 = 145.92)—use main jet number 146.

To Determine the Pilot Screw Setting and Jet Needle Clip Position
    If the C factor is above 0.95 no adjustment is necessary to the pilot screw or clip position on the jet needle for proper engine operation.
    If the C factor is 0.95 or below, turn the pilot screw *out* by 1/2 additional turn and raise the clip on the jet needle by one groove.

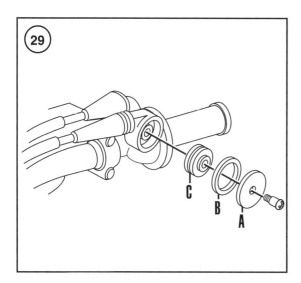

4. Remove the screw and throttle cover (A, **Figure 29**).

5. Remove the cover gasket (B, **Figure 29**).

6. Remove the throttle cable roller (C, **Figure 29**).

7. Disengage the throttle cables from the throttle grip and withdraw them from the upper half of the throttle body.

8. Loosen the throttle cable locknuts at the carburetor assembly.

9. Disconnect the throttle pull and return cables from the throttle pulley on the carburetor.

10. Tie a piece of heavy string or cord (approximately 2 m [7 ft.] long) to the carburetor end of both throttle cables. Wrap this end with masking tape or duct tape. Do not use an excessive amount of tape as it must be pulled through the frame during removal. Tie the other end of the string to the frame or air box.

11. At the throttle grip end of the cables, carefully pull the cables (and attached string) out through the frame. Make sure the attached string follows the same path as the cables through the frame.

12. Remove the tape and untie the string from the old cables.

13. Lubricate the new cables as described in Chapter Three.

14. Tie the string to the carburetor end of the new throttle cables and wrap them with tape.

15. Carefully pull the string back through the frame so the new cables route through the same path as the old cables.

16. Untie the string from the cables and remove it from the frame.

17. Attach the pull cable to the bottom receptacle in the throttle pulley on the carburetor.

18. Attach the return cable to the top receptacle in the throttle pulley on the carburetor.

19. Apply grease to the upper ends of the throttle cables and to the throttle cable roller.

20. Install the throttle cables through the upper half of the throttle body housing.

21. Attach the throttle cables onto the throttle grip.

22. Install the throttle cable roller (C, **Figure 29**).

23. Install the cover gasket (B, **Figure 29**).

24. Install the throttle cover and screw (A, **Figure 29**). Tighten the screw securely.

25. Install the lower half of the throttle body and install the screws securing the throttle body halves together. Tighten the screws securely.

26. Operate the throttle grip several times and make sure the throttle linkage operates correctly, with no binding. If operation is incorrect or there is binding, carefully check that the cables are attached correctly and there are no tight bends in the cables.

27. Adjust the throttle operation as described in Chapter Three.

28. Install the fuel tank as described in this chapter.

29. Install both side covers and the seat.

30. Test ride the bike slowly at first and make sure the throttle operates correctly.

FUEL TANK

Removal/Installation

1. Remove both side covers and the seat.

2. Turn the fuel shutoff valve to off.

3. Remove the fuel line to the carburetor assembly.

4. Unhook the rubber strap (A, **Figure 30**) securing the rear of the tank.

5. Remove the bolt and spacer on each side of the front of the fuel tank (B, **Figure 30**).

6. Pull the fuel filler cap vent tube (C, **Figure 30**) from the steering head receptacle.

7. Lift up and pull the tank to the rear and remove the fuel tank.

8. Inspect the rubber protective bands (**Figure 31**) or rubber covers (**Figure 32**) on the nuts of the engine upper hanger plate. Replace as a set if any are damaged or starting to deteriorate.

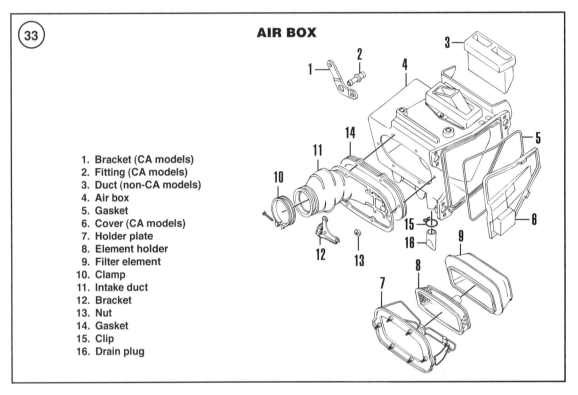

AIR BOX

1. Bracket (CA models)
2. Fitting (CA models)
3. Duct (non-CA models)
4. Air box
5. Gasket
6. Cover (CA models)
7. Holder plate
8. Element holder
9. Filter element
10. Clamp
11. Intake duct
12. Bracket
13. Nut
14. Gasket
15. Clip
16. Drain plug

WARNING
If the protective bands or rubber covers are worn through or not installed, the bolt heads or nuts may wear a hole through the fuel tank.

9. Install by reversing the removal steps.

FUEL VALVE

Removal/Installation

1. Remove the fuel tank as described in this chapter.
2. Drain the fuel tank of all gas. Store the gas in a can approved for gasoline storage.
3. Remove the screws securing the fuel valve to the bottom of the fuel tank, then remove the fuel valve.

4. Clean the strainer screen in a high-flash point solvent. The strainer screen is not available separately.
5. Install a new fuel valve O-ring.
6. Install the fuel valve by reversing the preceding removal steps while noting the following:
   a. Tighten the fuel valve mounting screws securely.
   b. After turning on the fuel valve, check the fuel valve and hose for leaks.

AIR BOX

Removal/Installation

Refer to **Figure 33**.
1. Remove the seat and both side covers.

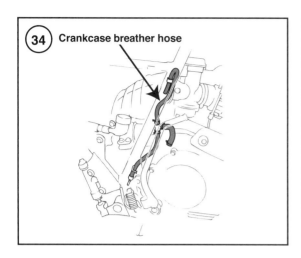

Crankcase breather hose

6. Remove the bolts securing the air box to the frame.
7. Remove the air box out the left side of the frame.
8. Install by reversing the removal steps.

CRANKCASE BREATHER SYSTEM

On all models except California models, crankcase gasses exit the crankcase through a fitting on the rear of the crankcase into the hoses shown in **Figure 34**. A drain plug at the bottom of the hose allows removal of residue. The upper hose end is open to the atmosphere.

California models are equipped with an air/oil canister that collects residue expelled from the engine. The upper hose end connects to a fitting on the air box. Refer to **Figure 35**.

On all models, make sure all hoses and clamps are in good condition and tight to prevent the entrance of water or debris into the engine.

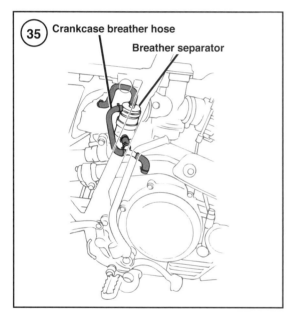

Crankcase breather hose
Breather separator

EXHAUST SYSTEM

Removal/Installation

1. Remove the seat and right side cover as described in Chapter Sixteen.
2. Remove the fuel tank as described in this chapter.
3. Loosen the clamp bolts (A, **Figure 36**) securing the exhaust pipe to the muffler.
4. Remove the bolt(s) and washer(s) (B, **Figure 36**) securing the muffler to the frame. Withdraw the muffler out through the rear and remove it.
5. Remove the nuts (**Figure 37**) securing the exhaust pipe flanges to the cylinder head. Remove the two individual exhaust pipe flanges from each exhaust pipe.
6. Remove the exhaust pipe.
7. Inspect the gaskets at all joints; replace as necessary.
8. Reverse the removal steps for installation while noting the following:

2. Loosen the clamp band screw on the carburetor for the air box inlet tube.
3. Remove the mud guard from the air box.
4. Detach the wire retaining bands.
5. Remove the duct from the air box.

a. Install a new gasket in each exhaust port in the cylinder head.
b. Install the exhaust pipe retaining flanges so they interlock as shown in **Figure 38**.
c. Tighten the exhaust pipe nuts to 27 N•m (20 ft.-lb.).
d. Tighten the muffler mounting bolts to 35 N•m (26 ft.-lb.).
e. Tighten the muffler clamp bolts to 17 N•m (13 ft.-lb.).
f. After installation is complete, start the engine and make sure there are no exhaust leaks.

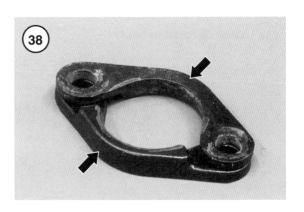

Table 1 CARBURETOR SPECIFICATIONS

Identification number	
1991-1997	PD8AF
1998-2000	
California	PDM1B
Except California	PD8AF
Float level	14.5 mm (0.57 in.)
Main jet	
1991-1997	152
1998-2000	
California	125
Except California	152
Slow jet	
1991-1997	62
1998-2000	
California	58
Except California	62
Jet needle clip position	3rd groove
Idle speed	1200-1400 rpm
Pilot screw adjustment (turns out)*	
1991-1997	2
1998-2000	
California	1 1/8
Except California	2

*Initial adjustment only. See text for procedure.

Table 2 FUEL TANK SPECIFICATIONS

	Liters	U.S. gal.
Fuel tank capacity	10.0	2.7
Reserve capacity	2.0	0.5

Table 3 EXHAUST SYSTEM TORQUE SPECIFICATIONS

	N•m	in.-lb.	ft.-lb.
Exhaust pipe nuts	27	–	20
Muffler clamp bolts	17	–	13
Muffler mounting bolts	35	–	26

CHAPTER NINE

FUEL, EMISSION CONTROL AND EXHAUST SYSTEMS (XR650L)

This chapter covers the fuel system. Air filter service is covered in Chapter Three. Refer to *Safety* in Chapter One when working around the fuel system and related components.

Specification **Tables 1-4** are located at the end of this chapter.

CARBURETOR

Removal/Installation

1. Remove both side covers and the seat as described in Chapter Sixteen.
2. Remove the fuel tank as described in this chapter.
3. Disconnect the negative battery lead (**Figure 1**).
4. Loosen and move the hose clamps off the hoses going to the crankcase ventilation system separator and remove the separator (**Figure 2**).
5. Loosen and move the hose clamp and slide the secondary air injection system hose from the carburetor (**Figure 3**).
6. On California models, disconnect the evaporative emission control vacuum hoses from the carburetor.
7. At the carburetor, slide back the rubber boot (A, **Figure 4**) and unscrew the starter enrichment valve nut (B), then remove the cable, valve and spring assembly from the carburetor. Move the cable out of the way.
8. Loosen the locknut (A, **Figure 5**) on each throttle cable. Detach each throttle cable (B, **Figure 5**) from the mounting bracket, then from the carburetor pulley. Label each throttle cable so it can be reinstalled in its original location.

9. Remove the bolt and bracket (A, **Figure 6**) securing the rear master cylinder reservoir to the frame. Move back the master cylinder reservoir (B, **Figure 6**) and tie it up out of the way. It is not necessary to disconnect the brake fluid hose from the reservoir. Keep the master cylinder upright to prevent air from entering the system.
10. Loosen the screw on the airbox tube clamping band (**Figure 7**).
11. Loosen the screw on the intake tube clamping band (A, **Figure 8**).
12. Pull the carburetor assembly toward the rear and free the assembly from the intake tube on the cylinder head.
13. Carefully remove the carburetor assembly out through the right side of the frame.
14. Install by reversing the preceding removal steps while noting the following:
   a. Make sure the carburetor is fully seated forward in the intake tube in the cylinder head.
   b. On the left side of the carburetor, align the raised tab on the carburetor (B, **Figure 8**) with the groove in the intake tube (C) on the cylinder head.
   c. Make sure the locating pin on the intake tube clamp (D, **Figure 8**) fits between the tabs (E) on the intake tube.
   d. Make sure the screws on the clamping bands are tight to avoid a vacuum leak.
   e. Adjust the throttle cable as described in Chapter Three.

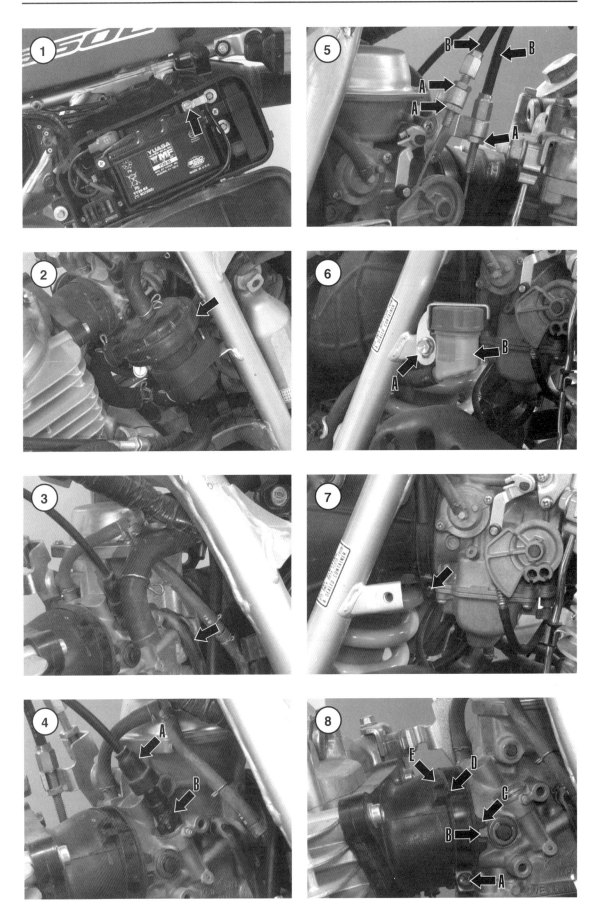

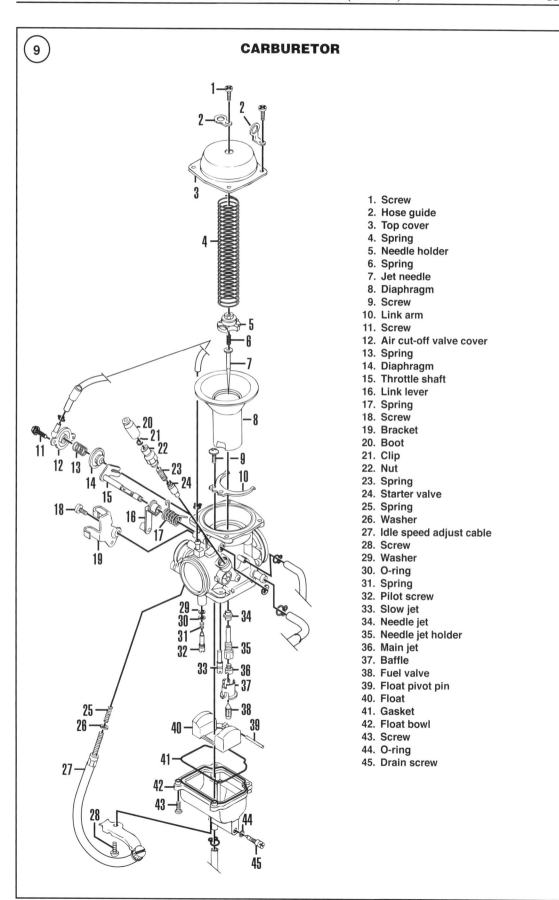

CARBURETOR

1. Screw
2. Hose guide
3. Top cover
4. Spring
5. Needle holder
6. Spring
7. Jet needle
8. Diaphragm
9. Screw
10. Link arm
11. Screw
12. Air cut-off valve cover
13. Spring
14. Diaphragm
15. Throttle shaft
16. Link lever
17. Spring
18. Screw
19. Bracket
20. Boot
21. Clip
22. Nut
23. Spring
24. Starter valve
25. Spring
26. Washer
27. Idle speed adjust cable
28. Screw
29. Washer
30. O-ring
31. Spring
32. Pilot screw
33. Slow jet
34. Needle jet
35. Needle jet holder
36. Main jet
37. Baffle
38. Fuel valve
39. Float pivot pin
40. Float
41. Gasket
42. Float bowl
43. Screw
44. O-ring
45. Drain screw

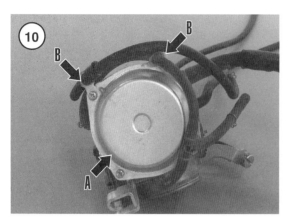

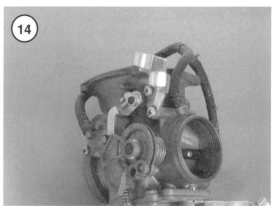

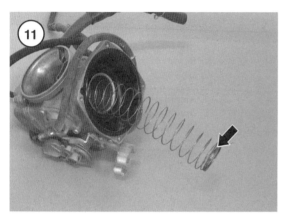

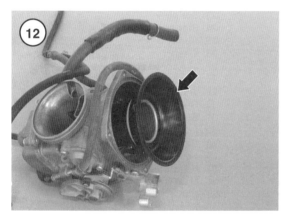

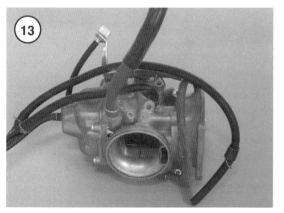

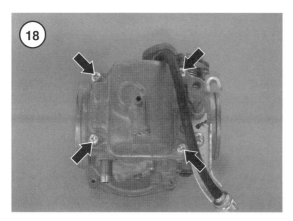

9

Disassembly/Assembly

Refer to **Figure 9**.

1. Remove the screws securing the diaphragm cover and remove the cover (A, **Figure 10**). Note the location of the hose clamps (B, **Figure 10**).

2. Remove the spring (**Figure 11**) and the diaphragm (**Figure 12**).

3. Note their location, then remove the various hoses from the carburetor body. Refer to **Figure 13** and **Figure 14**.

4. Remove the air cut-off valve as follows:
   a. Remove the screws (A, **Figure 15**) securing the air cut-off valve cover and remove the cover (B).
   b. Remove the spring (**Figure 16**) and the diaphragm (**Figure 17**).

5. Remove the screws (**Figure 18**) securing the float bowl and remove the float bowl and gasket.

6. Remove the main jet baffle (**Figure 19**).

7. Using a pin punch, loosen the float pivot pin by pushing it toward the fuel inlet side of the carburetor (**Figure 20**).

8. Remove the float pin (A, **Figure 21**).

9. Remove the float and the fuel valve (B, **Figure 21**).

10. Unscrew the main jet (A, **Figure 22**).

11. Unscrew the needle jet holder (B, **Figure 22**).

12. Turn the carburetor over and remove the needle jet (**Figure 23**).

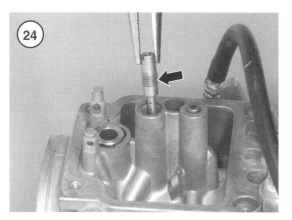

13. Loosen the slow jet, then remove it (**Figure 24**).

14. To disassemble the jet needle assembly, perform the following:

    a. Using an 8-mm socket or flat-nosed needle-nose pliers, turn the needle holder (**Figure 25**) 90° counterclockwise and remove the holder and small spring (**Figure 26**).

    b. Remove the jet needle (**Figure 27**).

> *NOTE*
> *Do not remove the pilot screw unless it is damaged or requires replacement.*

15. If pilot screw removal is necessary, remove the screw cap (**Figure 28**).

16. Unscrew and remove the pilot screw, spring, washer and O-ring (**Figure 29**).

> *NOTE*
> *Further disassembly is not necessary. Do not remove the throttle shaft and throttle valve assemblies (**Figure 30**). If these parts are damaged, replace the carburetor.*

17. Clean and inspect all parts as described in this section.

18. Assemble the carburetor by reversing the preceding disassembly steps while noting the following:

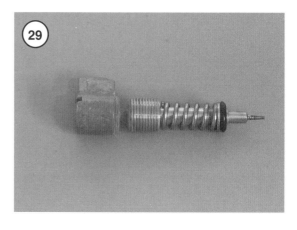

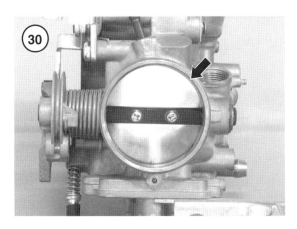

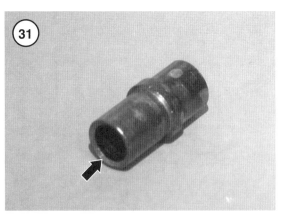

a. Position the needle jet with the larger diameter opening (**Figure 31**) entering first and install the needle jet (**Figure 32**).

b. After installing the needle jet, make sure it is completely seated as shown in **Figure 23**.

c. Install the fuel valve (**Figure 33**) on the float prior to installing the float.

d. When installing the diaphragm, position the tab on the diaphragm into the recess in the carburetor body (**Figure 34**).

e. Align the hole in the carburetor body with the raised boss (**Figure 35**) in the top cover. Install the top cover and tighten the screws securely.

f. After the top cover has been installed, move the piston valve up. The piston valve should slide back down immediately with no binding. If it binds or if the movement is sluggish, the diaphragm may have seated incorrectly or may be folded over. The diaphragm rubber is very soft and may fold over during spring and top cover installation.

g. Check the float level as described in *Carburetor Adjustments* in this chapter.

h. After the carburetor has been installed, adjust the pilot screw, the idle speed and the choke as described in this chapter and Chapter Three.

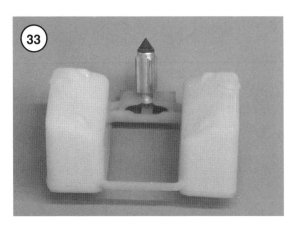

9

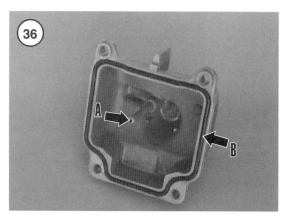

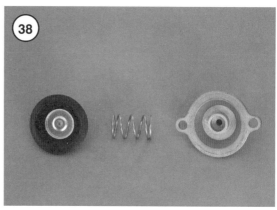

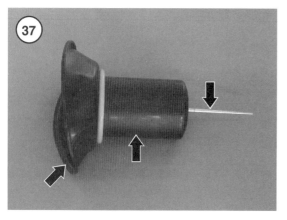

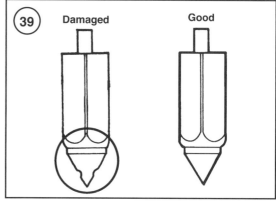

Cleaning and Inspection

1. Clean and dry the carburetor parts.

> *CAUTION*
> *Do not clean the carburetor body or the O-rings in a carburetor cleaner that damages rubber parts.*

> *CAUTION*
> *Do not use wire or drill bits to clean the jets. Minor gouges in the jets can alter the air/fuel mixture.*

2. Remove the drain screw from the float bowl.

3. Make sure the float bowl overflow tube (A, **Figure 36**) is clear. Blow out with compressed air if necessary.

4. Inspect the float bowl O-ring gasket (B, **Figure 36**) for damage, hardening or deterioration; replace if necessary.

5. Inspect the diaphragm, slide and needle (**Figure 37**) for wear, damage or deterioration; replace if necessary.

6. Inspect the air cut-off valve assembly (**Figure 38**) for wear, damage or deterioration; replace any defective part.

7. Inspect the end of the fuel valve (**Figure 39**) for wear or damage. Also check the inside of the valve

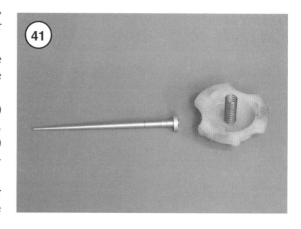

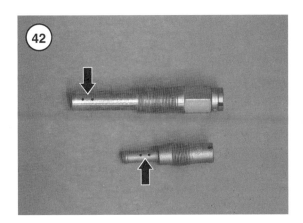

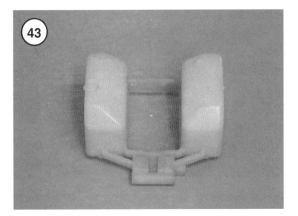

9

seat (**Figure 40**). If either part is damaged, replace as a set.

8. Inspect the needle jet, the jet holder and spring (**Figure 41**) for wear, damage or deterioration; replace any defective part.

9. Make sure the holes in the needle jet and slow jet (**Figure 42**) are clear. Clean out using compressed air if plugged.

10. Inspect the float (**Figure 43**) for deterioration or damage. Place the float in a container of water and push it down. If the float sinks or if bubbles appear (indicating a leak), replace the float.

11. Make sure the screws securing the link arm (**Figure 44**) are tight. Tighten if necessary.

12. Make sure the throttle valve screws (**Figure 45**) are tight. Tighten if necessary.

13. Move the throttle pulley (**Figure 46**) back and forth from stop-to-stop and check for free movement. If it does not move freely or if it sticks in any position, replace the carburetor body.

14. Make sure all openings in the carburetor body are clear. Clean out using compressed air if they are plugged. Refer to **Figures 47-49**.

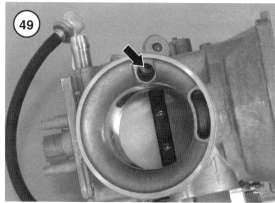

CARBURETOR ADJUSTMENTS

Idle Speed Adjustment

Refer to Chapter Three.

Float Level

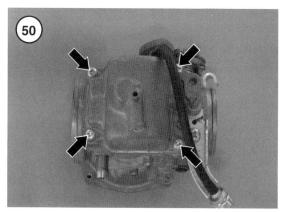

The fuel valve and float maintain a constant fuel level in the carburetor float bowl. Because the float level affects the fuel mixture throughout the engine's operating range, this level must be at the specification in **Table 1**.

1. Remove the carburetor as described in this chapter.
2. Remove the float bowl mounting screws and float bowl (**Figure 50**). Do not remove the O-ring from the float bowl groove.
3. Hold the carburetor so the fuel valve just touches the float arm without pushing it down. Measure the distance from the carburetor body gasket surface to the float (**Figure 51**) using a float level gauge, ruler or vernier caliper.
4. The float is non-adjustable. If the float level is incorrect, check the float pin and fuel valve for damage. If these parts are in good condition, replace the float and remeasure the float level.

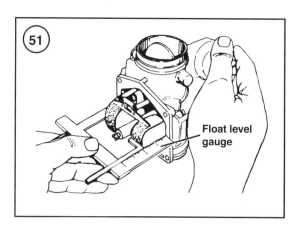

Float level gauge

5. Install the float bowl, O-ring and the mounting screws (**Figure 50**). Tighten the mounting screws securely.
6. Install the carburetor as described in this chapter.

Pilot Screw Adjustment

> *NOTE*
> *Pilot screw adjustment is not necessary unless the carburetor has been overhauled or it has been misadjusted.*

The air filter element must be clean before starting this procedure or the results will be inaccurate. Refer to Chapter Three.

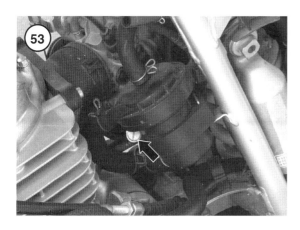

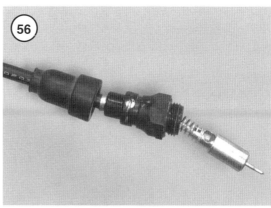

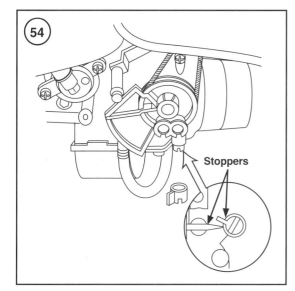

Stoppers

3. Connect a portable tachometer following the manufacturer's instructions.

4. Start the engine and turn the throttle stop screw (**Figure 53**) in or out to obtain the idle speed in **Table 1**.

5. Turn the pilot screw in or out to obtain the highest engine idle speed.

6. Reset the idle speed. Open and close the throttle several times; check for variation in idle speed. Readjust if necessary.

7. Turn the pilot screw (**Figure 54**) in gradually until the engine speed drops by 50 rpm.

8. Turn the pilot screw out 3/4 turn from the position obtained in Step 7.

9. On 2008-on models, use the throttle stop screw to readjust the idle speed.

10. Install a new limiter cap as follows:
   a. Apply Loctite No. 601, or equivalent, to the new limiter cap.
   b. Position the limiter cap against the stop on the float bowl (**Figure 54**) so the pilot screw can only turn clockwise, not counterclockwise.
   c. Install the limiter cap on the pilot screw. Make sure the pilot screw does not move while installing the limiter cap.

11. Disconnect the portable tachometer.

12. Test ride the bike for throttle response without hesitation.

Choke Cable Adjustment

Make sure the choke (starter enrichment valve) operates smoothly with no binding. If the cable binds, lubricate it as described in Chapter Three. If the cable still does not operate smoothly, replace it as described in this chapter.

1. Remove the fuel tank as described in this chapter.

2. Slide back the rubber boot (A, **Figure 55**) and unscrew the valve nut (B), then remove the valve and spring assembly from the carburetor (**Figure 56**).

1. Remove the limiter cap on the pilot screw (**Figure 52**), if so equipped. For a preliminary adjustment, carefully turn the pilot screw (**Figure 52**) in until it seats *lightly* and then back it out the number of turns in **Table 1**.

2. Start the engine and let it reach normal operating temperature. Approximately 5-10 minutes of stop-and-go riding is sufficient. Shut off the engine.

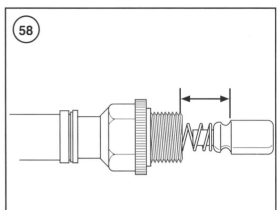

3. Push the choke lever (**Figure 57**) all the way toward the hand grip to the on position.

4. Using a vernier caliper, measure the distance between the end of the threads of the choke valve nut and the choke valve (**Figure 58**). The correct distance is 1-2 mm (0.04-0.08 in.).

5. To adjust, perform the following:

   a. Loosen the locknut (A, **Figure 59**) on the choke cable at the hand lever.

   b. Turn the adjuster (B, **Figure 59**) in either direction until the dimension at the cable end is correct.

   c. Tighten the locknut and recheck the dimension in Step 4. Readjust if necessary.

High Altitude Adjustment

> *CAUTION*
> *If the bike is returned to lower elevations, return the pilot screw to its original position, install the sea level main jet (**Table 2**) and readjust the idle speed. Failure to do so may result in engine damage.*

If the motorcycle will be operated for sustained periods at high elevations (above 2000 m [6500 ft.]), readjust the carburetor to improve performance.

1. Remove the carburetor as described in this chapter.

2. Install the main jet specified in **Table 2**.

3. Install the carburetor as described in this chapter.

4. Start the engine and let it reach normal operating temperature. Approximately 5-10 minutes of stop-and-go riding is sufficient. Shut off the engine.

5. Turn the pilot screw clockwise 1/2 turn (**Figure 60**).

6. Connect a portable tachometer following the manufacturer's instructions.

7. Start the engine and turn the throttle stop screw (**Figure 53**) in or out to obtain the idle speed in **Table 1**.

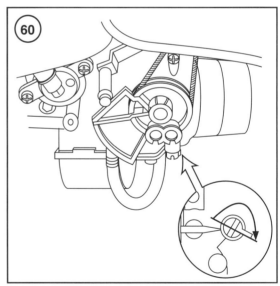

Carburetor Rejetting

Refer to Chapter Eight.

THROTTLE CABLE REPLACEMENT

> *WARNING*
> *Do not ride the motorcycle until the throttle cables are installed and adjusted properly.*

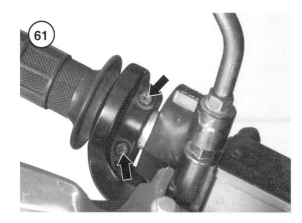

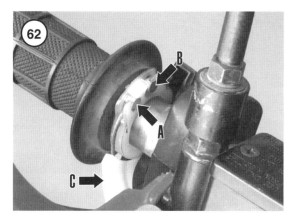

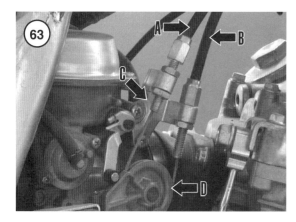

1. Remove the fuel tank as described in this chapter.
2. Slide the boot off the handlebar throttle housing.
3. Remove the throttle housing screws (**Figure 61**) and separate the housing.
4. Disconnect the throttle cables from the throttle grip pulley (**Figure 62**).
5. On the carburetor loosen the nuts on the pull cable (A, **Figure 63**) and return cable (B). Disengage the cables from the bracket (C, **Figure 63**) and throttle pulley (D).
6. Note the routing of the throttle cables.
7. Remove the throttle cables.
8. Route the new cables from the throttle control to the carburetor.
9. Attach the cables to the carburetor throttle pulley and bracket as shown in **Figure 63**. Note that the pull cable (A, **Figure 63**) is equipped with two nuts.
10. Lubricate the ends of the cable with lithium grease, then insert the ends into the handlebar throttle control.
11. Reconnect the pull (A, **Figure 62**) and return (B) throttle cables. Route the pull cable into the groove in the cable guide (C, **Figure 62**) and position the cable guide into the outer throttle housing.
12. Mate both housing covers together so the cable guide fits inside the housing (**Figure 64**) and install the mounting bolts finger-tight.
13. Slide the boot over the throttle housing.
14. Align the clamp mating surface on the throttle housing with the punch mark on the handlebar. Tighten the throttle housing bolts to 8.8 N•m (80 in.-lb.). Operate the throttle grip and make sure it turns smoothly. Turn the handlebar and check the throttle operation in both lock positions.
15. Adjust the throttle cables as described in Chapter Three.
16. Install the fuel tank as described in this chapter.

CHOKE CABLE REPLACEMENT

The choke cable operates the starter enrichment valve on the carburetor.
1. Remove the left hand guard as described in Chapter Sixteen.
2. Remove the fuel tank as described in this chapter.
3. Note the choke cable routing path from the handlebar to the carburetor.
4. At the carburetor, slide back the rubber boot (A, **Figure 65**) and unscrew the starter enrichment valve nut (B), then remove the cable, valve and spring assembly from the carburetor.
5. Remove the valve (A, **Figure 66**) and spring (B) from the end of the choke cable to prevent loss.
6. Disconnect the choke cable from the handlebar lever (**Figure 67**).

9

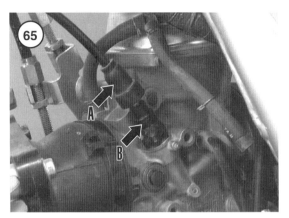

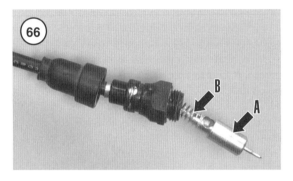

7. Detach the cable from any cable guides and re-move the choke cable.

8. Reverse the preceding steps to install the choke cable while noting the following:

    a. Adjust the choke cable as described in this chapter.

    b. Check the choke operation.

FUEL TANK

Removal/Installation

1. Remove the seat and both side covers as described in Chapter Sixteen.

2. Remove the air shroud on both sides as described in Chapter Sixteen.

3. Disconnect the battery negative lead (**Figure 68**).

4. Turn the fuel shutoff valve off.

5. Disconnect the fuel hose from the fuel valve (**Figure 69**).

6. Remove the bolt and washer (**Figure 70**) securing the rear of the fuel tank.

7. Pull the fuel tank partially up and disconnect the fuel line to the carburetor.

8. On California models, label and disconnect the evaporation emission control hoses.

9. Lift up and pull the tank to the rear and remove the fuel tank.

10. Install by reversing the preceding removal steps while noting the following:

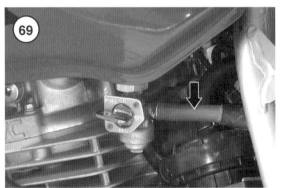

    a. Inspect the front rubber support cushions (**Figure 71**). Replace the cushions if damaged.

    b. Turn the fuel shutoff valve on and check for fuel leaks.

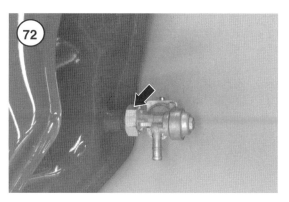

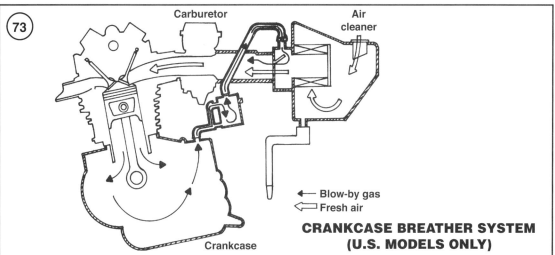

Carburetor

Air cleaner

← Blow-by gas

⇐ Fresh air

CRANKCASE BREATHER SYSTEM (U.S. MODELS ONLY)

Crankcase

FUEL VALVE

Removal/Installation

1. Remove the fuel tank as described in this chapter.
2. Drain the fuel tank of all gas. Store the gas in an approved gasoline storage container.
3. Turn the fuel valve nut (**Figure 72**) and remove the fuel valve.
4. Clean the strainer screen in a high-flash point solvent. If damaged, replace the strainer screen.
5. Install a new fuel valve O-ring.
6. Install the fuel valve by reversing the preceding removal steps while noting the following:
   a. Tighten the fuel valve nut securely.
   b. After turning on the fuel valve, check the fuel valve and hose for leaks.

CRANKCASE BREATHER SYSTEM

The crankcase breather system (**Figure 73**) captures blow-by gasses from the crankcase and recirculates them into the air/fuel mixture to be burned.

Inspection/Cleaning

Make sure all hose clamps are tight. Check all hoses for deterioration and replace as necessary.

Remove the drain hose from the base of the air filter case and drain out all residue. Perform this cleaning procedure more frequently if a considerable amount of riding is done at full throttle or in the rain. Make sure to reinstall the drain hose and push it on completely.

EVAPORATIVE EMISSION CONTROL SYSTEM (CALIFORNIA MODELS)

Fuel vapor from the fuel tank is routed into a charcoal canister located on the left side of the frame. This vapor is stored when the engine is not running. When the engine is running these vapors are drawn through a purge control valve and into the carburetor (**Figure 74**).

Make sure all hose clamps are tight. Check all hoses for deterioration and replace as necessary.

When removing the hoses from any component in the system, mark the hose and the fitting with a piece of masking tape and identify where the hose goes.

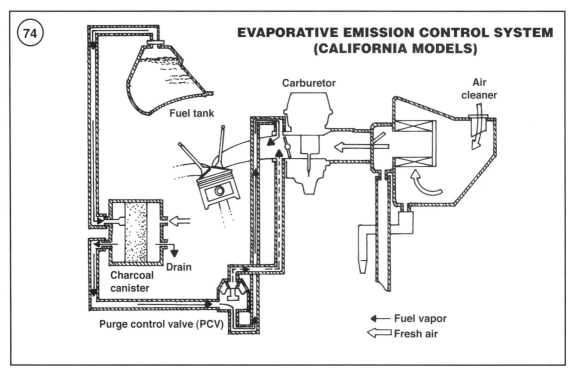

EVAPORATIVE EMISSION CONTROL SYSTEM (CALIFORNIA MODELS)

Carburetor

Air cleaner

Fuel tank

Charcoal canister

Drain

Purge control valve (PCV)

◄— Fuel vapor
⇐ Fresh air

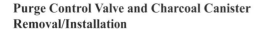

Purge Control Valve and Charcoal Canister Removal/Installation

1. Disconnect the hoses (A, **Figure 75**) routed to the charcoal canister.

2. Remove the bolts and washers securing the charcoal canister (B, **Figure 75**) to the frame bracket and remove the canister assembly.

3. Disconnect the hoses connected to the purge control valve (A, **Figure 76**).

4. Unhook the purge control valve assembly (B, **Figure 76**) from the frame tab and remove the valve assembly.

5. Install by reversing the preceding removal steps while noting the following:

   a. Make sure to install the hoses to the correct fitting on the charcoal canister and the vacuum control valves and that they are routed correctly through the frame.

   b. Make sure the hoses are not kinked, twisted or in contact with any sharp surfaces.

Purge Control Valve Test (2008-on XR650L)

1. Remove the purge control valve as described in this section.

2. Check the valve's output circuit by performing the following:

   a. Connect a vacuum pump to the output port on the bottom of the purge control valve (**Figure 74**). The output port's hose connects to the top of the carburetor's output horn.

   b. Operate the vacuum pump until the applied vacuum equals the purge control valve specified vacuum in **Table 1**.

   c. The valve should hold the vacuum at the specified level. Replace the purge control valve if vacuum is not maintained.

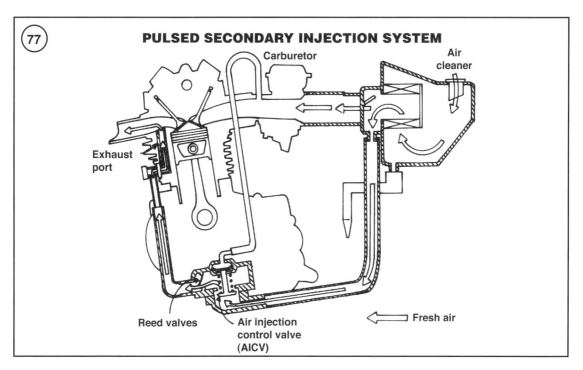

PULSED SECONDARY INJECTION SYSTEM

Carburetor

Air cleaner

Exhaust port

Reed valves

Air injection control valve (AICV)

Fresh air

d. Release the vacuum and remove the vacuum pump from the valve's output port.

3. Check the valve's vacuum circuit by performing the following:

a. Connect the vacuum pump to the vacuum port on the top of the purge control valve. The vacuum port's hose connects to the bottom of the carburetor's output horn.

b. Operate the vacuum pump until the applied vacuum equals the purge control valve specified vacuum in **Table 1**.

c. The valve should hold the vacuum at the specified level. Replace the purge control valve if vacuum is not maintained.

4. Check the valve's input circuit by performing the following:

a. While still applying the specified vacuum to the valve's vacuum port, blow into the input port on

the bottom of the purge control valve. The input port's hose connects to the EVAP canister.

b. Air should flow through the purge control valve and exit from the valve's output port.

c. Replace the purge control valve if air does not flow from the output port.

PULSED SECONDARY AIR INJECTION SYSTEM

The pulsed secondary air injection (PAIR) system consists of an air injection control valve incorporating reed valves and air and vacuum hoses (**Figure 77**). This system does not pressurize air, but uses the momentary pressure differentials generated by the exhaust gas pulses to introduce fresh air into the exhaust ports. Make sure all air and vacuum hoses are correctly routed and attached. Inspect the hoses and replace any if necessary.

Prior to removing any hoses, identify and locate each hose and fitting using masking tape.

Control Valve

Testing

1. Run the engine until it reaches normal operating temperature, then shut off the engine.

2. Remove the left side cover as described in Chapter Sixteen.

3. Disconnect the PAIR system inlet hose from the air box connector (A, **Figure 78**).

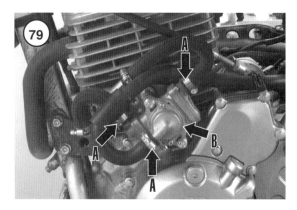

NOTE
The vacuum hose is the smallest hose
on the backside of the control valve.

4. Disconnect the control valve vacuum hose (B, **Figure 78**) from the PAIR control valve. Plug the disconnected end of the vacuum hose.

5. Connect a hand-operated vacuum pump to the vacuum fitting on the control valve.

6. Run the engine. Verify that air is drawn into the control valve-to-air box hose. If not, check for a clogged or blocked valve-to-air box hose or vacuum hose.

7. While the engine is running, operate the vacuum pump and apply 330 mm Hg (13.0 in. Hg) to the control valve vacuum fitting. Air flow should stop in the control valve-to-air box hose.

8. If air continues to flow into the control valve-to-air box hose with specified vacuum applied, replace the PAIR control valve.

9. If specified vacuum cannot be maintained, check for a damaged hose or leaking connection. If the hose is good, replace the PAIR control valve.

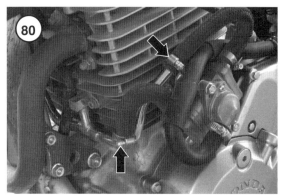

Removal/installation

1. Loosen and move the hose clamps (A, **Figure 79**) and slide the hoses off the control valve.

2. Remove the nuts securing the control valve (B, **Figure 79**) to the mounting bracket on the cylinder and remove the valve.

3. If necessary, remove the bolts securing the mounting bracket to the cylinder and remove it.

4. Install by reversing the preceding removal steps. Make sure to install each hose onto the correct fitting.

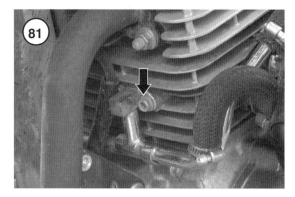

Air Injection Pipes

Removal/installation

1. Loosen and move the hose clamps (**Figure 80**) and slide the hoses off the air injection pipes.

2. Remove the bolts securing the air injection pipes to the cylinder head and remove the pipe assembly. Refer to **Figure 81** and **Figure 82**.

3. Install by reversing the preceding removal steps while noting the following:

    a. Make sure to connect each hose to the correct fitting.

    b. Tighten the bolts securely.

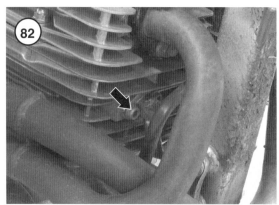

AIR BOX

Removal/Installation

1. Remove the seat and both side covers as described in Chapter Sixteen.

2. Remove the screws securing the mud guard to the rear of the air box and remove the mud guard.

3. Loosen and move the hose clamps and slide both crankcase breather hoses off the fitting on the top and on the base of the air box.

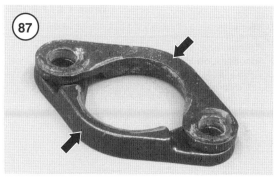

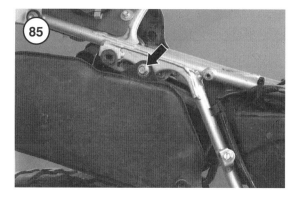

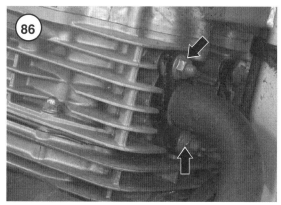

clamp off the carburetor air inlet hose at the front of the air box.

6. Remove the right bolt (B, **Figure 83**) and the left bolt and ground wire (C) securing the air box to the frame. Remove the bolt and washer from the right side of the air box.

7. Carefully slide the air box (D, **Figure 83**) out of the frame from the left side.

8. Install by reversing the preceding removal steps. Make sure all hoses are in place and that the hose clamps are tight.

EXHAUST SYSTEM

Removal/Installation

1. Remove the right side cover as described in Chapter Sixteen.

2. Loosen the clamping bolts (A, **Figure 84**) securing the exhaust pipe to the muffler.

3. Remove the front muffler mounting bolt (B, **Figure 84**).

4. While holding up the muffler, remove the rear muffler mounting bolt (**Figure 85**).

5. Separate the muffler from the exhaust pipe, then remove the muffler.

6. Remove the nuts (**Figure 86**) securing the exhaust pipe flanges to the cylinder head. Remove the two individual exhaust pipe flanges from each exhaust pipe.

7. Remove the exhaust pipe.

8. Inspect the gaskets at all joints; replace as necessary.

9. Reverse the removal steps for installation while noting the following:

    a. Install a new gasket in each exhaust port in the cylinder head.

    b. Install the exhaust pipe retaining flanges so they interlock as shown in **Figure 87**.

    c. Tighten the exhaust pipe nuts to 17 N•m (13 ft.-lb.).

    d. Tighten the muffler mounting bolts to the specification in **Table 4**.

    e. Tighten the muffler clamp bolts to 20 N•m (15 ft.-lb.).

    f. After installation is complete, start the engine and make sure there are no exhaust leaks.

4. Open the tie wraps (A, **Figure 83**) and disconnect the wiring harness from the top of the air box.

5. Loosen the clamp screw then move the hose

Table 1 CARBURETOR SPECIFICATIONS

Item	
Throttle bore size	42.5 mm (1.67 in.)
Identification number	
1993-1994	
California	VE86A
Except California	VE85A
1995-on	
U.S. except California	VE85C
California	VE86B
Canada	
1993-2007	VE85D
2008-on	VE85C
Float level	18.5 mm (0.73 in.)
Main jet	See Table 2
Slow jet	50
Idle speed	1200-1400 rpm
Pilot screw adjustment (turns out)*	
1993	
U.S. except California	
PM-000001~PM000958	2 3/4
After PM-000958	2 1/4
California	
PM-000001~PM-000078	2 3/4
After PM-000078	2 1/4
Canada (all units)	2 1/4
1994-on (all units)	2
Purge control valve specified vacuum (2008-on)	250 mm (33 kP)

*Initial adjustment only. See text for procedure and final pilot air screw adjustment (turns out).

Table 2 MAIN JET SIZE

	Frame serial no.	Main jet (sea level)	Main jet (high altitude)*
1993			
U.S. except California	PM-000001~PM-000958	155	152
	After PM-000958	152	150
California	PM-000001~PM-000078	155	152
	After PM-000078	152	150
Canada	All units	152	150
1994-on	All units	152	150

*Motorcycle operation at an altitude below 5000 ft. (1500 m) with a high altitude main jet installed may cause erratic engine operation and possible damage.

Table 3 FUEL TANK SPECIFICATIONS

	Liters	U.S. gal.
Fuel tank capacity	10.5 liters	2.8 U.S. gal. (2.31 Imp. gal.)
Reserve		
1993 - 2007	2.3 liters	0.60 U.S. gal. (0.50 Imp.gal.)
2008-on	2.8 liters	0.74 U.S. gal. (0.62 Imp.gal.)

Table 4 EXHAUST SYSTEM TORQUE SPECIFICATIONS

	N•m	in.-lb.	ft.-lb.
Exhaust pipe nuts	17	–	13
Muffler clamp bolts	20	–	15
Muffler mounting bolts			
1993-2007	35	–	26
2008-on	34	–	25

CHAPTER TEN

ELECTRICAL SYSTEM (XR600R)

This chapter contains service and test procedures for the electrical and ignition system components. The spark plug is covered in Chapter Three.

Refer to **Tables 1-3** at the end of this chapter. Wiring diagrams are located at the end of this manual.

ELECTRICAL COMPONENT REPLACEMENT

Most parts suppliers will not accept returned electrical components. If the exact cause of any electrical system malfunction has not been determined, do not attempt to remedy the problem through parts replacement. If an accurate diagnosis cannot be performed, have the suspect component or system tested by a professional technician before purchasing electrical components.

Consider any test results carefully before replacing a component that tests only slightly out of specification, especially resistance. A number of variables can affect test results dramatically. These include: the internal tester circuitry, ambient temperature and motorcycle operating conditions. All instructions and specifications have been checked for accuracy; however, successful test results depend to a great degree upon individual accuracy.

ELECTRICAL CONNECTORS

The position of the connectors may have been changed during previous repairs. Always confirm the wire colors to and from the connector and follow the wiring harness to the various components when performing tests.

Although connectors may appear rugged, the internal pins are easily damaged and dislodged, which may cause a malfunction. Exercise care when handling or testing the connectors.

Under normal operating conditions the connectors are weather-tight. If continuous operation in adverse operating conditions is expected, pack the connectors with dielectric grease to prevent the intrusion of water or other contaminants. Do not use a substitute that may interfere with current flow. Dielectric grease is specifically formulated to seal the connector and not increase current resistance.

An often overlooked area when troubleshooting are the ground connections. Make sure they are corrosion free and tight. Apply dielectric grease to the terminals before reconnecting them.

ALTERNATOR

The alternator consists of the flywheel, which contains the rotor magnets, and stator coil assembly. Flywheel removal and installation procedures are covered in Chapter Five.

Flywheel Testing

The flywheel is permanently magnetized and cannot be tested except by replacing it with a known good one. The rotor can loose magnetism over time or from a sharp blow. Replace the flywheel if defective or damaged.

Stator

The stator contains two coils: the exciter coil and the lighting coil. The exciter coil powers the ignition circuit while the lighting coil provides voltage for the headlight and taillight.

The exciter coil and lighting coil are not available individually, only as part of the stator plate assembly.

It is not necessary to remove the stator plate to perform the following tests. It is shown removed in the following procedure for clarity.

Testing

Refer to **Table 1** for specifications.

1. Remove the seat as described in Chapter Sixteen.
2. To test the lighting coil proceed as follows:
   a. Disconnect the connectors above the air box for the white/yellow and green wires.
   b. Use an ohmmeter and check resistance between the connectors of the stator wires.
   c. Check for continuity between each wire terminal and ground. If tester indicates continuity, check for a wire shorted to ground. If the wiring tests good, the coil is grounded. Replace the stator assembly.
3. To test the exciter coil proceed as follows:
   a. Disconnect the connector above the air box for the black/red wire.
   b. Use an ohmmeter and check resistance between the connector of the stator wire and ground.
   c. Check for continuity between the wire terminal and ground. If tester indicates continuity, check for a wire shorted to ground. If the wire tests good, the coil is grounded. Replace the stator assembly.
4. Connect the electrical connectors. Make sure all connectors are free of corrosion and are tight.

Removal/installation

1. Perform Steps 1-8 under *Flywheel, Removal* in Chapter Five.
2. Remove the bolts (A, **Figure 1**) securing the stator assembly to the alternator cover.
3. Pull the electrical harness and rubber grommet (B, **Figure 1**) from the notch in the cover.
4. Remove the stator assembly.
5. Install by reversing the removal steps. Make sure all electrical connectors are free of corrosion and are tight.

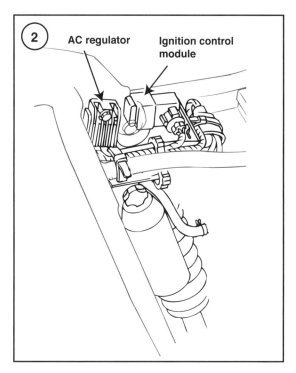

VOLTAGE REGULATOR

The regulator is attached to the left side of the upper frame tube under the seat (**Figure 2**).

Testing

1. Remove the headlight lens assembly from the housing as described in this chapter. Leave the electrical connector attached to the headlight bulb.
2. Connect a voltmeter to the headlight green and blue electrical wire terminals.
3. Start the engine and let it idle. Increase engine speed slowly until engine speed reaches 5000 rpm. The voltmeter should read 13.5-14.5 volts.
4. If the regulator fails the preceding test, check for open or shorted wires and corroded terminals. If faulty wiring or terminals are not found, replace the regulator.

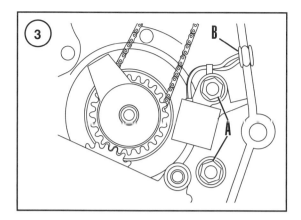

IGNITION CONTROL MODULE

The XR600R model is equipped with an ignition control module (ICM). The ICM controls ignition timing using an electrical signal from the ignition pulse generator as the timing source.

Alternating current from the alternator is rectified and used to charge the capacitor in the ICM. As the piston approaches the firing position, a pulse from the ignition pulse generator triggers the CDI system. This causes the capacitor to discharge into the primary windings of the ignition coil, which amplifies the voltage sufficiently to jump the spark plug gap.

Precautions

1. Never disconnect any of the electrical connections while the engine is running.
2. Keep all connections between the various units clean and tight. Apply dielectric grease to all electrical connectors before reconnecting them to seal out moisture.
3. When kicking the engine over with the spark plug removed, make sure the spark plug or a spark plug tester is installed in the plug cap, and grounded. If not, excessive resistance may damage the ICM.

4. The ICM is mounted to the frame in a rubber mount. Make sure the unit is mounted correctly.

Troubleshooting

Refer to Chapter Two.

Testing

Test specifications for the ICM are not available. Determining whether the ICM is faulty requires eliminating other possible causes through troubleshooting.

Replacement

The ICM is mounted on the right frame tube under the seat (**Figure 2**).
1. Remove the seat as described in Chapter Sixteen.
2. Disconnect the electrical connector from the ICM.
3. Remove the ICM from the rubber isolator on the frame.
4. When installing a new ICM make sure the electrical connector terminals are corrosion-free and tight.

PULSE GENERATOR

Testing

1. Remove the fuel tank as described in Chapter Eight.
2. Disconnect the electrical connector going to the pulse generator.
3. Measure the resistance between the connector terminals and compare the test results to the specified resistance in **Table 2**.
4. If the indicated resistance is not as specified, replace the pulse generator as described in this section.

Removal/Installation

1. Remove the right crankcase cover as described in Chapter Six.
2. Remove the bolts (A, **Figure 3**) securing the pulse generator to the crankcase.
3. Carefully remove the electrical harness and rubber grommet (B, **Figure 3**) from the crankcase.
4. Install by reversing the removal steps. Apply medium strength threadlock to the pulse generator mounting bolts and tighten securely.

IGNITION COIL

Refer to Chapter Eleven.

10

HEADLIGHT

Replacement

1. Unhook the rubber mounting bands (**Figure 4**) securing the number plate/headlight assembly to the front fork.
2. Pivot the number plate/headlight assembly out away from the fork and disconnect the electrical connectors from the bulb socket (**Figure 5**).
3. Remove the number plate.
4. Unhook the spring securing the electrical connector/socket to the backside of the headlight lens unit.
5. Remove the bulb from the electrical connector/socket and replace with a new bulb.
6. Install by reversing the removal steps. Adjust the headlight as described in this section.

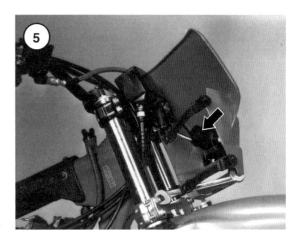

Adjustment

The headlight is limited to vertical adjustment only. For vertical adjustment, turn the adjust screw (**Figure 6**, typical) at the base of the headlight lens.

TAILLIGHT

Replacement

1. From underneath the rear fender, remove the screws, washers and metal collars securing the lens and remove the lens.
2. Wash the inside and outside of the lens with a mild detergent and wipe dry.
3. Replace the bulb and install the lens; do not overtighten the screws as the lens may crack.

ENGINE STOP SWITCH

Testing

1. Disconnect the electrical connector from the engine stop switch on the handlebar.

2. Connect an ohmmeter or continuity tester to the black/white and black switch wires.

3. Test the switch for continuity in both off positions. If the switch is good there will be continuity (very low resistance) in both off positions.

4. Turn the switch button to run. If the switch is good there will be no continuity (infinite resistance).

5. If the switch fails to pass any of these tests, replace the switch.

6. Reconnect the electrical connectors.

Table 1 ALTERNATOR SPECIFICATIONS

Alternator	
Capacity	45 W at 5000 rpm
Exciter coil resistance*	50-200 ohms
Lighting coil resistance*	0.1-1.0 ohms
Regulator	
Regulated voltage	13.5-14.5 volts at 5000 rpm
*Perform test at 20° C (68° F). Do not test if the engine or component is hot.	

Table 2 IGNITION SYSTEM SPECIFICATIONS

Ignition coil	
Primary resistance*	0.1-0.3 ohms
Secondary resistance	
With plug cap	3700-4500 ohms
Without plug cap	2000-4000 ohms
Ignition pulse generator resistance*	360-440 ohms

*Perform test at 20° C (68° F). Do not test if the engine or component is hot.

Table 3 BULB SPECIFICATIONS

	Voltage-wattage
Headlight	12V-35W
Taillight/brakelight	12V-3.8W

10

ELECTRICAL SYSTEM (XR650L)

This chapter contains service and test procedures for the electrical and ignition system components. The battery and spark plug are covered in Chapter Three.

Refer to **Tables 1-7** at the end of this chapter. Wiring diagrams are located at the end of this manual.

ELECTRICAL COMPONENT REPLACEMENT

Most parts suppliers will not accept returned electrical components. If the exact cause of any electrical system malfunction has not been determined, do not attempt to remedy the problem through parts replacement. If an accurate diagnosis cannot be performed, have the suspect component or system tested by a professional technician before purchasing electrical components.

Consider any test results carefully before replacing a component that tests only slightly out of specification, especially resistance. A number of variables can affect test results dramatically. These include: the internal tester circuitry, ambient temperature and motorcycle operating conditions. All instructions and specifications have been checked for accuracy; however, successful test results depend to a great degree upon individual accuracy.

ELECTRICAL CONNECTORS

The position of the connectors may have been changed during previous repairs. Always confirm the wire colors to and from the connector and follow the wiring harness to the various components when performing tests.

Although connectors may appear rugged, the internal pins are easily damaged and dislodged, which may cause a malfunction. Exercise care when handling or testing the connectors.

Under normal operating conditions the connectors are weather-tight. If continuous operation in adverse operating conditions is expected, pack the connectors with dielectric grease to prevent the intrusion of water or other contaminants. Do not use a substitute that may interfere with current flow. Dielectric grease is specifically formulated to seal the connector and not increase current resistance.

An often overlooked area when troubleshooting are the ground connections. Make sure they are corrosion free and tight. Apply dielectric grease to the terminals before reconnecting them.

CHARGING SYSTEM

The charging system consists of the battery, alternator and a voltage regulator/rectifier. Alternating

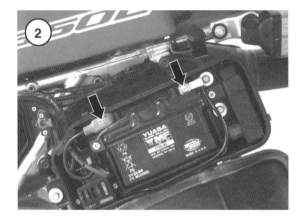

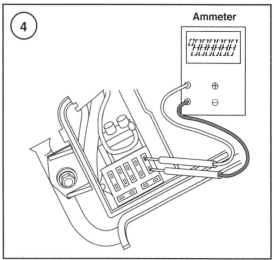

3. Release the rubber hooks at the top of the battery box cover (**Figure 1**) and lower the cover.

4. Leave the battery wires connected to the battery and connect a DC voltmeter between both battery terminals (**Figure 2**). The voltage should be greater than 13 volts. If the voltage is less, refer to Chapter Three for battery service.

5. Disconnect the voltmeter leads from the battery terminals.

> *CAUTION*
> *Do not short either of the voltmeter test probes during this test.*

6. Disconnect the main fuse (**Figure 3**).

7. Connect an ammeter (**Figure 4**) to the main fuse terminals in the fuse panel as follows:

   a. Connect the positive tester probe to the lower terminal.

   b. Connect the negative probe to the upper terminal.

8. Start the engine and let it idle.

9. Gradually increase engine speed to 5000 rpm. At 5000 rpm, the ammeter should read 13 amps. Disconnect the ammeter.

10. Repeat Step 7 and Step 8 using a voltmeter. Gradually increase engine speed to 5000 rpm. At 5000 rpm, the voltmeter should read 14.7-15.5 volts.

11. If the output amperage or voltage is not within specifications, first check the alternator-to-battery wire harness for loose or damaged connectors. If the wire harness connectors are correct, check the alternator stator and then the voltage regulator/rectifier as described in this chapter.

12. Disconnect the voltmeter and reinstall the main fuse.

13. Install the battery case cover and the left side cover.

current generated by the alternator is rectified to direct current. The voltage regulator maintains the correct voltage to the battery and additional electrical loads regardless of variations in engine speed and load. A 20-amp main fuse protects the circuit.

Testing

1. Remove the left side cover as described in Chapter Sixteen.

2. Start the engine and let it reach normal operating temperature. Turn off the engine.

11

ALTERNATOR

The alternator consists of the flywheel, which contains the rotor magnets, and stator coil assembly. Flywheel removal and installation procedures are covered in Chapter Five.

Flywheel Testing

The flywheel is permanently magnetized and cannot be tested except by replacing it with a known good one. The rotor can loose magnetism over time or from a sharp blow. Replace the flywheel if defective or damaged.

Stator

The stator coil or charge coil (A, **Figure 5**) is mounted inside the left crankcase cover.

Testing

The stator/charge coil can be tested with the left crankcase cover mounted on the engine.
1. Remove the right side cover as described in Chapter Sixteen.
2. Disconnect the 3-wire (yellow wires) alternator stator connector (**Figure 6**). Check the electrical wires to and within the electrical connector for damage or poor connections.
3. Use an ohmmeter and measure the resistance between each yellow wire at the stator end of the connector. Refer to **Table 1** for the specified stator coil resistance.
4. If the resistance is as specified, the stator coil is good. If the resistance is significantly higher than specified or the reading is infinite, the coil is damaged. Replace the stator assembly.
5. Use an ohmmeter and check continuity from each yellow wire terminal in the alternator stator end of the connector and to ground. Replace the stator coil if any yellow terminal has continuity to ground. Continuity indicates a short within the stator coil winding.
6. If the stator coil fails either of these tests, replace it as described in this section.
7. Apply a dielectric grease to the stator coil connector before reconnecting it to help seal out moisture.
8. Reconnect the alternator stator connector (**Figure 6**).

Removal/installation

1. Perform Steps 1-11 under *Flywheel, Removal* in Chapter Five.

2. Remove the bolt and wire clamp (A, **Figure 7**) securing the wire to the housing.
3. Remove the bolts (B, **Figure 5**) securing the alternator stator to the left crankcase cover.
4. Carefully pull the rubber grommet (B, **Figure 7**) and electrical wire harness from the left crankcase cover.
5. Install by reversing the preceding removal steps while noting the following:
    a. Make sure to install the wire clamp.
    b. Tighten the wire clamp bolt securely.

VOLTAGE REGULATOR/RECTIFIER

Wiring Harness Test

1. Remove both side covers and the seat as described in Chapter Sixteen.
2. Remove the fuel tank as described in Chapter Nine.
3. Disconnect the voltage regulator/rectifier electrical connector (**Figure 6**). The connector contains two wires (red/white and green).

NOTE
Make all tests (Steps 4-6) at the wiring harness side of the connectors, not at the regulator/rectifier side.

NOTE
When checking for faulty wiring also check for dirty or loose connector terminals.

4. Check the battery circuit lead as follows:
   a. Connect a voltmeter between the red wire connector terminal and a good engine ground.
   b. With the ignition switch off, the voltmeter should read battery voltage.
   c. If the measured voltage is less than battery voltage, check the wire for damage.
   d. Disconnect the voltmeter leads.
5. Check the ground wire as follows:
   a. Connect an ohmmeter between the green wire connector terminal and a good engine ground.
   b. The ohmmeter must read continuity.
   c. If there is no continuity, check the green wire for damage.
6. Check the stator coil and wires as described in this chapter. Refer to *Alternator*.
7. If the above tests do not indicate a fault, the regulator/rectifier may be defective. Substitute a known good unit, or have the regulator/rectifier tested by a dealership.

Removal/Installation

1. Remove both side covers and the seat as described in Chapter Sixteen.
2. Remove the fuel tank as described in Chapter Nine.
3. Disconnect the voltage regulator/rectifier two electrical connectors (**Figure 6**). One connector contains three yellow wires and the other contains two wires (red/white and green).
4. Unhook the electrical wires from any clips or tie-wraps on the frame.
5. Remove the nuts (**Figure 8**) securing the voltage regulator/rectifier to the right side of the frame and remove the voltage regulator/rectifier.
6. Carefully pull the voltage regulator/rectifier and all electrical wires and connectors out from the frame.
7. Install by reversing the preceding removal steps. Make sure all electrical connections are tight and corrosion-free.

IGNITION SYSTEM

All models are equipped with an electronic ignition system.

Precautions

1. Never disconnect any of the electrical connections while the engine is running.
2. Apply dielectric grease to all electrical connectors before reconnecting them to help seal out moisture.
3. The electrical connectors must be free of corrosion and properly connected.
4. The ignition control module (ICM) is held in a rubber mount. If removed, make sure to reinstall it into the rubber mount.

Troubleshooting

Refer to Chapter Two.

PEAK VOLTAGE TESTS

WARNING
High voltage is present during ignition system operation. Do not touch ignition components, wires or test leads while cranking or running the engine.

Peak voltage tests check the voltage output of the ignition system components at normal cranking speed, thus making it possible to accurately test the voltage output under operating conditions.

11

The peak voltage specifications listed in Table 3 are minimum values. If the measured voltage meets or exceeds the specification, the test results are satisfactory. In some cases, the voltage may greatly exceed the minimum specification.

A peak voltage tester is required. One of the following testers, or an equivalent, can be used to perform peak voltage tests described in this section. Refer to the manufacturer's instructions when using these tools.

1. Honda Peak voltage adapter, part No. 07HGJ-0020100. This tool must be used in combination with a digital multimeter with a minimum impedance of 10M ohms/DC V. A meter with lower impedance does not display accurate measurements. Refer to **Figure 8a.**

2. Ignition Mate (Motion Pro part No. 08-0193). Refer to **Figure 8b**.

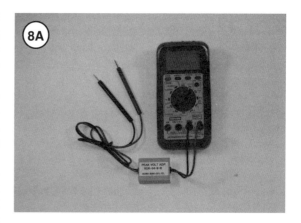

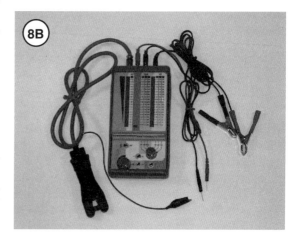

CRANKSHAFT POSITION SENSOR (2008-ON)

Peak Voltage Test

This test requires a peak voltage tester as described in this chapter.

1. Check the battery to make sure it is fully charged and in good condition. A weak battery causes a slow engine cranking speed and inaccurate peak voltage tests results.

2. Check engine compression as described in Chapter Three. If the compression is low, the following test results will be inaccurate.

3. Check all of the ignition component electrical connectors and wiring harnesses. Make sure the connectors are clean and properly connected.

4. Remove the ignition control module (ICM) as described under *Replacement* in Chapter Eleven.

5. Reconnect the battery cables to the battery.

> *WARNING*
> *High voltage is present during ignition system operation. Do not touch the spark plug, ignition components, connectors or test leads while cranking the engine.*

> *NOTE*
> *If using the Ignition Mate tester or a similar peak voltage tester, follow the manufacturer's instructions for connection.*

> *NOTE*
> *All peak voltage specifications in the text (Step 3 and Step 4) and Table 3 are minimum voltages. If the measured voltage meets or exceeds the specification, consider the test results satisfactory. On some components, the voltage*

may greatly exceed the minimum specification.

6. If using the Honda peak voltage adapter, connect it to the multimeter as shown in **Figure 1**.

7. Perform the following test:
   a. Connect the peak voltage positive test lead to the 4-pin ICM wiring harness connector blue/yellow wire terminal and the negative test lead to the green wire terminal.
   b. Shift the transmission into neutral.
   c. Turn the ignition switch on and the engine stop switch to RUN.
   d. Press the starter button while reading the meter. The meter should indicate a minimum peak voltage reading of 0.7 volts DC.
   e. Turn the ignition switch off and disconnect the test leads.

8. Perform the following test:
   a. Remove the fuel tank as described in Chapter Nine.
   b. Disconnect the crankshaft position sensor connector (**Figure 11**).
   c. Connect the tester to the sensor end of the connector.

d. Connect the peak voltage positive test lead to the blue/yellow wire terminal and the negative test lead to the green wire connector terminal.

e. Shift the transmission into neutral.

f. Turn the ignition switch on and the engine stop switch to RUN.

g. Press the starter button while reading the meter. The meter should indicate a minimum peak voltage reading of 0.7 volts DC.

h. Turn the ignition switch off and disconnect the test leads.

9A. If both tests were incorrect, check the following:

a. Low multimeter impedance; below 10M ohms/DCV.

b. Low cranking speed due to low battery voltage.

c. Faulty wiring.

d. Faulty crankshaft position sensor.

9B. If test in Step 7 was good, but test in Step 6 was incorrect, inspect the wiring harness and connections.

10. Install the removed parts.

Removal/Installation

1. Remove the right crankcase cover as described in Chapter Six.

2. Remove the bolts (A, **Figure 12**) securing the crankcase position sensor to the crankcase.

3. Carefully remove the electrical harness and rubber grommet (B, **Figure 12**) from the crankcase.

4. Install by reversing the preceding removal steps. Make sure all electrical connectors are clean and tight.

IGNITION COIL (2008-ON)

Peak Voltage Test

This test requires a peak voltage tester as described in this chapter.

1. Check the battery to make sure it is fully charged and in good condition. A weak battery causes a slow engine cranking speed and inaccurate peak voltage tests results.

2. Remove the fuel tank (Chapter Nine).

3. Check engine compression as described in Chapter Three. If the compression is low, the test results will be inaccurate.

4. Check all of the ignition component electrical connectors and wiring harnesses. Check the electrical wires to and within the connector for any opens or poor connections. Make sure the connectors are clean and properly connected.

5. Disconnect the spark plug cap. Then connect a new spark plug to the plug cap and ground the plug against the cylinder head. Do not remove the spark plug from the cylinder head. The spark plug must remain in the cylinder head to maintain engine compression.

6. If using the Honda peak voltage adapter, connect it to the multimeter as shown in **Figure 1**.

NOTE
If using the Ignition Mate tester or a similar peak voltage tester, follow the manufacturer's instructions for connection.

NOTE
Do not disconnect the ignition coil primary connectors when performing Step 8.

7. Connect the positive test lead to the ignition coil's black/yellow connector terminal and the negative test lead to ground.

8. Shift the transmission into neutral.

9. Turn the ignition switch on and the engine stop switch to RUN.

WARNING
High voltage is present during ignition system operation. Do not touch the spark plug, ignition components, connectors or test leads while cranking the engine.

10. Press the starter button while reading the meter. The meter should indicate a minimum peak voltage reading of 100 volts.

NOTE
The peak voltage specification is a minimum voltage. If the measured voltage meets or exceeds the specification, consider the test results satisfactory.

11. Turn off the ignition switch and disconnect the test leads.

12. Reinstall the spark plug cap.

13. Install the fuel tank (Chapter Nine).

IGNITION CONTROL MODULE

Wiring Harness Test

The following procedure tests the ignition control module (ICM) wiring harness as well as the connected components. Incorrect test results indicated either faulty wiring or connectors, or a defective component. To determine which component is faulty, isolate and test the component as described in this chapter.

11

1. Remove the left side cover as described in Chapter Sixteen.

2. Release the rubber hooks at the top of the battery box cover (**Figure 9**) and lower the cover.

3. Disconnect the battery negative lead (A, **Figure 10**), then the positive lead.

4. Remove the bolts securing the battery holder and remove the holder (B, **Figure 10**).

5. Slide the ICM (C, **Figure 10**) out of the battery case and disconnect the multi-pin electrical connector from it.

6. Refer to **Table 2** and measure the resistance values between each of the electrical connector terminals on the wire harness end of the electrical connector. Do not perform these tests on the ICM terminals.

7. If any of the test results do not meet the specifications, then test and inspect the following ignition system components as described in this chapter:

    a. Ignition coil: primary and secondary resistance.

    b. Pulse generator (1993-2007) or crankshaft position sensor (2008-on).

8. If all of the ignition components test good, then check the following:

    a. Check for an open or short in the wire harness between each component.

    b. Make sure all connections between the various components are clean and tight.

9. If Steps 6-8 meet all specifications, then the ICM is probably faulty and must be replaced as described in this section.

10. If the ICM tests good, reinstall the following components:

    a. Reconnect the electrical connector onto the ICM unit and slide it back into place in the battery case.

    b. Install the battery holder and tighten the bolts securely.

    c. Reconnect the positive then the negative battery leads.

    d. Install the battery case cover and the left side cover.

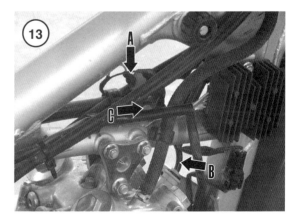

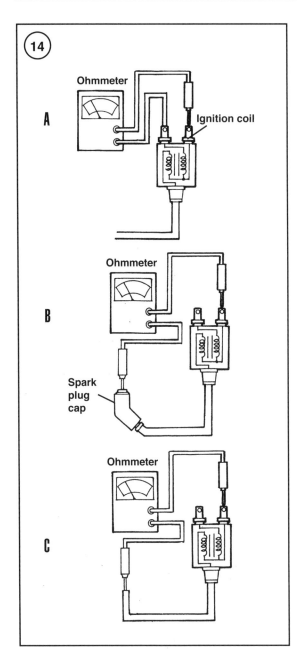

14

A

Ohmmeter

Ignition coil

B

Ohmmeter

Spark
plug
cap

C

Ohmmeter

Replacement

1. Remove the left side cover as described in Chapter Sixteen.
2. Release the rubber hooks at the top of the battery box cover (**Figure 9**) and lower the cover.
3. Disconnect the battery negative lead (A, **Figure 10**), then the positive lead.
4. Remove the bolts securing the battery holder and remove the holder (B, **Figure 10**).
5. Slide the ICM (C, **Figure 10**) out of the battery case and disconnect the multi-pin electrical connector from it.
6. Reconnect the electrical connector onto the new ICM and slide it back into place in the battery case.

7. Install the battery holder and tighten the bolts securely.
8. Install the battery case cover and the left side cover.

PULSE GENERATOR (1993-2007)

Testing

1. Disconnect the 2-pin electrical connector from the pulse generator (**Figure 11**).
2. Using an ohmmeter check the resistance between the terminals in the electrical connector. Refer to **Table 3** for the specified resistance.
3. If the pulse generator fails the resistance test in Step 2, replace it as described in this section.
4. If the pulse generator passes the resistance test, reconnect the 2-pin electrical connector.

Removal/Installation

1. Remove the right crankcase cover as described in Chapter Six.
2. Remove the bolts (A, **Figure 12**) securing the pulse generator to the crankcase cover.
3. Carefully remove the electrical harness and rubber grommet (B, **Figure 12**) from the crankcase.
4. Install by reversing the preceding removal steps. Make sure all electrical connectors are clean and tight.

IGNITION COIL (1993-2007)

Removal/Installation

1. Remove the fuel tank as described in Chapter Nine.
2. Disconnect the primary electrical wires (A, **Figure 13**) from the coil.
3. Disconnect the high voltage lead from the spark plug (B, **Figure 13**).
4. Remove the bolt (C, **Figure 13**) securing the ignition coil to the frame.
5. Carefully pull the ignition coil away from the frame and remove it.
6. Install by reversing the preceding removal steps. Make sure all electrical connections are tight and corrosion-free.

Testing

Refer to **Table 3** for specifications.
1. Remove the fuel tank as described in Chapter Nine.
2. Disconnect all ignition coil wires (including the spark plug lead from the spark plug) before testing.
3. Using an ohmmeter measure the primary coil resistance between the positive and the negative terminals on the top of the ignition coil (A, **Figure 14**).

11

4. Measure the secondary coil resistance between the ignition coil green wire lead and the spark plug lead with the spark plug cap attached (B, **Figure 14**).

5. Measure the secondary coil resistance between the ignition coil green wire lead and the spark plug lead with the spark plug cap removed (C, **Figure 14**).

6. If the coil resistance does not meet any of these specifications, replace the coil. If the coil exhibits visible damage, replace it.

7. If the ignition coil passes the preceding tests, reconnect all ignition coil wires to the ignition coil.

STARTING SYSTEM

The starting system consists of the starter, starter gears, starter relay and starter switch.

When the starter switch button is pressed, it engages the starter relay that completes the circuit allowing electricity to flow from the battery to the starter. The starter gears are covered in Chapter Five.

> *CAUTION*
> *Do not operate the starter for more than 5 seconds at a time. Wait for approximately 10 seconds between starting periods.*

Troubleshooting

Refer to Chapter Two.

STARTER

Removal/Installation

1. Remove the left side cover as described in Chapter Sixteen.

2. Release the rubber hooks at the top of the battery box cover (**Figure 9**) and lower the cover.

3. Disconnect the battery negative lead (A, **Figure 10**).

4. Remove the carburetor as described in Chapter Nine.

5. Remove the clutch cable bracket bolt (**Figure 15**).

6. Slide back the rubber boot (A, **Figure 16**) on the electrical cable connector.

7. Disconnect the starter electrical cable from the starter terminal (B, **Figure 16**).

8. Remove the bolts (and ground wire) (C, **Figure 16**) securing the starter to the crankcase.

9. Extract the starter (D, **Figure 16**) from the top of the crankcase.

10. Remove the starter spacer (A, **Figure 17**) and rubber mount (B) from the top of the crankcase.

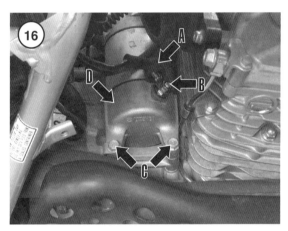

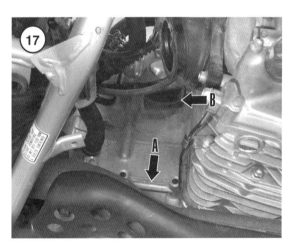

11. Install by reversing the preceding removal steps while noting the following:

   a. Make sure to reinstall the rubber mount under the left side of the starter.

   b. Install the ground cable under the starter rear mounting bolt.

Disassembly

Refer to **Figure 18**.

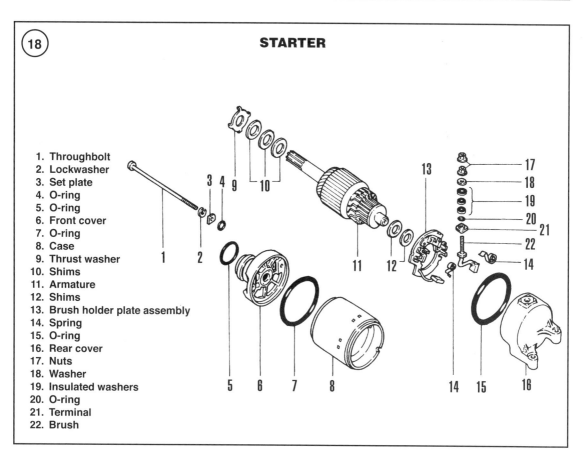

STARTER

1. Throughbolt
2. Lockwasher
3. Set plate
4. O-ring
5. O-ring
6. Front cover
7. O-ring
8. Case
9. Thrust washer
10. Shims
11. Armature
12. Shims
13. Brush holder plate assembly
14. Spring
15. O-ring
16. Rear cover
17. Nuts
18. Washer
19. Insulated washers
20. O-ring
21. Terminal
22. Brush

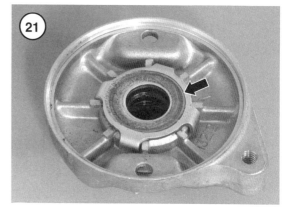

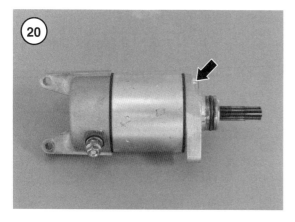

1. Remove the two case throughbolts, washers and lockwashers (**Figure 19**).

2. Slide the front cover (**Figure 20**) off the armature shaft.

3. Note the thrust washer which will remain in the front cover (**Figure 21**).

NOTE
The number of shims used in each starter varies and may not be the same as depicted in this procedure.

4. Slide the shims (**Figure 22**) off the armature shaft. Record the number and location of the shims.

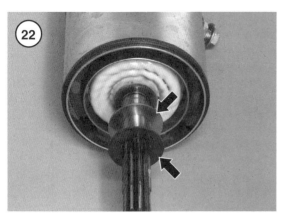

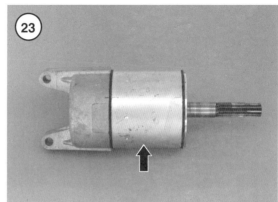

5. Slide the case (**Figure 23**) off the armature.

6. Remove the end cover (**Figure 24**) from the armature.

7. Slide the shims off the armature shaft (**Figure 25**). Record the number and location of the shims.

8. Clean all grease, dirt and carbon from the armature, case and end covers.

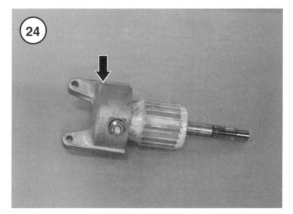

Inspection

> *CAUTION*
> *Do not immerse the wire windings in the case or the armature coil in solvent as the insulation may be damaged. Wipe the windings with a cloth lightly moistened with solvent and thoroughly dry.*

1. Pull the brush holder assembly (A, **Figure 26**) out of the end cover and carefully turn it over to expose the brushes (B).

2. Pull the spring away from each brush (B, **Figure 26**) and pull the brushes out of the guides.

3. Measure the length of each brush with a vernier caliper (**Figure 27**). If the length of any brush equals or is less than the service limit in **Table 4** replace the brush holder assembly. The brushes cannot be replaced individually.

4. To replace the brush holder assembly, perform the following:

> *CAUTION*
> *The cable terminal assembly (C, **Figure 26***) is composed of three insulated washers, a regular washer and nut. Label each component when removed, especially the insulated washers, as they must be reinstalled in the same order to insulate the brushes from the case.*

a. Remove the nut (A, **Figure 28**) from the cable terminal and slide off the regular washer (B).

b. Remove the large insulated washer (C, **Figure 28**) and the two small insulated washers (D).

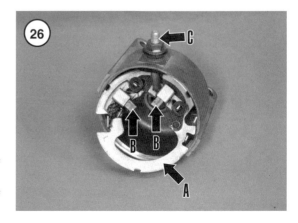

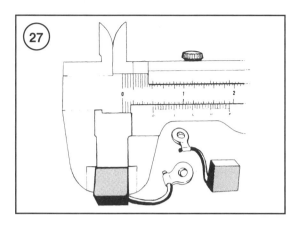

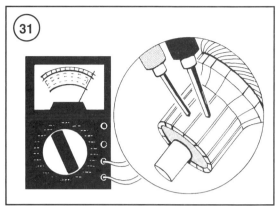

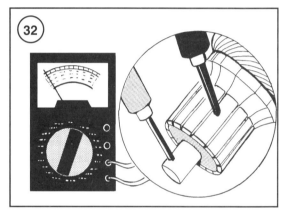

c. Slide the O-ring off the cable terminal.

d. Push the cable terminal into the end cover and remove the brush holder assembly.

e. Install the brush holder assembly by reversing the preceding removal steps. Make sure to install the nut and washers in their original order.

5. Inspect the commutator (**Figure 29**). The mica in a good commutator is below the surface of the copper bars. On a worn commutator the mica and copper bars may be worn to the same level (**Figure 30**). If necessary, have the commutator serviced by a dealer or electrical repair shop.

6. Inspect the commutator copper bars for discoloration. If a pair of bars are discolored, the armature coils are grounded.

7. Use an ohmmeter and perform the following:

a. Check for continuity between the commutator bars (**Figure 31**); there should be continuity (indicated resistance) between pairs of bars.

b. Check for continuity between the commutator bars and the shaft (**Figure 32**); there should be no continuity (infinite resistance).

c. If the unit fails either of these tests, replace the starter. The armature cannot be replaced individually.

8. Use an ohmmeter and perform the following:

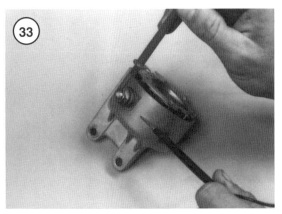

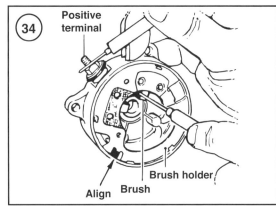

Positive terminal

Brush holder

Align   Brush

a. Check for continuity between the starter cable terminal and the rear case cover (**Figure 33**); there should be no continuity.

b. Check for continuity between the starter cable terminal and the brush black wire terminal (**Figure 34**); there should be continuity.

c. If the unit fails either of these tests, replace the starter. The case/field coil assembly cannot be replaced individually.

9. Inspect the seal and bearing in the front cover (**Figure 35**) for wear or damage. If either is damaged, replace the starter as these parts are not available separately.

10. Inspect the bushing in the rear cover (**Figure 36**) for wear or damage. If it is damaged, replace the starter as this part is not available separately.

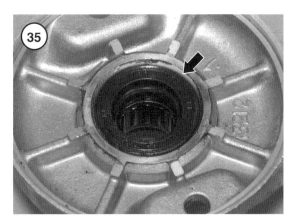

Assembly

1. If removed, install the brushes into the holders and secure the brushes with the springs.

2. Install the brush holder assembly in the rear cover. Align the holder locating tab with the notch in the rear cover (**Figure 37**).

3. Install the correct number of shims on the armature shaft next to the commutator.

4. Insert the armature coil assembly into the rear cover (**Figure 24**). Turn the armature during installation so the brushes engage the commutator properly. Make sure the armature is not turned upside down so the shims could slide off the end of the shaft. Do not damage the brushes during this step.

5. Make sure the two O-rings (**Figure 38**) are installed on the case. Then slide the case over the armature (**Figure 23**). Align the marks on the case and rear cover (**Figure 39**).

6. Install the correct number of shims onto the armature shaft.

7. Install the thrust washer onto the front cover so the tabs engage the cover slots (**Figure 40**).

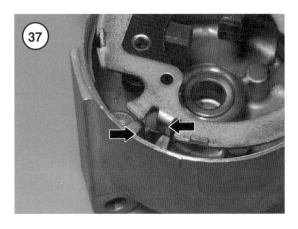

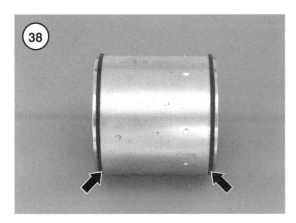

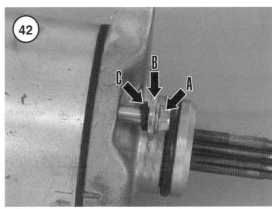

8. Install the front cover (A, **Figure 41**) onto the armature shaft. Align the marks on the front cover and the case.

9. Install the bolts (A, **Figure 42**), washers (B) and O-rings (C). Tighten the bolts securely.

10. Replace the front cover O-ring seal (B, **Figure 41**) if deteriorated or damaged. Apply engine oil onto the O-ring.

11. Clean the cover mounting lugs (C, **Figure 41**) as they act as the ground for the starter.

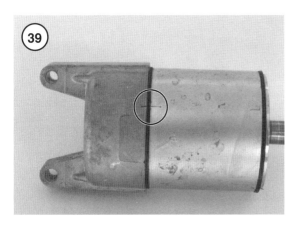

STARTER RELAY

The starter relay provides a circuit for high-amperage current to flow from the battery to the starter. Pushing the starter button actuates the magnetic coil switch within the starter relay, which closes the internal contacts for the starter circuit.

Testing

1. Troubleshoot the starting circuit as described in Chapter Two. If the problem has been isolated to the starter relay, perform the following test.

2. Remove the left side cover as described in Chapter Sixteen.

3. Release the rubber hooks at the top of the battery box cover and lower the cover.

4. Shift the transmission into neutral.

5. Turn the ignition switch on and press the starter button. The starter relay (A, **Figure 43**) should click. Note the following:

   a. Yes, the relay clicks: The starter relay is operating correctly.

   b. No, the relay does not click: Continue with Step 6.

6. Disconnect the starter relay electrical connector (B, **Figure 43**). Repair any dirty, loose fitting or damaged terminals. If the wiring is in good condition, leave the connector disconnected and continue with Step 7.

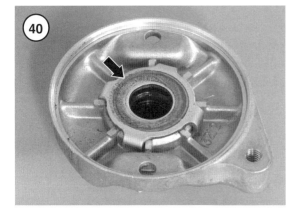

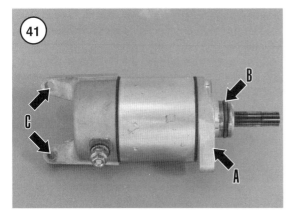

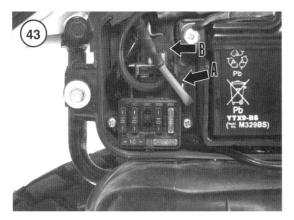

7. Ground circuit connection test: Shift the transmission into neutral. Check for continuity between the starter relay connector green/red wire and ground. There should be continuity or a slight resistance reading. Note the following:

NOTE
The ohmmeter should read 0 ohms when making a ground test. However, because of the diode in the circuit, it is normal for the ohmmeter to show a slight resistance reading.

a. There is continuity: Go to Step 8.
b. There is no continuity: Repair the open circuit in the green/red wire between the starter relay connector and the left handlebar switch connector.

8. Starter relay voltage check: Turn the ignition switch on and measure voltage between the starter relay yellow/red wire at the starter relay connector (B, **Figure 43**) and ground when pressing the starter button. There should be battery voltage. Note the following:

a. There is battery voltage: Go to Step 9.
b. There is no battery voltage: Repair the open in the yellow/red wire between the starter relay connector and the engine stop switch in the right-handlebar switch connector.

9. Bench test the starter relay as follows:
a. Remove the starter relay as described in this section. Clean the switch electrical terminals.
b. Connect test leads between the two large terminals on the starter relay (A, **Figure 44**). There should be no continuity.
c. If there is continuity, replace the starter relay.
d. If there is no continuity, leave the ohmmeter connected to the relay and continue with substep e.
e. Connect the positive lead from a fully charged 12-volt battery to the starter relay yellow/red wire terminal (B, **Figure 44**) and the negative battery lead to the green/red wire terminal (C). There should be continuity.
f. If there is no continuity, replace the starter relay.

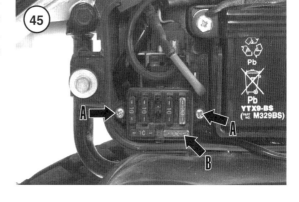

g. If there is continuity, the starter relay is operational. Reinstall the starter relay and test the integrity of the wires and cables in the starting circuit.

10. Install all parts previously removed.

Removal/Installation

1. Remove the left side cover as described in Chapter Sixteen.
2. Release the rubber hooks at the top of the battery box cover and lower the cover.
3. Disconnect the battery negative lead, then the positive lead.
4. Remove the fuse block mounting screws (A, **Figure 45**), then move the fuse block (B) out of the way.
5. Remove the starter relay (**Figure 46**) and rubber mount from the mounting prongs.
6. Disconnect the starter relay electrical connector (A, **Figure 47**) from the relay.
7. Disconnect the battery lead (B, **Figure 47**) and starter cable lead (C) from the starter relay.
8. Installation is the reverse of removal. Note the following:
a. Clean the battery and starter cable leads before connecting them to the relay.
b. Install the rubber mount so the rounded side is toward the cable terminal side of the relay.

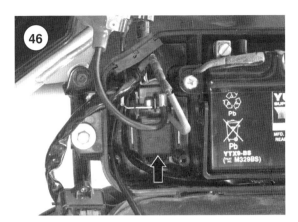

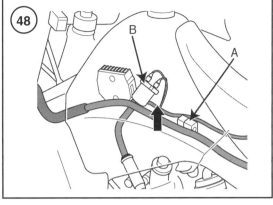

CLUTCH DIODE

The clutch diode is part of the starter circuit and is wired between the clutch switch and neutral switch. The diode prevents the flow of current from the neutral switch back through the clutch switch.

Suspect a faulty clutch diode if the neutral light comes on when the transmission is in gear and the clutch is disengaged. Also, look for a dirty or loose clutch diode connection if the starter does not operate when the transmission is in neutral.

Testing/Replacement

1. Remove the fuel tank as described in Chapter Nine.
2. Disconnect the 2-pin electrical connector from the clutch diode (A, **Figure 48**), which is adjacent to the wiring harness on the left side and rearward of the ignition coil (B).
3. Using an ohmmeter, connect a test lead to a diode terminal. Then touch the remaining ohmmeter test lead to the opposite diode terminal. Reverse the test leads and check continuity in the opposite direction. The ohmmeter should indicate continuity in one direction and no continuity when the test leads are reversed.
4. Replace the diode if it fails this test.

LIGHTING SYSTEM

Headlight Bulb and Lens Removal/Installation

Refer to **Figure 49**.
1. Remove the bolt and collar (A, **Figure 50**) on each side securing the headlight visor.
2. Lift up the visor to disengage it from the lower bracket and remove the visor (B, **Figure 50**).
3. Remove the bolt (A, **Figure 51**) on each side securing the headlight lens assembly to the mounting bracket and remove the assembly (B).
4. Disconnect the electrical connector from the backside of the bulb (A, **Figure 52**).
5. Remove the rubber cover (B, **Figure 52**) from the back of the headlight.

CAUTION
*The headlight uses a quartz-halogen bulb (**Figure 53**). Do not touch the bulb glass, as traces of oil on this type of bulb reduce its life. Clean oil or other contamination from the bulb with a cloth moistened in alcohol or lacquer thinner.*

6. Unhook the clip (A, **Figure 54**) and remove the light bulb (B). Replace with a new bulb.
7. Install by reversing the preceding removal steps while noting the following:
   a. Install the rubber bulb cover so the TOP arrow points toward the top of the headlight.
   b. Align the notches in the lens assembly arms (**Figure 55**) with the front edge of the mounting bracket.
   c. Adjust the headlight as described in this chapter.

Headlight Adjustment

To adjust the headlight horizontally, turn the adjuster located in the lower section of the visor (**Figure 56**). Turn the adjuster either clockwise or counterclockwise until the aim is correct.

11

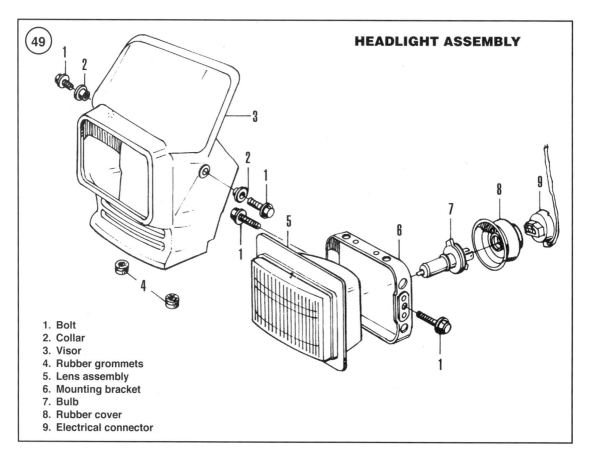

HEADLIGHT ASSEMBLY

1. Bolt
2. Collar
3. Visor
4. Rubber grommets
5. Lens assembly
6. Mounting bracket
7. Bulb
8. Rubber cover
9. Electrical connector

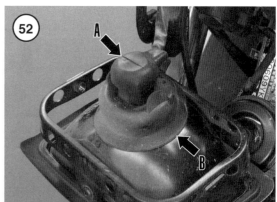

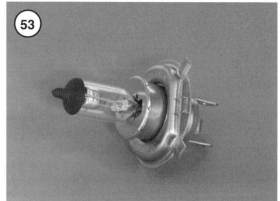

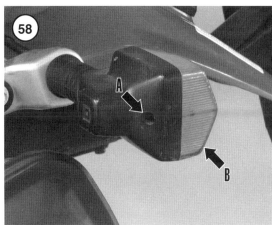

To adjust the headlight vertically, proceed as follows:
1. Remove the bolt and collar (A, **Figure 50**) on each side securing the headlight visor.
2. Lift up the visor to disengage it from the lower bracket and remove the visor (B, **Figure 50**).
3. Loosen the mounting bolts (A, **Figure 51**). Move the headlight assembly either up or down until the aim is correct.
4. Tighten the mounting bolt and reinstall the headlight visor.

Taillight/Brake Light Bulb Replacement

1. Remove the lens retaining screws (A, **Figure 57**), then remove the lens (B).
2. Push the defective bulb into the socket, turn it counterclockwise and remove it.
3. Carefully clean the lens and reflective surface on the bulb holder.
4. Install a new bulb.
5. Install the lens and gasket. Do not overtighten the screws, otherwise, the lens may crack.
6. Check light operation.

11

**Front and Rear Turn Signal
Bulb Replacement**

1. Remove the lens retaining screw (A, **Figure 58**), then remove the lens (B).
2. Push the defective bulb into the socket, turn it counterclockwise and remove it.
3. Carefully clean the lens and reflective surface on the bulb holder.
4. Install a new bulb.
5. Install the lens and gasket. Do not overtighten the screw, otherwise, the lens may crack.
6. Check the turn signal light operation.

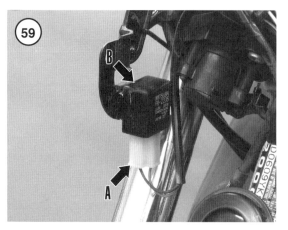

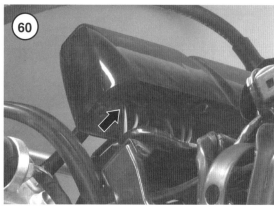

Turn Signal Relay

Testing

There is no specific test for the turn signal relay. Determine if the relay is causing a turn signal malfunction by testing and eliminating the other components in the turn signal system.

If all other turn signal components test good, proceed as follows:

1. Remove the bolt and collar (A, **Figure 50**) on each side securing the headlight visor.
2. Lift up the visor to disengage it from the lower bracket and remove the visor (B, **Figure 50**).
3. Remove the headlight visor as described in this section.
4. Disconnect the electrical connector (A, **Figure 59**) from the turn signal relay.
5. Connect a piece of wire between the terminals in the connector.
6. Operate the turn signals. If the turn signal light does not come on, check the turn signal components. If the turn signal light comes on, the turn signal relay is faulty.

Removal/installation

1. Remove the bolt and collar (A, **Figure 50**) on each side securing the headlight visor.
2. Lift up the visor to disengage it from the lower bracket and remove the visor (B, **Figure 50**).
3. Disconnect the electrical connector (A, **Figure 59**) from the turn signal relay.
4. Remove the turn signal relay (B, **Figure 59**) from the rubber mount.
5. Reverse the removal steps to install the relay.

Indicator Light Replacement

1. Remove the bolt and collar (A, **Figure 50**) on each side securing the headlight visor.

61   **IGNITION SWITCH**

	BAT 1	BAT 2
ON	•———————	———•
OFF		
LOCK		
Color	Red	Red/black

2. Lift the visor up to disengage it from the lower bracket and remove the visor (B, **Figure 50**).
3. Carefully pull the lamp holder/electrical wire assembly (**Figure 60**) down and out of the backside of the instrument cluster.
4. Remove and replace the defective bulb(s).
5. Push the lamp holder/electrical wire assembly back into the instrument cluster. Make sure it is completely seated to prevent the entry of water and moisture.
6. Install the visor and tighten the bolts securely.

SWITCHES

Testing

Test switches for continuity with an ohmmeter or test light (Chapter One) at the switch connector plug by operating the switch in each of its operating positions and comparing the results with its switch operation diagram. For example, **Figure 61** shows a continuity diagram for an ignition switch. The horizontal line indicates which terminals should show continuity when the switch is in that position.

When testing switches, refer to the appropriate continuity diagrams in the wiring diagrams at the end of this manual and note the following:

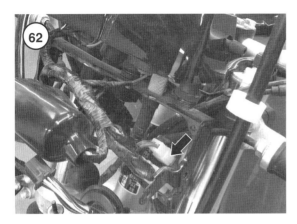

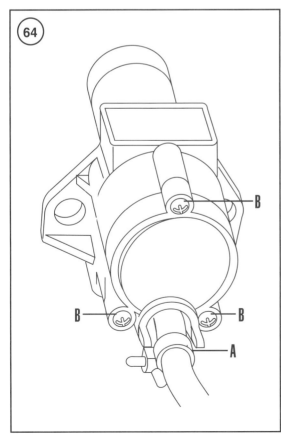

1. First check the fuse as described in *Fuses* in this chapter.
2. Make sure the battery state of charge is acceptable (Chapter Three).
3. Disconnect the switch from the circuit or disconnect the negative battery cable before performing continuity tests.
4. When separating two connectors, pull the connector housings and not the wires.
5. After isolating a defective circuit, check the connectors to make sure they are clean and properly connected. Check all wires going into a connector housing to make sure each wire is properly positioned and the wire end is not loose.
6. When reconnecting electrical connector halves, push them together until they click or snap into place.

Ignition Switch

Removal/installation

1. Remove the bolt and collar (A, **Figure 50**) on each side securing the headlight visor.
2. Lift the visor up to disengage it from the lower bracket and remove the visor (B, **Figure 50**).
3. Disconnect the ignition switch connector (**Figure 62**).
4. Remove the mounting bolts (A, **Figure 63**) and remove the switch assembly (B).
5. Install by reversing the removal steps.

Disassembly/assembly

1. Remove the ignition switch as described in this section.
2. Insert the ignition key in the switch and turn the tumbler so it is part way between on and off.
3. Open the wire retainer (A, **Figure 64**) securing the electrical harness to the switch.
4. Remove the screws (B, **Figure 64**) securing the electrical contact portion.
5. Push in on the lug of the electrical contact switch portion, depressing it enough to clear the slot in the mechanical portion of the switch assembly.
6. Withdraw the electrical portion of the switch from the mechanical portion of the switch assembly.
7. Replace the defective component.
8. Assemble by reversing the disassembly steps. Make sure the lugs are completely indexed into the slots in the mechanical portion of the switch.

Right Handlebar Switch Housing

The right handlebar switch housing contains the start button (A, **Figure 65**) and engine stop switch (B). Individual switches are not available.

11

Replacement

1. Remove the bolt and collar (A, **Figure 50**) on each side securing the headlight visor.
2. Lift the visor up to disengage it from the lower bracket and remove the visor (B, **Figure 50**).
3. Remove any clamps securing the switch wiring harness to the handlebar.
4. Disconnect the right handlebar switch electrical connector (**Figure 66**).

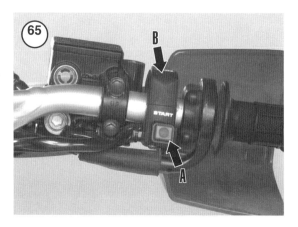

> *NOTE*
> *The handlebar switch wiring harness also includes wiring for the front brake light switch. If complete removal is necessary, also disconnect the brake light switch connectors as described in this section.*

5. Remove the switch housing screws and separate the switch halves. Remove the switch and wiring harness from the frame.
6. Install the switch housing by reversing the preceding removal steps. Align the lower switch housing pin with the hole in the handlebar, then install the housing.
7. Start the engine and check the switch in each of the operating positions.

Left Handlebar Switch Housing

The left handlebar switch housing contains the headlight dimmer switch (A, **Figure 67**), turn signal switch (B) and horn button (C). Individual switches are not available.

Replacement

1. Remove the bolt and collar (A, **Figure 50**) on each side securing the headlight visor.
2. Lift the visor up to disengage it from the lower bracket and remove the visor (B, **Figure 50**).
3. Remove any clamps securing the switch wiring harness to the handlebar.
4. Disconnect the left handlebar switch electrical connector (**Figure 68**).

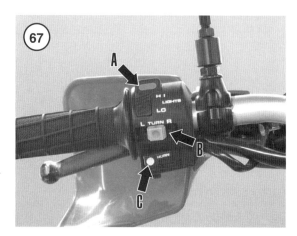

> *NOTE*
> *The handlebar switch wiring harness also includes wiring for the turn signal relay and clutch switch. If complete removal is necessary, also disconnect the relay and clutch switch connectors as described in this section.*

5. Remove the switch housing screws and separate the switch halves. Remove the switch and wiring harness from the frame.

6. Install the switch housing by reversing the preceding removal steps. Align the lower switch housing pin with the hole in the handlebar, then install the housing.
7. Start the engine and check the switch in each of the operating positions.

Neutral Switch

Testing

1. Remove the seat as described in Chapter Sixteen.

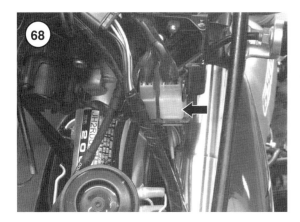

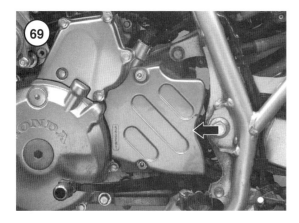

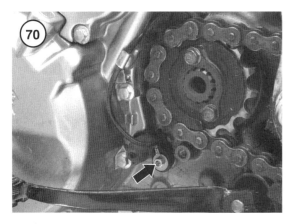

6. Repeat Step 3 at the neutral switch terminal.
7. If necessary, replace the switch.

Removal/installatiom

1. Remove the bolts securing the drive sprocket cover and remove the cover (**Figure 69**).
2. Move the boot, then remove the nut **(Figure 70)** and disconnect the wire from the neutral switch terminal.
3. Unscrew the neutral switch from the crankcase.
4. Install the new switch. Tighten the switch to 12 N•m (106 in.-lb.)
5. Connect the electrical wire to the switch terminal. Do not overtighten the nut on the switch terminal.
6. Install the drive sprocket cover.

Clutch/Front Brake Lever Switches

WARNING
Do not ride the motorcycle until the brake light switch works correctly.

Testing

1. Disconnect the connector from the switch.
2. Connect an ohmmeter to the switch terminals.
3. Pull in the lever. There should be continuity.
4. If there is no continuity, replace the switch.

Removal/installation

1. Disconnect the connector from the switch.
2. Remove the switch mounting screw and remove the switch.
3. Install the switch and tighten the mounting screw securely.
4. Connect the connector to the switch.
5. Check operation.

Rear Brake Light Switch

WARNING
Do not ride the motorcycle until the brake light switch works correctly.

Testing

1. Remove the seat as described in Chapter Sixteen.
2. Disconnect the brake light switch wires at the electrical connector above the air box.
3. Connect the leads of an ohmmeter or continuity tester between the connector terminals. The tester should indicate continuity when the rear brake

2. Disconnect the neutral switch wires at the electrical connector above the air box.
3. Connect the leads of an ohmmeter or continuity tester between the light green/red wire terminal and ground. The tester should indicate continuity when the transmission is in neutral and infinity when the transmission is in gear.
4. If the readings are incorrect, remove the bolts securing the drive sprocket cover and remove the cover (**Figure 69**).
5. Move the boot, then remove the nut (**Figure 70**) and disconnect the wire from the neutral switch terminal.

11

pedal is depressed and infinity when the pedal is released.

4. If necessary, replace the rear brake light switch if it fails to operate.

5. Connect the switch connector.

Removal/installation

1. Remove the seat as described in Chapter Sixteen.
2. Disconnect the brake light switch wires at the electrical connector above the air box.
3. Detach the spring (A, **Figure 71**) from the brake light switch.
4. Unscrew the brake light switch from the mounting nut (B, **Figure 71**).
5. Reverse these removal steps to install the brake light switch.
6. Refer to Chapter Three and adjust the rear brake light switch.

Sidestand Switch Removal/Installation

1. Remove the seat as described in Chapter Sixteen.
2. On top of the air filter air box, disconnect the 3-pin electrical connector (**Figure 72**).
3. Release all clamps and bands securing the electrical wire from the connector to the sidestand.
4. Remove the bolts securing the switch cover (A, **Figure 73**) and remove the cover (B).
5. Remove the bolt (C, **Figure 73**) securing the switch to the sidestand pivot bolt.
6. Remove the switch and wiring harness from the frame.
7. Install by reversing the preceding removal steps while noting the following:
   a. Align the switch pin with the sidestand hole.
   b. Align the switch groove with the sidestand return spring holding pin.
   c. Apply threadlock to the switch retaining bolt (C, **Figure 73**) threads and tighten securely.

INSTRUMENT CLUSTER

Removal/Installation

1. Remove the headlight lens assembly as described in this Chapter.
2. Remove the left side cover as described in Chapter Sixteen.
3. Release the rubber hooks at the top of the battery box cover (**Figure 74**) and lower the cover.
4. Disconnect the battery negative lead (**Figure 75**).
5. Unscrew the speedometer drive cable (A, **Figure 76**) from the back of the meter.

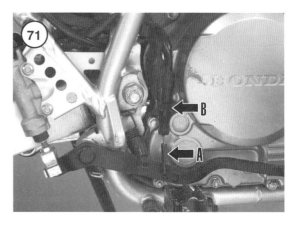

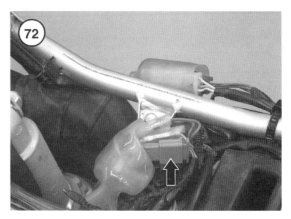

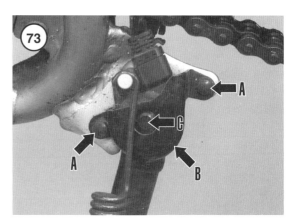

6. Carefully pull each lamp holder/electrical wire assembly (B, **Figure 76**) down and out of the backside of the instrument cluster.

7. Remove the nuts (C, **Figure 76**) securing the instrument cluster to the mounting bracket and remove the cluster.

8. Install by reversing the preceding removal steps, while making sure all electrical connectors are free of corrosion and tight.

HORN

Testing

1. Remove the bolt and collar (A, **Figure 50**) on each side securing the headlight visor.

2. Lift the visor up to disengage it from the lower bracket and remove the visor (B, **Figure 50**).

3. Disconnect the electrical connectors (A, **Figure 77**) from the horn.

4. Connect a 12-volt battery to the horn terminals. The horn should sound.

5. If it does not, replace the horn.

Removal/Installation

1. Remove the bolt and collar (A, **Figure 50**) on each side securing the headlight visor.

2. Lift the visor up to disengage it from the lower bracket and remove the visor (B, **Figure 50**).

3. Disconnect the electrical connectors (A, **Figure 77**) from the horn.

4. Remove the bolt (B, **Figure 77**) securing the horn to the mounting bracket.

5. Remove the horn.

6. Install by reversing the preceding removal steps while noting the following:

    a. Make sure the electrical connectors are tight and corrosion-free.

    b. Test the horn to make sure it operates correctly.

FUSES

Replacement

1. Remove the left side cover as described in Chapter Sixteen.

2. Release the rubber hooks at the top of the battery box cover (**Figure 74**) and lower the cover.

3. Remove the blown fuse (A, **Figure 78**) and install a new one.

4. Spare fuses (B, **Figure 78**) are located at the base of the fuse panel.

5. Install the battery box cover.

6. Install the left side cover.

11

Table 1 CHARGING SYSTEM SPECIFICATIONS

Alternator	
Capacity	186 W at 5000 rpm
Stator coil resistance*	0.2-1.2 ohms
Battery	
Capacity	12 V – 8 amp hours
Current leakage	0.1 mA max.
Voltage	
Fully charged	13.0-13.2 V
Needs charging	Less than 12.3 V
Charging current	
Normal	0.9 amps, 5-10 hours
Quick	4.0 amps, 1.0 hour
Regulator/rectifier	
Type	Triple phase/full-wave rectification
Regulated voltage	
1993-2007	14.7-15.5 volts @ 5000 rpm
2008-on	< 15.5 volts @ 5000 rpm
*Perform test at 20° C (68° F).	

Table 2 IGNITION SYSTEM TESTS

Item	Terminal	Reading
Engine stop switch (in RUN position)	Black/white and Black/red	No continuity
Ignition switch (in ON position)	Black/white and Black/red	Continuity
Neutral switch line		
In neutral position	Light green/red and ground	Continuity
In any gear position	Light green/red and ground	No continuity
Sidestand switch line		
Sidestand in up position	Green/white and ground	Continuity
Sidestand in down position	Green/white and ground	No continuity
Sidestand in down position	Yellow/black and ground	Continuity
Sidestand in up position	Yellow/black and ground	No continuity

Table 3 IGNITION SYSTEM SPECIFICATIONS

1993-2007	
Ignition coil	
Primary resistance*	0.19-0.23 ohms
Secondary resistance	
With plug cap	6500-9700 ohms
Without plug cap	2800-3400 ohms
Ignition pulse generator resistance*	423-517 ohms
2008-on	
Crankshaft position sensor peak voltage	0.7 volts minimum
Ignition coil peak voltage	100 volts minimum
*Perform test at 20° C (68° F).	

Table 4 STARTER SERVICE SPECIFICATIONS

	New mm (in.)	Service limit mm (in.)
Starter motor brush length		
1993 - 2007	12.5 (0.49)	6.5 (0.26)
2008-on	12.5 (0.49)	9.0 (0.35)

Table 5 BULB SPECIFICATIONS

	Voltage-wattage
Headlight	12V-60/55W
Indicator lights	
High beam	12V-1.7W
Neutral	12V-3.4W
Sidestand	12V-1.7W
Turn signal	12V-3.4W
Instrument light	12V-3.4W
Taillight/brakelight	12V-8/27W
Turn signal	12V-23W

Table 6 FUSES

	Fuse rating
Main fuse	20 amp
Sub-fuses located in fuse box	
Headlight	10 amp
Ignition	10 amp
Lights	10 amp

Table 7 ELECTRICAL SYSTEM TORQUE SPECIFICATIONS

	N.m	in.-lb.	ft.-lb.
Neutral switch	12	106	–
Speedometer cable nut	10	88	–

CHAPTER TWELVE

WHEELS, TIRES AND DRIVE CHAIN

This chapter covers the wheels, wheel bearings, tires, drive chain and sprockets. Maintenance procedures for these components are in Chapter Three.

Specifications are in **Tables 1-3** at the end of this chapter.

FRONT WHEEL

Removal

1. Support the motorcycle with the front wheel off the ground.
2. Remove the speedometer or tripmeter cable retaining screw (A, **Figure 1**).
3. Withdraw the speedometer or tripmeter cable end (B, **Figure 1**) from the drive unit.
4. Loosen the axle holder nuts (A, **Figure 2**) sufficiently to reduce the grip of the axle holder on the axle. Nut removal is not necessary.
5. Unscrew the front axle (B, **Figure 2**) from the left fork leg.
6. Remove the front axle from the right side and roll the wheel forward.

CAUTION
To prevent damage to the brake disc, do not set the wheel down so it rests on the brake disc.

NOTE
Do not operate the front brake lever with the wheel removed. Insert a spacer block, between the pads until the wheel is installed. This prevents the caliper pistons from extending if the lever is operated.

7. Inspect the front wheel as described in this section.

Installation

1. Clean the axle bearing surfaces on the fork tube and axle holder.
2. Remove the spacer block from between the brake pads.
3. If removed, install the left-side spacer with the flange side facing out (**Figure 3**). Lubricate the seal lips with grease prior to spacer insertion.
4. If removed, install the speedometer or tripmeter gear unit by aligning the two drive tangs (A, **Figure 4**) with the slots (B) in the gear hub.
5. Carefully insert the disc between the brake pads, then install the front axle from the right side. Tighten the axle finger-tight.
6. Check that the arm on the speedometer or tripmeter gear unit fits over the lug (**Figure 5**) on the fork tube.

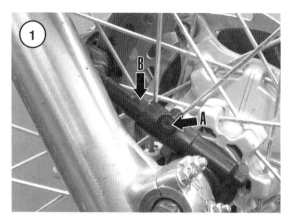

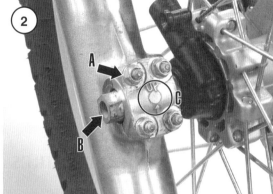

7. If removed, install the axle holder so the UP mark faces upward (C, **Figure 2**). Install the axle holder nuts and tighten finger-tight.

8. Tighten the front axle (B, **Figure 2**) to the specification in **Table 3**.

9. Tighten the axle holder nuts (A, **Figure 2**) to 12 N•m (106 in.-lb.).

NOTE
Make sure the cable end and drive unit
tangs mesh when installing the cable
end in Step 10.

10. Install the speedometer or tripmeter cable end into the gear unit, then install the retaining screw (A, **Figure 1**).

11. Remove the motorcycle from the stand so the front wheel is on the ground. Apply the front brake, then compress and release the front suspension several times to reposition the pads against the disc.

12. Check that the wheel spins freely and the brake operates properly.

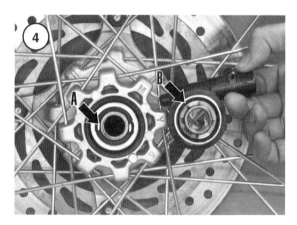

Inspection

1. Inspect the seals (A, **Figure 6**) for wear, hardness, cracks or other damage. If necessary, replace the seals as described under *Front and Rear Hubs* in this chapter.

2. Inspect the bearings on both sides of the wheel for:

    a. Roughness. Turn each bearing inner race by hand and check for smooth and quiet operation.

    b. Radial and lateral play (**Figure 7**). Try to push the bearing in and out to check for lateral play.

3. Slight play is normal. Try to push the bearing up and down to check for radial play. Any radial play should be difficult to feel. If play is easily felt, the bearing is worn out. If necessary, replace both bear-

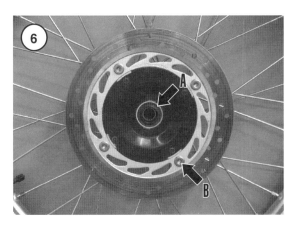

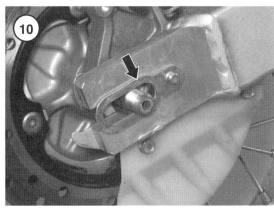

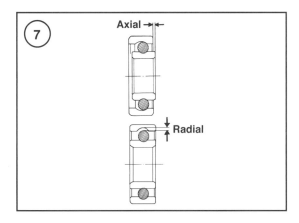

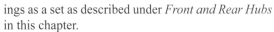

ings as a set as described under *Front and Rear Hubs* in this chapter.

4. Clean the axle and spacers in solvent to remove all grease and dirt. Make sure the axle contact surfaces are clean.

5. Check the axle for straightness with a set of V-blocks and dial indicator (**Figure 8**). Refer to **Table 2** for maximum axle runout. Actual runout is one-half of the gauge reading. Do not attempt to straighten a bent axle.

6. Check the brake disc bolts (B, **Figure 6**) for tightness. To service the brake disc, refer to Chapter Fifteen.

7. Inspect the speedometer or tripmeter gear unit. Inspect the plastic gear for damage. Inspect the seal for hardness, cracks and other damage. Replace the O-ring if damaged.

8. Refer to *Wheel Service* in this chapter and inspect the wheel.

12

REAR WHEEL

Removal

> *NOTE*
> *On XR600R models, the rear axle nut is on the left side. On XR650L models, it is on the right side. This procedure is shown on a XR650L model. The removal and installation are the same for both models except for the axle direction.*

1. Loosen the rear axle nut (A, **Figure 9**).

2. Rotate the adjuster (B, **Figure 9**) forward for maximum chain slack.

3. Remove the rear axle nut, washer, adjuster and lockplate (**Figure 10**).

4. Support the motorcycle securely with the rear wheel off the ground.

5. Move the wheel forward and derail the drive chain from the driven sprocket.

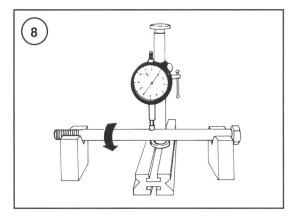

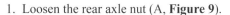

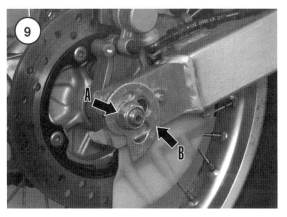

6. Withdraw the rear axle (A, **Figure 11**) and adjuster (B) from the wheel and swing arm.

7. Slide the wheel to the rear and remove it. Do not lose the spacer on each side of the wheel hub.

> *CAUTION*
> *To prevent damage to the brake disc, do not set the wheel down so it rests on the brake disc.*

8. Tie the caliper and bracket assembly and the torque link to the frame.

> *NOTE*
> *Do not operate the rear brake pedal with the wheel removed. Insert a spacer block, between the pads until the wheel is installed. This prevents the caliper pistons from extending if the pedal is operated.*

9. Inspect the rear wheel as described in this section.

Installation

1. Clean the axle bearing surfaces.

2. Remove the spacer block from between the brake pads.

3. Lubricate the seal lips with grease prior to spacer insertion.

4. Position the hub spacers with the flange side facing out away from the bearings (**Figure 12**). Install the wide spacer onto the left side of the wheel.

5. Align the raised bar on the rear caliper bracket with the groove in the swing arm and make sure the dowel pin (**Figure 13**) is correctly positioned in the swing arm. These two items must be installed correctly for proper brake operation.

6. Install the wheel while also installing the drive chain around the drive sprocket.

7. Install the axle bolt, adjusters, washer and nut. Do not tighten the nut. Make sure the axle passes through the caliper mounting bracket.

8. Adjust the drive chain as described in Chapter Three.

9. After the wheel is completely installed, rotate it several times to make sure that it rotates freely.

10. Apply the rear brake several times to make sure the brake pads contact the brake disc correctly.

Inspection

1. Inspect the seals (A, **Figure 14**) for excessive wear, hardness, cracks or other damage. If necessary, replace seals as described under *Front and Rear Hubs* in this chapter.

2. Inspect the bearings on both sides of the wheel for:
   a. Roughness. Turn each bearing inner race by hand and check for smooth and quiet operation.
   b. Try to push the bearing in and out to check for lateral play (**Figure 7**). Slight play is normal.
   c. Try to push the bearing up and down to check for radial play. Any radial play should be difficult to feel. If play is easily felt, the bearing is worn out.
   d. If necessary, replace the bearings as a set as described under *Front and Rear Hubs* in this chapter.

3. Clean the axle and spacers in solvent to remove all grease and dirt. Make sure all axle contact surfaces are clean.

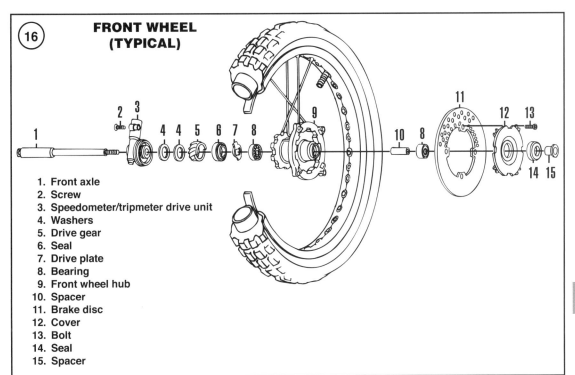

FRONT WHEEL (TYPICAL)

1. Front axle
2. Screw
3. Speedometer/tripmeter drive unit
4. Washers
5. Drive gear
6. Seal
7. Drive plate
8. Bearing
9. Front wheel hub
10. Spacer
11. Brake disc
12. Cover
13. Bolt
14. Seal
15. Spacer

4. Check the axle for straightness with a set of V-blocks and dial indicator (**Figure 8**). Refer to **Table 2** for maximum axle runout. Actual runout is one-half of the gauge reading. Do not attempt to straighten a bent axle.

5. Check the brake disc bolts (B, **Figure 14**) for tightness. To service the brake disc, refer to Chapter Fifteen.

CAUTION
The driven sprocket is attached to the rear hub with Allen bolts and nuts. Do not loosen these fasteners by turning the Allen bolt. Instead, hold the Allen bolt and loosen the nut to avoid rounding out the Allen bolt heads.

7. Check the driven sprocket bolts (**Figure 15**) for tightness. If loose, tighten the driven sprocket nuts to 64 N•m (47 ft.-lb.).

8. Refer to *Wheel Service* in this chapter and inspect the wheel.

FRONT AND REAR HUBS

The front and rear hubs contain the seals, wheel bearings and a spacer. Both hubs support a brake disc and the rear hub carries the driven sprocket. A retainer secures the right wheel bearing in the rear hub. Refer to **Figure 16** (front) or **Figure 17** (rear) when servicing the front and rear hubs in this section.

Procedures for servicing the front and rear hubs are essentially the same. Where differences occur, they are described in the procedure.

12

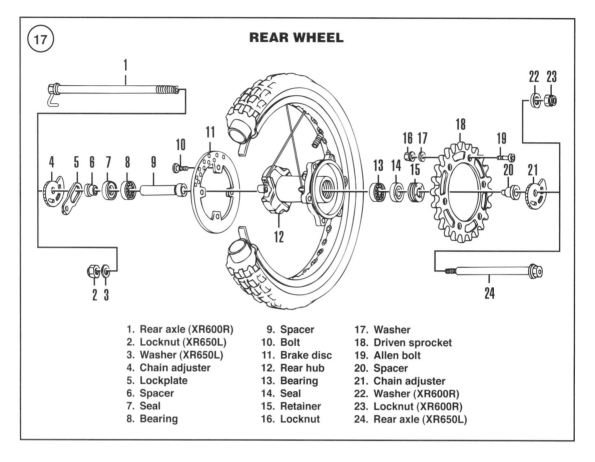

REAR WHEEL

1. Rear axle (XR600R)
2. Locknut (XR650L)
3. Washer (XR650L)
4. Chain adjuster
5. Lockplate
6. Spacer
7. Seal
8. Bearing
9. Spacer
10. Bolt
11. Brake disc
12. Rear hub
13. Bearing
14. Seal
15. Retainer
16. Locknut
17. Washer
18. Driven sprocket
19. Allen bolt
20. Spacer
21. Chain adjuster
22. Washer (XR600R)
23. Locknut (XR600R)
24. Rear axle (XR650L)

Bearing Inspection

Inspect bearings with the wheels installed on the motorcycle. With the wheels installed, leverage can be applied to the bearings to detect wear. In addition, the wheels can be spun to listen for roughness in the bearings. If the wheels must be removed, perform the checks in the wheel removal procedures described in this chapter. Do not remove the wheel bearings to check their condition. If the bearings are removed, replace them.

1. Support the motorcycle with the wheel off the ground. The axle bolt or nut must be tight.

2. Grasp the wheel with both hands, 180° apart. Rock the wheel up and down, and side to side, to check for radial and lateral play. Have an assistant apply the brake while the test is repeated. Play will be detected in severely worn bearings, even though the wheel is locked.

3. Push the front or rear brake caliper in by hand. This forces the caliper piston(s) away from the pads so that the wheel can spin without the brake pads contacting the brake disc.

4. Spin the wheel and listen for bearing noise. A grinding or catching noise indicates worn bearings. If the disc brake drags and the bearing cannot be

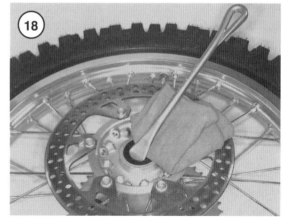

heard, remove the wheel and support it on a truing stand.

5. If damage is evident, replace the bearings as a set. Always install new seals.

6. Apply the front and rear brakes to reposition the brake pads against the brake disc.

Seal Replacement

Seals protect the bearings from dirt and moisture contamination. Always install new seals when replacing bearings.

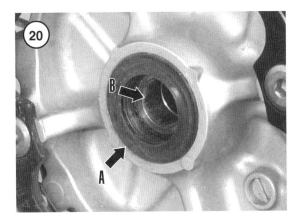

CAUTION
In the following procedure, do not set the wheel on the brake disc. Support the wheel on wooden blocks.

1. Pry the seals out of the hub with a seal puller, tire iron or wide-blade screwdriver (**Figure 18**). Place a shop cloth under the tool to protect the hub from damage.
2. Clean the seal bore.
3. Pack grease into the lip of the new seal.
4. Place the seal in the bore with the closed side of the seal facing out. The seal must be square in the bore.
5. Use a seal driver or socket (**Figure 19**) to install the seal in the bore. Install the seal so it is flush with the top of the hub bore surface. See A, **Figure 20**, typical.

CAUTION
When driving seals, the edge of the driver must fit at the perimeter of the seal. If the driver outside diameter is appreciably smaller than that of the seal, the driver will press against the center of the seal and damage it.

Wheel Bearing Replacement

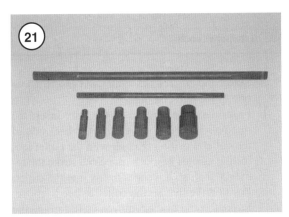

Wheel bearings are installed with a slight press fit and are not generally difficult to remove when the seals have been properly serviced. However, when damaged seals are not replaced, corrosion can seize the bearings in the hub bore, making removal very difficult. Work carefully to avoid damaging the hub when replacing the bearings. Discard the bearings after removing them.

Refer to Chapter One for general bearing replacement procedures.

Tools

Refer to the following for tools described in the text:
1. Collets and remover shafts (**Figure 21**) are available in sets, or can be purchased individually.
   a. For the front hub, use a 15 mm (1991-1992) or 17 mm (1993-on) expanding collet.
   b. For the rear hub, use a 17 mm (XR600R and XR650L) and 20 mm (XR600R) expanding collet.
2. Use one of the following tools to remove the bearing retainer (**Figure 22**) installed in the rear hub:

12

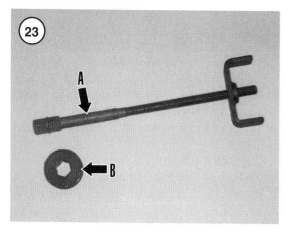

a. Retainer wrench body (Honda part No. 07710-0010401 [A, **Figure 23**]) and retainer wrench (Honda part No. 07710-0010100 [B, **Figure 23**]).

b. Motion Pro XR Seal/Bearing Retainer Tool (part No. 08-0227).

3. The wheel bearings can also be removed with a propane torch, drift and hammer.

Removal

> *CAUTION*
> *In the following procedure, do not set the wheel on the brake disc. Support the wheel with wooden blocks.*

1. Remove the seals (A, **Figure 20**) as described in this section.

2. Examine the wheel bearings for damage, especially the inner race (B, **Figure 20**). If the inner race of one bearing is damaged, remove the opposite bearing first. If both bearings are damaged, select the bearing with the least amount of damage and remove it first. On rusted and damaged bearings, applying pressure against the inner race can cause the inner race to pop out, leaving the outer race pressed in the hub. Refer to *Damaged Bearings* in this section.

3. On the front wheel, remove the speedometer or tripmeter drive plate (**Figure 24**).

4. On the rear wheel, remove the bearing retainer (**Figure 22**) with one of the tools described under *Tools*. Make sure that the pins on the removal tool engage with the holes in the bearing retainer. **Figure 25** and **Figure 26** show the Honda tools assembled through the hub and onto the retainer.

> *WARNING*
> *Wear safety glasses when removing the bearings in the following steps.*

5A. Remove the wheel bearings using expanding collets (**Figure 27**):

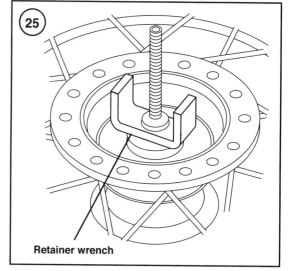

Retainer wrench

a. Select the correct size collet and insert it into one of the hub bearings.

b. From the opposite side of the hub, insert the remover shaft into the slot in the backside of the collet. Position the hub with the collet tool resting against a solid surface and strike the remover shaft so it wedges firmly into the collet.

c. Position the hub so the collet is free to move. Strike the end of the remover shaft, forcing the bearing out of the hub. Remove the bearing and tool. Release the collet from the bearing. Discard the bearing.

d. Remove the spacer from the hub.

e. Repeat the procedure to remove the remaining bearing.

5B. Remove the wheel bearings using a hammer, drift and propane torch as follows:

> *WARNING*
> *When using a propane torch to heat the hub, work in a well-ventilated area away from combustible materials. Wear protective clothing, including eye protection and insulated gloves.*

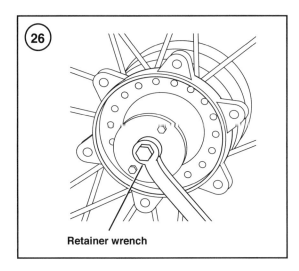

Retainer wrench

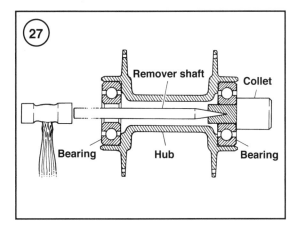

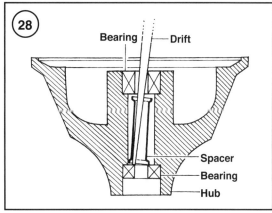

6. Clean and dry the hub and spacer.

7. Check the hub mounting bore for cracks or other damage. If the bearings were a loose fit in the hub, the hub mounting bore and hub may be damaged.

CAUTION
The spacer contacts the wheel bearing inner races to prevent them from moving inward when the axle is tightened. If a spacer is too short, or if it is not installed, the inner bearing races will move inward and bind on the axle, causing bearing damage.

8. Inspect the spacer for flared ends. Check the ends for cracks or other damage. Do not try to repair the spacer by cutting or grinding its end surfaces as this will shorten the spacer. Replace the spacer if one or both ends are damaged.

a. Clean all lubricants from the wheel.

b. Heat the hub around the bearing to be removed. Work the torch in a circular motion around the hub, taking care not to hold the torch in one area. Turn the wheel over and remove the bearing as described in the following steps.

c. Tilt the spacer away from one side of the bearing using a long driver (**Figure 28**).

CAUTION
Do not damage the spacer when removing the bearing. If necessary, grind a clearance groove in the drift to enable it to contact the bearing while clearing the spacer.

d. Tap around the inner bearing race. Make several passes until the bearing exits the hub.

e. Remove the spacer from the hub.

f. Turn the hub over and heat the opposite side.

g. Drive out the opposite bearing using a large socket or bearing driver inserted through the hub.

h. Inspect the spacer for burrs created during removal. Remove burrs with a file.

Installation

1. Before installing the new bearings and seals, note the following:

a. Install bearings so the closed side faces out. If a bearing is sealed on both sides, install the bearing so the manufacturer's marks face out. If a shield is installed on one side of the bearing, the shield side must face out.

b. Apply grease (NLGI No. 2) to bearings that are open on one or both sides. Work the grease into the cavities between the balls and races.

c. Support the bottom side of the hub, near the bore, when installing bearings.

d. At the front hub, install the right bearing first, then the left bearing.

e. At the rear hub, install the left bearing first, then the right bearing.

2. Heat the hub evenly around the bearing bore.

3. Place the first bearing squarely against the bore opening with the closed side facing out. Select a driver with an outside diameter slightly smaller than

12

the bearing outside diameter. Then drive the bearing into the bore until it bottoms (**Figure 29**).

> *NOTE*
> *Install the rear wheel hub spacer on XR600R models so the flanged end (marked LH) is toward the left side of the hub.*

4. Turn the hub over. Install the spacer and center it against the center race.
5. Position the opposite bearing squarely against the bore opening with its closed side facing out. Drive the bearing partway into the bearing bore. Make sure the spacer is centered in the hub. If not, install the axle through the hub to align the spacer with the bearing. Then remove the axle and continue installing the bearing until it bottoms.
6. Insert the axle though the hub and turn it by hand. Check for any roughness or binding, indicating bearing damage.

> *NOTE*
> *If the axle does not go in, the spacer is not aligned correctly with one of the bearings.*

7. Install the rear wheel bearing retainer (**Figure 22**) and tighten it securely against the bearing. Peen the edge of the retainer against the hub in four places.
8. Install the speedometer or tripmeter drive plate (**Figure 24**). Make sure the drive tangs face out.
9. Install the seals as previously described.

Damaged bearings

If damaged wheel bearings remain in use, the inner race can break apart, leaving the outer race pressed in the hub. Removal is difficult because only a small part of the race is accessible above the hub shoulder, leaving little material to drive against. To remove an outer bearing race under these conditions, first heat the hub evenly with a propane torch. Drive out the

outer race with a drift and hammer. It may be necessary to grind a clearance tip on the end of the drift, to avoid damaging the hub bore. Remove the race evenly by applying force at different points around the race. Do not allow the race to bind in its bore. After removing the race, inspect the hub mounting bore for cracks or other damage.

WHEEL SERVICE

To prevent wheel failure, inspect the wheels, bearings and tires at the intervals specified in Chapter Three.

Component Condition

Off-road motorcycle wheels receive a lot of abuse. It is important to inspect the wheel regularly for lateral (side-to-side) and radial (up-and-down) runout, spoke tension, and damage. When a wheel has a noticeable wobble, it is out of true. This is usually caused by loose spokes, but it can be caused by impact damage.

Truing a wheel corrects the lateral and radial runout to bring the wheel back into specification.

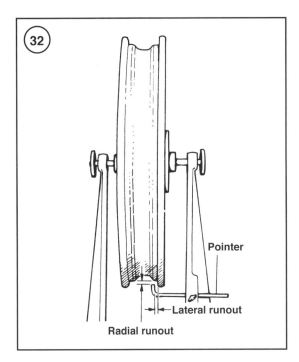

Pointer

Lateral runout

Radial runout

The condition of the individual wheel components will affect the ability to successfully true the wheel. Note the following;

1. Spoke condition: Do not attempt to true a wheel with bent or damaged spokes. Doing so places an excessive amount of tension on the spoke, hub and wheel. Overtightening the spoke may damage the spoke nipple hole in the hub or wheel. Inspect for and replace damaged spokes.

NOTE
When a properly trued wheel hits a sharp object, all the torque or wheel impact is equally divided or trans-ferred among all of the wheel spokes. The spokes are able to bend or bow slightly, thus absorbing the shock and usually preventing wheel and hub dam-age. When the spokes are overtight-ened, they are unable to flex, causing all the impact to be absorbed by the hub or wheel. When the spokes are too loose, the torque or wheel impact is divided unequally between the spokes, with the tighter spokes receiving most of the torque and isolating the impact in one area along the wheel and hub. This eventually causes a cracked or broken hub or wheel.

2. Nipple condition: When truing the wheels the nip-ples must turn freely on the spokes. However, corroded and rusted spoke threads are common and difficult to adjust. Spray a penetrating liquid onto the nipples and allow sufficient time for it to penetrate before trying to turn the nipples. Turn the spoke wrench in both direc-tions and continue to apply penetrating liquid. If the spoke wrench rounds off the nipple, it is necessary to remove the tire from the wheel, cut the spokes out of the wheel and install new spokes.

3. Wheel condition: Minor wheel runout can be cor-rected by truing the wheel; however, overtightening the spokes to correct a wheel may damage the hub and wheel. Inspect the wheels for cracks, flat spots or dents (**Figure 30**). Check the spoke holes for cracks or enlargement. Replace damaged wheels.

Wheel Truing Preliminaries

Before checking the runout and truing the wheel, note the following:

1. Clean the wheel and spoke nipples.
2. Make sure the wheel bearings are in good con-dition. Refer to the front and rear wheel inspection procedures in this chapter.
3. Inspect the spoke holes in the wheel for cracks, hole elongation and other damage. Replace the wheel if damaged.
4. A small amount of wheel runout is acceptable. Attempting to true the wheel to a zero reading may damage the wheel and hub from overtightened spokes.
5. Check runout by mounting a pointer against the fork or swing arm and slowly rotating the wheel. When checking the rear wheel, it will be easier if the chain is first removed from the driven sprocket. If the wheel needs major tuning, remove the tire and mount the wheel on a truing stand (**Figure 31**). An adjustable pointer or dial indicator mounted next to the rim allows runout measurement in both direc-tions **Figure 32**.
6. Use the correct size spoke wrench (**Figure 33**). Using the wrong type of tool or incorrect size spoke wrench may round off the spoke nipples, making ad-justment difficult.

12

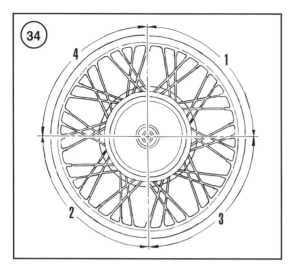

Tightening Loose Spokes

This section describes steps for checking and tightening loose spokes without affecting the wheel runout. When many spokes are loose and the wheel is running out of true, refer to the *Wheel Truing Procedure* in this section.

1. Support the wheel so that it can turn freely. If the rear wheel is being checked while on the motorcycle, remove the chain from the driven sprocket.

2. Spokes can be checked for looseness by one of three ways:

    a. Spoke Torque: Spoke torque wrenches are available from different tool companies. When using s spoke torque wrench, refer to the specification in **Table 3**.

    b. Hand check: Grasp and squeeze two spokes where they cross. Loose spokes can be flexed by hand. Tight spokes feel stiff with little noticeable movement. Tighten the spokes until the tension between the different spoke groups feels the same.

    c. Spoke tone: Tapping a spoke causes it to vibrate and produce sound waves. Loose and tight spokes produce different sounds or tones. A tight spoke will ring. A loose spoke has a soft or dull ring. Tap each spoke with a spoke wrench or screwdriver to identify loose spokes.

3. Check the spokes using one of the methods described in Step 2. If there are loose spokes, spin the wheel and note the following:

    a. If the wheel is running true, continue with Step 4 to tighten the loose spokes.

    b. If the wheel is running out of true, go to the *Wheel Truing Procedure* to measure runout and true the wheel.

4. Use tape and divide the wheel into four equally spaced sections. Number the sections as shown in **Figure 34**.

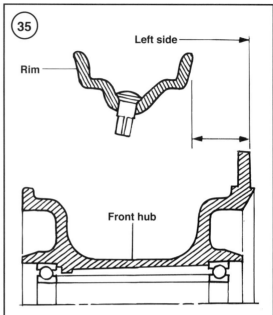

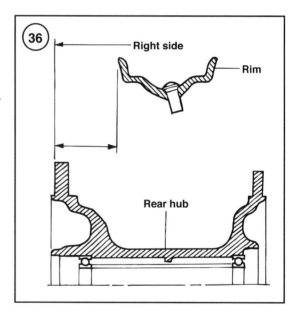

5. Start by tightening the loose spokes in Section 1, then in sections 2, 3 and 4. Do not turn each spoke more than a fourth to a half turn at a time as this over-tightens the spokes and forces the wheel out of true. Work slowly while checking spoke tightness. Continue until all of the spokes are tightened evenly.

NOTE
If the spokes are hard to turn, spray penetrating oil into the top of the nipple. Wipe off excess oil.

6. When all the spokes are tightened evenly, spin the wheel. If there is any noticeable runout, true the wheel as described in the following procedure.

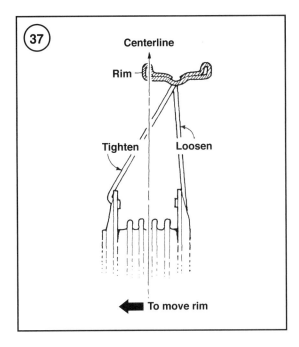

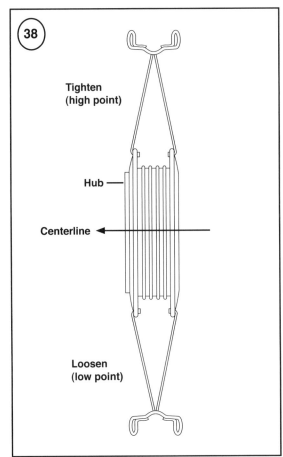

Wheel Truing Procedure

Refer to **Table 1** for lateral and radial wheel runout specifications.

1. Clean the wheel, spokes and nipples.

2. Position a pointer against the rim as shown in **Figure 32**. If the tire is mounted on the wheel, position the pointer as shown in **Figure 31**.

3. Spin the wheel slowly and check the lateral and radial wheel runout. If the wheel is out of adjustment, continue with Step 4.

> *NOTE*
> *It is normal for the wheel to jump at the point where the wheel was welded together. Also small imperfections in the wheel will affect the runout reading, especially when using a dial indicator.*

4. Spray penetrating oil into the top of each nipple. Wipe off excess oil.

> *NOTE*
> *If the runout is minimal, the tire can be left on the wheel. However, if the runout is excessive, or if the wheel must be centered with the hub (Step 5), remove the tire from the wheel.*

5. If there are a large number of loose spokes, or if some or all of the spokes were replaced, measure the hub to wheel offset as shown in **Figure 35** (front) or **Figure 36** (rear) and compare to the specifications in **Table 1**. If necessary, reposition the hub before truing the wheel.

6. Lateral runout adjustment: If the side-to-side runout is out of specification, adjust the wheel. For example, to pull the wheel to the left side (**Figure 37**), tighten the spokes on the left side of the hub (at the runout point) and loosen the adjacent spokes on the right side of the hub. Always loosen and tighten the spokes in equal number of turns.

> *NOTE*
> *Determining the number of spokes to loosen and tighten depends on how far the runout is out of adjustment. Loosen two or three spokes, then tighten the opposite two or three spokes. If the runout is excessive and affects a greater area along the wheel, loosen and tighten a greater number of spokes.*

7. Radial runout adjustment: If the up and down runout is out of specification, the hub is not centered in the wheel. Draw the high point of the wheel toward the centerline by tightening the spokes in the area of the high point, and loosening the spokes on the side opposite the high point (**Figure 38**). Tighten the spokes in equal amounts to prevent distortion.

NOTE
Alternate between checking and adjusting lateral and radial runout. Remember, changing spoke tension on one side of the wheel will affect the tension on the other side.

8. After truing the wheel, seat each spoke in the hub by tapping it with a flat nose punch and hammer. Then recheck the spoke tension and wheel runout. Readjust if necessary as described under *Tightening Loose Spokes* in this section.

9. Check the ends of the spokes where they are threaded in the nipples. Grind off any ends that protrude through the nipples to prevent them from puncturing the tube.

DRIVE CHAIN

Refer to **Table 2** for drive chain specifications. Refer to *Drive Chain* in Chapter Three for routine drive chain inspection, adjustment and lubrication procedures.

When checking the condition of the chain, also check the condition of the sprockets, as described in Chapter Three. If either the chain or sprockets are worn, replace all drive components at the same time. Using new sprockets with a worn chain, or a new chain on worn sprockets will shorten the life of the new part.

A drive chain equipped with a spring-clip master link (**Figure 39**) is standard equipment on XR600R models. A drive chain equipped with a staked-pin master link (**Figure 40**) is standard equipment on XR650L models.

Clip Master Link Drive Chain Removal/Installation

1. Support the motorcycle on a workstand with its rear wheel off the ground and shift the transmission into neutral.

2. Find the master link on the chain. Remove the spring clip (**Figure 41**) with pliers, then remove the link from the chain (**Figure 39**).

3. Remove the drive chain.

4. Clean and inspect the chain (Chapter Three).

5. Clean the drive and driven sprockets.

6. Check the drive chain sliders for worn or damaged parts (Chapter Three).

7. Reverse this procedure to install the chain. Note the following:

   a. Install the chain and reassemble a new master link (**Figure 39**).

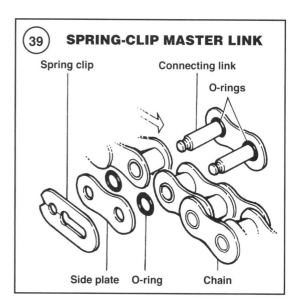

39 **SPRING-CLIP MASTER LINK**

Spring clip   Connecting link

O-rings

Side plate   O-ring   Chain

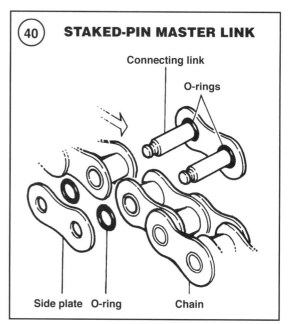

40 **STAKED-PIN MASTER LINK**

Connecting link

O-rings

Side plate O-ring   Chain

   b. Install the spring clip on the master link with the closed end of the clip pointing toward the direction of travel (**Figure 41**).

   c. Adjust the chain (Chapter Three).

Staked Master Link Drive Chain Removal/Installation

WARNING
Never reuse the connecting link, side plate and O-rings after removing them as they could break and cause the chain to separate. A chain that comes apart can lock the rear wheel, causing a serious accident.

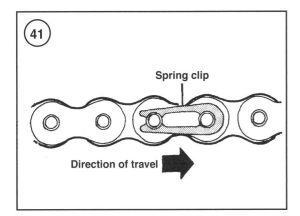

Spring clip

Direction of travel

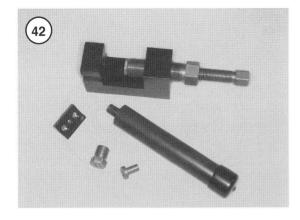

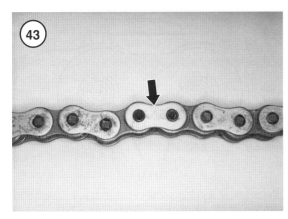

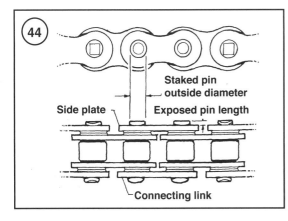

Staked pin
outside diameter

Side plate

Exposed pin length

Connecting link

A staked master link drive chain (**Figure 40**) can be removed/replaced with the swing arm on the motorcycle. The following describes chain removal and installation using a Jumbo Chain Tool (Motion Pro part No. 08-0135 [**Figure 42**]). The tool can be used to break roller chains up to No. 630 and can be used to rivet chain sizes up to No. 530. Always follow the tool manufacturer's instructions provided with the tool. Use the following steps to supplement the instructions.

1. Support the motorcycle with the rear wheel off the ground.

2. Loosen the rear axle nut and the chain adjusters. Push the rear wheel forward until maximum chain slack is obtained.

3. Assemble the extractor bolt onto the body bolt. Then turn the extractor bolt until its pin is withdrawn into the pin guide chain tool, following the manufacturer's instructions.

4. Turn the chain to locate the crimped pin ends (**Figure 43**) on the master link. Break the chain at this point.

5. Install the chain tool across the master link, then operate the tool and push the connecting link out of the side plate to break the chain. Remove the side plate, connecting link and O-rings (**Figure 40**) and discard them.

6. If installing a new drive chain, count the links of the new chain, and if necessary, cut the chain to length as described under *Cutting A Drive Chain to Length*. Refer to **Table 2** for the original equipment chain sizes and lengths.

7. Install the chain around the drive sprocket, swing arm and driven sprocket.

NOTE
Always install the drive chain around the swing arm before connecting and staking the master link.

8. Assemble the new master link as follows:
   a. Install an O-ring on each connecting link pin (**Figure 40**).
   b. Insert the connecting link through the inside of the chain and connect both chain ends together.
   c. Install the remaining two O-rings onto the connecting link pins.
   d. Install the side plate so the identification mark faces out (away from chain).

9. Refer to **Table 2** and stake each connecting link pin as follows:
   a. Measure the height of the connecting link from the outer side plate surface to the top of the connecting link (**Figure 44**). If the height measurement is incorrect, confirm that the correct master

12

link is being installed. If so, readjust the side plate height position on the connecting link.

b. Assemble the chain tool onto the master link and carefully stake each connecting link pin until its outside diameter (**Figure 44**) is as specified in **Table 2**. Work carefully and do not exceed the specified outside diameter measurement. Measure with a vernier caliper (**Figure 45**) in two places on each pin, 90° apart.

WARNING
If the diameter of one pin end is out of specification, remove and discard the master link. Then install a new master link assembly. An incorrectly installed master link may cause the chain to come apart and lock the rear wheel, causing a serious accident. Do not ride the motorcycle unless absolutely certain the master link is installed correctly.

10. Remove the chain tool and inspect the master link for any cracks or other damage. Check the staked area for cracks (**Figure 46**). Then make sure the master link O-rings were not crushed. If there are cracks on the staked link surfaces or other damage, remove the master link and install a new one.

11. If there are no cracks, pivot the chain ends where they hook onto the master link. Each chain end must pivot freely. Compare by pivoting other links of the chain. If one or both drive chain ends cannot pivot on the master link, the chain is too tight. Remove and install a new master link assembly.

12. Adjust the drive chain and tighten the rear axle nut as described in Chapter Three.

Cutting a Drive Chain To Length

Refer to **Table 2** for the number of chain links required for original equipment gearing. If the replacement drive chain is too long, cut it to length as follows.

1. Stretch the new chain on a workbench.

2. If installing a new chain over original equipment gearing, refer to **Table 2** for the number of links. If sprocket sizes were changed, install the new chain over both sprockets, with the rear wheel moved forward, to determine the correct number of links to remove (**Figure 47**). Make a chalk mark on the two chain pins to cut. Count the chain links one more time or check the chain length before cutting. Include the master link when counting the drive chain links.

WARNING
Wear eye protection when using a hand or bench grinder.

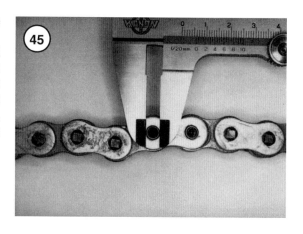

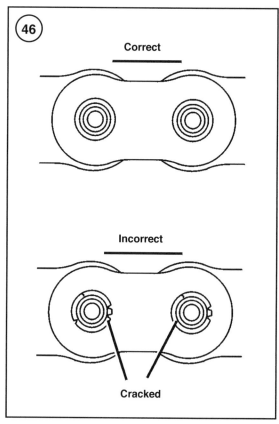

Correct

Incorrect

Cracked

3A. If using a chain breaker, use it to break the drive chain.

3B. To break the drive chain with a grinder, perform the following:

a. Grind the head of two pins flush with the face of the side plate with a grinder or suitable grinding tool.

b. Press the side plate out of the chain with a chain breaker; support the chain carefully while doing this. If the pins are still tight, grind more material from the end of the pins and then try again.

c. Remove the side plate and push out the connecting link.

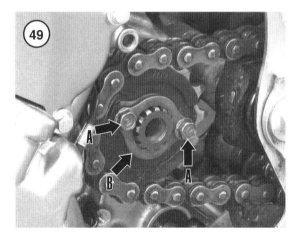

4. Install the new drive chain as described in this section.

SPROCKETS

This section describes service procedures for replacing the drive (front) and driven (rear) sprockets. Refer to **Table 2** for sprocket sizes.

After replacing the chain and sprockets, check the drive chain sliders for worn or damaged parts (Chapter Three).

Drive Sprocket Removal/Installation

1. Remove the bolts securing the drive sprocket cover and remove the cover (**Figure 48**).
2. Remove the bolts (A, **Figure 49**) securing the drive sprocket.
3. Rotate the drive sprocket holder (B, **Figure 49**) in either direction and slide it off the shaft.
4. Clean and inspect the parts.
5. Reverse the removal steps to install the drive sprocket while noting the following:
   a. Install the drive sprocket so the OUT mark is visible.
   b. Adjust the drive chain as described in Chapter Three.

Driven Sprocket Removal and Installation

> *CAUTION*
> *The driven sprocket is attached to the rear hub with Allen bolts and nuts. Do not loosen these fasteners by turning the Allen bolt. Instead, hold the Allen bolt and loosen the nut to avoid rounding out the Allen bolt heads.*

1. Remove the rear wheel as described in this chapter.
2. Remove the nuts, washers, Allen bolts and driven sprocket (**Figure 50**) from the rear hub.
3. Inspect the sprocket mounting tabs for cracks or other damage. Replace the hub if damaged.
4. Clean and dry the sprocket fasteners. Replace damaged fasteners.
5. Install the new sprocket onto the rear hub.
6. Install the Allen bolts, washers, and nuts and tighten finger-tight.
7. Install the rear wheel as described in this chapter.
8. Hold the Allen bolts and tighten the nuts in two or three steps and in a crossing pattern to 64 N•m (47

12

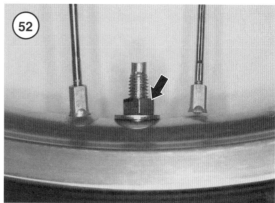

ft.-lb.). Use a torque adapter (Motion Pro part No. 08-0134) to access the nuts (**Figure 51**, typical).

9. Adjust the drive chain and tighten the rear axle nut to the specification in **Table 3**.

TIRES

Removal

1. Remove the valve core and deflate the tire.
2. On wheels so equipped, loosen the rim locknut(s) (**Figure 52**).

> *NOTE*
> *Warming the tire makes it softer and more pliable. Place the tire and wheel assembly in the sun or in a completely closed automobile. Place the new tire in the same location.*

3. Press the entire bead on both sides of the tire into the center of the rim.
4. Lubricate the beads with soapy water.

> *CAUTION*
> *Use tire irons without sharp edges. If necessary, file the ends of the tire irons to remove any rough edges.*

5. Insert the tire iron under the bead next to the valve stem (**Figure 53**). Force the bead on the opposite side of the tire into the center of the rim, then pry the bead over the rim with the tire iron.
6. Insert a second tire iron next to the first to hold the bead over the rim (**Figure 54**). While holding the tire with one iron, work around the tire with the second iron, prying the tire over the rim. Be careful not to pinch the inner tube with the tire irons.
7. Remove the inner tube from the tire (**Figure 55**). If necessary, reach inside the tire and remove the valve from the hole in the rim.
8. Remove the nut and washer and remove the rim lock(s) from the rim.

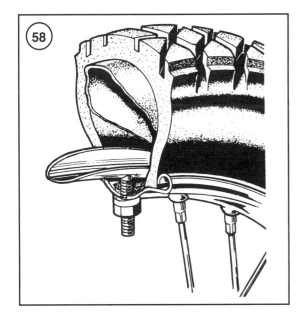

3. Check the rim locks and replace if damaged.

4. Make sure the spoke ends do not protrude above the nipple heads and into the center of the rim. Grind or file off any protruding spoke ends.

NOTE
If water and dirt entered the rim, discard the rubber rim band. Wrap the center of the rim with two separate revolutions of duct tape. Punch holes through the tape at the rim lock and valve stem hole positions.

Installation

NOTE
Installation will be easier if the tire is pliable. This can be achieved by warming the tire in the sun or in an enclosed vehicle.

1. Sprinkle talcum powder around the interior of the tire casing. Distribute the powder so it is on all surfaces that will touch the inner tube. The powder minimizes chafing and helps the tube distribute itself when inflated.

NOTE
Depending on the make and type of tire installed, check the sidewall and determine if it must be installed in a specific direction. A direction arrow is often embossed in the sidewall.

2. If a rubber rim band is used, make sure the band is in place with the rough side toward the rim. Align the holes in the band with the holes in the rim.

3. Lubricate one bead and push it onto the rim (**Figure 57**). When necessary, work the tire from the opposite side of the rim.

4. Install the rim lock, lockwasher and nut. Do not tighten at this time. The rim lock must be over the edge of both tire beads when installation is completed (**Figure 58**).

5. Install the core into the valve stem, then insert the tube into the tire. Make sure that the tube is not twisted as it is tucked into the tire. Put the locknut on the upper end of the valve stem to prevent the stem from falling out of the hole.

6. Inflate the tube until it is rounded and no longer wrinkled. Too much air makes tire installation difficult and too little air increases the chance of pinching the tube.

7. Lubricate the second tire bead, then start installation opposite the valve stem. Fit the rim lock over the tire bead, then work around the rim, hand-fitting

9. Stand the tire upright and pry the second tire bead (**Figure 56**) over the rim.

Inspection

1. Inspect the tire for any damage.

2. Fill the tube with air to check for leaks.

as much of the tire as possible. If necessary, relubricate the bead. Before final installation, make sure that the valve stem is straight and the inner tube is not pinched. Use the tire irons to pry the remaining section of bead onto the rim (**Figure 59**).

8. Check the bead for uniform fit, on both sides of the tire.

WARNING
If the tire does not seat at the recommended pressure, do not continue to overinflate the tire. Deflate the tire and reinflate to the recommended seating pressure. Relubricate the beads, if necessary.

9. Lubricate both beads and inflate the tire to seat the beads onto the rim. Inflate the tire to 1 1/2 times the recommended air pressure in **Table 1**.

10. If so equipped, tighten the rim locknut(s) securely.

11. Bleed the tire pressure to the specification in **Table 1**.

12. Finger-tighten the valve stem locknut and install the cap.

WHEEL BALANCE

Check wheels for balance either statically (single plane balance) or dynamically (dual plane balance). This section describes how to static balance the wheels using a wheel balancing stand. To obtain a higher degree of accuracy, take the wheels to a dealership and have them balanced with a two plane computer dynamic wheel balancer. This machine spins the wheel to accurately detect any imbalance.

Balance weights are used to balance the wheel and are attached to the spokes (**Figure 60**). Weight kits are available from motorcycle dealerships.

The wheel must be able to rotate freely when checking wheel balance. Because excessively worn or damaged wheel bearings affect the accuracy of this procedure, check the wheel bearings as described in this chapter. Also confirm that the tire balance mark, a paint mark on the tire, is aligned with the valve stem (**Figure 61**).

NOTE
Leave the brake disc mounted on the front wheel when checking and adjusting wheel balance.

1. Remove the wheel as described in this chapter.
2. Clean the seals and inspect the wheel bearings as described in this chapter.
3. Clean the tire, rim and spokes. Remove any stones or pebbles stuck in the tire tread.

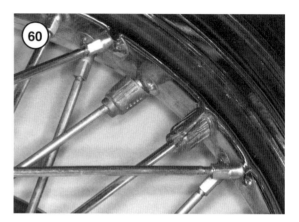

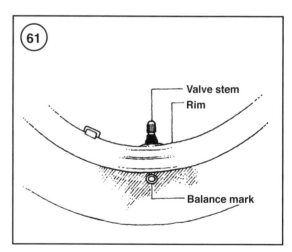

4A. Mount the front wheel (with brake disc attached) on a balance stand.

4B. Mount the rear wheel (with driven flange assembly and sprocket) on a balance stand (**Figure 62**).

NOTE
To check the original balance of the wheel, leave the original weights attached to the spokes.

5. Spin the wheel by hand and let it coast to a stop. Mark the tire at its bottom point with chalk.

6. Spin the wheel several more times. If the same spot on the tire stops at the bottom each time, the wheel is out of balance. This is the heaviest part of the tire. When an unbalanced wheel is spun, it always comes to rest with the heaviest spot at the bottom.

7. Attach a test weight to the wheel at the point opposite the heaviest spot and spin the wheel again.

8. Experiment with different weights until the wheel, when spun, comes to rest at a different position each time. When a wheel is correctly balanced, the weight of the tire and wheel assembly is distributed equally around the wheel.

9. Remove the test weight and install the correct size weight or weights to the wheel. Crimp the weight tightly against the spoke and nipple (**Figure 60**).

NOTE
Do not exceed 60 grams (2.1 oz.) on the front wheel or 70 grams (2.5 oz.) on the rear wheel. If a wheel requires an excessive amount of weight, make sure the weight mark on the tire aligns with the valve stem.

10. Record the weight, number and position of the weights in the maintenance log at the end of the manual. Then, if the motorcycle experiences a handling or vibration problem in the future, check for any missing balance weights as previously recorded.

11. Install the wheel as described in this chapter.

Table 1 TIRE AND WHEEL SPECIFICATIONS

Item Tire type	Front Tube	Rear Tube
Size	80/100-21 or 3.00-21	110/100-18 or 4.60-18
Manufacturer		
XR600R	Inoue VE32	Inoue VE37
XR650L	Bridgestone TW301 or Dunlop K850	Bridgestone TW52 or Dunlop K850
Minimum tread depth	3.0 mm (0.12 in.)	3.0 mm (0.12 in.)
Inflation pressure (cold)[1]		
XR600R	15 psi (100 kPa)[2]	15 psi (100 kPa)[2]
XR650L	22 psi (150 kPa)[2]	22 psi (150 kPa)[2]

1. Tire inflation pressure is for original equipment tires. Aftermarket tires may require different inflation pressure.
2. Up to maximum weight capacity.

Table 2 WHEELS, TIRES AND DRIVE CHAIN SPECIFICATIONS

Item	Specification
Axle runout (max.)	0.2 mm (0.008 in.)
Drive chain	
XR600R	DID 520V8 (110 links)
	RK 520MO4X (110 links)
XR650L	DID 520V8 (110 links)
	RK 520MOZ6 (110 links)
Drive chain slack	35-45 mm (1 3/8-1 3/4 in.)
Drive chain master link	
Pin length	
XR600R and 1993-2007 XR650L	1.2-1.4 mm (0.47-0.55 in.)
2008-on XR650L	
DID	1.15-1.55 mm (0.045-0.061 in.)
RK	1.2-1.4 mm (0.47-0.55 in.)
Staked diameter	
XR600R and 1993-2007 XR650L	5.50-5.80 mm (0.217-0.228 in.)
2008-on XR650L	
DID	5.4-5.6 mm (0.21-0.22 in.)
RK	5.50-5.80 mm (0.217-0.228 in.)
(continued)	

12

Table 2 WHEELS, TIRES AND DRIVE CHAIN SPECIFICATIONS (continued)

Sprocket sizes	
XR600R	
Drive (front)	14 teeth
Driven (rear)	48 teeth
XR650L	
Drive (front)	15 teeth
Driven (rear)	45 teeth
Wheel axial runout (max.)	2.0 mm (0.08 in.)
Wheel radial runout (max.)	2.0 mm (0.08 in.)
Wheel hub-to-rim distance*	
XR650L	
1993-2007	
Front	20.25 mm (0.797 in.)
Rear	19.0 mm (0.75 in.)
2008-on	
Front	19.25-21.25 mm (0.757-0.837 in.)
Rear	18-20 mm (0.71-0.79 in.)

*Manufacturer does not specify for XR600R.

Table 3 WHEELS, TIRES AND DRIVE CHAIN TORQUE SPECIFICATIONS

Item	N•m	in.-lb.	ft.-lb.
Driven sprocket nuts	64	-	47
Front axle			
XR600R and 1993-2007 XR650L	87	-	64
2008-on XR650L	85	-	63
Front axle holder nut	12	106	-
Rear axle nut			
XR600R	95	-	70
XR650L			
1993-2007	90	-	66
2008-on	88	-	65
Wheel spoke nipple			
XR600R & 1993-2007 XR650L	4	35.00	-
2008-on XR650L	3.7	32.75	-

CHAPTER THIRTEEN

FRONT SUSPENSION AND STEERING

This chapter covers procedures for the front fork and steering components. Refer to Chapter Twelve for front wheel and tire service. Front suspension specifications are in **Table 1** and **Table 2** at the end of this chapter.

HANDLEBAR

Removal/Installation

1. Remove the headlight housing as described Chapter Ten or Chapter Eleven.

> *CAUTION*
> *The fuel tank is easily damaged when removing the handlebar. Either protect the fuel tank or remove it.*

2. On XR650L models, remove the right rear view mirror (A, **Figure 1**).
3. On XR650L models, disconnect the front brake light switch electrical connectors (B, **Figure 1**).
4. Remove the screws securing the right handlebar switch assembly (C, **Figure 1**) and remove the electrical wires from the clips on the handlebar.
5. On XR600R models, perform the following:
   a. Remove the screws securing the throttle body together and separate the parts.

b. Remove the screw and throttle cover (A, **Figure 2**).
c. Remove the cover gasket (B, **Figure 2**).
d. Remove the throttle cable roller (C, **Figure 2**).
e. Disengage the throttle cables from the throttle grip and withdraw them from the upper half of the throttle body.
f. Lay the throttle cables over the fender or back over the frame. Be careful that the cables are not kinked.

6. On XR650L models, remove the bolts securing the throttle assembly (D, **Figure 1**) and carefully lay the throttle assembly and cables over the fender or back over the frame. Be careful that the cables are not kinked.

> *CAUTION*
> *Cover the frame with a heavy cloth or plastic tarp to protect it from accidental spilling of brake fluid. Wash any spilled brake fluid off any painted or plated surface immediately, as it will damage the finish. Use soapy water and rinse thoroughly.*

7. Remove the bolts (E, **Figure 1**) securing the brake master cylinder and lay it over the frame. Keep the reservoir in the upright position to minimize loss of brake fluid and to keep air from entering the brake

13

system. It is not necessary to disconnect the brake line.

8. On XR650L models, remove the left rear view mirror (A, **Figure 3**).

9. Remove the bolts securing the clutch lever assembly (B, **Figure 3**).

10. Lay the clutch and choke lever assemblies and cable over the frame or front fender. Be careful that the cables are not kinked.

11. Remove the screws securing the left handlebar switch assembly (C, **Figure 3**) and remove the electrical wires from the clips on the handlebar.

12. On XR600R models, loosen the decompressor lever bracket bolt.

13. Remove the bolts securing the handlebar upper holders (**Figure 4**), then remove the handlebar upper holders.

14. Remove the handlebar. On XR600R models, slide the decompressor lever bracket off the handlebar.

15. Install by reversing the preceding removal steps while noting the following.

16. To maintain a good grip on the handlebar and to prevent it from slipping down, clean the knurled section of the handlebar with a wire brush. It should be rough so it will be held securely by the holders. Also clean the holders.

17. Position the handlebar on the lower handlebar holders so the punch mark on the handlebar is aligned with the top surface of the handlebar holder (**Figure 5**).

18. Install the upper handlebar holders so the punch mark is to the front (**Figure 6**).

19. Tighten the front bolts first and then the rear bolts. A gap should exist between the rear mating surfaces of the upper and lower holders. Tighten all bolts to the specification in **Table 2**.

20. On XR650L models, align the lower switch housing pin with the hole in the handlebar when installing the handlebar switches.

21. Align the clamp parting line of the brake and clutch brackets with the punch mark on the handlebar.

22. Apply a light coat of multipurpose grease to the throttle grip area on the handlebar before installing the throttle grip assembly.

23. Install the brake master cylinder onto the handlebar. Install the clamp with the UP arrow facing up and align the clamp mating surface with the punch mark on the handlebar. Tighten the upper bolt first and then the lower bolt. Tighten the bolts to 27 N•m (20 ft.-lb.) on XR600R models and to the specification in **Table 2** on XR650L models.

24. On XR600R models, perform the following:

   a. Lubricate the upper ends of the throttle cables and the throttle cable roller.

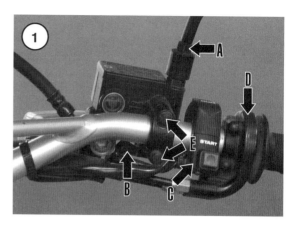

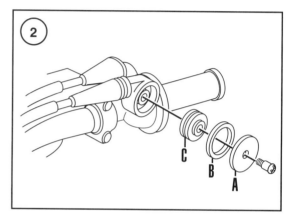

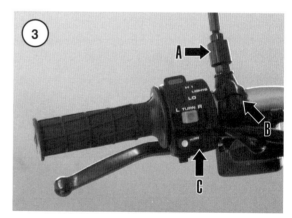

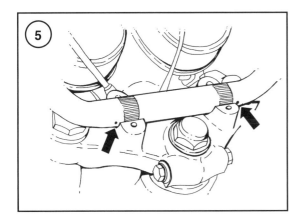

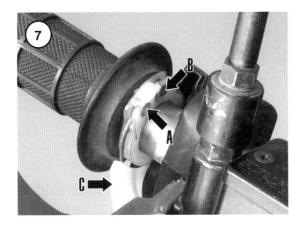

a. Lubricate the ends of the throttle cables with lithium grease, then insert the ends into the handlebar throttle control.

b. Reconnect the pull (A, **Figure** 7) and return (B) throttle cables. Route the cables into the cable guide (C, **Figure** 7) and position the cable guide into the throttle housing. Make sure the cables fit into the grooves in the guide.

c. Install the throttle housing cover. Mate both housings together and install the mounting bolts finger-tight.

d. Slide the boot over the throttle housing.

e. Align the clamp mating surface on the throttle housing with the punch mark on the handlebar. Tighten the throttle housing bolts to the specification in **Table 2**.

26. Operate the throttle grip and make sure it turns smoothly. Turn the handlebar and check the throttle operation in both lock positions.

27. Adjust the throttle operation as described in Chapter Three.

HANDLEBAR GRIPS

Replacement

Depending on the condition of the handlebar grips, different removal methods are available. Use contact cleaner and compressed air to remove the grips if they are to be reused. If the grips are torn and damaged, it may be possible to push them off by hand. This section lists some different ways for removing grips. While some riders cut the grips off, the tool used in this method can score the throttle tube or the aluminum handlebar (if used), so use caution if using this method. Replace the grips with the handlebar installed on the motorcycle.

NOTE
When removing handlebar grips that are in good condition, it is best to use a technique that pushes them off the handlebar. Trying to pull a grip off the handlebar stretches the grip and tightens it against the handlebar.

1. If the grips are to be reused, note any alignment marks on the grips or make your own.

2. If the grips are torn and damaged, grab the inner grip flange and pull it off the handlebar or throttle tube, inside out.

3. If cutting the grips, carefully cut through the grip flange and pull it back to expose the handlebar or throttle pipe. Continue to pull the grip away from the handlebar or throttle pipe while cutting it lengthwise. Pulling the grip helps prevent the blade from contacting the handlebar or throttle pipe. After cutting the grip, spread it and pull it off, inside out.

b. Install the throttle cables through the upper half of the throttle body housing.

c. Attach the throttle cables onto the throttle grip.

d. Install the throttle cable roller (C, **Figure 2**).

e. Install the cover gasket (B, **Figure 2**).

f. Install the throttle cover and screw (A, **Figure 2**). Tighten the screw securely.

g. Install the lower half of the throttle body and install the screws securing the throttle body halves together. Tighten the screws securely.

25. On XR650L models, perform the following:

4. To remove the left grip so it can be reused, insert a thin screwdriver between the grip and handlebar. Work carefully to prevent tearing the grip or gouging the handlebar. Then squirt contact cleaner into the open area under the grip (**Figure 8**). Immediately remove the screwdriver and turn the grip by hand to break the adhesive bond between the grip and handlebar, then push or slide the grip off. If necessary, repeat this step at different points around the grip until it slides off.

5. To remove the right grip from the throttle tube so it can be reused:

    a. Make sure the grip is in good condition. This technique does not work on cut or damaged grips.

    b. Disconnect the throttle cables and remove the throttle tube as described under *Handlebar* in this chapter.

    c. Insert the nozzle from an air gun between the grip and throttle tube and carefully blow the grip slowly off the throttle pipe (**Figure 9**).

6. Remove grip adhesive from the handlebar and throttle tube with solvent or WD-40. Then clean with contact cleaner to remove any oil residue.

7. Inspect the throttle tube for any cracks and damage and replace if necessary.

> *CAUTION*
> *Do not install a new grip over a damaged or broken throttle tube. The glue will leak through and stick to the handlebar and the inner throttle tube surfaces.*

8. Inspect the handlebar ends for scoring, grooves and other damage. Sand or file until the surface is smooth.

9. Reinstall the throttle tube (without the new grip) and the throttle cables as described under *Handlebar* in this chapter.

10A. If installing original equipment grips, note the following:

    a. Align the index mark on the throttle grip flange with the edge of the throttle tube (**Figure 10**).

    b. Align the index mark on the left grip flange with the punch or paint mark on the handlebar (**Figure 10**).

10B. On aftermarket grips, some are directional as to how they mount on the handlebar and throttle tube. Check the manufacturer's instructions before installing them.

11. Recheck the riding position and adjust the handlebar, if necessary.

12. Identify the left and right (throttle tube) grips.

> *WARNING*
> *Make sure the grip cement used is applicable to the grips being installed. A specific cement may be required when installing Gel grips and other soft com-*

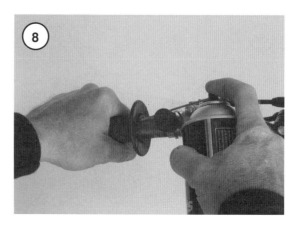

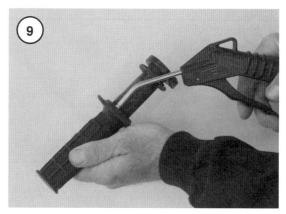

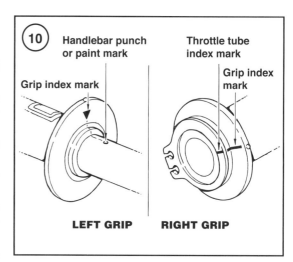

pound grips. Always refer to the grip manufacturer's instructions for application and drying time.

13. Install the grips as follows:

    a. Cover the hole in the end of the throttle tube with duct tape to prevent the cement from contacting the handlebar and inner throttle tube surface.

    b. If hidden end caps are used, install them into the handlebar ends before installing the grips.

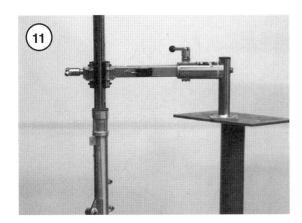

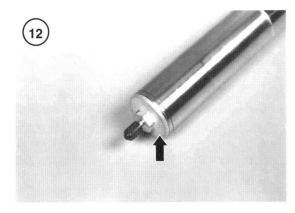

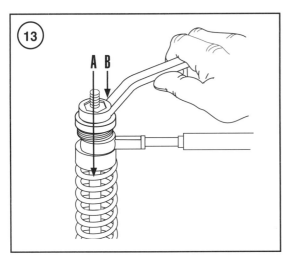

c. Apply grip cement to the inside surface of the grip and to the grip contact surface on the left side of the handlebar or on the throttle tube.

d. Install the grip with a twisting motion to spread the cement evenly. Then quickly align the grip with the handlebar or throttle tube. Squeeze the outer end of the left grip to make sure it contacts the end of the handlebar. For the right grip, make sure there is a small gap between the grip and the throttle housing, and the grip contacts the end of the throttle pipe.

14. Observe the grip cement manufacturer's drying time before riding the motorcycle.

FRONT FORK

Adjustment

Refer to Chapter Three.

Oil Change

1. Remove the fork assembly as described in this section.

> *WARNING*
> *Wear eye protection when releasing air pressure from the fork leg. Slowly release the air pressure to prevent loss of fork oil.*

> *NOTE*
> *Recommended fork oil is Pro Honda Suspension Fluid SS-7 or HP Fork Oil SS-19. Refer to Table 1 for fluid level and fluid capacity specifications.*

2. Remove the air valve cap and bleed off all air pressure by depressing the valve stem.

> *CAUTION*
> *Workstands (**Figure 11** [www.park-tool.com]), with quick adjustability and padded clamps are ideal for fork service. If using a vise, make sure it has soft jaw inserts.*

3. If not loosened during the removal sequence, hold the upper fork tube and unscrew the fork cap/air valve assembly (**Figure 12**) from the fork tube.

> *WARNING*
> *Be careful when unscrewing the fork cap/air valve assembly as the spring under it is under pressure.*

4. Place a wrench on the fork damper locknut (A, **Figure 13**).
5. Place a wrench (B, **Figure 13**) on the fork cap assembly, and loosen the fork damper locknut.
6. Remove the fork cap assembly, the spring seat and the fork spring from the top of the piston rod (1991-2007 models) or from the top of the fork damper (2008-on models).
7. Do not remove the piston rod and piston.
8. Remove the fork from the vise, pour out the fork oil and discard it. Pump the fork several times by hand to expel most of the remaining oil.
9. Fill the fork tube with Pro-Honda Suspension Fluid SS-7, or equivalent fork oil. Refer to **Table 1** for the specified quantity for each fork leg.
10. Hold the fork assembly upright and slowly pump the fork several times.

13

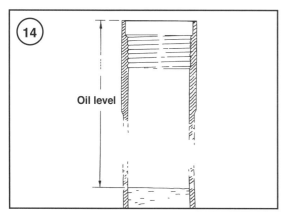

Oil level

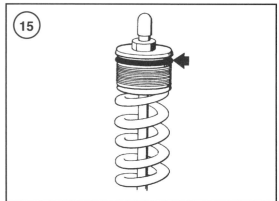

11. Compress the fork completely and measure the fluid level from the top of the fork tube (**Figure 14**) after the fork oil settles. Refer to **Table 1** for the specified fork oil level.

12. Wipe the fork spring with a lint-free cloth.

13A. On XR600R models, install the fork spring with the narrow wound coils toward the top.

13B. On XR650L models, install the fork spring with the narrow wound coils toward the bottom.

14. Install the spring seat.

15. Make sure the O-ring seal (**Figure 15**) is in place on the fork cap assembly and is in good condition; replace if necessary. On 1991-2007 models, turn the fork cap assembly onto the threads of the piston rod. On 2008-on models, turn the fork cap assembly onto the threads of the fork damper. On all models make sure the cap bottoms on the rod threads.

16. To tighten the fork cap assembly, perform the following:

    a. Place a wrench on the fork damper locknut (A, **Figure 13**).

    b. Place a wrench (B, **Figure 13**) on the fork cap assembly, and tighten the locknut against the fork cap assembly. Tighten the locknut to 20 Nm (15 ft-lb.)

17. Screw the fork cap assembly into the fork tube while pushing down on the spring. Start the bolt slowly; do not cross-thread it.

18. Place the fork tube in a vise or holder and tighten the fork cap to 23 N•m (17 ft.-lb.).

19. Install the fork assembly as described in this section.

20. Repeat for the other fork assembly.

Removal/Installation

> *WARNING*
> *Wear eye protection when releasing air pressure from the fork leg. Slowly re-lease the air pressure to prevent loss of fork oil.*

1. Remove the air valve cap and bleed off all air pressure by depressing the valve stem.

2. If the fork is going to be disassembled, perform the following:

    a. Remove the cap (**Figure 16**) from the base of the slider.

    b. Loosen the damper adjust bolt (**Figure 17**) just enough to break it loose, otherwise, fork oil may flow out of the slider.

    c. Loosen the upper fork bridge bolts (A, **Figure 18**).

    d. Loosen the fork cap assembly (B, **Figure 18**).

3. Remove the front wheel as described in Chapter Twelve.

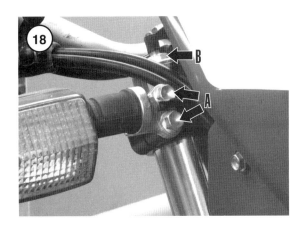

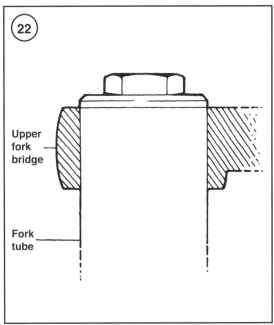

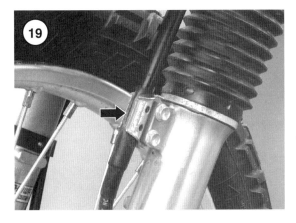

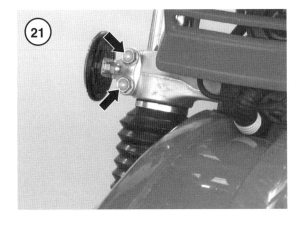

4. On XR600R models, remove the headlight as described in Chapter Ten.

5. Remove the bolts securing the brake hose bracket (**Figure 19**) to the left fork leg. Move the bracket and hose out of the way.

6. Remove the speedometer/tripmeter cable clamp on the right fork tube.

> *CAUTION*
> *Do not allow the front brake caliper to hang from the brake hose in Step 7.*

7. Remove the front brake caliper mounting bolts (**Figure 20**), then remove the caliper. Suspend or support the caliper so it is out of the way.

8. If not already loosened, loosen the upper fork bridge bolts (A, **Figure 18**).

9. Loosen the lower fork bridge bolts (**Figure 21**).

10. Slide the fork tube from the upper and lower fork bridge. It may be necessary to slightly rotate the fork tube while pulling it down and out.

11. Install by reversing the preceding removal steps while noting the following:

    a. Install the fork tubes so that the top of the fork tube aligns with the top surface of the upper fork bridge (**Figure 22**).

    b. If the fork was disassembled, tighten the fork cap to 23 N•m (17 ft.-lb.).

    c. Tighten the lower fork bridge bolts to 33 N•m (24 ft.-lb.).

    d. Tighten the upper fork bridge bolts to 28 N•m (20 ft.-lb.).

    e. Install the front brake caliper mounting bolts. Tighten the bolts to the specification in **Table 2**.

13

FRONT FORK

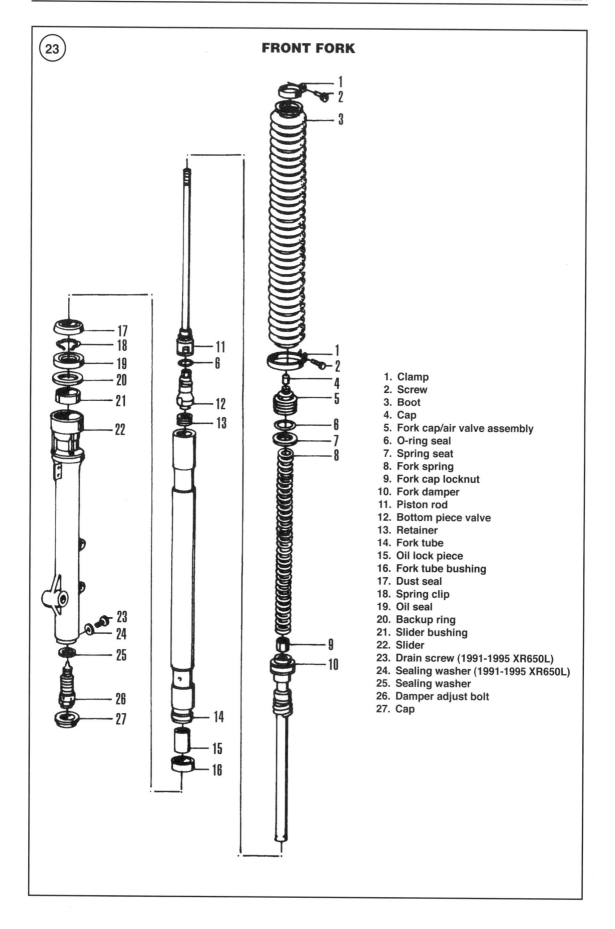

1. Clamp
2. Screw
3. Boot
4. Cap
5. Fork cap/air valve assembly
6. O-ring seal
7. Spring seat
8. Fork spring
9. Fork cap locknut
10. Fork damper
11. Piston rod
12. Bottom piece valve
13. Retainer
14. Fork tube
15. Oil lock piece
16. Fork tube bushing
17. Dust seal
18. Spring clip
19. Oil seal
20. Backup ring
21. Slider bushing
22. Slider
23. Drain screw (1991-1995 XR650L)
24. Sealing washer (1991-1995 XR650L)
25. Sealing washer
26. Damper adjust bolt
27. Cap

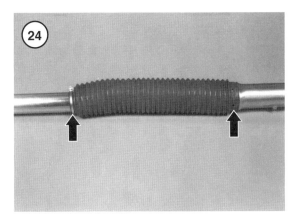

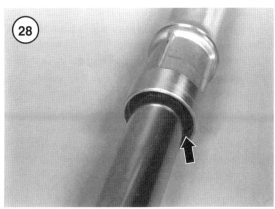

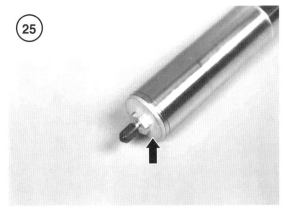

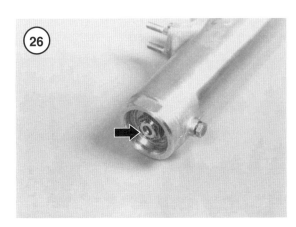

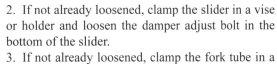

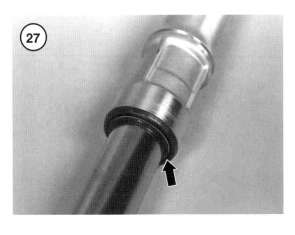

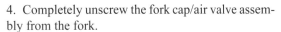

Disassembly

Refer to **Figure 23**.

1. Remove the clamping screws and clamps (**Figure 24**) at the top and bottom of the rubber boot. Remove the rubber boot from the groove in the top of the slider. Slide the rubber boot off the top of the fork tube.

> *CAUTION*
> *Workstands (**Figure 11** [www.parktool. com]), with quick adjustability and padded clamps are ideal for fork service. If using a vise, make sure it has soft jaw inserts.*

2. If not already loosened, clamp the slider in a vise or holder and loosen the damper adjust bolt in the bottom of the slider.

3. If not already loosened, clamp the fork tube in a vise with soft jaws and loosen the fork cap/air valve assembly (**Figure 25**).

> *WARNING*
> *Be careful when unscrewing the fork cap/air valve assembly as the spring is under pressure.*

4. Completely unscrew the fork cap/air valve assembly from the fork.

5. Slide the fork tube down into the slider to expose the fork spring assembly.

6. Pour out the fork oil and discard it. Pump the fork several times by hand to expel most of the remaining oil.

7. Turn the damping adjuster in the damper adjust bolt counterclockwise to its fully soft position so the adjuster needle will not be damaged. Note the total number of turns this takes so the adjuster can be reset to its original setting. Remove the damper adjust bolt and sealing washer (**Figure 26**). Discard the sealing washer.

8. On 1991-2007 models, withdraw the fork piston/fork spring assembly from the fork tube. On 2008-on models, withdraw the fork damper/fork spring assembly.

13

9. Install the slider in a vise with soft jaws or holder.

10. Remove the dust seal (**Figure 27**) from the fork slider.

11. Remove the stopper ring (**Figure 28**) from the fork slider.

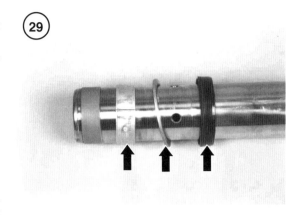

> *NOTE*
> *It may be necessary to slightly heat the slider area around the oil seal prior to removal. Use a rag soaked in hot water; do not apply a flame directly to the fork slider.*

12. To separate the fork tube from the slider, hold the slider and pull hard on the fork tube using quick in and out strokes. Doing this will withdraw the bushing, backup ring and oil seal from the slider.

> *NOTE*
> *There is an interference fit between the bushing in the fork slider and the bushing on the fork tube.*

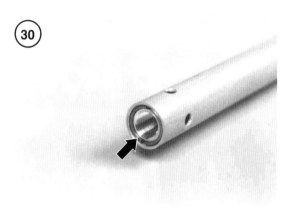

13. Turn the fork tube upside down and slide off the oil seal, backup ring and slider bushing from the fork tube (**Figure 29**).

> *NOTE*
> *Do not discard the slider bushing at this time. It will be used during the installation procedure.*

> *NOTE*
> *Do not remove the fork tube bushing unless replacement is required. Inspect it as described in this chapter.*

14. Remove the oil lock piece from the slider.

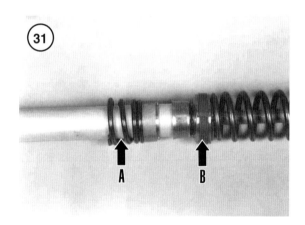

> *NOTE*
> *Before performing Step 15, make sure the parts and special tool are available. Honda factory parts catalogs list only the complete piston assembly, which includes the retainer and bottom valve piece, for all model years.*

15. On 1991-2007 models, if necessary, use piston tool (Honda part No. 07GMA-KS70100) and remove the retainer and bottom piece valve (**Figure 30**) from the piston. It is not necessary to remove these two parts unless they are damaged.

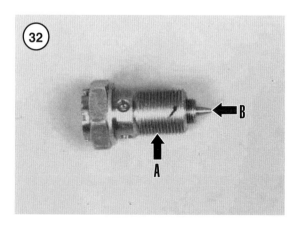

> *NOTE*
> *The following step is not necessary for inspection; only if replacement is required.*

16. On 1991-2007 models, perform the following to disassemble the fork piston/fork spring assembly:

    a. Place a wrench on the fork damper locknut (A, **Figure 13**).

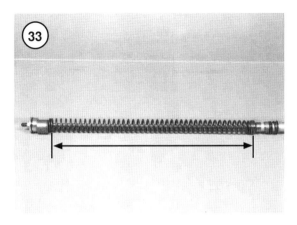

33

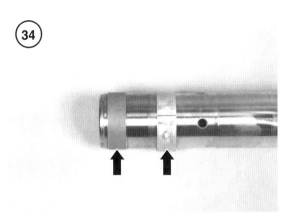

34

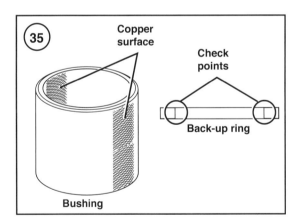

35

Copper surface

Check points

Back-up ring

Bushing

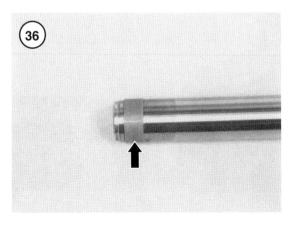

36

b. Place a wrench (B, **Figure 13**) on the fork cap assembly, and loosen the fork damper locknut.

c. Remove the fork cap assembly, the spring seat and the fork spring from on top of the piston rod.

d. Unscrew the fork cap locknut.

e. Withdraw the piston rod from the piston.

17. Inspect the components as described in this section.

Inspection

1. Thoroughly clean all parts in solvent and dry them.

2. Check the fork tube for signs of wear or scratches.

3. Inspect the fork piston rebound spring (A, **Figure 31**) for wear or damage; replace if worn or sagged.

4. Inspect the piston ring (B, **Figure 31**) for wear or damage; replace if necessary.

5. On 1991-2007 models, inspect the fork tube, fork piston, and piston rod for wear or damage if they were removed. On all models, inspect the fork tube and fork damper for wear or damage. Replace any damaged part.

6. Inspect the lower portion of the slider for dents or exterior damage that may cause binding. Replace if necessary.

7. Inspect the threads (A, **Figure 32**) and the needle edge (B) of the damper adjust bolt for damage; replace if necessary.

8. Measure the uncompressed length of the fork spring (not rebound spring) as shown in **Figure 33**. If the spring has sagged to the service limit in **Table 1**, replace the spring:

9. Inspect the slider and fork tube bushings (**Figure 34**). If either is scratched or scored, replace it. If the Teflon coating is worn off so that the copper base material is showing on approximately 3/4 of the total surface, replace the bushing. Also check for distortion on the check points of the backup ring; replace as necessary. Refer to **Figure 35**.

10. Replace any parts that are worn or damaged. Simply cleaning and reinstalling unserviceable components will not improve performance of the front suspension.

Assembly

1. Coat all parts with fresh Pro-Honda Suspension Fluid SS-7, or equivalent fork oil, prior to installation.

2. If removed, install a new fork tube bushing (**Figure 36**).

3. On 1991-2007 models, if disassembled assemble the fork piston/fork spring assembly as follows:

> *CAUTION*
> *Be careful not to damage the guide bushing inside the fork piston with the threads on the piston rod during installation.*

a. Carefully install the piston rod into the fork piston from the bottom.

13

b. Position the locknut with the sharp side facing up (**Figure 37**) and screw the locknut onto the piston rod. Screw the locknut on all the way.

c. Install the fork spring, spring seat, spring spacer and the fork cap assembly onto the piston rod.

d. Tighten the fork cap assembly only finger-tight at this time.

4. On 1991-2007 models, if removed, install the bottom piece valve and retainer into the fork piston (**Figure 30**). Tighten the retainer to 35 N•m (26 ft.-lb.). Use the same tool set-up used for disassembly.

5. On 1991-2007 models, install the fork piston/fork spring assembly into the fork tube. On 2008-on models, install the fork damper/fork spring assembly into the fork tube. Refer to **Figure 38** and **Figure 39**. Temporarily tighten the fork cap assembly securely.

6. Install the oil lock piece onto the damper rod (**Figure 40**).

7. Install the fork tube assembly into the slider (**Figure 41**).

8. Install a new sealing washer and the damper adjust bolt into the base of the slider (**Figure 26**).

9. Place the fork slider in a vise with soft jaws or holder and tighten the damper adjust bolt to 35 N•m (26 ft.-lb.).

10. Slide a new fork slider bushing (A, **Figure 42**) down the fork tube and rest it on the slider.

11. Slide the fork slider backup ring (B, **Figure 42**) (flange side up) down the fork tube and rest it on top of the fork slider bushing.

NOTE
*A fork seal driver (**Figure 43**) is required to install the fork slider bushing and fork seal into the slider. A number of after-market fork seal drivers are available for this purpose. Another method is to use a piece of pipe or metal collar with the correct dimensions to slide over the fork tube and seat against the seal. When selecting or fabricating a driver tool, it must have sufficient weight to drive the bushing and oil seal into the slider.*

12. Place the old fork slider bushing on top of the backup ring. Drive the bushing into the fork slider using a fork seal driver. Drive the bushing into place until it seats completely in the recess in the slider. Remove the installation tool and the old fork slider bushing.

13. To prevent damage to the inner surface of the oil seal, place a plastic bag over the end of the fork tube and coat it with fork oil. This will prevent damage to the dust seal and the oil seal lips when installing them over the top of the fork tube.

14. Coat the new seal with Pro-Honda Suspension Fluid SS-7, or equivalent fork oil. Position the seal

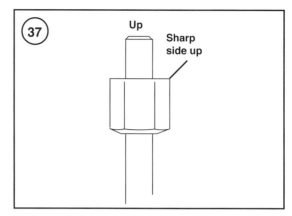
37 — Up — Sharp side up

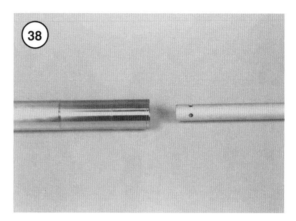
38

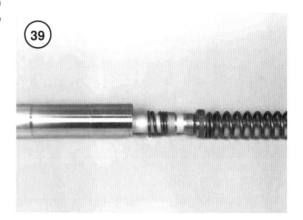
39

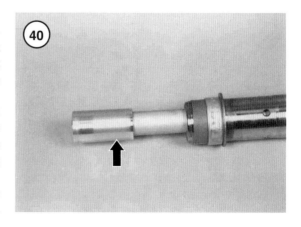
40

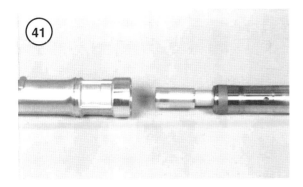

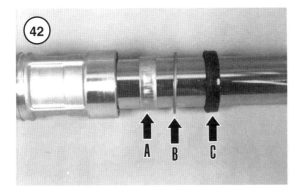

with the marked face upward and slide it down onto the fork tube (C, **Figure 42**).

15. Drive the seal into the slider using a fork seal driver. Drive the oil seal in until the stopper ring groove in the slider can be seen above the top surface of the oil seal.

16. Install the stopper ring (**Figure 28**). Make sure the stopper ring is completely seated in the groove in the fork slider.

17. Slide the dust seal (**Figure 27**) down and into place on the fork slider.

18. Unscrew the fork cap assembly from the fork tube.

NOTE
All of the sub-steps in Step 19 may not be necessary, depending on how tight the fork cap/air valve assembly was tightened against the fork cap locknut in Step 3.

19. To remove the fork spring, perform the following:

WARNING
Be careful, when unscrewing the fork cap/air valve assembly as the spring under it is under pressure.

a. Unscrew the fork cap assembly from the fork tube.
b. Place a wrench on the fork damper locknut (A, **Figure 13**).
c. Place a wrench (B, **Figure 13**) on the fork cap assembly and loosen the fork cap assembly.
d. Remove the fork cap assembly, the spring seat and the fork spring from on top of the piston rod.

20. If removed, install the sealing washer and drain bolt in the fork slider. Tighten the bolt securely.

21. Fill the fork tube with Pro-Honda Suspension Fluid SS-7, or equivalent fork oil. Refer to **Table 1** for the specified quantity for each fork leg.

22. Hold the fork assembly upright and slowly pump the fork several times.

23. Compress the fork completely and measure the fluid level from the top of the fork tube (**Figure 14**) after the fork oil settles. Refer to **Table 1** for the specified fork oil level.

24. Wipe the fork spring with a lint-free cloth.

25A. On XR600R models, install the fork spring with the narrow wound coils toward the top.

25B. On XR650L models, install the fork spring with the narrow wound coils toward the bottom.

26. Install the spring seat.

27. Make sure the O-ring seal (**Figure 15**) is in place on the fork cap assembly and is in good condition; replace if necessary.

28. To tighten the fork cap/air valve assembly, perform the following:

a. Place a wrench on the fork damper locknut (A, **Figure 13**).
b. Place a wrench (B, **Figure 13**) on the fork cap assembly and tighten the locknut against the fork cap assembly. Tighten the locknut to 20 Nm (15 ft.-lb.).

29. Screw the fork cap assembly into the fork tube while pushing down on the spring. Make sure the cap is not cross threaded.

30. Place the fork tube in a vise with soft jaws and tighten the fork cap assembly to 23 N•m (17 ft.-lb.).

31. Slide the rubber boot and clamps onto the fork tube. Install the rubber boot into the groove in the top of the slider. Do not tighten the clamp screws at this time.

32. Install the fork assembly as described in this chapter.

33. Repeat for the other fork assembly.

34. After the fork assemblies and the front wheel are installed, rotate the rubber boot so the breather holes face toward the rear.

13

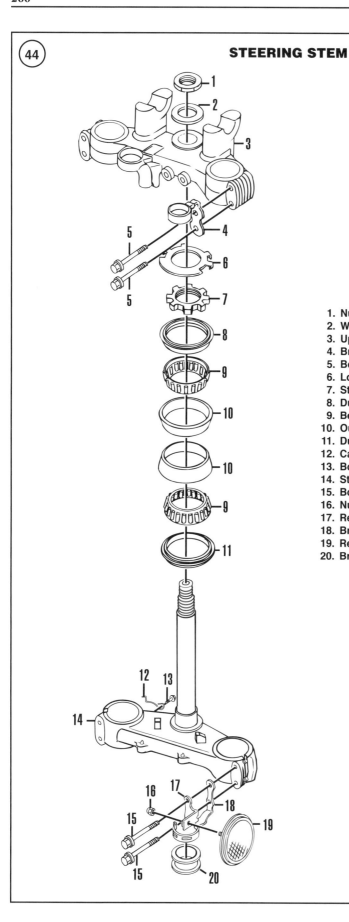

(44) **STEERING STEM**

1. Nut
2. Washer
3. Upper fork bridge
4. Brake hose guide
5. Bolt
6. Lockplate
7. Steering adjust nut
8. Dust seal
9. Bearing
10. Outer bearing race
11. Dust seal
12. Cable guide
13. Bolt
14. Steering stem
15. Bolt
16. Nut
17. Reflector bracket (XR650L)
18. Brake hose guide bracket
19. Reflector (XR650L)
20. Brake hose guide

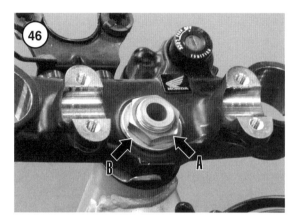

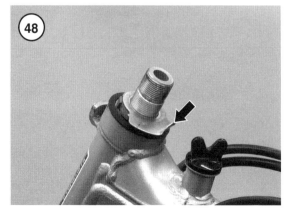

35. Push the rubber boot up until it touches the bottom surface of the lower fork bridge. Tighten all clamps screws securely.

36. Refer to Chapter Three for adjustment.

STEERING HEAD

The steering stem pivots on tapered roller bearings contained in the steering head (**Figure 44**). The bearing races (mounted in the frame) and the lower bearing (mounted on the steering stem) should not be removed unless they require replacement.

Remove the steering stem and lubricate the bearings at the intervals specified in Chapter Three.

Tools

One of the following tools is required to turn the steering adjust nut on the steering stem for bearing adjustment, disassembly and assembly:

1. T-stem nut wrench and bearing adjustment spanner (Motion Pro part No. 08-0232).

2. Steering stem socket (Honda part No. 07916-KA50100).

3. Universal spanner wrench that can be used as a torque adapter (**Figure 45**).

Disassembly

1. Remove the fender as described in Chapter Sixteen.

2. Remove the headlight as described in Chapter Ten or Chapter Eleven.

3. Remove the instrument cluster or speedometer as described in Chapter Ten or Chapter Eleven.

4. On XR650L models, remove the horn as described in Chapter Eleven. Remove the horn mounting bracket from the steering stem.

5. Remove the handlebar as described in this chapter.

6. Loosen the steering stem nut (A, **Figure 46**).

7. Remove the front fork as described in this chapter.

8. Suspend the master cylinder and caliper so there is no tension on the brake hose.

9. On XR650L models, remove the front turn signal and fork clamp bolts on each side of the upper fork bridge, as well as the brake hose guide on the left side.

10. Remove the brake hose guide on the left side of the lower fork bridge.

11. Remove the steering stem nut (A, **Figure 46**) and washer (B).

12. Remove the upper fork bridge (**Figure 47**).

13. Remove and discard the lockplate (**Figure 48**).

> *CAUTION*
> *Hold the steering stem in Step 14 so it cannot fall out of the steering head.*

14. Remove the steering adjust nut (**Figure 49**) using a spanner wrench.

15. Remove the steering stem.

13

16. Remove the dust seal (**Figure 50**) and upper bearing (**Figure 51**).

Inspection

Replace worn or damaged parts as described. If impact damage has occurred, check the frame, steering stem and upper fork bridge.

> *CAUTION*
> *Steering bearings are usually damaged from a lack of lubrication and incorrect adjustment. A loose steering adjustment increases clearance between bearings and races. Pounding from off-road use damages the bearings and races. Overtightening the bearing during adjustment can also damage the bearings and races.*

> *NOTE*
> *Do not remove the lower bearing (***Figure 52***) for cleaning or lubrication. If the bearing can be reused, service it while it is mounted on the steering stem. Remove the bearing only to replace it.*

1. Clean the bearings and races in solvent.
2. Clean the steering stem, steering adjust nut and steering stem nut threads thoroughly to ensure accurate torque readings and steering adjustment during reassembly.
3. Check the steering head frame welds for cracks and fractures. Refer repair to a qualified frame shop or welding service.
4. Check the steering stem nut and steering adjust nut for damage.
5. Check the steering stem and upper fork bridge for cracks and damage. Check the steering stem for straightness.
6. Check the bearing races (**Figure 53**) in the frame for dimples, pitting, galling and impact damage. If a race is worn or damaged, replace both races and bearings as described under *Steering Head Bearing Races* in this chapter.
7. Check the tapered roller bearings (**Figure 54**) for flat spots, pitting, wear and other damage. If a bearing is damaged, replace both races and bearings as described in this chapter.
8. When reusing bearings, clean them thoroughly with a degreaser. Pack the bearings with waterproof bearing grease.

Assembly and Adjustment

Refer to **Figure 44**.
1. Make sure the upper and lower bearing races are properly seated in the frame.
2. Lubricate the bearings and races with a waterproof bearing grease.

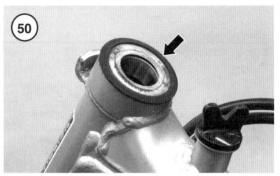

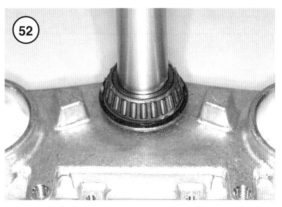

3. Install the steering stem (A, **Figure 55**) through the bottom of the frame and hold it in place.
4. Install the upper bearing (B, **Figure 55**) over the steering stem and seat it into its race.
5. Install the dust seal and the steering adjust nut (**Figure 49**). Tighten the nut finger-tight.

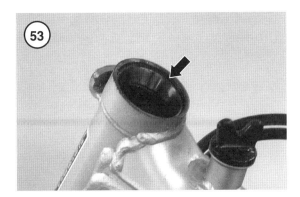

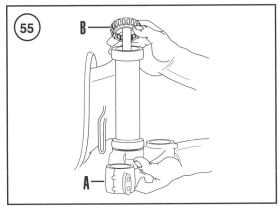

CAUTION
In Step 6A and Step 6B, the steering adjust nut must be tight enough to remove play, both horizontal and verti-

cal, yet loose enough so the steering assembly will turn to both lock positions without binding.

6A. To seat the bearings using a torque adapter and torque wrench, perform the following:

    a. Tighten the steering adjust nut (**Figure 56**) to 25 N•m (18 ft.-lb.).

    b. Turn the steering stem from lock-to-lock several times to seat the bearings.

    c. Retighten the steering adjust nut (**Figure 56**) to 25 N•m (18 ft.-lb.).

    d. Loosen the steering adjust nut.

    e. Tighten the steering adjust nut to the final torque specification in **Table 2**.

    f. Check bearing play by turning the steering stem from lock-to-lock several times. The steering stem must pivot smoothly with no binding or roughness.

6B. If the tools described in Step 6A are not available, tighten the steering adjust nut as follows:

    a. Tighten the steering adjust nut (**Figure 56**) to seat the bearings. Turn the steering stem several times to seat the bearings, then tighten the nut again.

    b. Loosen the steering adjust nut.

    c. Tighten the steering adjust nut while checking bearing play.

NOTE
Inspect the lockplate before installation in Step 7. If the tab portion of the lockplate is creased and may break when bent, install a new lockplate.

7. Install the lockplate (**Figure 48**) so the tab is toward the rear.

8. Install the upper fork bridge, washer and steering stem nut. Tighten the nut finger-tight.

9. Slide both fork tubes into position and tighten the upper and lower fork tube clamp bolts so the fork legs cannot slide out.

10. Tighten the steering stem nut to the specification in **Table 2**.

NOTE
Because tightening the steering stem nut affects the steering bearing preload, it may be necessary to repeat these steps several times until the steering adjustment is correct.

11. Check bearing play by turning the steering stem from side to side. The steering stem must pivot smoothly. If the steering stem adjustment is incorrect, readjust the bearing play as follows:

    a. Loosen the steering stem nut (A, **Figure 46**).

    b. Loosen or tighten the steering adjust nut as required to adjust the steering play.

13

c. Retighten the steering stem nut to the specification in **Table 2**.

d. Recheck bearing play by turning the steering stem from side to side. If the play feels correct, turn the steering stem so the front fork is facing straight ahead. While an assistant steadies the motorcycle, grasp the fork tubes, and try to move them front to back. If there is play and the bearing adjustment feels correct, the bearings and races are probably worn and require replacement.

12. Bend the tab of the lockplate against the upper fork bridge (**Figure 57**).

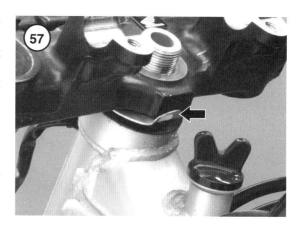

NOTE
The front turn signals on XR650L models are marked R and L to indicate location.

13. Install the turn signals and brake hose guides on the fork tubes. Install the fork tubes as described in this chapter.

14. On XR650L models, install the horn mounting bracket onto the steering stem. Install the horn as described in Chapter Eleven.

15. Install the instrument cluster or speedometer as described in Chapter Ten or Chapter Eleven.

16. Install the headlight as described in Chapter Ten or Chapter Eleven.

17. Install the fender as described in Chapter Sixteen.

18. Install the front wheel as described in Chapter Twelve.

19. After 30 minutes to 1 hour of riding time, check the steering adjustment. If necessary, adjust as described under *Steering Play Check and Adjustment* in this chapter.

STEERING PLAY CHECK AND ADJUSTMENT

Steering adjustment removes free play in the steering stem and bearings while allowing free steering stem rotation. Excessive play or roughness in the steering stem produces imprecise steering and possible bearing damage. Improper bearing lubrication or an incorrect steering adjustment (too loose or tight) usually causes these conditions. Incorrect clutch and throttle cable routing can also affect steering operation.

Because tightening the steering stem nut affects the steering bearing preload, it may be necessary to repeat the procedure a few times until the steering adjustment is correct. If the steering adjustment cannot be corrected, the steering bearings may require lubrication or are damaged. Remove the steering stem and inspect the bearings as described in this chapter.

1. Support the motorcycle with the front wheel off the ground.

2. Turn the handlebar from side to side. The steering stem should move freely and without any binding or

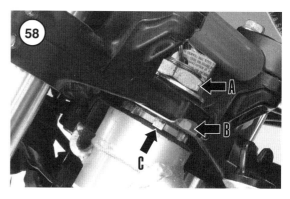

roughness. If it feels as if the bearings are catching, the bearing races are probably damaged.

3. Turn the handlebar so the front wheel points straight ahead. Alternately push (slightly) one end of the handlebar and then the other. The front end should turn to each side from the center under its own weight. Note the following:

a. If the steering stem moved roughly or stopped before hitting the frame stop, check the clutch and throttle cable routing. Reroute the cable(s) if necessary.

b. If the cable routing is correct and the steering is tight, the steering adjustment is too tight or the bearings require lubrication or replacement.

c. If the steering stem moved from side to side correctly, perform Step 4 to check for excessive looseness.

NOTE
When checking for excessive steering play in Step 4, have an assistant steady the motorcycle.

4. Grasp the fork tubes firmly (near the axle) and attempt to move the wheel front to back. Note the following:

a. If movement can be felt at the steering stem, the steering adjustment is probably loose. Go to Step 5 to adjust the steering.

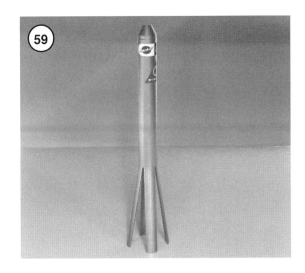

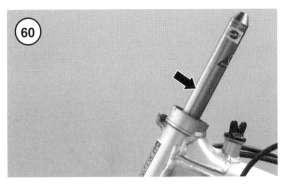

b. If there is no movement and the front end turns correctly as described in Steps 2-4, the steering adjustment is correct.

5. Loosen the steering stem nut (A, **Figure 58**).

6. Push down the locking tab on the lockplate (B, **Figure 58**).

7. Adjust the steering adjust nut (C, **Figure 58**) as follows:

   a. If the steering is too loose, tighten the steering adjust nut.

   b. If the steering is too tight, loosen the steering adjust nut.

NOTE
If the tab on the lockplate breaks or will not stay in place against the fork bridge, replace the lockplate.

8. Bend the tab of the lockplate (B, **Figure 58**) against the upper fork bridge.

NOTE
If a torque adapter is not available to tighten the steering stem nut, remove the handlebar for access to the nut.

9. Tighten the steering stem nut to the specification in **Table 2**.

10. Recheck the steering adjustment as described in this procedure.

STEERING BEARING PRELOAD (2008-ON XR650L)

1. Securely support the motorcycle on a level surface with the front wheel off the ground.

2. Turn the handlebar so the steering stem points straight ahead.

3. Connect a spring scale to a fork leg between the upper and lower fork bridges. Make sure no cable or wiring harness will interfere with steering stem movement.

4. While keeping the scale perpendicular to the steering stem, pull the spring scale rearward. Read the scale at the point where the steering stem begins to move.

5. Compare the scale reading to the steering bearing preload specified in Table 1. If the reading is outside the specified range, adjust the steering play.

STEERING HEAD BEARING RACES

The steering head bearing races (**Figure 44**) are pressed into the steering head. Do not remove the bearing races unless they require replacement.

Outer Bearing Race Replacement

Do not remove the upper and lower outer bearing races unless they require replacement. Replace a bearing race and bearing as a set.

1A. Use a bearing race removal tool (**Figure 59**, [www.parktool.com]) as follows:

   a. Insert the tool through the steering head.

   b. Position the tool so the legs contact the bearing race edge (**Figure 60**).

   c. Strike the end of the tool to force the bearing race out of the steering head.

1B. Use hand tools as follows:

   a. Insert an aluminum drift into the steering head (**Figure 61**).

   b. Carefully drive the race out from the inside. Strike at different spots around the race to prevent it from binding in the mounting bore.

2. Repeat for the other race.

3. Clean the race bore and check for cracks or other damage.

4. Place the new race squarely into the mounting bore opening with its tapered side facing out (**Figure 62**).

CAUTION
When using a tool to install the bearing races in the following steps, do not allow the rod or tool to contact the face of the bearing race as it may damage it.

13

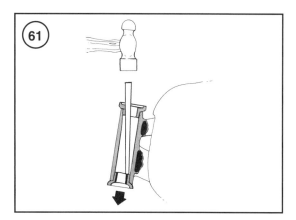

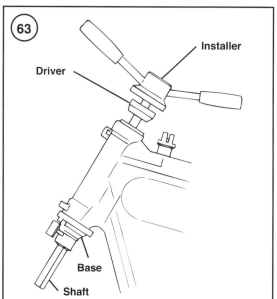

5A. Use a bearing race installation tool (**Figure 63**, [www.parktool.com]) as follows:

a. Place the correct size race installer on the tool shaft.

b. Insert the tool shaft into the steering head so the installer contacts the bearing race.

c. Install the clamp on the shaft end.

d. Turn the tool handle until the bearing race is seated in the steering head.

e. Disassemble the tool. Verify that the race is properly seated.

5B. Use a fabricated bearing race installation tool (**Figure 64**). The tool shown consists of a threaded rod and appropriately sized discs. One disc fits the outer diameter of the race, while the other disc is slightly larger than the diameter of the steering head.

a. Assemble the tool as shown in **Figure 65**.

b. Tighten the nut to pull in and seat the race **Figure 66**.

c. Remove the tool and verify that the race is properly seated.

6. Lubricate the upper and lower bearing races with grease.

Steering Stem Bearing Replacement

Perform the following steps to replace the steering stem bearing (**Figure 67**).

1. Install the steering stem nut onto the steering stem to protect the threads.

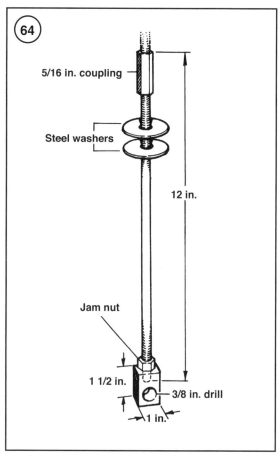

WARNING
Wear safety glasses when removing the
steering stem bearing in Step 2.

2. Remove the steering stem bearing and dust seal using a hammer and chisel as shown in **Figure 68**.

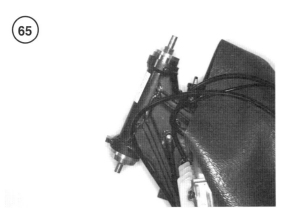

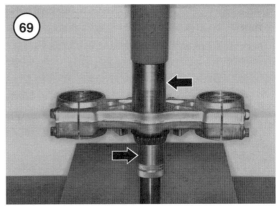

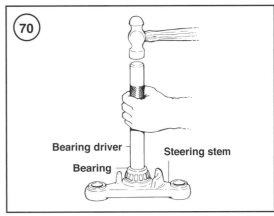

Bearing driver — | Steering stem
Bearing

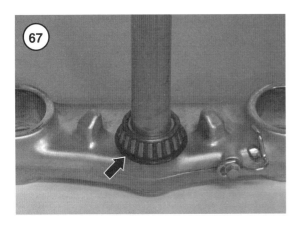

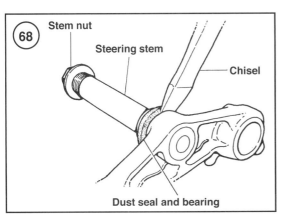

Stem nut
Steering stem
Chisel
Dust seal and bearing

Strike at different spots underneath the bearing to prevent it from binding on the steering stem.

3. Clean the steering stem with solvent and dry thoroughly.

4. Inspect the steering stem and replace if damaged.

5. Install a new dust seal onto the steering stem. Lubricate the seal lip with grease.

6. Pack the new bearing with waterproof bearing grease.

7. Slide the new bearing onto the steering stem until it stops.

8A. To install the new steering stem bearing with a press, perform the following:

   a. Install the steering stem and the new bearing in a press and support it with two bearing drivers as shown in **Figure 69**. Make sure the lower bearing driver seats against the inner bearing race and does not contact the bearing rollers.

   b. Press the bearing onto the steering stem until it bottoms (**Figure 67**).

8B. To install the new steering stem bearing using a bearing driver perform the following:

   a. Slide a bearing driver or long pipe over the steering stem until it seats against the bearing inner race (**Figure 70**).

   b. Drive the bearing onto the steering stem until it bottoms (**Figure 67**).

13

Table 1 FRONT SUSPENSION AND STEERING SPECIFICATIONS

Item	Specification	Service limit
Fork air pressure		
Standard	0 psi (0 kPa)	
Maximum		
1993-2007	6 psi (40 kPa)	
2008-on	5.7 psi (39 kPa)	
Fork oil		
Type	Pro Honda Suspension Fluid SS-7, HP Fork Oil SS-19 or an equivalent	
Capacity		
XR600R		
1991-1992	580 ml (19.6 U.S. oz.)	
1993-1997	585 ml (19.8 U.S. oz.)	
XR650L		
1993-2007	564 ml (19.1 U.S. oz.)	
2008-on		
HP Fork Oil SS-19	558 ml (18.9 U.S. oz.)	
Pro Honda Suspension Fluid SS-7	564 ml (19.1 U.S. oz.)	
Oil level		
XR600R	125 mm (4.9 in.)	
XR650L		
1993-2007	145 mm (5.7 in.)	
2008-on		
HP Fork Oil SS-19	150 mm (5.9 in.)	
Pro Honda Suspension Fluid SS-7	145 mm (5.7 in.)	
Fork spring free length	576 mm (22.68 in.)	570 mm (22.44 in.)
Front fork travel		
1993-2007	295 mm (11.6 in.)	–
2008-on	260 mm (10.2 in.)	–
Steering bearing preload		
XR600R	NA	NA
XR650L	1.1-1.6 kgf (2.4-3.5 lbf)	–

Table 2 FRONT SUSPENSION AND STEERING TORQUE SPECIFICATIONS

Item	N•m	in.-lb.	ft.-lb.
Brake caliper mounting bolts			
XR600R and 1993-2007 XR650L	31	–	23
2008-on XR650L	30	–	22
Fork bottom piece valve retainer	35	–	25
Fork bridge bolts			
Lower	33	–	24
Upper	28	–	20
Fork damper adjust bolt	35	–	26
Fork damper locknut	20	–	15
Fork cap assembly	23	–	17
Fork cap locknut	20	–	15
Front brake master cylinder clamp			
XR600R	27	–	20
XR650L			
1993-2007	12	106	–
2008-on	NA	NA	–
Handlebar holder bolts			
XR600R and 1993-2007 XR650L	27	–	20
2008-on XR650L	26	–	19
Steering adjust nut			
XR600R			
1991-1992	1	8.8	–
1993-1997	1.5	13.2	–
XR650L	1	8.8	–
Steering stem nut			
XR600R and 1993-2007 XR650L	118	–	87
2008-on XR650L	116	–	86
Throttle housing bolts (XR650L)			
1993-2007	8.8	78	–
2008-on	NA	NA	–

CHAPTER FOURTEEN

REAR SUSPENSION

This chapter covers the rear shock absorber, shock linkage assembly and swing arm. Refer to Chapter Twelve for rear wheel, rear axle and tire service information.

Rear suspension specifications are in **Tables 1-3** at the end of this chapter.

The rear suspension is a progressive rising rate design. When the swing arm is slightly compressed over small bumps, the spring and damping rates are soft. When riding conditions become more severe, the swing arm travel increases. This causes the linkage system to pivot into a position to increase the travel of the spring and damper. This provides a progressively firmer shock absorbing action, greater control and better transfer of power to the ground.

SHOCK ABSORBER

The single shock absorber is a spring-loaded hydraulically damped unit with an integral oil/nitrogen reservoir. To adjust the rear shock absorber, refer to *Rear Suspension Adjustment* in Chapter Three.

Shock Absorber Removal/Installation

1. Support the motorcycle with the rear wheel off the ground.
2. Remove the air box as described Chapter Eight or Chapter Nine.

> *NOTE*
> *If the spring will be removed after shock absorber removal, refer to Chapter Three and turn the spring retaining nut to lessen spring pressure.*

3. On XR600R models, remove the ICM as described in Chapter Ten.
4. Remove the upper shock absorber nut and mounting bolt (**Figure 1**) and allow the rear wheel to drop to the ground.
5. On XR650L models, remove the shock link to arm bolt (**Figure 2**), then remove the dust seal caps (**Figure 3**).
6. Move the upper end of the shock absorber rearward, then turn the upper end so the reservoir is to the rear.
7. Remove the lower shock absorber bolt (**Figure 4**), then remove the shock absorber from the left side.
8. Clean and service the seals, collar and spherical bearing as described in this section.

14

9. Service the shock spring as described in this chapter.

10. Installation is the reverse of removal. Note the following:

a. Clean and dry the shock absorber fasteners. Inspect and replace damaged fasteners.

b. Install the shock absorber so the reservoir is on the left side.

c. Install the lower shock mounting bolt from the right side. Tighten the bolt to the specification in **Table 3**.

d. On XR650L models, lubricate the shock link dust seal caps with molybdenum grease. Install the shock link bolt from the left side. Tighten the nut to 45 N•m (33 ft.-lb.).

e. On XR600R models, install the upper shock mounting bolt from the right side. Tighten the nut to 45 N•m (33 ft.-lb.).

f. On XR650L models, install the upper shock mounting bolt from the left side. Tighten the nut to the specification in **Table 3**.

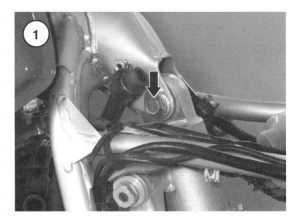

Shock Absorber Inspection

1. Inspect the shock absorber for gas or oil leaks.

2. Check the damper rod for bending, rust or other damage. If parts of the damper rod have turned blue, the rod is overheating, probably due to a lack of oil in the shock.

3. Check the reservoir for dents or other damage.

4. Inspect the seals and spherical bearing in the upper shock mount as described in this section.

5. If necessary, remove and inspect the spring as described in this section.

6. If the shock is leaking, or if it is time to change the shock oil, refer service to a Honda dealership or suspension specialist.

Seal and Bearing Inspection/Lubrication

Refer to **Figure 5**.

Use a waterproof bearing grease when lubricating the seals and bearing in this section.

1. Insert a thin screwdriver or similar tool between the seal and bearing and carefully pry the dust seal from the bearing bore (A, **Figure 6**). Repeat for the other seal.

2. Clean and dry both seals, then check them for damage. If the seals are not damaged, they can be reused.

3. Move the spherical bearing (B, **Figure 6**) by hand. If any roughness, damage or excessive looseness is evident, replace the bearing as described in this section.

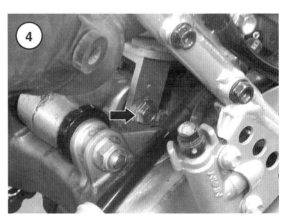

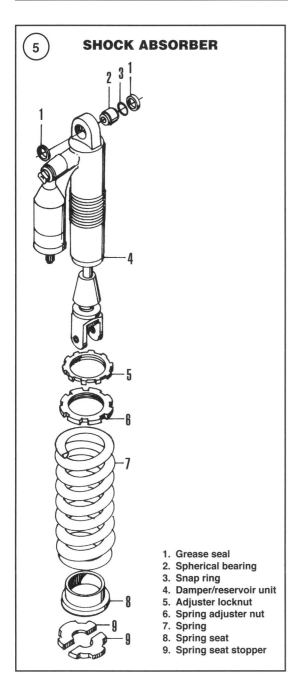

SHOCK ABSORBER

1. Grease seal
2. Spherical bearing
3. Snap ring
4. Damper/reservoir unit
5. Adjuster locknut
6. Spring adjuster nut
7. Spring
8. Spring seat
9. Spring seat stopper

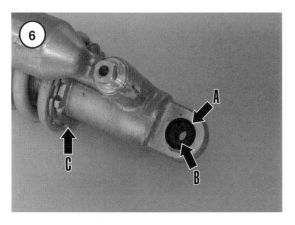

4. If the bearing is in good condition, lubricate it with grease.

5. Lubricate the dust seal lips with grease and then install them into the shock mount with the open side facing out. Make sure the outer edge of the seals are positioned flush with the shock body.

Spherical Bearing Replacement

The stop ring is installed in a groove in the right side of the bearing bore and must be removed before the bearing can be pressed out.

NOTE
On XR600R models, the bearing and stop ring are available. On XR650L models, replacement parts are not available.

This section describes bearing replacement using a bolt, washers, and pieces of pipe or metal tubing.

1. Remove the stop ring as follows:

NOTE
During initial bearing installation the bearing was pressed against the stop ring to prevent the stop ring from coming out of its groove. Before the stop ring can be removed, the bearing must be pressed away from it.

a. Use a bolt and nut to hold a piece of tubing (A, **Figure 7**) against the bearing and a thick washer (B) against the shock absorber.

b. Hold the nut and turn the bolt to press the bearing away from the top ring. Then remove the assembled pieces.

c. Pry the stop ring out of the groove with a scribe or similar tool.

2. Remove the bearing as follows:

NOTE
*The stop ring depicted in **Figure 8** was removed in Step 1c. The drawing illustrates the tool assembly described in substep a.*

a. Assemble the bolt and pipe assembly against the shock absorber and bearing as shown in **Figure 8**.

b. Hold the nut and turn the bolt to force the bearing out of the shock mount.

3. Clean the bearing bore. Check the bore and stop ring groove (**Figure 9**) for cracks and other damage.

4. Lubricate the new bearing with waterproof grease.

5. Install the new bearing as follows:

14

a. Assemble the bolt, spacer, bearing and washer assembly (**Figure 8**) onto the shock mount as shown in **Figure 10**. Make sure the bearing seats squarely in the bore.

b. Hold the nut and tighten the bolt to press the bearing into the shock mount. Install a new stop ring into the groove.

c. Remove the assembled parts, and then reassemble them onto the shock mount to move the bearing until it seats against the stop ring (**Figure 8**).

d. Remove the assembled parts from the shock mount. Make sure the stop ring and bearing are properly installed.

6. Install new seals as described in this section.

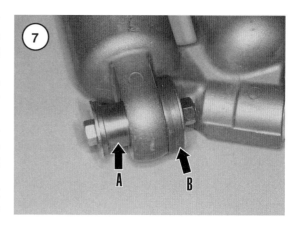

Spring Removal/Installation

Refer to **Figure 5**.

1. Remove the shock absorber as described in this section.

2. Turn the locknut and spring adjustment nut (C, **Figure 6**) to the top of the threads, but do not remove the nuts.

3. With all preload removed from the spring, remove the spring seat stoppers.

4. Remove the spring seat and spring.

5. Clean and dry the shock assembly.

6. Check the spring for cracks and other damage.

7. Slide the rubber stopper on the damper rod to expose different areas on the rod and inspect the rod surface for nicks, bluing or other damage. This surface must be smooth.

8. Install the spring so the end with the large diameter is toward the upper end of the shock absorber.

9. Install the spring seat and spring seat stoppers.

10. Install the shock absorber as described in this chapter.

11. Adjust the spring preload as described in Chapter Three.

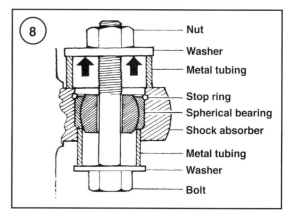

Nut
Washer
Metal tubing
Stop ring
Spherical bearing
Shock absorber
Metal tubing
Washer
Bolt

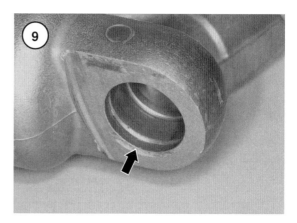

SHOCK LINKAGE

The shock linkage consists of the shock arm, shock link, pivot bolts, seals and bearings. Service the assembly at the intervals specified in Chapter Three, or more frequently if operated in extreme conditions.

Removal/Installation

1. Clean the shock linkage assembly (**Figure 11**) to prevent dirt from contaminating the bearings when removing the linkage components.

2. Support the motorcycle with the rear wheel off the ground.

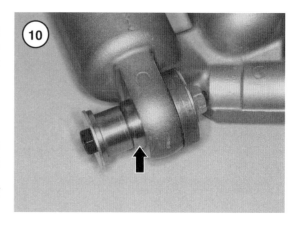

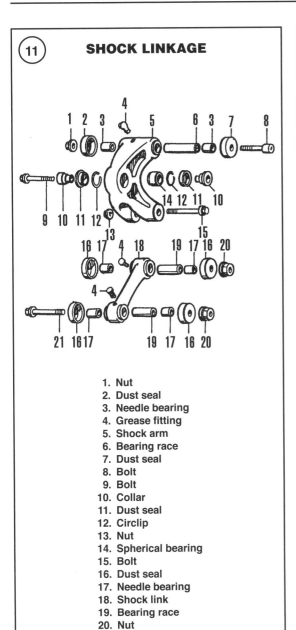

SHOCK LINKAGE

1. Nut
2. Dust seal
3. Needle bearing
4. Grease fitting
5. Shock arm
6. Bearing race
7. Dust seal
8. Bolt
9. Bolt
10. Collar
11. Dust seal
12. Circlip
13. Nut
14. Spherical bearing
15. Bolt
16. Dust seal
17. Needle bearing
18. Shock link
19. Bearing race
20. Nut
21. Bolt

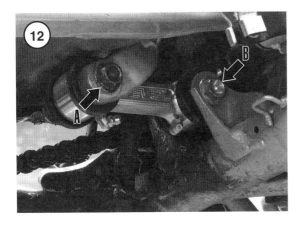

3. Remove the shock absorber as described in this chapter.

4. On XR600R models, remove the pivot bolt securing the shock arm to the shock link (A, **Figure 12**).

5. On XR650L models, remove the pivot bolt cover (**Figure 13**).

6. Remove the pivot bolt securing the shock arm to the swing arm (**Figure 14**).

7. Remove pivot bolt securing the shock link to the frame (B, **Figure 12**).

NOTE
The dust seals on each side of the pivot hubs are easily dislodged during disassembly.

8. Remove the shock link and shock arm from the frame.

9. Inspect the components as described in this chapter.

10. Reverse the removal steps for installation while noting the following:

    a. Apply molybdenum disulfide paste grease to all spacers and dust seals prior to installation.

    b. Install the shock arm-to-swing arm pivot bolt from the left side. Tighten to the specification in **Table 3**.

    c. Install the shock link so the grease fittings point away from the drive chain.

    d. On XR600R models, install the shock link-to-frame pivot bolt from the left side and tighten to 45 N•m (33 ft.-lb.).

    e. On XR650L models, install the shock link-to-frame pivot bolt from the right side and tighten to the specification in **Table 3**.

    f. Install the shock link-to-shock arm pivot bolt from the left side and tighten to 45 N•m (33 ft.-lb.).

    g. Move the swing arm up and down several times to make sure all components are properly seated.

14

Inspection

1. Inspect the shock link and shock arm for cracks or damage; replace if necessary.

2. Remove the dust seals and push out the inner bearing races (**Figure 15**).

3. Clean all parts in solvent and thoroughly dry with compressed air.

4. Inspect the races for scratches, abrasion or abnormal wear; replace if necessary.

5. Inspect the bearings (**Figure 16**). If damaged or worn, replace as described in *Bearing Replacement*.

6. Inspect the dust seals. Replace all of them as a set if any are worn or starting to deteriorate. If the dust seals are in poor condition they will allow dirt to enter into the pivot areas and cause bearing wear.

7. Coat all bearings, inner races and the inside of the dust seals with molybdenum disulfide grease. Insert the inner races into the bearings and install the dust seals.

> *NOTE*
> *Make sure the dust seal lips seat correctly. If not, they will allow dirt and moisture into the bearings and cause wear.*

Bearing Replacement

> *NOTE*
> *Refer to Table 2 for Honda bearing tool information when replacing the needle bearings in the shock arm and shock link.*

Shock arm needle bearing replacement

1. Support the shock arm so the dust seal sealing surface will not be damaged.

2. Install the bearing removal tool (**Table 2**) into the shock arm (**Figure 17**) and drive out both needle bearings. Discard the needle bearings.

3. Thoroughly clean the shock arm in solvent and blow dry with compressed air.

4. Apply a light coat of oil to the inner surface of the shock arm prior to installation of the needle bearings.

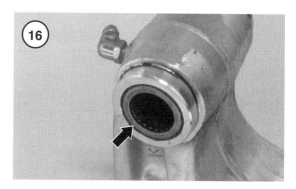

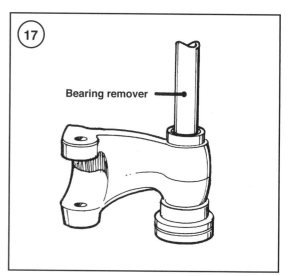

Bearing remover

5. Support the shock arm so the dust seal sealing surface will not be damaged.

6. Position the needle bearings with the end marking facing toward the outside.

7. Correctly position one of the needle bearings onto the shock arm.

8. Install the bearing installation tools (**Table 2**) into the needle bearing and the shock arm (**Figure 18**).

9. Drive in the needle bearing.

10. Turn the shock arm over and install the remaining bearing.

11. Repeat Steps 6-9 for the other needle bearing.

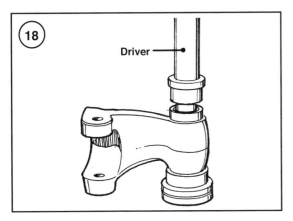

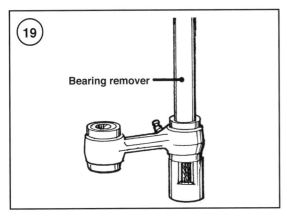

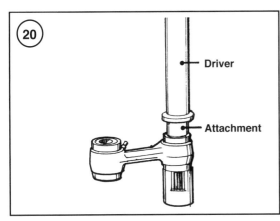

6. Support the shock link so the dust seal sealing surface will not be damaged.
7. Position the needle bearings with the end marking facing toward the outside.
8. Correctly position one of the needle bearings onto the shock link.
9. Install the bearing installation tools (**Table 2**) into the needle bearing and the shock link (**Figure 20**).
10. Drive in the needle bearing.
11. Repeat Steps 7-9 for the other needle bearing.
12. Repeat Steps 7-11 for the other set of needle bearings at the other end of the shock link.

Shock link spherical bearing replacement

This procedure requires a hydraulic press.

1. Remove the side collars (A, **Figure 21**) and dust seals (B).
2. Remove the circlip (**Figure 22**) from each side of the spherical bearing.
3. Support the shock link on the bearing driver base special tool (Honda part No. 07HMF-KS60100).
4. Install the spherical bearing driver (Honda part No. 07946-KA30200) into the shock link (**Figure 23**).
5. Use a hydraulic press and force the spherical bearing out of the shock link. Discard the spherical bearing.
6. Thoroughly clean the shock link in solvent and blow dry with compressed air.
7. Apply a light coat of oil to the inner surface of the shock link prior to installation of the spherical bearing.
8. Install a circlip into one side of the shock link.
9. Using the same tool set-up used for removal, install the new spherical bearing until it bottoms against the circlip.
10. Install the other circlip.
11. Apply molybdenum disulfide paste grease to the side collars and dust seals prior to installation.
12. Install the side collars and the dust seals.

Shock link needle bearing replacement

1. Support the shock link so the dust seal sealing surface will not be damaged.
2. Install the bearing installation tools (**Table 2**) into the shock link (**Figure 19**) and drive out both needle bearings. Discard the needle bearings.
3. Repeat Step 2 for the bearings at the other end of the shock link.
4. Thoroughly clean the shock link in solvent and blow dry with compressed air.
5. Apply a light coat of oil to the inner surface of the shock link prior to installation of the needle bearings.

SWING ARM

The swing arm is supported by needle bearings that ride on the pivot bolt. The condition of the bearings can greatly affect handling performance and if worn parts are not replaced they can produce wheel hop, pulling to one side during acceleration and pulling to the other side during braking.

Removal

1. Remove the drive chain cover (A, **Figure 24**) from the swing arm.

14

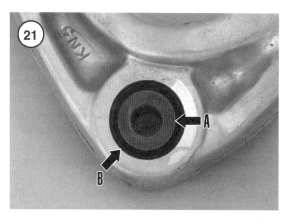

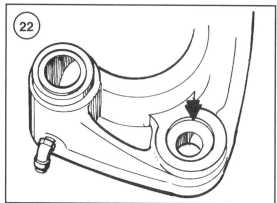

2. Detach the drive chain guide (B, **Figure 24**) from the swing arm.

3. Remove the rear wheel as described in Chapter Twelve.

> *CAUTION*
> *Do not allow the rear brake caliper to hang from the brake hose in Step 4. Suspend or support the caliper so it is out of the way.*

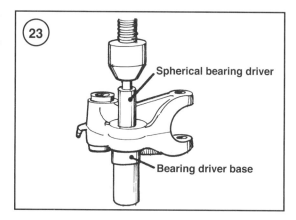

4. Detach the rear brake hose from the retaining clamps on the swing arm.

5. Remove the mud guard from the front of the rear fender.

6. Pull the air box breather tube out of the wire loop on the swing arm.

7. Note the location of fuel system breather and drain hoses in the swing arm wire loop guide.

8. Remove the shock link-to-shock arm bolt (**Figure 25**).

9. Remove the lower shock absorber bolt (**Figure 26**).

10. Grasp the rear end of the swing arm and try to move it from side to side in a horizontal arc. There should be no noticeable side play. If play is evident and the pivot bolt is tightened correctly, the bearings or pivot collar should be replaced.

11. Remove the locknut (**Figure 27**) and withdraw the pivot bolt from the left side.

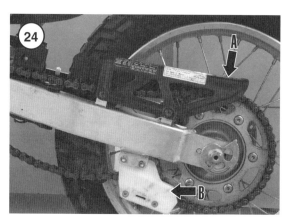

> *NOTE*
> *The shock arm remains on the swing arm and may be removed from the swing arm after removal.*

> *NOTE*
> *The dust seals on each side of the pivot hubs may fall off during swing arm removal.*

12. Pull back on the swing arm, free it from the drive chain and remove the swing arm from the frame.

13. To remove the shock arm from the swing arm proceed as follows:

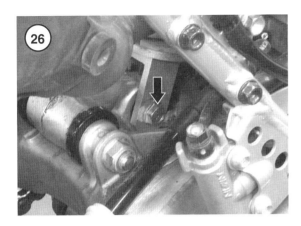

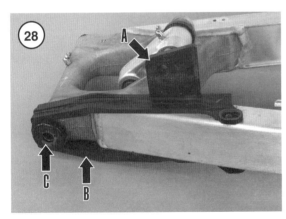

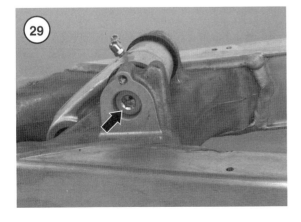

a. On XR650L models, remove the pivot bolt cover (A, **Figure 28**).

b. Remove the pivot bolt securing the shock arm to the swing arm (**Figure 29**).

c. Remove the shock arm from the swing arm.

14. Inspect the swing arm as described in this chapter.

NOTE
The dust seals on each side of the pivot hubs may fall off during swing arm removal.

Installation

1. If removed, install the shock arm onto the swing arm as follows:

a. Apply molybdenum disulfide paste grease to the dust seals prior to installation.

b. Install the bolt from the left side. Tighten the nut to the specification in **Table 3**.

c. On XR650L models, install the pivot bolt cover.

2. If the pivot seals where removed, apply molybdenum disulfide paste grease to the dust seals and install them on the swing arm pivot hubs.

3. Position the drive chain over the left side of the swing arm.

4. Insert the swing arm into the mounting area of the frame. Align the holes in the swing arm with the holes in the frame. To help align the holes, insert a drift in from the right side.

5. Apply a light coat of molybdenum disulfide grease to the pivot bolt and install the pivot bolt from the left side.

6. Install the locknut and tighten to the specification in **Table 3**.

7. Move the swing arm up and down several times to make sure all components are properly seated.

8. Install the lower shock mounting bolt from the right side. Tighten the bolt to the specification in **Table 3**.

9. Install the shock link-to-shock arm pivot bolt from the left side and tighten to 45 N•m (33 ft.-lb.).

10. Install the mud guard onto the rear fender.

11. Install the rear wheel as described in Chapter Twelve.

12. Install the drive chain cover and drive chain guide onto the swing arm.

13. Install the rear brake hose into the retaining clamps on the swing arm.

Disassembly/Inspection/Assembly

Refer to **Figure 30**.

1. Remove the swing arm as described in this section.

2. To remove the shock arm from the swing arm proceed as follows:

14

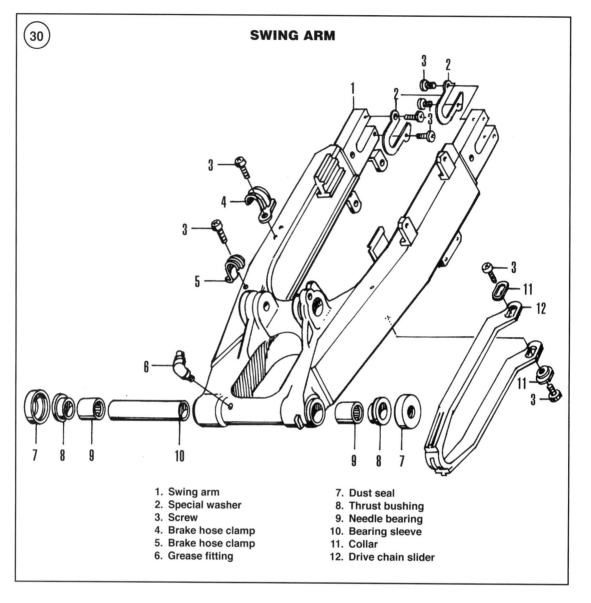

SWING ARM

1. Swing arm
2. Special washer
3. Screw
4. Brake hose clamp
5. Brake hose clamp
6. Grease fitting
7. Dust seal
8. Thrust bushing
9. Needle bearing
10. Bearing sleeve
11. Collar
12. Drive chain slider

a. On XR650L models, remove the pivot bolt cover (A, **Figure 28**).

b. Remove the pivot bolt securing the shock arm to the swing arm (**Figure 29**).

c. Remove the shock arm from the swing arm.

3. Remove the drive chain slider (B, **Figure 28**) from the swing arm.

4. Remove both dust seals (C, **Figure 28**) if they did not fall off during swing arm removal.

NOTE
The pivot sleeve serves as the inner race for the needle bearings.

5. Remove the pivot sleeve (A, **Figure 31**), clean in solvent and dry thoroughly.

6. Inspect the pivot sleeve for scoring, excessive wear, corrosion or other damage.

7. Remove the thrust bushings from the pivot hubs (B, **Figure 31**), clean in solvent and dry thoroughly.

NOTE
There are no specifications for the pivot sleeve or thrust bushings.

8. Inspect the thrust bushing for abnormal wear, scratches or score marks. Replace if necessary.

9. Inspect the needle bearings (**Figure 32**) as follows:

a. Wipe off any excess grease from the needle bearing at each end of the swing arm.

b. Turn each bearing and make sure they rotate smoothly. The needle bearings wear very slowly and wear is very difficult to measure.

c. Check the rollers for evidence of wear, pitting or color change (bluish tint) indicating heat from lack of lubrication.

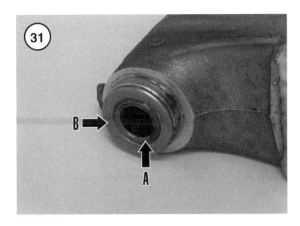

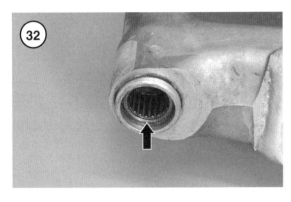

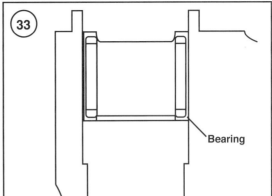

Bearing

NOTE
Always replace both needle bearings even though only one may be worn.

10. Prior to installing the thrust bushings, coat the bushings and needle bearings with molybdenum disulfide grease.

11. Insert the thrust bushing.

12. Lubricate the pivot sleeve with molybdenum disulfide grease, and then insert it into the swing arm (A, **Figure 31**).

13. Coat the inside of both dust caps with molybdenum disulfide grease and install them onto the hubs of the swing arm.

14. If removed, install the shock arm onto the swing arm as follows:

    a. Apply molybdenum disulfide paste grease to the dust seals prior to installation.

    b. Install the pivot bolt from the left side. Tighten the nut to the specification in **Table 3**.

    c. On XR650L models, install the pivot bolt cover.

15. Install the drive chain slider.

16. Install the swing arm as described in this section.

Needle Bearing Replacement

The swing arm is equipped with a needle bearing on each side. The bearing is pressed in place; bearing removal requires replacement.

1. Remove the swing arm as described in this section.

2. Remove the dust seal from each side of the swing arm.

3. Remove the pivot sleeve (A, **Figure 31**).

4. Remove the thrust bushing (B, **Figure 31**) from each side of the swing arm.

5. Using a blind bearing puller (Chapter One), withdraw the needle bearing (**Figure 32**) from the swing arm. Discard the needle bearing.

6. Remove the remaining needle bearing on the other side of the swing arm.

7. Thoroughly clean out the inside of the swing arm with solvent and dry with compressed air.

NOTE
Either bearing may be installed first.

8. Apply a light coat of molybdenum disulfide grease to all parts prior to installation.

CAUTION
Make sure the bearing is square with the swing arm bore during installation. If installed incorrectly, the needle bearing can be damaged during installation and may not be aligned correctly.

9. Position the new needle bearing with the end marks facing up toward the outside.

10. Press or drive the bearing into the swing arm so the outer end of the bearing is recessed 2-3 mm (0.08-0.12 in.) into the swing arm (**Figure 33**).

11. Install the bearing into the other side of the swing arm.

12. Install the thrust bushing (B, **Figure 31**) into each side of the swing arm.

13. Install the pivot sleeve (A, **Figure 31**).

14. Install a new dust seal on each end of the swing arm.

15. Install the swing arm as described in this section.

14

Table 1 REAR SUSPENSION SPECIFICATIONS

Item	Specification	Service limit
Shock absorber spring free length		
XR600R	215.5 mm (8.48 in.)	213.3 mm (8.40 in.)
XR650L	225.3 mm (8.87 in.)	223.1 mm (8.78 in.)
Shock absorber spring installed length		
2008-on XR650L	206.5 mm (8.13 in.)	–

Table 2 SHOCK ARM AND SHOCK LINK BEARING TOOLS

Item	Honda Part Number
Shock arm needle bearing replacement	
Bearing removal tool	
XR600R and 1993-2007 XR650L	
Bearing remover	07946-MJ00100
2008-on XR650L	
Driver	07949-3710001
Bearing Installation tools	
XR600R and 1993-2007 XR650L	
Driver	07749-0010000
32 x 35 mm attachment	07746-0010100
2008-on XR650L	
Driver	07749-0010000
28 x 30 mm attachment	07946-1870100
17 mm pilot	07746-0040400
Shock link needle bearing replacement	
Bearing removal tool	
XR600R and 1993-2007 XR650L	
Bearing remover	07946-MJ00100
2008-on XR650L	
Driver	07949-3710001
Bearing Installation tools	
XR600R and 1993-2007 XR650L	
Driver	07749-0010000
32 x 35 mm attachment	07746-0010100
2008-on XR650L	
Driver	07749-0010000
24 x 26 mm attachment	07746-0010700
15 mm pilot	07746-0040400

Table 3 REAR SUSPENSION TORQUE SPECIFICATIONS

Item	N•m	in.-lb.	ft.-lb.
Rear axle nut			
XR600R	95	–	70
XR650L			
1993-2007	90	–	66
2008-on	88	–	65
Shock absorber			
XR600R and 1993-2007 XR650L			
Lower mounting bolt	35	–	26
Upper mounting bolt	45	–	33
2008-on XR650L			
Lower mounting bolt	34	–	25
Upper mounting bolt	44	–	32
Shock link-to-frame pivot bolt			
XR600R	45	—	33
XR650L			
1993-2007	55	–	41
2008-on	54	–	40
Shock link-to-shock arm pivot bolt	45	–	33
Shock arm-to-swing arm pivot bolt			
XR600R and 1993-2007 XR650L	70	–	52
2008-on XR650L	69	–	51
Swing arm pivot bolt			
XR600R and 1993-2007 XR650L	90	–	66
2008-on XR650L	88	–	65

CHAPTER FIFTEEN

BRAKES

This chapter covers the brake system. Brake specifications are in **Tables 1-4** at the end of this chapter.

BRAKE FLUID

WARNING
Do not intermix silicone DOT 5 brake fluid with DOT 4 brake fluid as it can cause brake system failure.

When adding brake fluid, use DOT 4 brake fluid from a sealed container. Brake fluid absorbs moisture from the atmosphere, which reduces its ability to perform correctly. Purchase brake fluid in small containers and discard small leftover quantities. Do not store a container of brake fluid with less than 1/4 of the fluid remaining.

Do not reuse drained fluid. Discard old fluid properly.

BRAKE SERVICE

WARNING
After performing any of the procedures in this chapter, make sure that the brake system operates correctly before riding the motorcycle. Make sure the lever/ pedal travel is correct and that full hydraulic pressure is available.

WARNING
Whenever working on the brake system, do not inhale brake dust. It may contain asbestos, which can cause lung injury and cancer. Wear a facemask that meets requirements for trapping asbestos particles, and wash hands and forearms thoroughly after completing the work. Never use compressed air to clean any part of the brake system. This releases the harmful brake pad dust. Use an aerosol brake cleaner to clean parts when servicing any component still installed on the bike.

The disc brake system transmits hydraulic pressure from the master cylinder to the brake caliper. This pressure is transmitted from the caliper to the brake pads, which grip both sides of the brake disc and slow the motorcycle. As the pads wear, the caliper piston moves out of the caliper bore to automatically compensate for pad wear. As this occurs the fluid level in the reservoir goes down, which must be raised with additional fluid.

The brake caliper piston self-adjusts to compensate for brake pad wear. When the brake is applied, hydraulic pressure against the piston causes the piston seal to stretch and deflect slightly. This allows the piston to move out where it contacts the brake pad and pushes it against the brake disc. When the brake is released, pressure against the piston seal is reduced and this allows it to retract and return to its original

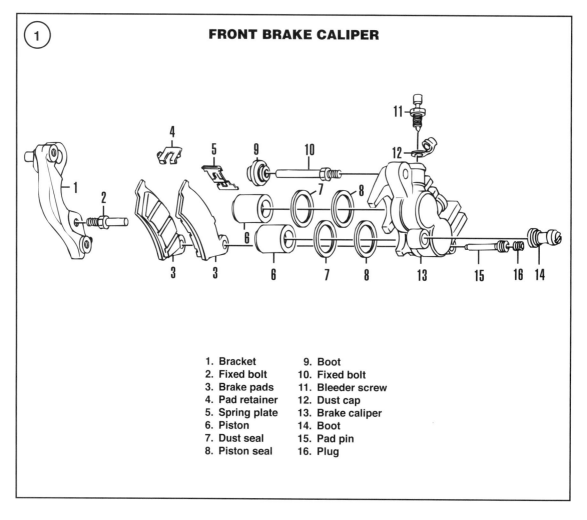

FRONT BRAKE CALIPER

1. Bracket
2. Fixed bolt
3. Brake pads
4. Pad retainer
5. Spring plate
6. Piston
7. Dust seal
8. Piston seal
9. Boot
10. Fixed bolt
11. Bleeder screw
12. Dust cap
13. Brake caliper
14. Boot
15. Pad pin
16. Plug

shape. This action draws the piston away from the brake pad and disengages the brake. As the brake pads wear, the piston will travel farther through the seals in order to contact the brake pads.

Proper service includes carefully performed procedures and a clean work environment. Debris that enters the system can damage the components and cause poor brake performance. Do not use sharp tools while servicing the master cylinder, caliper or piston. Any damage to these components could cause a loss of hydraulic pressure in the system. If there is any doubt about having the ability to correctly and safely service the brake system, have a professional technician perform the task.

Consider the following whenever servicing the brake system:

1. When properly maintained, hydraulic components rarely require disassembly. Make sure it is necessary.

2. Keep the reservoir covers in place to prevent the entry of moisture and debris.

3. Clean parts with DOT 4 brake fluid or an aerosol brake parts cleaner. Never use petroleum-based

solvents on internal brake system components. They cause seals to swell and distort.

4. Do not allow brake fluid to contact plastic, painted or plated parts. It will damage the surface.

5. Dispose of brake fluid properly.

6. If the hydraulic system has been opened (not including the reservoir cover), the system must be bled to remove air from the system. Refer to *Brake Bleeding* in this chapter.

FRONT BRAKE PADS

There is no recommended time interval for changing the pads in the front brake caliper. Pad wear depends on riding habits and conditions. The brake pads have wear grooves that allow inspection without removal. Refer to *Brakes* in Chapter Three. Always replace brake pads as a set.

Replacement

Refer to **Figure 1**.

1. Read *Brake Service* in this chapter.

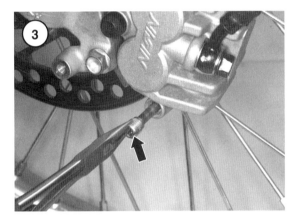

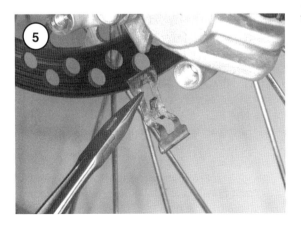

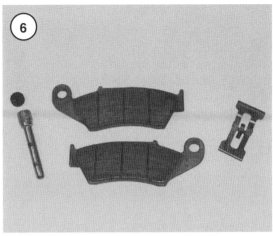

> *CAUTION*
> *Do not allow the master cylinder reservoir to overflow when performing Step 2. If the fluid level is high, remove the cover and draw some of the fluid from the reservoir with a syringe.*

> *CAUTION*
> *Before pushing the pistons into the caliper in Step 2, check for debris buildup on the end of the pistons. When the pistons are pushed back into the caliper, this material can damage the caliper seals. If there is residue build up, clean the end of the pistons with a soft brush and denatured alcohol while the caliper is assembled or remove and disassemble the caliper to clean the pistons.*

2. Push the caliper body in by hand to push the pistons back into the caliper to make room for the new pads.
3. Remove the pad pin plug (**Figure 2**).
4. Loosen and remove the pad pin bolt (**Figure 3**).
5. Remove the brake pads (**Figure 4**).
6. Remove the pad spring (**Figure 5**).
7. Inspect the brake pads (**Figure 6**) for uneven wear, damage or contamination. Note the following:
    a. Remove surface contamination by lightly sanding the lining surface with a piece of sandpaper placed on a flat surface. If the lining material is contaminated, replace both brake pads.
    b. Wear should be approximately the same for both brake pads. If the inner pad is worn more than the outer pad, the caliper may be binding on the caliper bracket. Uneven wear can also be caused by worn or damaged piston seals that have lost their resilience to self-adjust (returning the piston and disengaging the brake after the brake lever is released).

15

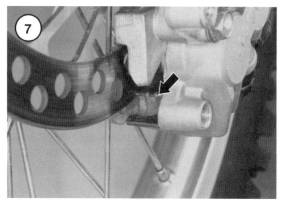

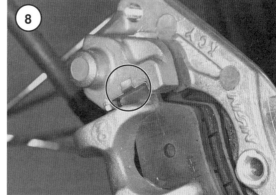

8. Replace the pads as a set if the thickness of any one pad has worn down to its wear groove.

9. Check the caliper for leaks around the pistons. If brake fluid is leaking from the caliper bores, overhaul the brake caliper as described in this chapter.

10. Clean the pad pin and plug. Remove rust and corrosion from the pad pin and inspect for excessive wear, grooves or other damage. Replace if damaged.

11. Inspect the pad spring (**Figure 6**) and replace if damaged.

12. Inspect the brake disc for oil contamination (especially if the fork seal was leaking). Spray both sides of the brake disc with brake cleaner. Inspect the brake disc for wear as described in this chapter.

13. Install the pad spring (**Figure 5**) so it grips the brake caliper (**Figure 7**) tightly. Replace the pad spring if it does not stay in position.

14. Install the inner and outer brake pads as shown in **Figure 4**. Push them in place so the upper end of each pad seats against the pad retainer (**Figure 8**) in the caliper bracket.

15. Push both pads against the pad spring and install the pad pin bolt (**Figure 3**) into the caliper and through the hole in the bottom of each brake pad.

16. Tighten the pad pin bolt (**Figure 3**) to the specification in **Table 4**.

17. Install and tighten the pad pin plug (**Figure 2**) to the specification in **Table 4**.

18. Operate the brake lever to seat the pads against the disc. The brake lever should feel firm when applied.

19. Check the brake fluid level in the reservoir. If necessary, add new DOT 4 brake fluid.

20. Raise the front wheel and make sure the wheel spins freely and the brake operates properly.

21. Install the brake disc cover.

22. Break in the pads by braking slowly at first and then increase braking pressure. Do not overheat new brake pads.

FRONT BRAKE CALIPER

Refer to *Brake Service* in this chapter.

Removal/Installation

1. If the caliper will be disconnected from the brake hose, drain the system as described in this chapter. After draining, remove the brake hose union bolt (A, **Figure 9**) and both washers while the caliper is mounted on the fork. Tie a plastic bag over the end of the hose.

2A. If the caliper will be removed from the motorcycle, remove the caliper mounting bolts (B, **Figure 9**).

2B. If the caliper will be left attached to the brake hose:

    a. Remove the caliper mounting bolts (B, **Figure 9**) and secure the caliper with a length of wire. Do not allow the caliper to hang by the brake hose.

    b. Insert a spacer block between the brake pads to prevent the pistons from being forced out of the caliper if the front brake lever is applied with the brake caliper removed.

3. Service the caliper as described in this section.

4. Installation is the reverse of removal. Note the following:

    a. If the pads are installed in the caliper, press the caliper pistons back into the caliper so the pads will clear the disc.

    b. Apply a medium strength threadlock onto the front brake caliper mounting bolts and tighten to the specification in **Table 4**.

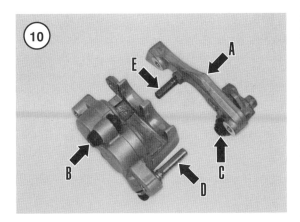

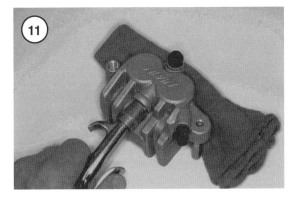

c. Check the brake fluid level in the reservoir and fill or remove fluid as necessary.

d. After installing the brake caliper, operate the brake lever several times to seat the pads against the brake disc.

e. If the brake hose was disconnected from the caliper, install a new washer on each side of the brake hose fitting, and tighten the union bolt to the specification in **Table 4**. Fill and bleed the brake system as described in this chapter.

f. With the front wheel raised, make sure the wheel spins freely and the brake operates properly.

Disassembly

Refer to **Figure 1**.

Removing the pistons hydraulically

If the piston and dust seals are in good condition and there are no signs of brake fluid leaking from the bores, it may be possible to remove the pistons hydraulically. However, note that brake fluid will spill from the caliper once the pistons are free.

Read this procedure through to understand the steps and tools required.

1. Remove the front brake caliper as described in this section. Do not loosen or remove the brake hose.

2. Remove the caliper bracket from the caliper. Have a rag and a pan available to catch and wipe up spilled brake fluid.

3. Hold the caliper with the pistons facing down and slowly operate the brake lever to push the pistons out of their bores. If both pistons move evenly, continue until they extend far enough to be removed by hand.

4. If the pistons do not move evenly, stop and push the extended piston back into its bore by hand so that both pistons are even, and then repeat. If the results are the same, reposition the extended piston again, and then operate the brake lever while preventing the moving piston from extending. Install a strip of wood across the caliper to block the piston. If the other piston now starts to move, continue with this technique until both pistons move evenly and can be gripped and removed by hand. After removing the pistons, hold the caliper over the drain pan to catch the brake fluid draining through the caliper.

5. Remove the union bolt with an impact gun, if available. Otherwise, hold the caliper in a secure manner and remove the union bolt with hand tools. If the caliper cannot be held securely to remove the bolt, stuff rags into the caliper bores to absorb brake fluid leaking from the hose and reservoir. Temporarily re-install the caliper bracket and mount the caliper onto the slider with its mounting bolts to hold it in place, then remove the union bolt and both washers.

6. Perform the relevant steps in the following section to complete caliper disassembly.

Removing the pistons with compressed air

1. Remove the brake caliper as described in this section.

2. Slide the caliper bracket (A, **Figure 10**) out of the caliper.

3. Remove the caliper's rubber boot (B, **Figure 10**) by grasping its thick outer edge and pulling it out of its mounting hole. Then remove the rubber boot (C, **Figure 10**) from the caliper bracket.

4. Remove the pad retainer from the caliper bracket.

5. Close the bleed valve so air cannot escape.

WARNING
Wear eye protection when using compressed air to remove the pistons, and keep your fingers away from the piston.

6. Cushion the caliper pistons with a shop rag and position the caliper with the piston bores facing down. Apply compressed air through the brake hose port (**Figure 11**) to pop the pistons out. If only one piston came out, block its bore opening with a piece of thick rubber (old inner tube), wooden block and clamp as shown in **Figure 12**. Apply compressed air again and remove the remaining piston. See **Figure 13**.

15

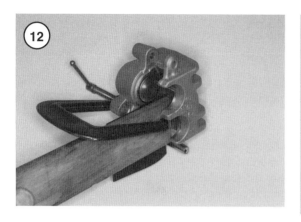

CAUTION
Do not pry the piston out. This will
damage the piston and caliper bore.

7. Use a small wooden or plastic tool and remove the dust (A, **Figure 14**) and piston seals (B) from the caliper bore grooves and discard them.
8. Remove the bleed valve and its cover from the caliper.
9. Clean and inspect the brake caliper assembly as described in this section.

Assembly

NOTE
Use new DOT 4 brake fluid when lu-
bricating the piston seals, pistons and
caliper bores in the following steps.

1. Install the bleed valve and its cover into the caliper.
2. Soak the new piston and dust seals in brake fluid.
3. Lubricate the cylinder bores with brake fluid.

NOTE
*The piston seals (A, **Figure 15**) are*
thicker than the dust seals (B).

4. Install a new piston seal into each rear bore groove (B, **Figure 14**).
5. Install a new dust seal into each front bore groove (A, **Figure 14**).

NOTE
Make sure each seal fits squarely inside
its bore groove.

6. Lubricate the pistons with brake fluid.

CAUTION
The tight piston-to-seal fit can make
piston installation difficult. Do not
install the pistons by pushing them
straight in as they may bind in their
bores and tear the seals.

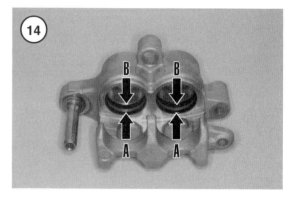

7. With the open side facing out, align a piston with the caliper bore. Rock the piston slightly to center it in the bore while at the same time pushing the lower end past the seals. When the lower end of the piston passes through both seals, push and bottom the piston in the bore (**Figure 16**). After installing the other piston, clean brake fluid from the area in front of the pistons to prevent brake pad contamination.
8. Pinch the open end of the large rubber boot and push this end through the mounting hole in the caliper until its outer shoulder bottoms (B, **Figure 10**). Make sure the boot opening faces toward the inside of the caliper. Partially fill the boot with silicone brake grease.
9. Install the small boot into the groove in the caliper bracket (A, **Figure 17**). Partially fill the boot with silicone brake grease.
10. Hook the pad retainer (B, **Figure 17**) onto the caliper bracket.
11. Lubricate the fixed shafts on the caliper (D, **Figure 10**) and caliper bracket (E) with silicone brake grease.
12. Align and slide the mounting bracket onto the caliper body. Hold the caliper and slide the caliper bracket (A, **Figure 10**) in and out by hand. Make sure there is no roughness or binding.
13. Install the brake caliper assembly and brake pads as described in this chapter.

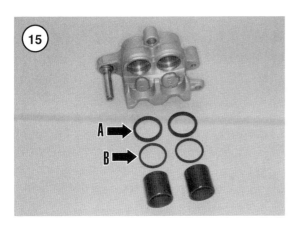

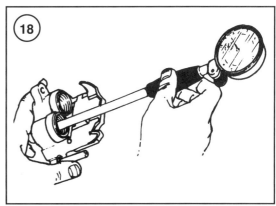

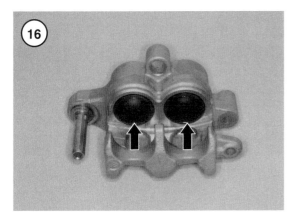

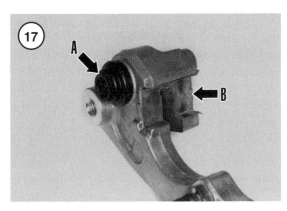

Inspection

WARNING
Do not allow any oil or grease on any of the brake components. Do not clean the parts with kerosene or other petroleum products. These chemicals cause the rubber brake system components to swell, which may cause brake failure.

All models use a floating caliper design, in which the caliper slides or floats on shafts mounted parallel with each other on the caliper and caliper bracket. Rubber boots around each shaft prevent dirt from damaging the shafts. If the shafts are worn or damaged the caliper can move out of alignment on the caliper bracket. This will cause brake drag, uneven pad wear and overheating. Inspect the rubber boots and shafts during caliper inspection as they play a vital role in brake performance.

Refer to **Figure 1** when servicing the front brake caliper assembly. Replace parts that are out of specification or show damage as described in this section.

1. Clean and dry the caliper and the other metal components. Clean the seal grooves carefully to avoid damaging the grooves and bore surfaces. If the contamination is difficult to remove, soak the caliper in a suitable solvent and then reclean. If any of the rubber parts are to be reused, clean them with denatured alcohol or new DOT 4 brake fluid. Do not use a petroleum-based solvent.

2. Inspect the caliper bracket, fixed shafts and rubber boots (**Figure 10**) as follows:
   a. Inspect the rubber boots for cracks, tearing, weakness or other damage.
   b. Inspect the fixed shafts (D and E, **Figure 10**) on the caliper housing and caliper bracket for excessive or uneven wear. If the fixed shaft is damaged, remove and discard the shaft. Install a new fixed shaft with threadlock and tighten to the specification in **Table 4**. If the caliper bracket fixed shaft is damaged, replace the caliper bracket assembly. However, if the fixed shaft on the caliper body is loose, remove the shaft and clean the threads on the shaft and the caliper bracket of all threadlock residue. Apply a threadlock to the shaft threads and tighten as described in **Table 4**.

3. Check each cylinder bore for corrosion, pitting, deep scratches or other wear.

4. Measure the inside diameter of the caliper bores (**Figure 18**).

5. Check the pistons for wear marks, scoring, cracks or other damage.

6. Measure the outside diameter of the pistons (**Figure 19**).

15

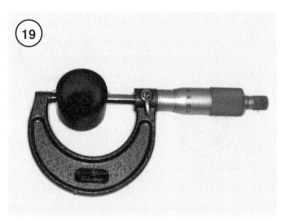

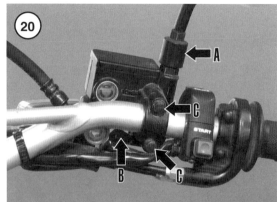

7. Check the bleed valve and cap for wear or damage. Make sure air can pass through the bleed valve.
8. Check the union bolt for wear or damage. Discard the washers.
9. Inspect the brake pads, pad spring, pad retainer, pad pin plug and pad pin bolt as described under *Front Brake Pads* in this chapter.

FRONT BRAKE MASTER CYLINDER

Refer to *Brake Service* in this chapter.

Removal/Installation

1. On XR650L models, remove the right rear view mirror (A, **Figure 20**).
2. On XR650L models, disconnect the front brake light switch electrical connectors (B, **Figure 20**).
3. Remove the master cylinder cover (**Figure 21**) and diaphragm. Use a syringe to draw brake fluid from the master cylinder reservoir. Discard the brake fluid. Reinstall the diaphragm and master cylinder cover.
4. Remove the union bolt (**Figure 22**) and washers securing the brake hose to the master cylinder. Seal the brake hose to prevent brake fluid from dripping out.
5. Remove the bolts and clamp holding the master cylinder (C, **Figure 20**) to the handlebar and remove the master cylinder (**Figure 23**).
6. If necessary, service the master cylinder as described in this section.
7. Clean the handlebar, master cylinder and clamp mating surfaces.
8. Mount the master cylinder onto the handlebar, then install the clamp and both mounting bolts. Install the clamp with the UP mark facing up. Align the clamp mating surface with the punch mark on the handlebar.
9. Tighten the upper clamp bolt first and then the lower bolt. On XR600R models, tighten the bolts

to 27 N•m (20 ft.-lb.). On XR650L models, tighten the bolts to the specification in **Table 4**.
10. Secure the brake hose to the master cylinder with the union bolt and two new washers. Install a washer on each side of the fitting. Position the fitting against the master cylinder boss. Tighten the union bolt to the specification in **Table 4**.
11. Bleed the front brake as described in this chapter.

Disassembly

Refer to **Figure 24**.
1. Remove the master cylinder as described in this section.
2A. On XR600R models, remove the brake lever pivot bolt and nut, and then remove the brake lever, hand guard, if so equipped, and brake lever spring from the master cylinder.
2B. On XR650L models, remove the brake lever pivot bolt and nut, and then remove the brake lever and hand guard, if so equipped, from the master cylinder.
3. Remove the brake light switch retaining screw (A, **Figure 23**), then remove the switch (B).
4. Remove the master cylinder cap screws and remove the cap, diaphragm plate and diaphragm from the master cylinder.

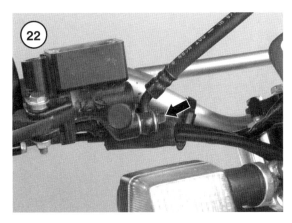

FRONT BRAKE MASTER CYLINDER

1. Mirror (XR650L)
2. Screw
3. Cover
4. Plate
5. Diaphragm
6. Master cylinder
7. Bolt
8. Clamp
9. Dust cover
10. Snap ring
11. Piston assembly
12. Spring
13. Brake switch (XR650L)
14. Screw (XR650L)
15. Pivot bolt
16. Hand guard
17. Brake lever
18. Sleeve
19. Nut

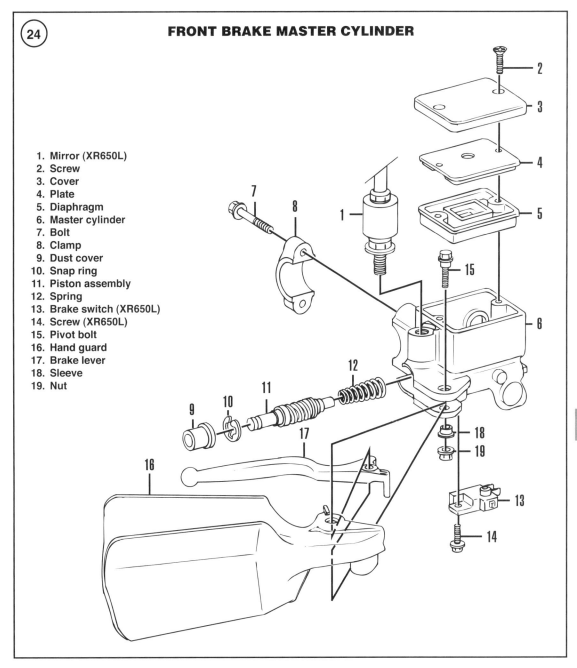

15

5. Thread a bolt and nut into the master cylinder. Tighten the nut against the master cylinder, then clamp the bolt and nut in a vise as shown in **Figure 25**.
6. Remove the dust cover (**Figure 25**) from the groove in the end of the piston.

WARNING
If brake fluid is leaking from the piston bore, the piston cups are worn or damaged. Replace the piston assembly.

7. Compress the piston and remove the snap ring (**Figure 26**) from the groove in the master cylinder.
8. Remove the snap ring and piston assembly (**Figure 27**) from the master cylinder bore.

Inspection

1. Wash the piston and cylinder with brake fluid.

CAUTION
Do not remove the primary and secondary cups from the piston assembly.

2. Check the piston assembly for the following defects:
   a. Broken, distorted or collapsed piston return spring (A, **Figure 28**).
   b. Worn, cracked, damaged or swollen primary (B, **Figure 28**) and secondary cups (C).
   c. Scratched, scored or damaged piston (D, **Figure 28**).
   d. Corroded, weak or damaged snap ring.
   e. Worn or damaged dust cover.
3. Replace the piston assembly if any part is worn or damaged.
4. Measure the piston outside diameter (**Figure 29**). Replace the piston if its diameter is less than the service limit in **Table 1**.
5. To assemble a new piston assembly, perform the following:
   a. When replacing the piston, install new primary (A, **Figure 30**) and secondary cups (B).

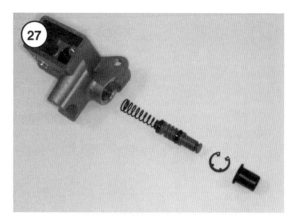

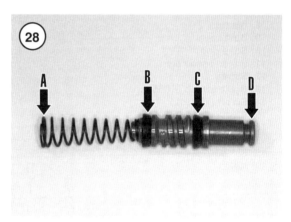

   b. Use the original piston assembly (C, **Figure 30**) as a reference when installing the new cups onto the piston.
   c. Before installing the new piston cups, soak them in brake fluid for approximately 5-10 minutes. This will soften them and ease installation. Clean the new piston in brake fluid.
   d. Install the secondary (B, **Figure 30**) then the primary (A) cups onto the piston.
6. Inspect the master cylinder bore. Replace the master cylinder if the bore is corroded, scored or damaged in any way. Do not hone the master cylinder bore to remove scratches or other damage.

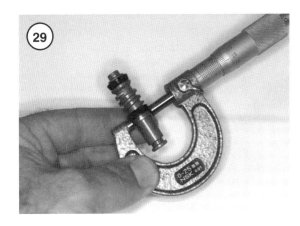

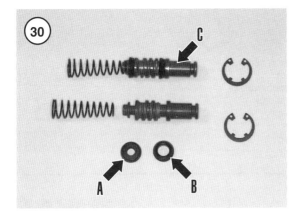

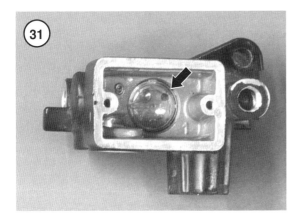

7. Measure the master cylinder bore. Replace the master cylinder assembly if the bore diameter exceeds the service limit in **Table 1**.

NOTE
*The ports are covered by a clear plastic disc (**Figure 31**) to prevent debris from entering the ports. Remove the disc only if it is necessary to clean the ports.*

8. Check for plugged supply and relief ports in the master cylinder. Clean with compressed air.
9. Inspect the brake lever and pivot bolt and replace if worn or damaged.

10. Inspect the reservoir cap, diaphragm plate and diaphragm for damage. Inspect the diaphragm for cracks or deterioration. Replace damaged parts as required.

Assembly

Refer to **Figure 24**. Lubricate the parts with DOT 4 brake fluid.
1. If installing a new piston, assemble it as described under *Inspection* in this section.
2. Lubricate the piston assembly and cylinder bore with brake fluid.
3. Install the spring-small end first-onto the piston as shown in A, **Figure 28**.

CAUTION
Do not allow the piston cups to tear or turn inside out when installing the piston into the master cylinder bore. Both cups are larger than the bore. To ease installation, lubricate the cups and piston with brake fluid.

4. Insert the piston assembly-spring end first- into the master cylinder bore (**Figure 27**).
5. Mount the master cylinder in a vise (**Figure 25**). Compress the piston assembly and install the snap ring (**Figure 26**).
6. The snap ring must seat in the groove completely. Push and release the piston a few times to make sure it moves smoothly and that the snap ring does not pop out.
7. Slide the dust cover onto the piston. Seat the cover in the cylinder bore and in the piston groove.
8A. Install the lever spring into the master cylinder, then install the brake lever, hand guard, if so equipped, pivot bolt and nut. Tighten the pivot bolt and nut. Then operate the hand lever and make sure it moves freely with no binding or roughness.
8B. Install the brake lever, hand guard, if so equipped, pivot bolt and nut. Tighten the pivot bolt and nut. Then operate the hand lever and make sure it moves freely with no binding or roughness.
9. Install the master cylinder as described in this section.

REAR BRAKE PADS

There is no recommended time interval for changing the pads in the rear brake caliper. Pad wear depends on riding habits and conditions. The brake pads have wear grooves that allow inspection without removal. Refer to *Brakes* in Chapter Three. Always replace brake pads as a set.

15

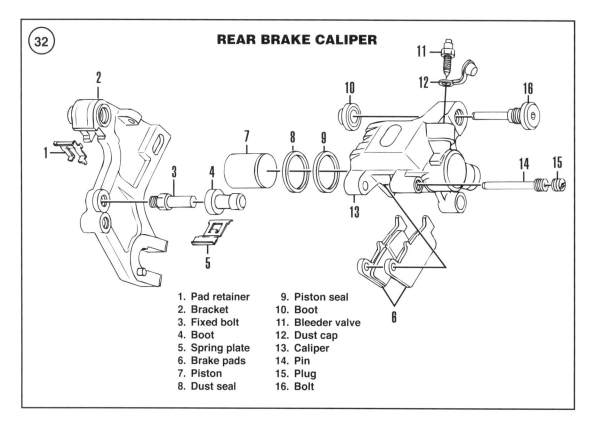

REAL BRAKE CALIPER

1. Pad retainer
2. Bracket
3. Fixed bolt
4. Boot
5. Spring plate
6. Brake pads
7. Piston
8. Dust seal
9. Piston seal
10. Boot
11. Bleeder valve
12. Dust cap
13. Caliper
14. Pin
15. Plug
16. Bolt

Replacement

Refer to **Figure 32**.

1. Read *Brake Service* in this chapter.

> *CAUTION*
> *Do not allow the master cylinder reservoir to overflow when performing Step 2. If the fluid level is high, remove the cap and draw some of the fluid from the reservoir with a syringe.*

> *CAUTION*
> *Before pushing the piston into the caliper in Step 2, check for corrosion and dirt buildup on the exposed end of the piston. When the piston is pushed back into the caliper, this material can damage the caliper seals. If there is residue built up on the ends of the piston, clean the end of the piston with a soft brush and denatured alcohol while the caliper is assembled or remove and disassemble the caliper to clean the piston.*

2. Push the caliper body in by hand to push the piston back into the caliper to make room for the new pads.
3. Unscrew the pad pin plug (**Figure 33**).
4. Remove the pad pin retainer bolt.
5. Remove the inboard and outboard brake pads from the caliper.

6. If necessary, remove the pad spring.
7. Inspect the brake pads (**Figure 34**) for uneven wear, damage or contamination. Note the following:

   a. Remove surface contamination by lightly sanding the lining surface with a piece of sandpaper placed on a flat surface. If lining material is contaminated, replace both brake pads.

   b. Wear should be approximately the same for both brake pads. If the inner pad is worn more than the outer pad, the caliper may be binding on the caliper bracket. Uneven wear can also be caused by worn or damaged piston seals that have lost their resilience to self-adjust (returning the pistons and disengaging the brakes after the brake lever is released).

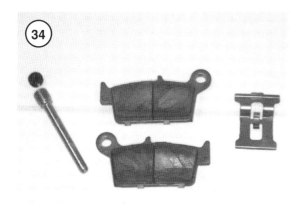

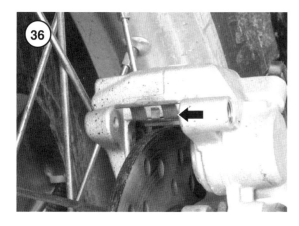

8. Replace the pads as a set if the thickness of any one pad has worn down to its wear groove.

9. Check the caliper for leaks around the pistons. If brake fluid is leaking from the caliper bores, overhaul the brake caliper as described in this chapter.

10. Clean the pad pin and plug. Remove rust and corrosion from the pad pin and inspect for excessive wear, grooves or other damage. Replace if damaged.

11. Inspect the pad spring (**Figure 34**) and replace if damaged.

12. Inspect the brake disc for oil contamination. Spray both sides of the brake disc with brake cleaner. Inspect the brake disc for wear as described in this chapter.

13A. On XR600R models, when new pads are installed in the caliper, the master cylinder brake fluid will rise as the caliper piston is repositioned. Perform the following:

    a. Clean the top of the master cylinder of all debris.

    b. Unscrew the top cover (B, **Figure 35**), set plate and diaphragm from the master cylinder reservoir.

    c. Slowly push the caliper piston into the caliper. Constantly check the reservoir to make sure brake fluid does not overflow. Remove fluid, if necessary, before it overflows.

    d. The piston should move freely. If it does not and there is evidence of it sticking in the cylinder, remove the caliper and service it as described in this chapter.

13B. On XR650L models, when new pads are installed in the caliper, the master cylinder brake fluid will rise as the caliper piston is repositioned. Perform the following:

    a. Clean the top of the master cylinder of all debris.

    b. Remove the mounting bolt and bracket (A, **Figure 35**).

    c. Reposition the reservoir onto the frame and install the mounting bolt without the bracket.

    d. Unscrew the top cover (B, **Figure 35**), set plate and diaphragm from the master cylinder reservoir.

    e. Slowly push the caliper piston into the caliper. Constantly check the reservoir to make sure brake fluid does not overflow. Remove fluid, if necessary, before it overflows.

    f. The piston should move freely. If it does not and there is evidence of it sticking in the cylinder, remove the caliper and service it as described in this chapter.

14. Push the caliper piston in all the way to allow room for the new pads.

15. If removed, install the pad spring as shown in **Figure 36**.

16. Insert the inboard brake pad (**Figure 37**) into the caliper and hook the front edge onto the caliper boss.

15

17. Insert the outboard brake pad (**Figure 38**) into the caliper and hook the front edge onto the caliper boss.

18. Align the outboard pad pin hole with the bore of the caliper and push the pad pin (A, **Figure 39**) through the outboard pad (B).

19. Continue to push the pad pin through the inboard pad and caliper. Push the pin in until it bottoms out.

20. Tighten the pad pin bolt to the specification in **Table 4**.

21. Install the pad pin plug and tighten to the specification in **Table 4**.

22. Operate the brake pedal to seat the pads against the disc. The brake pedal should feel firm when applied.

23. Check the brake fluid level in the reservoir. If necessary, add new DOT 4 brake fluid.

24. Raise the rear wheel and check that the wheel spins freely and the brake operates properly.

25. Break in the pads by braking slowly at first and then increase braking pressure. Do not overheat new brake pads.

REAR BRAKE CALIPER

Refer to *Brake Service* in this chapter.

Removal/Installation

NOTE
If hydraulic pressure will be used to remove the pistion during disassembly, disregard Step 1.

1. If caliper disassembly is required, perform the following:
   a. Place a container under the brake line at the caliper.
   b. Remove the union bolt and sealing washers (**Figure 40**) securing the brake line fitting to the caliper assembly. Remove the brake line and drain the brake fluid into the container.

   c. To prevent the entry of moisture and dirt, cap the end of the brake line and tie the loose end up to the frame.

2. Remove the rear wheel (Chapter Twelve).

3. If necessary, remove the brake pads as described in this chapter.

4. On XR600R models, remove the caliper cover.

NOTE
If the caliper will not be disconnected from the brake hose during this procedure, insert a small wooden block between the brake pads to prevent the caliper piston from extending out of the caliper if the brake pedal is actuated.

5. If the caliper will be disassembled using hydraulic force to expel the piston, refer to *Disassembly* in this section.

6. Remove the caliper and bracket assembly.

7. Remove the caliper bracket from the caliper, if necessary.

8. Install the brake caliper by reversing the preceding steps while performing the following:
   a. If the brake hose was not disconnected, remove the spacer block from between the brake pads and slide the caliper bracket onto the

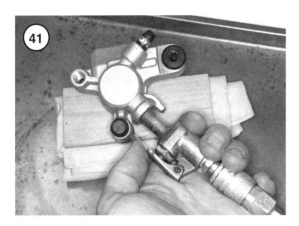

2. Remove the caliper bracket from the caliper. Have a supply of shop rags and a pan available to catch and wipe up spilled brake fluid.

3. Hold the caliper with the piston facing out and operate the brake pedal to push the piston out of the caliper bore.

4. If available, remove the union bolt with an impact gun. Otherwise, hold the caliper and caliper bracket against the swing arm with an adjustable wrench and remove the union bolt with hand tools.

Removing the piston with compressed air

1. Remove the brake caliper as described in this section.

2. Slide the caliper bracket out of the caliper.

WARNING
Wear eye protection when using compressed air to remove the piston. Keep your fingers away from the piston.

3. Cushion the piston with a shop rag and position the caliper with the piston bore facing down. Apply compressed air through the brake hose port (**Figure 41**) to force out the piston (A, **Figure 42**).

CAUTION
Do not pry the piston out. This will damage the piston and caliper bore.

4. Remove the caliper rubber boot (B, **Figure 42**) by grasping its thick outer edge and pulling it out of its mounting hole.

5. Remove the rubber boot from the caliper bracket.

6. Remove the pad retainer from the caliper bracket.

7. Remove the dust and piston seals (**Figure 43**) from the caliper bore grooves and discard them.

8. Remove the bleed valve and its cover from the caliper.

9. Clean and inspect the brake caliper assembly as described in this section.

swing arm. Make sure the brake pads were not contaminated with brake fluid.

b. If the brake hose was disconnected, install the brake hose with a new sealing washer on each side of the fitting. Install the union bolt and tighten to the specification in **Table 4**.

c. If the brake hose was disconnected, refill the master cylinder and bleed the rear brake as described in this chapter.

d. Operate the rear brake pedal to seat the pads against the brake disc.

Disassembly

Refer to **Figure 32**.

Removing the piston hydraulically

If the piston and dust seals are in good condition and there are no signs of brake fluid leaking from the bore, it may be possible to remove the piston hydraulically. However, note that brake fluid will spill from the caliper once the piston is free.

1. Remove the rear brake caliper as described in this section. Do not loosen or remove the brake hose.

15

Assembly

1. Install the bleed valve and the cover into the caliper.
2. Soak the new piston and dust seals in clean DOT 4 brake fluid.
3. Lubricate the cylinder bore with brake fluid.

> *NOTE*
> *The piston seal (A, **Figure 44**) is thicker than the dust seal (B).*

4. Install a new piston seal into the rear bore groove (**Figure 45**).
5. Install a new dust seal into the front bore groove.
6. Make sure each seal fits squarely inside its bore groove.
7. Lubricate the piston with DOT 4 brake fluid.

> *CAUTION*
> *The tight piston-to-seal fit can make piston installation difficult. Do not install the piston by pushing it straight in as it may bind in the bore and tear the seals.*

8. Align the piston with the caliper bore so the open side faces out. Rock the piston slightly to center it in the bore while at the same time pushing its lower end past the seals. When the lower end of the piston clears both seals, push and bottom the piston into the bore (A, **Figure 46**). Clean spilled brake fluid from the area in front of the piston to prevent brake pad contamination.
9. Install the rubber boot through the mounting hole in the caliper (B, **Figure 42**). Make sure the boot opening faces toward the inside of the caliper. Partially fill the boot with silicone brake grease.
10. Install the bleed valve and tighten finger-tight.
11. Install the pad spring onto the caliper.
12. Install the boot into the caliper bracket (A, **Figure 47**). Partially fill the boot with silicone brake grease.
13. Install the pad retainer onto the caliper bracket.
14. Lubricate the fixed shafts on the caliper (B, **Figure 46**) and caliper bracket (B, **Figure 47**) with silicone brake grease.
15. Align and slide the caliper bracket onto the caliper body (**Figure 48**). Hold the caliper and slide the caliper bracket in and out by hand. Make sure there is no roughness or binding.
16. Install the brake caliper assembly and brake pads as described in this chapter.

Inspection

> *WARNING*
> *Do not allow oil or grease on any of the brake components. Do not clean the parts with kerosene or other petro-*

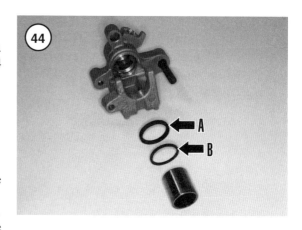

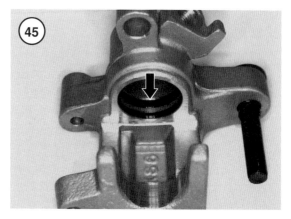

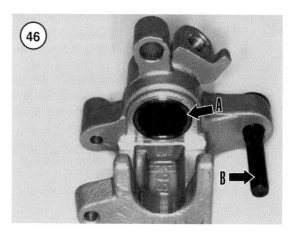

> *leum products. These chemicals cause the rubber brake system components to swell, which may cause brake failure.*

All models use a floating caliper design, in which the caliper slides or floats on shafts mounted parallel with each other on the caliper and caliper bracket. Rubber boots around each shaft prevent dirt from damaging the shafts. If the shafts are worn or damaged the caliper can move out of alignment on the caliper bracket. This causes brake drag, uneven pad wear and overheating. Inspect the rubber boots and

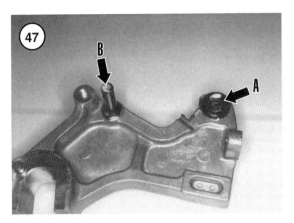

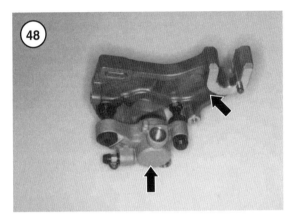

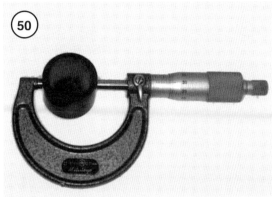

2. Inspect the caliper bracket, fixed shafts and rubber boots as follows:

    a. Inspect the rubber boots for cracks, tearing, weakness or other damage.

    b. Inspect the fixed shafts on the caliper (B, **Figure 46**) and caliper bracket (B, **Figure 47**) for excessive or uneven wear. If the caliper fixed shaft is damaged, remove and discard the shaft. Install a new fixed shaft with threadlock and tighten to the specification in **Table 4**. If the caliper bracket fixed shaft is damaged, remove and discard the shaft. Install a new fixed shaft with threadlock and tighten to the specification in **Table 4**.

3. Check the caliper bore for corrosion, pitting, deep scratches or other wear.

4. Measure the inside diameter of the caliper bore (**Figure 49**).

5. Check the piston for wear marks, scoring, cracks or other damage.

6. Measure the outside diameter of the piston (**Figure 50**).

7. Check the bleed valve and cap for wear or damage. Make sure air can pass through the bleed valve.

8. Check the union bolt for wear or damage. Discard the washers.

9. Inspect the brake pads, pad retainer, pad spring and pad pin bolt as described under *Rear Brake Pads* in this chapter.

15

REAR BRAKE MASTER CYLINDER

Removal/Installation

Refer to **Figure 51**.

1. Remove the right side cover as described in Chapter Sixteen.

2. Clean the top of the master cylinder of all debris.

3A. On XR600R models, unscrew the cap. Pull up and loosen the cap and the diaphragm. This will allow air to enter the reservoir so the brake fluid can drain out more quickly in the next steps.

shafts during caliper inspection as they play a vital role in brake performance. Replace parts that are out of specification (**Table 3**) or show damage as described in this section.

1. Clean and dry the caliper, and the other metal components. Clean the seal grooves carefully to avoid damaging the grooves and bore surfaces. If the contamination is difficult to remove, soak the caliper in a suitable solvent and then reclean. If any of the rubber parts are to be reused, clean them with denatured alcohol or new DOT 4 brake fluid. Do not use a petroleum-based solvent.

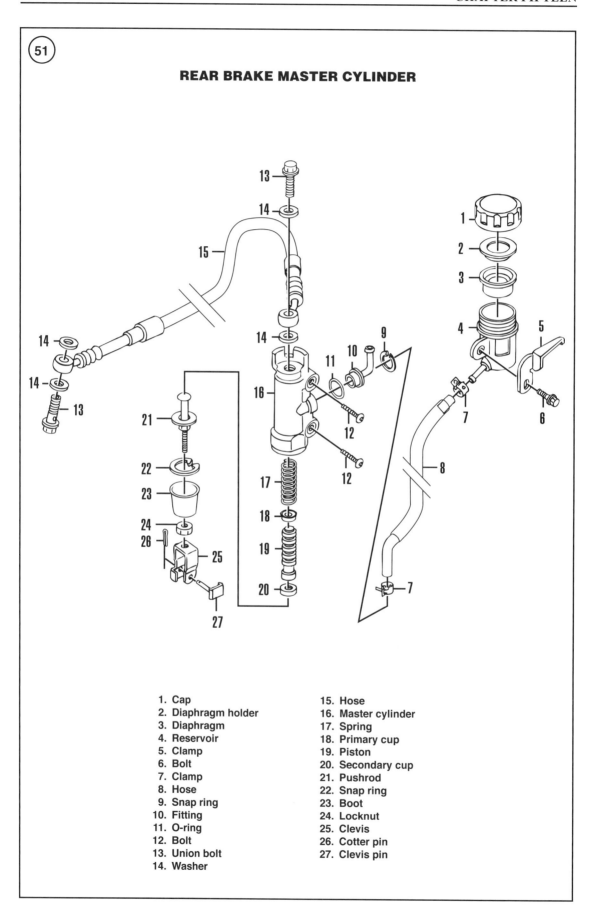

REAR BRAKE MASTER CYLINDER

1. Cap
2. Diaphragm holder
3. Diaphragm
4. Reservoir
5. Clamp
6. Bolt
7. Clamp
8. Hose
9. Snap ring
10. Fitting
11. O-ring
12. Bolt
13. Union bolt
14. Washer
15. Hose
16. Master cylinder
17. Spring
18. Primary cup
19. Piston
20. Secondary cup
21. Pushrod
22. Snap ring
23. Boot
24. Locknut
25. Clevis
26. Cotter pin
27. Clevis pin

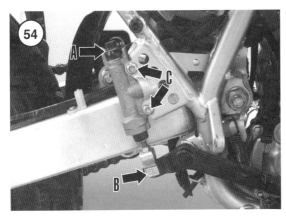

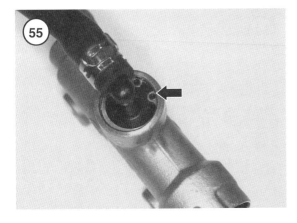

3B. On XR650L models, perform the following:
    a. Remove the mounting bolt and bracket (A, **Figure 52**).
    b. Reposition the reservoir on the frame and reinstall the mounting bolt without the bracket.
    c. Unscrew the cap (B, **Figure 52**). Pull up and loosen the cap and the diaphragm. This will allow air to enter the reservoir so the brake fluid can drain out more quickly in the next steps.

4. Place a tight fitting hose onto the rear caliper bleed screw (**Figure 53**), then loosen the bleed screw. Place the other end of the hose in a container to catch the brake fluid.

5. Apply the rear brake pedal as many times as necessary to pump the fluid out of the rear hydraulic brake lines. Remove the hose and tighten the bleed screw securely.

6. Remove the union bolt (A, **Figure 54**) and sealing washers from the top of the master cylinder. Do not lose the sealing washer on each side of the hose fitting.

7. Remove the caliper brake hose from the top of the master cylinder and plug the end of the hose to prevent the entry of debris.

8. Remove the cotter pin and withdraw the joint pin (B, **Figure 54**) securing the push rod to the brake pedal. Discard the cotter pin.

9. Remove the bolts (C, **Figure 54**) securing the master cylinder to the frame.

10. Pull the master cylinder away from the frame and remove the snap ring (**Figure 55**) securing the reservoir hose fitting to the backside of the master cylinder body.

11. Remove the master cylinder.

12. To remove the reservoir, perform the following:
    a. Remove the mounting bolt and bracket (A, **Figure 52**) securing the reservoir to the frame.
    b. Open the clip securing the reservoir hose to the frame and remove the reservoir and the attached hose from the frame.

13. During installation, install a new O-ring onto the reservoir hose fitting. Lubricate the O-ring with brake fluid.

14. Install new sealing washers and the union bolt in the reverse order of removal. Tighten the union bolt to 35 N•m (26 ft.-lb.).

15. Tighten the master cylinder mounting bolts to 15 N•m (133 in.-lb.).

16. Refill the master cylinder reservoir to maintain the correct fluid level as seen through the transparent side of the reservoir. Install the diaphragm and screw on the cap. Do not tighten at this time.

17. Bleed the brake as described in this chapter.

18. Adjust the rear brake pedal height as described in the Chapter Three.

15

Disassembly

Refer to **Figure 51**.

1. Remove the rear master cylinder as described in this section.

2. To hold the master cylinder during servicing, screw a bolt into the union bolt hole in the cylinder. Clamp the bolt in a vise (not the cylinder) as shown in **Figure 56**.

3. Pull the rubber boot away from the cylinder, then remove the snap ring (**Figure 57**). Pliers (Kowa Seiki part No. AKS-316-2010) with long tips make it easier to access to the recessed snap ring.

4. Remove the pushrod and piston assemblies from the cylinder (**Figure 58**).

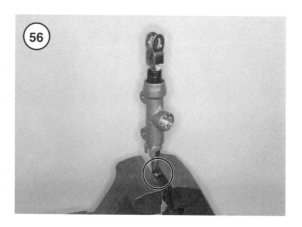

> *CAUTION*
> *Do not remove the primary cup from the piston.*

Inspection

1. Clean all parts (**Figure 58**) in denatured alcohol or brake fluid.

2. Inspect the body cylinder bore surface for wear and damage. If less than perfect, replace the master cylinder assembly. The body cannot be replaced separately.

3. Inspect the piston contact surfaces for wear and damage. If less than perfect, replace the piston assembly.

4. Check the end of the piston for wear caused by the pushrod. If worn, replace the piston assembly.

5. Measure the cylinder bore (**Figure 59**). Replace the master cylinder if the bore exceeds the specification in **Table 3**.

6. Measure the outside diameter of the piston as shown in **Figure 60** with a micrometer. Replace the piston assembly if it is less than the specification in **Table 3**.

7. Make sure the passages in the body of the master cylinder are clear.

8. Inspect the pushrod assembly (**Figure 61**). Check for stripped threads and inspect the rubber boot for tears or deterioration; replace if necessary.

9. Inspect the snap ring grooves in the master cylinder body for damage; replace the master cylinder if necessary.

10. Check the spring for cracks or other damage; replace if necessary.

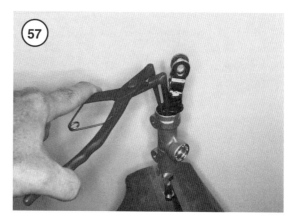

Assembly

1. Soak the new piston assembly in brake fluid for at least 15 minutes to make the cups pliable. Coat the inside of the cylinder bore with fresh brake fluid prior to the assembly of parts.

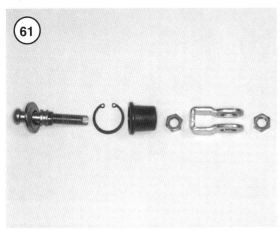

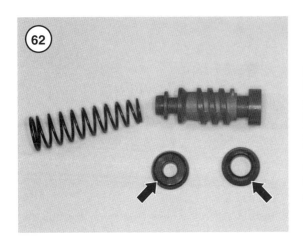

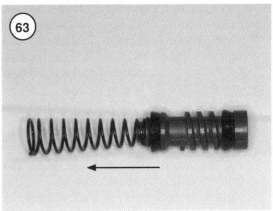

must face in the direction of the arrow (**Figure 63**). Install the secondary cup onto the piston.

   d. Install the small end of the spring onto the piston.

3. Lubricate the cylinder bore, piston and cups with brake fluid.

CAUTION
When installing the piston assembly, do not allow the cups to turn inside out.

4. Install the spring and piston assembly into the cylinder as an assembly (**Figure 58**).

5. Install the pushrod assembly into the body (**Figure 57**).

NOTE
Install the snap ring so the flat side is out.

6. Compress the pushrod and install the snap ring into the groove in the body. Make sure it seats completely. If the master cylinder pushrod was disassembled, adjust the pushrod height as described in *Rear Brake Pedal Height Adjustment* in Chapter Three.

7. Slide on the rubber boot so it seals the lower end of the body.

8. Install the master cylinder as described in this section.

BRAKE HOSE REPLACEMENT

Refer to *Brake Service* in this chapter.

1. Drain the brake system for the hose to be replaced. Refer to *Brake System Draining* in this chapter.

2. Before disconnecting the brake hoses, note how they are routed and mounted onto the master cylinder and brake caliper. Install the new hoses so they face in the same direction. Note also how the ends of the brake hoses are routed through guides or positioned next to a stop at the master cylinders and brake calipers. These hold the brake hoses in position when

2. Assemble the piston, cups and springs as follows.

   a. Apply brake fluid to the piston so the cups will slide over the ends.

   b. Identify the wide (open) side of the primary cup (**Figure 62**). When installed, the wide side of the cup must face in the direction of the arrow (**Figure 63**). Install the primary cup onto the piston.

   c. Identify the wide (open) side of the secondary cup. When installed, the wide side of the cup

the union bolts are tightened. See **Figure 64** and **Figure 65**, typical.

3. Remove the union bolts and washers for the brake hose requiring replacement.

4. Install the new brake hose in the reverse order of removal and perform the following:

   a. Install new sealing washers when installing the union bolts.

   b. Tighten the union bolts to the specification in **Table 4**.

   c. Fill the master cylinder(s) and bleed the brake(s) as described in this chapter.

   d. Operate the brake lever or brake pedal while observing the brake hose connections. Check for a loose connection or other damage.

BRAKE DISC

The brake discs are separate from the wheel hubs and can be removed after removing the wheel. See **Figure 66**, typical.

Inspection

The brake disc can be inspected while mounted on the motorcycle. Small marks on the disc are not important, but radial scratches that run all the way around the disc surface and are deep can reduce braking effectiveness and increase brake pad wear. If these grooves are evident, and the brake pads are wearing rapidly, replace the brake disc.

Refer to **Tables 1-3** for brake disc specifications. The minimum thickness dimension is also stamped on the outside of each disc (**Figure 67**).

1. Support the motorcycle on a workstand.

2. Measure the disc thickness at several locations with a micrometer (**Figure 68**). Replace the disc if its thickness at any point is less than the service limit or the dimension stamped on the disc.

> *NOTE*
> *Before checking disc runout in Step 3, make sure the wheel bearings are in good condition and the wheel is running true as described in Chapter Twelve.*

3. Measure disc runout with a dial indicator (**Figure 69**). Replace the disc if the runout exceeds the service limit.

Removal/Installation

1. Remove the wheel as described in Chapter Twelve.

2. Remove the bolts securing the brake disc to the wheel hub. Remove the brake disc.

3. Inspect the brake disc flanges on the hub for cracks or other damage. Replace the hub if damage is evident.

4. Clean the nuts and bolts of all threadlock residue. Replace the bolts if the hex end has started to round out.

5. Install the brake disc onto the hub with the side of the disc marked DRIVE facing out.

> *WARNING*
> *The brake disc mounting bolts are self locking. Discard the old bolts and install new bolts.*

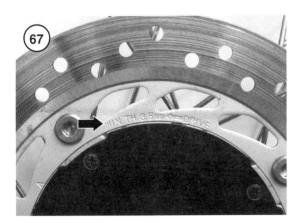

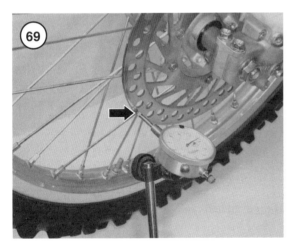

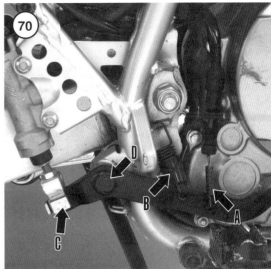

On front and rear wheels, tighten the brake disk bolts to the specification in **Table 4**.

7. Install the wheel as described in Chapter Twelve.

REAR BRAKE PEDAL

Removal/Installation

1A. On XR600R models, disconnect the return spring from the pedal.

1B. On XR650L models, disconnect the brake switch spring (A, **Figure 70**) and return spring (B) from the pedal.

2. Remove the cotter pin from the clevis pin (C, **Figure 70**), then remove the clevis pin.

3. Remove the cotter pin and washer from the pedal pivot pin (D, **Figure 70**).

4. Remove the brake pedal.

5. Inspect the grease seals in the frame. Replace if necessary.

6. Clean the pivot bore in the frame and the pedal pivot pin. Inspect the bore and pivot pin for damage and excessive wear.

7. Install the brake pedal by reversing the removal steps. Apply lithium-based multipurpose grease to the pivot pin. Install new cotter pins.

8. Operate the rear brake pedal, making sure it pivots and returns correctly.

BRAKE SYSTEM DRAINING

Refer to *Brake Service* in this chapter.

The brake system can be drained either manually or with a vacuum pump. When draining the system manually, the master cylinder is used to expel brake fluid from the system. An empty bottle, a length of clear hose that fits tightly onto the caliper bleed valve

NOTE
On XR600R models, the brake disc and disc cover are secured to the front wheel with the same bolts.

6A. On XR600R models, install new brake disc mounting bolts. Apply a threadlock onto the bolts. On the front wheel, install the disc cover and tighten the bolts to 20 N•m (177 in.-lb.). On the rear wheel, tighten the bolts to 42 N•m (31 ft.-lb.).

6B. On XR650L models, install new brake disc mounting bolts. Apply a threadlock onto the bolts.

15

and a wrench (**Figure 71**) are required. When using vacuum to drain the system, a hand-operated vacuum pump (**Figure 72**) is required.

1. Remove the diaphragm from the reservoir.

2A. When draining the system manually, perform the following:

    a. Connect the hose to the caliper bleed valve (**Figure 73**). Then insert the other end of the hose into a clean container.

    b. Apply (do not pump) the brake lever or brake pedal until it stops and then hold in this position.

    c. Open the bleed valve with a wrench, then apply the brake lever or brake pedal until it reaches the end of its travel. This expels some of the brake fluid from the system.

    d. Hold the lever or pedal in this position and close the bleed valve, then slowly release the lever or pedal.

    e. Repeat this sequence to remove as much brake fluid as possible.

2B. When using a vacuum pump, perform the following:

    a. Assemble the pump and connect it onto the caliper bleed valve (**Figure 74**) following the manufacturer's instructions.

    b. Operate the pump lever five to ten times to create a vacuum in the line, then open the bleed valve with a wrench. Brake fluid will begin to flow into the bottle connected to the vacuum pump.

    c. When the fluid draining from the system begins to slow down and before the gauge on the pump (if so equipped) reads 0 HG of vacuum, close the bleed valve.

    d. Repeat this sequence to remove as much brake fluid as possible.

3. Close the bleed valve and disconnect the hose or vacuum pump.

4. If necessary, use a syringe to remove brake fluid remaining in the bottom of the master cylinder reservoir.

5. Reinstall the diaphragm cover.

6. Discard the brake fluid removed from the system.

BRAKE BLEEDING

Refer to *Brake Service* in this chapter.

Whenever air enters the brake system, bleed the system to remove the air. Air can enter the system when the brake fluid level drops too low, after flushing the system, or when a union bolt or brake hose is loosened. Air in the brake system will increase lever or pedal travel while causing it to feel spongy and less responsive. In some cases, it can cause complete loss of the brake pressure.

Bleed the brakes manually or with a vacuum pump. Both methods are described in this section.

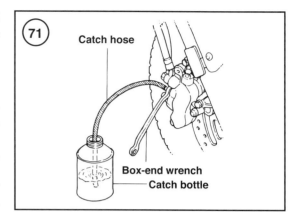

Catch hose

Box-end wrench

Catch bottle

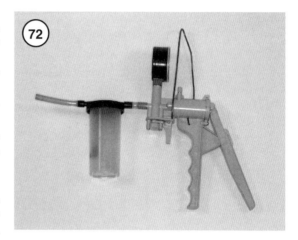

When adding brake fluid during the bleeding process, use new DOT 4 brake fluid. Do not reuse brake fluid drained from the system or use a silicone based DOT 5 brake fluid. Because brake fluid is very harmful to most surfaces, wipe up any spills immediately with soapy water.

When bleeding the brakes, check the fluid level in the master cylinder frequently. If the reservoir runs dry, air will enter the system.

Manual Bleeding

This procedure describes how to bleed the brake system manually. An empty bottle, length of clear hose and a wrench (**Figure 71**) are required.

1. Make sure both brake system union bolts are tight.

2. Remove the dust cap from the brake bleed valve and clean the valve and its opening of all debris. If a dust cap was not used, use a thin screwdriver or similar tool and compressed air to remove all debris from inside the bleed valve opening.

3. Connect the clear hose to the bleed valve on the caliper (**Figure 73**). Place the other end of the hose into a container filled with enough new brake fluid to keep the end submerged. Loop the hose higher than

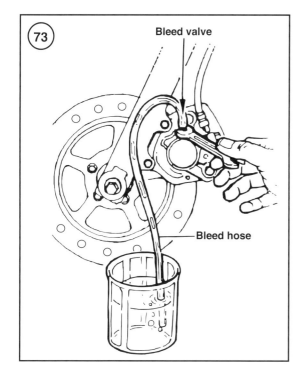

Bleed valve

Bleed hose

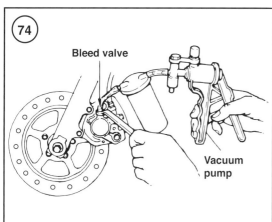

Bleed valve

Vacuum pump

housing with a soft-faced mallet to dislodge internal air bubbles so they can be released.

NOTE
If the brake lever or pedal feel firm, indicating that air has been bled from the system, but air bubbles are still visible in the hose connected to the bleed valve, air may be entering the hose from its connection around the bleed valve.

7. The system is bled when the brake lever or pedal feels firm, and there are no air bubbles exiting the system. Close the bleed valve and remove the bleed hose.
8. If necessary, add brake fluid to correct the level in the master cylinder reservoir. It must be above the level line.

Vacuum Bleeding

This procedure describes how to bleed the brake system with a vacuum pump (**Figure 72**).
1. Make sure both brake system union bolts are tight.
2. Remove the dust cap from the bleed valve and clean the valve and its opening of all debris. If a dust cap was not used, use a thin screwdriver or similar tool and compressed air to remove all debris from inside the bleed valve opening.
3. Remove the master cylinder cover and diaphragm. Fill the reservoir to about 10 mm (3/8 in.) from the top.
4. Assemble the vacuum tool according to the manufacturer's instructions.
5. Attach the pump hose to the bleed valve (**Figure 74**).
6. Operate the pump handle five to ten times to create a vacuum in the line between the pump and caliper, then open the bleed valve with a wrench. Doing so forces air and brake fluid from the system. Close the bleed valve before the brake fluid stops flowing from the valve or before the master cylinder reservoir runs empty. If the vacuum pump is equipped with a vacuum gauge, close the bleed valve before the vacuum reading on the gauge reaches 0 HG of vacuum.
7. Repeat Step 6 until the brake fluid exiting the system is clear, with no air bubbles. If the system is difficult to bleed, tap the master cylinder and caliper housing with a soft-faced mallet to dislodge the internal air bubbles so they can be released.
8. The system is bled when the brake lever or pedal feels firm, and there are no air bubbles exiting the system. Tighten the bleed valve and disconnect the pump hose.
9. If necessary, add fluid to correct the level in the master cylinder reservoir. It must be above the level line.

the bleed valve to prevent air from being drawn into the caliper during bleeding.
4. Remove the master cylinder cover and diaphragm. Fill the reservoir to about 10 mm (3/8 in.) from the top.
5. Apply the brake lever or brake pedal, and open the bleed valve. This will force air and brake fluid from the brake system. Close the bleed valve before the brake lever or pedal reaches its maximum limit or before brake fluid stops flowing from the bleed valve. Do not release the brake lever or pedal while the bleed valve is open. If the system was previously drained or new parts installed, brake fluid will not start draining from the system until after several repeated attempts are made. This is normal.
6. Repeat Step 5 until the brake fluid exiting the system is clear, with no air bubbles. If the system is difficult to bleed, tap the master cylinder and caliper

15

Table 1 FRONT BRAKE SPECIFICATIONS (XR600R)

	New mm (in.)	Service limit mm (in.)
Brake disc thickness	3.0 (0.12)	2.5 (0.10)
Brake disc runout	–	0.3 (0.01)
Caliper bore inside diameter	27.000-27.050 (1.0630-1.0650)	27.06 (1.065)
Caliper piston outside diameter	26.900-26.950 (1.0591-1.0610)	26.85 (1.057)
Master cylinder bore inside diameter	11.000-11.043 (0.4331-0.4348)	11.06 (0.435)
Master cylinder piston outside diameter	10.957-10.984 (0.4314-0.4324)	10.88 (0.428)

Table 2 FRONT BRAKE SPECIFICATIONS (XR650L)

	New mm (in.)	Service limit mm (in.)
Brake disc thickness		
1993-2007	4.0 (0.16)	3.5 (0.14)
2008-on	3.8-4.2 (3.15-3.17)	3.5 (0.14)
Brake disc runout	–	0.3 (0.01)
Caliper bore inside diameter	27.000-27.050 (1.0630-1.0650)	27.06 (1.065)
Caliper piston outside diameter	26.900-26.950 (1.0591-1.0610)	26.85 (1.057)
Master cylinder bore inside diameter	12.700-12.743 (0.5000-0.5017)	12.75 (0.502)
Master cylinder piston outside diameter	12.657-12.684 (0.4983-0.4994)	12.64 (0.498)

Table 3 REAR BRAKE SPECIFICATIONS

	New mm (in.)	Service limit mm (in.)
Brake disc thickness		
XR600R	4.5 (0.18)	4.0 (0.16)
XR650L		
1993-2007	5.0 (0.20)	4.0 (0.16)
2008-on	4.8-5.2 (0.19-0.20)	4.0 (0.16)
Brake disc runout		
XR600R and 1993-2007 XR650L	–	0.4 (0.02)
2008-on XR650L	–	0.3 (0.01)
Brake disc runout	–	0.4 (0.02)
Caliper bore inside diameter	27.000-27.050 (1.0630-1.0650)	27.06 (1.065)
Caliper piston outside diameter	26.935-26.968 (1.0604-1.0617)	26.91 (1.059)
Master cylinder bore inside diameter	12.700-12.743 (0.5000-0.5017)	12.75 (0.502)
Master cylinder piston outside diameter	12.657-12.684 (0.4983-0.4994)	12.64 (0.498)

Table 4 BRAKE SYSTEM TORQUE SPECIFICATIONS

	N•m	in.-lb.	ft.-lb.
Brake bleed valve			
XR600R and 1993-2007 XR650L	6	53	-
2008-on XR650L	5.4	48	-
Brake caliper bracket fixed shaft			
XR600R and 1993-2007 XR650L	13	115	-
2008-on XR650L	12	106	-
Brake caliper fixed shaft		-	
XR600R	28	-	21
XR650L			
Front			
1993-2007	23	-	17
2008-on	22	-	16
Rear			
1993-2007	28	-	21
2008-on	27	-	20
Brake caliper pad pin bolt			
XR600R and 1993-2007 XR650L	18	159	-
2008-on XR650L	17	150	-
Brake caliper pad pin plug			
XR600R and 1993-2007 XR650L	3	26	-
2008-on XR650L	2.5	22	-
Brake disc bolts			
Front			
XR600R	20	177	-
XR650L			
1993-2007	37	-	27
2008-on	NA	-	NA
Rear			
XR600R and1993-2007 XR650L	42	-	31
2008-on XR650L	NA	-	NA
Front brake caliper mounting bolts			
XR600R and1993-2007 XR650L	31	-	23
2008-on XR650L	30	-	22
Front brake master cylinder clamp bolts			
XR600R	27	-	20
XR650L			
1993-2007	12	106	-
2008-on	NA	NA	-
Rear brake master cylinder bolts	15	133	-
Brake hose union bolt			
XR600R and 1993-2007 XR650L	35	-	26
2008-on XR650L	34	-	25

CHAPTER SIXTEEN

BODY

LEFT SIDE COVER

Removal/Installation

1. Turn the clip rings (**Figure 1**) counterclockwise and disengage the clip pins from the frame plates.
2. Reverse the removal step to install the left side cover. Make sure the clip pins properly engage the plates on the frame.

RIGHT SIDE COVER

Removal/Installation

1. Remove the bolt securing the right side cover to the frame (**Figure 2**).
2. Pull out the right side cover to disengage the retaining pins on the backside of the cover from the mounting grommets on the frame.
3. Reverse the removal steps to install the right side cover.

SEAT

Removal/Installation

1. Remove the side covers as described in this chapter.
2. On XR650L models, remove the bolts securing the seat belt on each side (**Figure 3**) and remove the belt.
3. On the underside of the seat remove the seat retaining bolts on each side (**Figure 4**).
4. Lift up the rear of the seat, then remove the seat by pulling it rearward.
5. Reverse the removal steps to install the seat. Be sure the seat tab engages the frame notch. Tighten all bolts securely.

LEFT HAND GUARD

Removal/Installation

1. Remove the locknut on the underside of the clutch lever pivot bolt.

2. Remove the hand guard retaining bolt (**Figure 5**).

> *NOTE*
> *Be prepared to catch the flanged collars in the hand guard.*

3. Remove the hand guard.

4. Reverse the removal steps to install the hand guard. Tighten the pivot bolt nut to 9 N•m (80 in.-lb.).

RIGHT HAND GUARD

Removal/Installation

1. Remove the locknut on the underside of the brake lever pivot bolt (A, **Figure 6**).

> *NOTE*
> *Hold the control lever in Step 2 to prevent it from dropping out.*

> *NOTE*
> *Be prepared to catch the flanged collar in the bottom of the hand guard (B, Figure 6).*

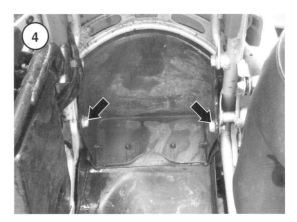

2. Remove the pivot bolt (C, **Figure 6**) and the hand guard.

3. Reverse the removal steps to install the hand guard. Tighten the pivot bolt nut to 6 N•m (53 in.-lb.).

FRONT FENDER

Removal/Installation

1. Remove the mounting bolts, then remove the front fender.

2. Reverse the removal step to install the front fender while noting the following:

    a. Flanged collars are located in the two rear, upper mounting holes.

    b. Flat washers (A, **Figure 7**) are installed on the two rear mounting bolts.

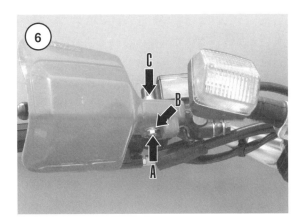

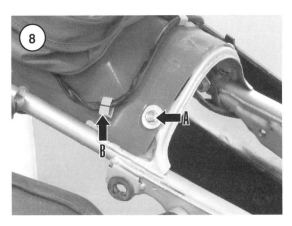

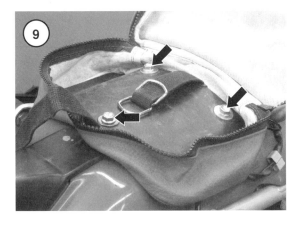

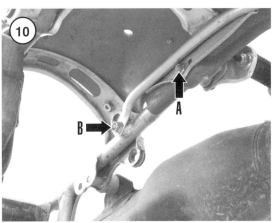

c. Flanged collars (B, **Figure 7**) are installed on the two front mounting bolts.

REAR FENDER

Removal/Installation (XR600R)

NOTE
Note the location of the flanged collars during disassembly.

1. Remove the seat as described in this chapter.
2. Disconnect the taillight electrical connector above the air box.
3. Remove the rear fender mounting bolt (A, **Figure 8**) on each side.
4. Remove the rear fender frame retaining bolts on the underside of the fender, then remove the rear fender assembly.
5. Reverse the removal steps to install the rear fender.

Removal/Installation (XR650L)

NOTE
Note the location of the flanged collars during disassembly.

1. Remove the seat as described in this chapter.
2. Disconnect the taillight and turn signal electrical connectors above the air box.
3. Remove the rear fender mounting bolt (A, **Figure 8**) on each side.
4. Remove the bolts (**Figure 9**) securing the tool bag, then remove the tool bag.
5. Detach the turn signal wires from the retaining clips (B, **Figure 8**).
6. Remove the turn signal retaining nut (A, **Figure 10**) for each turn signal, then remove the turn signal, bolt, flanged collar and grommet on each side.

16

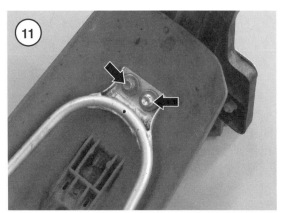

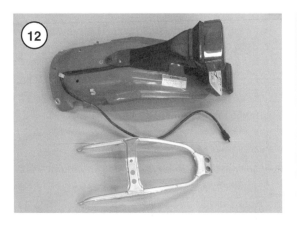

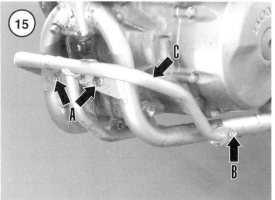

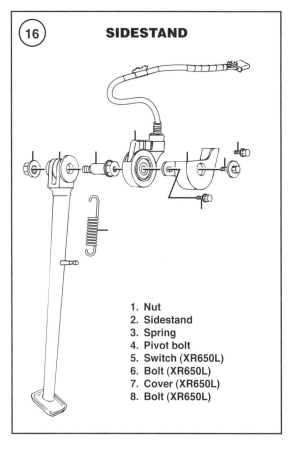

SIDESTAND

1. Nut
2. Sidestand
3. Spring
4. Pivot bolt
5. Switch (XR650L)
6. Bolt (XR650L)
7. Cover (XR650L)
8. Bolt (XR650L)

7. Remove the rear fender frame retaining bolt (B, **Figure 10**) on each side, then remove the rear fender assembly.

8. Remove the license bracket retaining bolts (**Figure 11**), flanged collars and grommets, then separate the fender frame from the fender (**Figure 12**).

9. Reverse the removal steps to install the rear fender.

AIR SHROUD (XR650L)

Removal/Installation

1. Remove the bolt (**Figure 13**).

2. Remove the lower bolt (A, **Figure 14**).

3. Hold the shroud, then remove the upper bolt, flanged collar and grommet (B, **Figure 14**).

4. Remove the shroud.

5. Reverse the removal steps for installation.

FRAME GUARD

Removal/Installation

1. Remove the front bolts (A, **Figure 15**).

2. Remove the side bolts (B, **Figure 15**), then remove the guard (C).

3. Reverse the removal steps for installation.

SIDESTAND

Removal/Installation

Refer to **Figure 16**.

1. On XR650L models, remove the sidestand switch as described in Chapter Eleven.

2. Detach the sidestand return spring.

3. Remove the pivot bolt, then remove the sidestand.

4. Reverse the removal steps for installation. Lubricate the pivot bolt and sidestand with lithium-based multipurpose grease. Tighten the pivot bolt nut to the specification in **Table 1**. Install the spring so the long end is up.

Table 1 BODY TORQUE SPECIFICATIONS

	N•m	in.-lb.	ft.-lb.
Brake lever pivot bolt nut	6	53	–
Clutch lever pivot bolt nut	9	80	–
Sidestand pivot bolt nut			
XR600R and 1993-2007 XR650L	40	–	30
2008-on XR650L	39	–	29

16

INDEX

17

17

1991-2000 XR600R

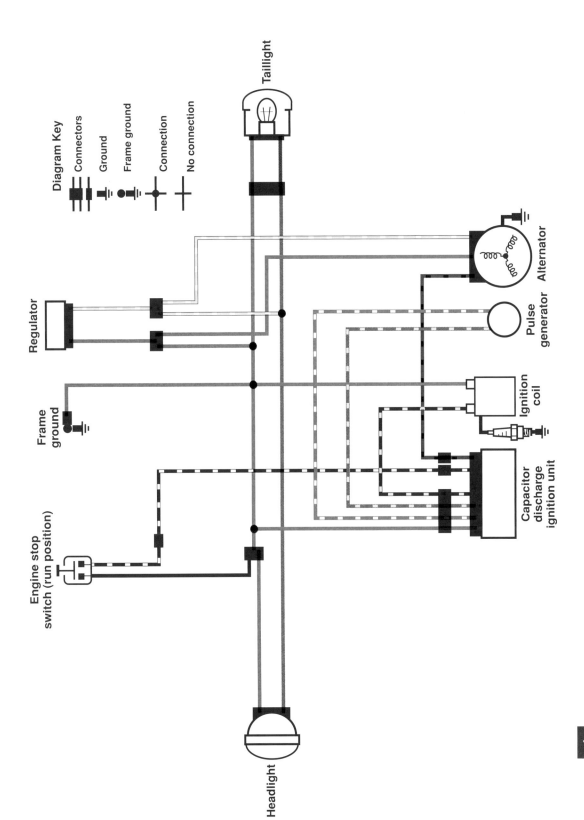

18

1993-2019 XR650L

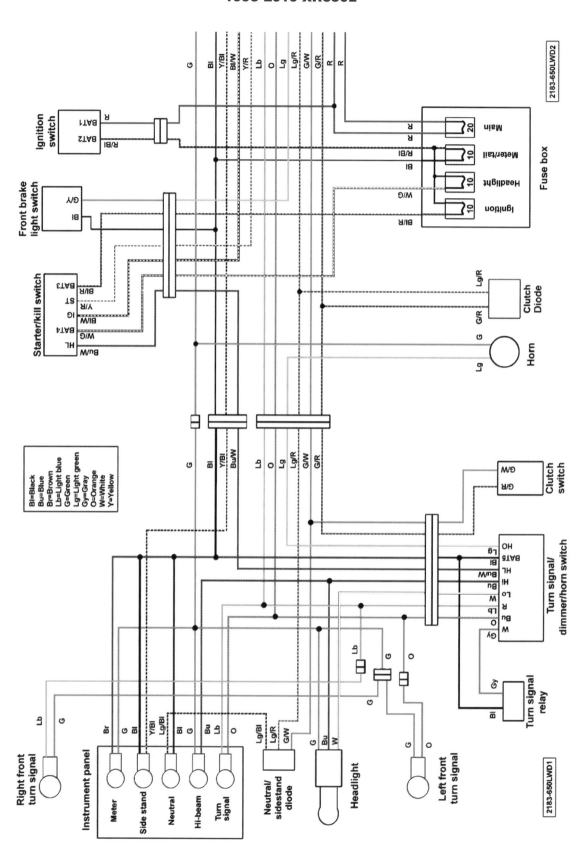

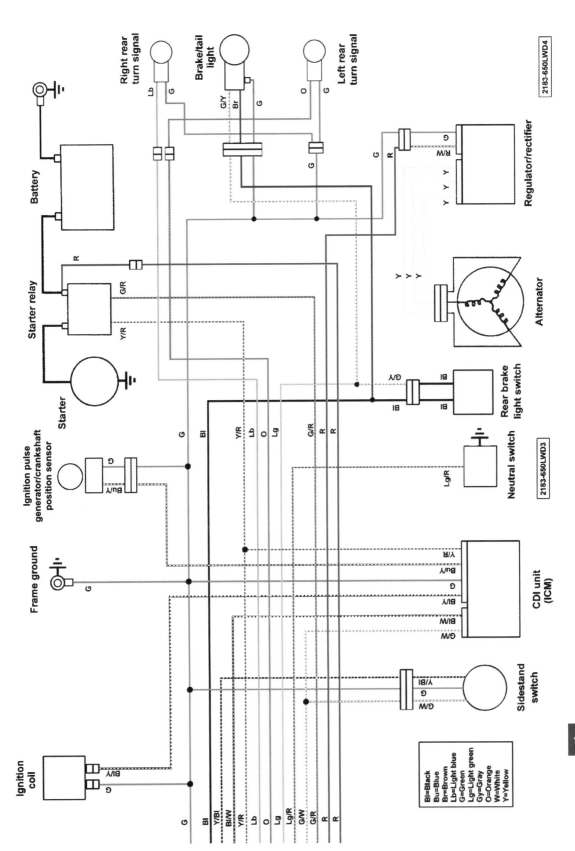

Check out *clymer.com* for our full line of powersport repair manuals.

BMW
M308 500 & 600cc Twins, 55-69
M502-3 BMW R50/5-R100GS PD, 70-96
M500-3 BMW K-Series, 85-97
M501-3 K1200RS, GT & LT, 98-10
M503-3 R850, R1100, R1150 & R1200C, 93-05
M309 F650, 1994-2000

HARLEY-DAVIDSON
M419 Sportsters, 59-85
M429-5 XL/XLH Sportster, 86-03
M427-4 XL Sportster, 04-13
M418 Panheads, 48-65
M420 Shovelheads,66-84
M421-3 FLS/FXS Evolution,84-99
M423-2 FLS/FXS Twin Cam, 00-05
M250 FLS/FXS/FXC Softail, 06-09
M422-3 FLH/FLT/FXR Evolution, 84-98
M430-4 FLH/FLT Twin Cam, 99-05
M252 FLH/FLT, 06-09
M426 VRSC Series, 02-07
M424-2 FXD Evolution, 91-98
M425-3 FXD Twin Cam, 99-05
M254 Dyna Series, 06-11

HONDA
ATVs
M316 Odyssey FL250, 77-84
M311 ATC, TRX & Fourtrax 70-125, 70-87
M433 Fourtrax 90, 93-00
M326 ATC185 & 200, 80-86
M347 ATC200X & Fourtrax 200SX, 86-88
M455 ATC250 & Fourtrax 200/250, 84-87
M342 ATC250R, 81-84
M348 TRX250R/Fourtrax 250R & ATC250R, 85-89
M456-4 TRX250X 87-92; TRX300EX 93-06
M446-3 TRX250 Recon & Recon ES, 97-07
M215-2 TTRX250EX Sportrax and TRX250X, 01-12
M346-3 TRX300/Fourtrax 300 & TRX300FW/Fourtrax 4x4, 88-00
M200-2 TRX350 Rancher, 00-06
M459-3 TRX400 Foreman 95-03
M454-5 TRX400EX Fourtrax & Sportrax 99-13
M201 TRX450R & TRX450ER, 04-09
M205 TRX450 Foreman, 98-04
M210 TRX500 Rubicon, 01-04
M206 TRX500 Foreman, 05-11

Singles
M310-13 50-110cc OHC Singles, 65-99
M315 100-350cc OHC, 69-82
M317 125-250cc Elsinore, 73-80
M442 CR60-125R Pro-Link, 81-88
M431-2 CR80R, 89-95, CR125R, 89-91
M435 CR80R &CR80RB, 96-02
M457-2 CR125R, 92-97; CR250R, 92-96
M464 CR125R, 1998-2002
M443 CR250R-500R Pro-Link, 81-87
M432-3 CR250R, 88-91 & CR500R, 88-01
M437 CR250R, 97-01
M352 CRF250R, CRF250X, CRF450R & CRF450X, 02-05
M319-3 XR50R, CRF50F, XR70R & CRF70F, 97-09
M312-14 XL/XR75-100, 75-91
M222 XR80R, CRF80F, XR100R, & CRF100F, 92-09
M318-4 XL/XR/TLR 125-200, 79-03
M328-4 XL/XR250, 78-00; XL/XR350R 83-85; XR200R, 84-85; XR250L, 91-96
M320-2 XR400R, 96-04
M221 XR600R, 91-07; XR650L, 93-07
M339-8 XL/XR 500-600, 79-90
M225 XR650R, 00-07

Twins
M321 125-200cc Twins, 65-78
M322 250-350cc Twins, 64-74
M323 250-360cc Twins, 74-77
M324-5 Twinstar, Rebel 250 & Nighthawk 250, 78-03
M334 400-450cc Twins, 78-87
M333 450 & 500cc Twins, 65-76
M335 CX & GL500/650, 78-83
M344 VT500, 83-88
M313 VT700 & 750, 83-87
M314-3 VT750 Shadow Chain Drive, 98-06
M440 VT1100C Shadow, 85-96
M460-4 VT1100 Series, 95-07
M230 VTX1800 Series, 02-08
M231 VTX1300 Series, 03-09

Fours
M332 CB350-550, SOHC, 71-78
M345 CB550 & 650, 83-85
M336 CB650,79-82
M341 CB750 SOHC, 69-78
M337 CB750 DOHC, 79-82
M436 CB750 Nighthawk, 91-93 & 95-99
M325 CB900, 1000 & 1100, 80-83
M439 600 Hurricane, 87-90
M441-2 CBR600F2 & F3, 91-98
M445-2 CBR600F4, 99-06
M220 CBR600RR, 03-06
M434-2 CBR900RR Fireblade, 93-99
M329 500cc V-Fours, 84-86
M349 700-1000cc Interceptor, 83-85
M458-2 VFR700F-750F, 86-97
M438 VFR800FI Interceptor, 98-00
M327 700-1100cc V-Fours, 82-88
M508 ST1100/Pan European, 90-02
M340 GL1000 & 1100, 75-83
M504 GL1200, 84-87

Sixes
M505 GL1500 Gold Wing, 88-92
M506-2 GL1500 Gold Wing, 93-00
M507-3 GL1800 Gold Wing, 01-10
M462-2 GL1500C Valkyrie, 97-03

KAWASAKI
ATVs
M465-3 Bayou KLF220 & KLF250, 88-10
M466-4 Bayou KLF300, 86-04
M467 Bayou KLF400, 93-99
M470 Lakota KEF300, 95-99
M385-2 Mojave KSF250, 87-04

Singles
M350-9 80-350cc Rotary Valve, 66-01
M444-2 KX60, 83-02; KX80 83-90
M448-2 KX80, 91-00; KX85, 01-10 & KX100, 89-09
M351 KDX200, 83-88
M447-3 KX125 & KX250, 82-91; KX500, 83-04
M472-2 KX125, 92-00
M473-2 KX250, 92-00
M474-3 KLR650, 87-07
M240-2 KLR650, 08-12

Twins
M355 KZ400, KZ/Z440, EN450 & EN500, 74-95
M241 Ninja 250R (EX250), 88-12
M360-3 EX500, GPZ500S, & Ninja 500R, 87-02
M356-5 Vulcan 700 & 750, 85-06
M354-3 Vulcan 800, 95-05
M246 Vulcan 900, 06-12
M357-2 Vulcan 1500, 87-99
M471-3 Vulcan 1500 Series, 96-08
M245 Vulcan 1600 Series, 03-08

Fours
M449 KZ500/550 & ZX550, 79-85
M450 KZ, Z & ZX750, 80-85
M358 KZ650, 77-83
M359-3 Z & KZ 900-1000cc, 73-81
M451-3 KZ, ZX & ZN 1000 &1100cc, 81-02
M452-3 ZX500 & Ninja ZX600, 85-97
M468-2 Ninja ZX-6, 90-04
M469 Ninja ZX-7, ZX7R & ZX7RR, 91-98
M453-3 Ninja ZX900, ZX1000 & ZX1100, 84-01
M409-2 Concours, 86-06

POLARIS
ATVs
M496 3-, 4- and 6-Wheel Models w/250-425cc Engines, 85-95
M362-2 Magnum & Big Boss, 96-99
M363 Scrambler 500 4X4, 97-00
M365-5 Sportsman/Xplorer, 96-13
M366 Sportsman 600/700/800 Twins, 02-10
M367 Predator 500, 03-07

SUZUKI
ATVs
M381 ALT/LT 125 & 185, 83-87
M475 LT230 & LT250, 85-90
M380-2 LT250R Quad Racer, 85-92
M483-2 LT-4WD, LT-F4WDX & LT-F250, 87-98
M270-2 LT-Z400, 03-08
M343-2 LT-F500F Quadrunner, 98-02

Singles
M369 125-400cc, 64-81
M371 RM50-400 Twin Shock, 75-81
M379 RM125-500 Single Shock, 81-88
M386 RM80-250, 89-95
M400 RM125, 96-00
M401 RM250, 96-02
M476 DR250-350, 90-94
M477-4 DR-Z400E, S & SM, 00-12
M272 DR650, 96-12
M384-5 LS650 Savage/S40, 86-12

Twins
M372 GS400-450 Chain Drive, 77-87
M484-3 GS500E Twins, 89-02
M361 SV650, 1999-2002
M481-6 VS700-800 Intruder/S50, 85-09
M261-2 1500 Intruder/C90, 98-09
M260-3 Volusia/Boulevard C50, 01-11
M482-3 VS1400 Intruder/S83, 87-07

Triple
M368 GT380, 550 & 750, 72-77

Fours
M373 GS550, 77-86
M364 GS650, 81-83
M370 GS750, 77-82
M376 GS850-1100 Shaft Drive, 79-84
M378 GS1100 Chain Drive, 80-81
M383-3 Katana 600, 88-96 GSX-R750-1100, 86-87
M331 GSX-R600, 97-00
M264 GSX-R600, 01-05
M478-2 GSX-R750, 88-92; GSX750F Katana, 89-96
M485 GSX-R750, 96-99
M377 GSX-R1000, 01-04
M266 GSX-R1000, 05-06
M265 GSX1300R Hayabusa, 99-07
M338 Bandit 600, 95-00
M353 GSF1200 Bandit, 96-03

YAMAHA
ATVs
M499-2 YFM80 Moto-4, Badger & Raptor, 85-08
M394 YTM200, 225 & YFM200, 83-86
M488-5 Blaster, 88-05
M489-2 Timberwolf, 89-00
M487-5 Warrior, 87-04
M486-6 Banshee, 87-06
M490-3 Moto-4 & Big Bear, 87-04
M493 Kodiak, 93-98
M287-2 YFZ450, 04-13
M285-2 Grizzly 660, 02-08
M280-2 Raptor 660R, 01-05
M290 Raptor 700R, 06-09
M291 Rhino 700, 2008-2012

Singles
M492-2 PW50 & 80 Y-Zinger & BW80 Big Wheel 80, 81-02
M410 80-175 Piston Port, 68-76
M415 250-400 Piston Port, 68-76
M412 DT & MX Series, 77-83
M414 IT125-490, 76-86
M393 YZ50-80 Monoshock, 78-90
M413 YZ100-490 Monoshock, 76-84
M390 YZ125-250, 85-87 YZ490, 85-90
M391 YZ125-250, 88-93 & WR250Z, 91-93
M497-2 YZ125, 94-01
M498 YZ250, 94-98; WR250Z, 94-97
M406 YZ250F & WR250F, 01-03
M491-2 YZ400F, 98-99 & 426F, 00-02; WR400F, 98-00 & 426F, 00-01
M417 XT125-250, 80-84
M480-3 XT350, 85-00; TT350, 86-87
M405 XT/TT 500, 76-81
M416 XT/TT 600, 83-89

Twins
M403 650cc Twins, 70-82
M395-10 XV535-1100 Virago, 81-03
M495-7 V-Star 650, 98-11
M284 V-Star 950, 09-12
M281-4 V-Star 1100, 99-09
M283 V-Star 1300, 07-10
M282-2 Road Star, 99-07

Triple
M404 XS750 & XS850, 77-81

Fours
M387 XJ550, XJ600 & FJ600, 81-92
M494 XJ600 Seca II/Diversion, 92-98
M388 YX600 Radian & FZ600, 86-90
M396 FZR600, 89-93
M392 FZ700-750 & Fazer, 85-87
M411 XS1100, 78-81
M461 YZF-R6, 99-04
M398 YZF-R1, 98-03
M399 FZ1, 01-05
M397 FJ1100 & 1200, 84-93
M375-2 V-Max, 85-07
M374-2 Royal Star, 96-10

VINTAGE MOTORCYCLES
Clymer® Collection Series
M330 Vintage British Street Bikes, BSA 500–650cc Unit Twins; Norton 750 & 850cc Commandos; Triumph 500-750cc Twins
M300 Vintage Dirt Bikes, V. 1 Bultaco, 125-370cc Singles; Montesa, 123-360cc Singles; Ossa, 125-250cc Singles
M305 Vintage Japanese Street Bikes Honda, 250 & 305cc Twins; Kawasaki, 250-750cc Triples; Kawasaki, 900 & 1000cc Fours